Dimensions of Property in Reproductive Economies

Structural Change of Property

Edited by Silke van Dyk, Tilman Reitz and Hartmut Rosa

Volume 5

Stefanie Graefe, PD Dr., is a senior researcher and lecturer at the Department of Sociology at Friedrich Schiller University Jena. *Irina Herb,* MPhil, is a research assistant at the Collaborative Research Center 294 ›Structural Change of Property‹ at Friedrich Schiller University Jena. *Susanne Lettow,* PD Dr., is a senior researcher and lecturer at the Margherita-von-Brentano-Centre for Gender Studies at Freie Universität Berlin.

Stefanie Graefe, Irina Herb, Susanne Lettow (eds.)

Dimensions of Property in Reproductive Economies

Practices, Structures, and Discourses

Campus Verlag
Frankfurt/New York

Funded by the Deutsche Forschungsgemeinschaft (DFG) – SFB TRR 294/1–424638267.

STRUCTURAL CHANGE OF PROPERTY

ISBN 978-3-593-51926-5 Print
ISBN 978-3-593-45840-3 E-Book (PDF)
DOI 10.12907/978-3-593-45764-2

Werderstr. 10, 69469 Weinheim, info@campus.de.
Cover design: Verlagsgruppe Beltz
Typesetting: le-tex xerif
Printing office and bookbinder: Beltz Grafische Betriebe GmbH, Bad Langensalza.
Beltz Grafische Betriebe is a company with a financial contribution to climate protection (ID 15985-2104-1001).
Printed in Germany

www.campus.de
www.press.uchicago.edu

Contents

Series Introduction

Property is a largely under-examined institutional basis of the contemporary global economic order. Yet property in the early twenty-first century is being challenged and politically contested in seemingly unprecedented ways. Property is being called into question not only because of the accelerated, global implementation of private property after the collapse of state socialism at the end of the twentieth century spurred an extreme increase in inequality, but also because established forms of property in various sectors prove to be dysfunctional with respect to such phenomena as environmental sustainability and even economic growth. The changing significance of what it means to own something such as an apartment, a forest, or stock options, has been set in motion. The meaning of ownership has been further called into question as a result of new technological developments, indefinitely transferable objects appear to be replacing scarce material goods, a process through which completely new questions related to intellectual property are being posed. Questions of what, if anything, lends itself to constituting or conceptualising property abound: works of art? Human organs? DNA sequences? Raw materials? Algorithms? Forests? Asteroids? What alternatives to private property are observable? What new property arrangements are being formed, and what alternatives to the property-wrought order of society are even thinkable?

The series at hand is a product of the German Research Foundation-sponsored Collaborative Research Centre TRR 294 "Structural Change of Property," based primarily at the universities of Jena and Erfurt. This series is dedicated to the systematic, interdisciplinary study of the topics outlined above and features outstanding scholarly works on the past, present and future of property.

Dimensions of Property: Introduction

Susanne Lettow and Stefanie Graefe

Assisted reproductive technologies (ARTs) have become normalised in today's society. So too have associated services such as surrogacy and gamete donation, and with them practices of extracting bodily substances such as eggs and sperm and transferring them to other bodies. The vast majority of these practices are monetised—that is to say, bodily substances are exchanged for money—and they are embedded within a rapidly growing transnational reproductive economy in which reproductive clinics, tissue banks and fertility brokers frequently interact across national borders. Since the 1980s, technologically assisted reproduction has developed dynamically to become a globally expanding sector with ever more diversified service offerings and market players (van de Wiel 2020; Vertommen et al. 2022b; König and Jacobson 2023). Most of the fertility clinics, gamete banks, broker and marketing agencies, consultancies and insurance companies active in the ART sector are privately owned for-profit businesses. Some of these entities even serve as "investment assets" for larger corporations (cf. Irina Herb's and Kathrin Braun's chapters in this volume; see also Herb and Wenner 2023). Researchers now refer to a "third phase" of the reproductive economy, characterised by a globalisation and interconnection of reproductive medical services and the emergence of new private business models (Simpson and Hampshire 2015; König and Jacobson 2023; Patrizio et al. 2022). In this context, accelerated and complex dynamics involving the appropriation and commodification of bodily substances, reproductive capacities and medical infrastructures can be observed. Human tissues are being extracted, transferred, appropriated by others and made profitable in historically novel ways.

1. Paradoxes of an "oblivion of property" in research on ART

We believe that these dynamics reveal the significance of property in ART contexts at a number of different levels. Firstly, they raise the very basic question of how bodily substances and reproductive capacities become property and what social, economic and cultural consequences this has. A second, related question is how actors involved in the reproductive economy—those who donate, receive, manage, transfer or store bodily substances—actually experience and perceive these developments, both in the present and prospectively, and how these issues are negotiated in legal regulations, media coverage and public or academic discourse. Thirdly, given the historically novel marketisation of reproductive substances, it must also be asked who owns the clinics, agencies and other companies and the profits they generate, and how these developments have contributed to a sweeping transformation of the contemporary property order (van Dyk et al. 2024). It is notable that questions around property and propertisation, that is, the extension of the logic of ownership to the realm of human generativity, have so far been addressed only marginally in the relevant debates and analyses. Put simply, one could say that property is a kind of "forgotten" category here.

This does not mean that the concept of property is entirely absent in academic and public debates about ART and the reproductive economy. On the contrary, the question of whether, and if so under what conditions, it is legitimate to alienate and commercialise "property in the human body" has long been a subject of intense debate, especially within bioethics. The conception of one's own body as property that can be sold and bought is usually formulated in terms of John Locke's theory of property. In his *Second Treatise of Government* (1689), Locke introduced his theory of property as a product of labour as follows:

> Every Man has a property in his own person. This no body has any right to but himself. The Labour of his Body and, and the Work of his Hands, we may say, are properly his.
>
> *Locke 1988 [1689], Second Treatise, § 27*

In bioethical discourse, this idea of property in "one's own person" is translated into that of property "in one's own body". That involves an important shift in meaning. While Locke sought to legitimise private property by reference to a person's "own" embodied labour and personal autonomy,[1] the bioethical conception centres on the body as an "arbitrarily divisible and available material substance" (Gehring 2006, 41). Locke's theory of property is thus being applied to a question—concerning the alienability of the human body or bodily substances—that is foreign to it (see Janice Richardson's chapter in this volume). Within the bioethical debate, the notion of property in the body is utilised both for positions that are largely supportive of commercialisation and for ones that emphasise individual rights of self-determination in order to *oppose* biomedical interventions made solely for the benefit of other people. However, the bioethical notion of property in one's own body is fundamentally too narrow to account for current developments in the reproductive economy (see Susanne Lettow's chapter in this volume). There is a lack of systematic reflection within bioethics on the economic structures, property relations and processes of propertisation involved in the transnational reproductive economy. Many questions go unaddressed, for instance: under what conditions does the human body—which in the context of bio- and reproductive medicine is increasingly fragmented and viewed through an economic lens—come to be addressed as (potential) property in the first place? And should the bioethical discourse around property in the human body not itself be regarded as an aspect of propertisation processes? Paradoxically, the bioethical notion of "property in the human body" thus contributes to an "oblivion of property" in academic and public debates about ART.

Critical discourses and debates in the social sciences, by contrast, have repeatedly pointed to how the ART economy (re)produces social inequalities new and old. It has been widely shown that transnational reproductive economies are gendered, racialised, and highly stratified systems, in which, alongside socioeconomic inequalities, characteristics such as ethnicity, age and educational level also play a central role (Pande 2014; 2022; Schurr 2018; Vertommen et al. 2022a; Waldby 2019; Namberger 2019; Nahman 2018; Mamo and Alston-Stepnitz 2015; cf. Charlotte Kroløkke and Katherine Carroll's and Daisy Deomampo's chapters in this volume). However, there is still a need for more specific analysis of property relations and processes of property formation: where critical social science perspectives focus on the political economy of ART, the concept of property as an analytical category

1 On colonial articulations of Locke's theory of property and for a critical, intersectional analysis, see Arneil 1996 and 2001.

usually does not play a systematic role. Many critical studies have instead focused on how practices of making bodily substances available can be analysed as forms of *labour* and, relatedly, as practices of exploitation. These studies show that, like the globalised services economy, the circulation of bodily substances is based on a stratified labour market in which historically novel forms of waged services are organised, including surrogacy, egg donation and participation in clinical trials (see e.g. Pande 2014; Namberger 2019; Siegl 2023). Egg donation is widely understood in this context as a form of "clinical" (Cooper and Waldby 2014), "embodied" (Pande 2014) or "biological" (Vora 2015) labour that is outsourced in a manner similar to other forms of labour in post-Fordist economies; Melinda Cooper and Catherine Waldby have introduced the term "fertility outsourcing" to describe this phenomenon (see Cooper and Waldby 2014; Waldby 2019). At the same time, some authors have critically reflected on how equating reproductive services and (wage) labour with bodily processes risks reducing the economic productivity of those services and forms of labour to (female) biology and conflating highly divergent regional and social contexts (Schultz and Braun 2014; Parry 2015; Oksala 2019). Nonetheless, the concept of "labour" and the related discussions do undoubtedly make an important contribution to the analysis of current globalised reproductive economies and also provide valuable insights for the still-nascent analysis of property relations. Recent analyses that deploy concepts such as "global fertility chains" (Cooper and Waldby 2014, Vertommen et al. 2022b, Vertommen, et al. 2022a), "oocyte commodity chain" (Bergmann 2012), or "reproductive geopolitics" (Perler et al. 2024) are especially instructive for a property-based analysis of globalised reproductive economies because these studies address the transnational and global nature of reproductive economies. Although they do not make systematic use of property as an analytic category, they do provide important insights for the study of property relations, processes of propertisation and practices of "doing property", and thus help to counteract the above-described "oblivion of property" in this field. In contrast to the bioethical debate, which focuses on the human body as a property object, the social sciences have not yet developed a specific tool for critically analysing property relations and processes of propertisation; the various property objects and property subjects that produce and are produced by the structures of the global ART economy are, however, implicitly addressed in relevant critical debates (see Susanne Schultz's chapter).

2. Property, propertisation, doing property

In our view, there are three main reasons why it is helpful to give a central place to property in our analysis and critique of the global ART economy. Firstly, doing so allows us to analyse how patterns of thought and action are increasingly structured by the category of property which we refer to with the term "propertisation". Secondly, a property-based perspective allows for a better understanding of the actors and structures of profit-driven ART economies and the interactions between different property objects and property subjects. Thirdly, sets of practices and interpretative schemas in which struggles over the meaning of ownership, property, belonging, and boundaries between "mine" and "yours" play out can be understood as constitutive elements of the global ART economy (see Daisy Deomampo's chapter in this volume). Not least in light of the global expansion of the ART economy, the question of ownership of bodily materials and fertility, as well as reproductive medical infrastructures and companies, emerges as an important subject of analysis (see Irina Herb's chapter in this volume).

We see the concept of *propertisation* as crucial to developing a property-based theoretical perspective on the dynamics of the global ART economy. Following Hannes Siegrist (2006), we understand propertisation to refer to historically specific processes by which property is strengthened and extended. This encompasses not just property in a legal sense, but also the

> cultural construction and mediation of property-related concepts, symbols, orders of meaning and knowledge, [...] social norms, role scripts, forms of habitus, customs and guiding principles.
>
> *ibid., 31*

Thus, propertisation is not just a legal or economic process, but one that spans right across society. It holds significance both for the production and distribution of goods, resources and wealth and for people's self-relations, intersubjective practices and normative orientations, whether individual or collective. Accordingly, it is possible to speak of different *dimensions* of property, with the use of the term "dimensions" signaling that we do not understand property solely as a legal category. Of course, the different dimensions of property cannot be viewed in isolation, but stand in a relation of mutual influence. For instance, although talk of "my" eggs or "my" child only rarely articulates an explicitly legal understanding of property, the subjective interpretive schemas in which such expressions occur are bound up with the ethical and societal debates around "property in the body" and with the economically and legally coded property relations and property structures of the transnational reproductive economy. Processes of propertisation always also involve specific (inter)subjective forms of "doing property" which can, paradoxically, also consist in denying or downplaying the role of property that significantly structures subjects' day-to-day lives (cf. Stefanie Graefe's chapter in this volume).

In addition, processes of propertisation are often closely linked to processes of commodification—that is, processes by which things, substances and capacities are made into commodities that can be exchanged for money. Accordingly, propertisation can be understood on the one hand as a *condition* of commodification and on the other as one of its possible *effects*—for instance, in cases where the transformation of non-commodities into commodities feeds into a codification of property rights or ideas about what objects are "ownable" in the first place. Propertisation and commodification are therefore not the same, but these processes can mutually reinforce each other. Within the political economy of ART, we can see this for instance when donors provide consent to the transfer of their gametes on the basis of their personality rights, and thereby transfer extensive usage rights and opportunities for profit (see Rebecca Rahe's and Sara Lafuente-Funes's chapters in this volume). Whether and in what sense donors, recipients, clinics and egg banks view these bodily substances as property is an open question, as several of the articles collected in this volume make clear. At the same time, the ability to generate profits in this sector is not always dependent on legal property titles; "*functional equivalents* of property" (van den Ecker et al. 2023, 267, emphasis in original), such as the aforementioned "personality rights", can substitute for them instead. Conversely, in ART contexts bodily substances can become transferrable and exchangeable property objects even without being directly commodified (see Carroll and Kroløkke's chapter). However, that rarely happens in practice in the globalised ART economy. Rather, the legal and normative construct of non-marketised, altruistic bodily "donation" paradoxically often serves to legitimise and drive forward the propertisation *and* commodification of bodily substances (see Kathrin Braun's and Stefanie Graefe's chapters in this volume).

Discourses and social practices that negotiate what can be considered as property in a legal sense or as a person's "own" property, are therefore of particular importance for processes of commodification. They are often also ambiguous. Above all, the limits of the existing legal norm that only things can be owned and that the human body, which categorically does not qualify as a thing, therefore cannot be considered an object of property in the legal sense, are being tested by newly emerging practices within the ART economy (see Gehring 2006 and Rebecca Rahe's chapter in this volume). One particular reason for this is that the distinction between person and thing that is of constitutive importance for both modern property rights and the legal status of civic subjects is often difficult to draw precisely in the context of biomedicine. This distinction must be continually restabilised to prevent the human body being reduced to an alienable, tradable property object.

However, it is not just property rights that are relevant to legal processes of propertisation in the context of the ART economy. Many countries have specific legal regulations governing modern reproductive medicine, which structure the possibilities for propertisation and commercialisation, and these regulations are often contested. One example is the dispute over whether to replace the German Embryo Protection Act with a Reproductive Medicine Act (see Kommission zur reproduktiven Selbstbestimmung und Fortpflanzungsmedizin 2024 and Sara Lafuente-Funes's chapter in this volume). Although legal regulations are important, we argue that the legal expansion of property relations and the associated shifts in understandings of property must always be viewed in relation to political and ethical discourses and everyday interpretive practices. In our view, examining the interconnections and interactions between the legal, cultural, political, ethical and affective dimensions of property contributes to a greater the understanding of the structures and dynamics of the ART economy and to an analysis of potential fault lines and contradictions in processes of propertisation.

In addition, the above-mentioned concept of global fertility chains (Vertommen et al. 2022b) is central to developing the property-based approach to which this volume seeks to contribute. Global fertility chains are

> a nexus of *intraconnected* practices, operations, and transactions among firms, states, and households through which a particular reproductive service (such as egg provision or surrogacy), commodity (such as a baby, stem cell line, regenerative drug, or therapy), or data are produced, distributed and consumed across the globe.
>
> *ibid., 119–120*

In her analysis of the patenting of human genes, Sabrina Safrin (2007) has instructively described how propertisation processes often take the form of self-reinforcing chain reactions, which ultimately lead to more propertisation and in the long term potentially also "hyper-privatisation". In our field of study, this can be observed for example in cases where, initially, eggs were propertised and commodified, and then further down the line embryos also became the object of propertisation processes—facilitated in particular by improved freezing techniques (cf. Lafuente-Funes's chapter). The financial gains resulting from these processes are often appropriated by large transnational clinic chains that drive processes of propertisation and commercialisation even further. What this shows is that chain reactions can potentially lead to property and power becoming highly concentrated.

Based on the multidimensional understanding of property set out here, we think that it is crucial to ask how the sociocultural, discursive, economic and legal dimensions of property interact at different "nodes" and influence the expansionist dynamics of the global ART economy. Although this volume cannot comprehensively answer this question, our intention in bringing together the essays collected here is to demonstrate how fruitful the property-based approach we propose can be for the analysis and critique of the global ART economy, as it makes it possible to build links between previously separate strands of research and debate. For instance, reconstructing the economic dynamics of the booming ART industry reveals the discursive construct of altruism and individual interpretive practices to constitute a form of work on a "moral economy" that is itself a part of processes of propertisation, precisely because questions about property relations are "forgotten". Moreover, in light of socioeconomic processes of propertisation, ethical debates are likewise revealed to be a discursive terrain on which the limits of the propertisation of human reproduction are negotiated. The systematic gaps and omissions in bioethical concepts and debates affect whether, and if so in what respects, the global ART economy and its intersectional structures of inequality are seen as problematic or not (see Elizabeth Lanphier's, Janice Richardson's and Susanne Lettow's chapters in this volume). In addition, the discursive distinction that is drawn from the direct, coercive and violent propertisation of the human body in transatlantic slavery, which features prominently in the legal and public debates on ART and abortion legislation in the United States, circumscribes the space of what can be problematised in relation to current processes of the propertisation of reproduction (see Penelope Deutscher's chapter in this volume). And even though such debates and discourses around property and propertisation do not have an immediate impact on property law or the economic dynamics of the ART economy, they do affect whether and how those dynamics are addressed at the political and societal level.

Overall, we see it as an important task to highlight the gaps and inconsistencies in discourses around property and practices of doing property, since they show that the global ART economy does not simply develop according to an inexorable logic of propertisation and commodification but is, to at least some degree, fragile and contested. This in turn opens up potential for critical and emancipatory perspectives. Many critics, who have long pointed to the inequalities within the global ART economy from various perspectives, refer to the concept of reproductive justice —originally developed in Black feminism—to highlight the importance of socio-economic conditions and infrastructures for a substantively "free" decision to have or not have children (Ross 2021). Applied to the context of the ART economy, the concept of reproductive justice offers an important framework for discussing exploitative relations and inequality, and makes it possible to address different, sometimes conflicting perspectives and claims (Ediger et al. 2021; see also Elizabeth Lanphier's and Susanne Schultz's chapters in this volume). Of course, the question of whether critics should aim to dismantle the multiple structures of inequality that shape the global ART economy, or—more modestly—focus on reducing some of the most glaring inequalities is open to debate. But regardless of the answer, we believe that critically analysing propertisation processes and property relations can make an important contribution to the project of reproductive justice, which seeks to restructure material and sociocultural conditions in such a way that diverse modes of living—with or without children, with or without technological support—emerge outside the profit-oriented dynamics of the global ART economy.

3. Structure of the volume

We have divided the volume into four parts. The first, *Dynamics of the ART Economy*, describes and analyses current economic developments in the field of technologically assisted reproduction. In "Dynamics, Displacement and Disembedding: An Analysis of the Oocyte Economy in Contemporary Capitalism", *Kathrin Braun* explores trends that are shaping the oocyte market. She shows that this sector of the global ART economy is increasingly dominated by non-medical stakeholders, including investors, brokers and commercial egg banks. These stakeholders operate according to an economic rationality that tends to sideline established medical norms, such as the norm of non-maleficence. To describe the shift towards economic rationality, Braun draws on the work of Nancy Fraser, in particular her analysis of capitalism as reliant on non-economic conditions and her distinction between exploitation and expropriation. Braun argues that there is a close relation in the oocyte economy between commodification and an altruistic framing: procurement models that invoke the notion of altruism occur along a continuum between commodification and expropriation, with altruism-cum-compensation enabling cost-effective access to oocytes while sustaining capital accumulation.

Rebecca Rahe's chapter, "'My Eggs Belong to Me': Commodification and Property in the Fertility Economy", then explores the commodification of human oocytes through the lens of a critical legal analysis inspired by Marxist feminist theory. By analysing the German legal debate about "property in the body", Rahe shows that although bodily substances are systematically distinguished from tradable "things" and procedures such as egg cell transfer are currently prohibited in Germany, the application of economic principles is *de facto* already firmly established and normalised, thus providing legitimation for the commodification of bodily substances on transnational reproductive. She argues that the compensation of egg donors should be understood neither as "remuneration" nor as a "wage". Rather, it represents a form of rent economy in which bodies or bodily materials do not function as commodities in their own right but rather as a kind of raw material that can be profitably cultivated.

In addition, property in technological infrastructures, patents and companies is a basic condition for the functioning and growth of the global ART economy. In her chapter "Who Has Seized Assisted Reproductive Technologies? The Role of Private Investors in the Fertility Sector", *Irina Herb* analyses current processes of assetisation, with a particular focus on patenting ART-related knowledge and on investments in fertility clinics in the United States and Germany. She shows how ART has been absorbed into global market mechanisms, with private investors and asset managers increasingly owning and profiting from reproductive technologies. This assetisation marks a significant shift that has increased the influence of wealthy individuals and firms. Based on this analysis, Herb asks whether we might be witnessing the emergence of a new era of more centralised control, dominated by "biofinanciers".

Part two, *Contested Objects of Property*, focuses on objects—including eggs, embryos and breastmilk—that have become propertised and in some cases also commodified in recent decades. The chapters in this section describe how processes of propertisation build on and reinforce intersectional structures of power and inequality, and rely in various ways on juridical and political regulation. In "Purchasing Race: Commodifying 'Asian' Eggs in Assisted Reproduction", *Daisy Deomampo* offers a critical perspective on the intersections of race, reproduction and capitalism with a specific focus on Asian Americans. She shows how eggs become objects that can be bought, sold and produced based on contractual relations. In this process, race is constructed as inheritable genetic property, so that racial identity becomes an asset to be purchased and sold. This has ethical implications for how to imagine possibilities for racial and reproductive justice.

Sara Lafuente-Funes argues that the propertisation of eggs does not necessarily result in overt commodification. Whether that happens depends, among other things, on the legal frameworks that establish what can or cannot be done with reproductive bodily substances. In her chapter, "Who Owns What Remains in the Cryotanks? Turning Sperm, Eggs and Embryos into Reproductive Materials and Duties in the Spanish Context", she analyses how and to what extent state regulations contribute to the propertisation and commodification of bodily substances and reproductive capacities. This happens not only where eggs or sperm are sold to potential recipients in return for money but also, interestingly, at the points where the question of how to *dispose* of the numerous "surplus" cryopreserved eggs or embryos is negotiated. Drawing on the history of relevant Spanish case law, the chapter shows how strongly state regulations reproduce moral axioms rooted in cultural traditions, in particular women's "reproductive duties". Furthermore, it demonstrates that, even though they are intended to prevent the commercialisation of reproductive bodily materials and embryos, the morally legitimised regulations themselves play a key role in supporting the propertisation of these substances and the expansion of reproductive markets. According to Lafuente-Funes, the explanation for this apparently paradoxical state of affairs is that state regulations are primarily aimed at limiting the ability of women or people with uteruses to choose what they do with their own reproductive bodily materials, which in turn gives other actors, such as private clinics, greater control over those materials.

In the next chapter, "Liquid Gold: The Monetisation of Breastmilk", *Charlotte Kroløkke and Katherine Carroll* explore another contested property object. They show how Danish health authorities, private companies and other relevant organisations have conferred on breastmilk the status of property that can be owned and sold by lactating mothers. At the same time, breastmilk serves as a vehicle for the Danish welfare system to pursue its goals of enhancing population health and creating a shared resource that can be redistributed to premature infants. The propertisation of breastmilk, Kroløkke and Carroll argue, is situated within a web of relations between the breastfeeding mothers, their reproductive bodies, babies, imagined recipients, technologies and the Danish welfare and healthcare sectors. With reference to the development of the Danish milk banking sector, they explain that breastmilk transcends the gift/commodity dichotomy. It is both a bio-commodity that can be exchanged for money and a biopolitical object through which an imagined community of providers and recipients is constituted. In this context, the Danish state is revealed to be a central player in the process of propertisation.

The chapters in part three, *Conceptualising Property, Propertisation and Moral Economies*, analyse how notions of property, propertisation and moral economies are or have been used in previous research and in everyday understandings of the ART economy. Although the authors draw on different textual archives, ranging from philosophy and social theory literature to interviews with various ART stakeholders, a common finding is that property and propertisation are largely undertheorised. They propose various theoretical approaches to address this lacuna. In her chapter "Subordination, Surrogacy and the Body: Feminist Perspectives on Locke's Individualism and His Conception of 'Property in the Person'", *Janice Richardson* argues that Locke's concepts of work and "property in the person", which are pervasive in liberal and neoliberal thought, are incompatible with a proper understanding of commercial surrogacy. Richardson reconstructs central passages of Locke's *Second Treatise* and critically evaluates them through the lens of multiple feminist interventions, drawing on Sophie Lewis's notion of surrogacy as work, Verena Namberger's analysis of the work of egg donors, Amrita Pande's analysis of the emotional labour of surrogacy and Carol Pateman's theory of how subordination is perpetuated and managed through marriage and employment contracts. She then turns to Spinoza's ontology, which she believes is better suited to conceptualising surrogates' labour and political agency than Locke's understanding of labour as appropriation. Richardson thus brings a fresh perspective to feminist criticism of bioethical endorsements and rearticulations of the Lockean theory of property.

Susanne Lettow's chapter, "Beyond the Lockean Paradigm: Property and Propertisation in the Reproductive Economy", discusses how earlier feminist critiques of the Lockean paradigm that were formulated by Anne Philips, Rosalind Petchesky and Donna Dickenson contribute to rethinking property and propertisation in the context of the ART economy. In particular, she builds on Dickenson's exploration of the bundle theory of property and of Hegel's intersubjective theory of property. Lettow argues that both theoretical moves should be further developed: firstly, by adopting a praxeological understanding of the bundle theory and insights from new materialism; secondly, by undertaking a critical rereading of Hegel's theory of ethical life that helps us to understand propertisation as not merely a one-dimensional process of extending an economic logic to a non-economic milieu, but rather as a process that is shaped by the active involvement of all three aspects of "ethical life": namely (in Hegel's terminology) the family, civil society and the state. Both theoretical moves, Lettow contends, are crucial for developing a critical property-based theory of global fertility chains.

Based on a detailed qualitative study conducted in Spain and Germany, *Stefanie Graefe*'s chapter, "Altruism and (De-)Propertisation: On the Moral Economy of Egg Donation", presents empirical findings on the ways in which the various parties involved in the egg transfer process (donors, recipients and professionals) "do" and "undo" property. Interestingly, questions of property only play a subordinate role for most of the interviewees, whereas the commodification of eggs is seen as potentially morally critical. Graefe shows that moral perspectives are brought to bear at all levels and by all interviewee groups. However, the intensity and breadth of this moralisation varies significantly; the "moral work" is unequally distributed, with a greater burden being placed on the donors. This distribution is inversely proportionate to socioeconomic status: the most (socioeconomically) vulnerable group, the egg donors, does the most (moral) work. The construct of "altruistic donation" plays a central role in this stratification. In this respect, it can be understood as an essential component of the reproductive industry's moral economy, not only because it serves to disguise the *de facto* economisation of technologically assisted reproduction, but above all because it takes the supposed contradiction between moral and economic activity and turns it into a marketing tool.

Part four, *Reproductive Justice Perspectives on the ART Economy*, explores ways of transcending or dismantling the intersectional relations of power, exploitation and expropriation that shape the sector's current dynamics.

In her chapter "Contested Property Relations: Feminist Debates on Labour, Biocapitalist 'Land Grabbing' and Geneticised Kinship", *Susanne Schultz* explores three interrelated framings that shape critical debates and research on the global ART economy. Schultz argues that each of these framings confronts a certain form of property and ownership. The labour framing highlights the fact that egg provision and surrogacy perpetuate historical patterns of reproductive labour exploitation, and criticises the property relations that enable this exploitation; the biocapitalist "land grab" framing directs its critique at processes of propertisation that are understood in terms of extractivism; and the geneticised kinship framing is primarily concerned with the genetic understanding of kinship that fuels the ART economy, and problematises the very notion and promise of having your "own" child. Schultz argues that the focus of feminist analysis of, and political positions on, egg provision and surrogacy should not be restricted to just one of the three framings. A comprehensive understanding of property and propertisation in the ART economy that seeks to promote reproductive justice must combine insights provided by all three framings.

In "Abortion, Surrogacy and Propertisation: Unthinkability as Analogy's Negation", *Penelope Deutscher* analyses how analogies to slavery have been deployed in jurisprudence and in the public debate around reproductive politics (specifically, access to abortion and IVF) in the United States since the 1980s. She shows how "techniques of echoing" that evoke slavery as an extreme form of reproductive injustice constitute a kind of "unthinkability" and delegitimise criticisms of contemporary forms of reproductive injustice. Deutscher draws on analyses by Alys Weinbaum ("the afterlife of slavery") and Eva von Redecker ("phantom possession") to understand how historical analogies function and how modes of domination and dominion that have been legally abolished still haunt present-day societies and modes of interaction. In contrast to Weinbaum and von Redecker, Deutscher emphasises the role of negation—articulations of what "*may not* be"—in semantic processes that seek, in paradoxical fashion, to limit possibilities of critique.

Finally, in "Life, Liberty or Property: Reparative Reproductive Justice without Self-Ownership", *Elizabeth Lanphier* discusses the concept of reproductive justice, and seeks to expand it to address theoretical, political and ethical shortcomings of the notion of self-ownership that is used in bioethical discourse to describe people's ownership and control of their own genetic and reproductive materials. While the notion of bodily self-ownership implies freedom from interference, it does not entail the positive liberties required for reproductive justice. Lanphier argues for a reparative worldbuilding approach to these matters that builds on Olúfẹ́mi O. Táíwò's political philosophy, in particular his understanding of reparation. According to Lanphier, political regulation of reproductive technologies should aim to repair and redress prior harm through structural change. An attentiveness to power and to historical and cultural context can and should inform ethical policies and practices regarding the use of and access to reproductive technologies on a local and global scale.

This volume is based on two workshops and a series of online lectures held as part of the research project "Property in the human body in the context of transnational economies of reproduction", a subproject of the Collaborative Research Centre TRR 294 "Structural Change of Property" at Freie Universität Berlin and the University of Jena. We are grateful to the German Research Foundation (DFG) for financially supporting both our project and the overall research centre, which has provided an inspiring setting for research and collaboration. Without the stimulating discussions hosted by the participating institutions, the volume would not have been possible in the form in which it exists today, so we would like to take this opportunity to thank all workshop participants for their contributions. We would also like to thank the colleagues without whose dedicated, highly professional work this volume would never have been published, in particular Irina Herb, research assistant in the "Property in the human body" project and co-editor of the present volume, who coordinated the overall editing process. She was supported by fellow research assistant Abibi Stewart, who joined the project in its final stages. Our student colleagues Franziska Wohlfarth and Lilith Poßner did a final check of the manuscripts and took care of layout and formatting. We are also grateful to Andrew Godfrey-Collins and Übersetzungsbüro Denzig for meticulous language editing and for translations of several chapters.[2]

2 This introduction and the chapters by Graefe, Rahe and Schultz, including all quotations from German-language sources, were translated by Andrew Godfrey-Collins and revised by Hilla Czinczoll and by the editors.

Works Cited

Arneil, Barbara (1996). *John Locke and America: The Defence of English Colonialism*. Oxford: Clarendon Press.

Arneil, Barbara (2001). Women as Wives, Servants and Slaves: Rethinking the Public/Private Divide. *Canadian Journal of Political Science*, 34(1), 29–54.

Bergmann, Sven (2014). *Ausweichrouten der Reproduktion: Biomedizinische Mobilität und die Praxis der Eizellspende*. Wiesbaden: Springer.

Cooper, Melinda, and Catherine Waldby (2014). *Clinical Labour: Tissue Donors and Research Subjects in the Global Bioeconomy*. Durham, NC: Duke University Press.

Dyk, Silke van, Hartmut Rosa and Tilman Reitz (2024). *Nach dem Privateigentum? Güter, Infrastrukturen und Weltverhältnisse im Kapitalismus des 21. Jahrhunderts*. Frankfurt: Campus.

Ecker, Marlen van den, Tilman Reitz and Sebastian Sevignani (2023). Between Openness and Exclusion: Property and Profitability in the Information Economy. https://sfb294-eigentum.de/media/filer_public/b5/d3/b5d3f479-4a50-43bf-8e56-dc31389819eb/wp_02_ffinal.pdf.

Ediger, Gülden, Anthea Kyere, Ute Kalender and Valle Mazzaferro (2021). *Reproduktionstechnologien: Queere Perspektiven und reproduktive Gerechtigkeit*. Göttingen: Wallstein.

Gehring, Petra (2006). *Was ist Biomacht? Vom zweifelhaften Mehrwert des Lebens*. Frankfurt: Campus.

Herb, Irina, and Zelda Wenner (2023). Who Owns and Controls the Means of Reproduction? Assisted Fertility and Pregnancy as a Multi-Billion Dollar Market. https://sfb294-eigentum.de/de/blog/who-owns-and-controls-the-means-of-reproduction-assisted-fertility-and-pregnancy-as-a-multi-billion-dollar-market/.

Kommission zur reproduktiven Selbstbestimmung und Fortpflanzungsmedizin (2024). Bericht der Kommission zur reproduktiven Selbstbestimmung und Fortpflanzungsmedizin: Kurzbericht. https://www.bmfsfj.de/resource/blob/238404/08fd14b5eb28265c8201b69d12e456f4/kurzbericht-kommission-zur-reproduktiven-selbstbestimmung-und-fortpflanzungsmedizin-data.pdf.

König, Anika, and Heather Jacobson (2023). Reprowebs: A Conceptual Approach to Elasticity in the Global Assisted Reproduction Industry. *BioSocieties*, 18(1), 174–196.

Locke, John (1988 [1689]). *Two Treatises of Government*. Cambridge: Cambridge University Press.

Mamo, Laura and Eli Alston-Stepnitz (2015). Queer Intimacies and Structural Inequalities: New Directions in Stratified Reproduction. *Journal of Family Issues*, 36(4), 519–540.

Namberger, Verena (2019). *The Reproductive Body at Work: The South African Bioeconomy of Egg Donation*. London: Routledge.

Nahman, Michal (2018). Migrant Extractability: Centring the Voices of Egg Providers in Cross-Border Reproduction. *Reproductive BioMedicine & Society Online*, 7, 82–90.

Oksala, Johanna (2019). Feminism against Biocapitalism: Gestational Surrogacy and the Limits of the Labor Paradigm. *SIGNS: Journal of Women in Culture and Society*, 44(4), 883–904.

Pande, Amrita (2014). *Wombs in Labor: Transnational Commercial Surrogacy in India*. New York: Columbia University Press.

Pande, Amrita (ed.) (2022). *Birth Controlled: Selective Reproduction and Neoliberal Eugenics in South Africa and India*. Manchester: Manchester University Press.

Parry, Bronwyn (2015). Narratives of Neoliberalism: "Clinical Labour" in Context. *Critical Medical Humanities*, 41, 32–37.

Patrizio, Pasquale, David F. Albertini, Norbert Gleicher and Arthur Caplan (2022). The Changing World of IVF: The Pros and Cons of New Business Models Offering Assisted Reproductive Technologies. *Journal of Assisted Reproduction and Genetics*, 39, 305–313.

Perler, Laura, Carolin Schurr, Nora Komposch, Mirko Winkel and Pedro Alejandro Cervantez Rodríguez (2024). *Reproductive Geopolitics: Governing In/fertile Bodies in Mexico's Past and Present. Environment and Planning C: Politics and Space*, 42(1), 102–124.

Ross, Loretta (2021). Reproduktive Gerechtigkeit: Ein Rahmen für eine anti-essentialistische und intersektionale Politik. In Kitchen Politics (ed.). *Mehr als Selbstbestimmung! Kämpfe für reproduktive Gerechtigkeit*, 17–59. Münster: edition assemblage.

Safrin, Sabrina (2013). *Chain Reaction: How Property Begets Property. Notre Dame Law Review*, 82(5), 1917–1969. https://scholarship.law.nd.edu/cgi/viewcontent.cgi?article=1310&context=ndlr.

Siegrist, Hannes (2006). Die Propertisierung von Gesellschaft und Kultur: Konstruktion und Institutionalisierung des Eigentums in der Moderne. *Comparativ*, 16(5–6), 9–52.

Simpson, Bob, and Kate Hampshire (eds) (2015). *Assisted Reproductive Technologies: A Third Phase? Global Encounters and Emerging Moral Worlds*. New York: Berghahn.

Schultz, Susanne, and Kathrin Braun (2012). Der bioökonomische Zugriff auf Körpermaterialien: Eine politische Positionssuche am Beispiel der Forschung mit Eizellen. In Susanne Lettow (ed.). *Bioökonomie: Die Lebenswissenschaften und die Bewirtschaftung der Körper*, 61–83. Bielefeld: transcript.

Schurr, Carolin (2018). The Baby Business Booms: Economic Geographies of Assisted Reproduction. *Geography Compass*, 12(8), 1–15.

Siegl, Veronika (2023). *Intimate Strangers: Commercial Surrogacy in Russia and Ukraine and the Making of Truth*. Ithaca, NY: Cornell University Press.

Vertommen, Sigrid, Bronwyn Parry and Michal Nahman (eds.) (2022a). Global Fertility Chains and the Colonial Present of Assisted Reproductive Technologies. Special section of *Catalyst: Feminism, Theory, Technoscience*.

Vertommen, Sigrid, Vincenzo Pavone and Michal Nahman (2022b). An Integrative Political Economy Approach to Understanding the Reproductive Bioeconomy. *Science, Technology and Human Values*, 47(1), 112–145.

Vora, Kalindi (2015). *Life Support: Biocapital and the New History of Outsourced Labour*. Minneapolis: University of Minesota Press.

Waldby, Catherine (2019). *The Oocyte Economy: The Changing Meaning of Human Eggs*. Durham, NC: Duke University Press.

I
Dynamics of the ART Economy

Dynamics, Displacement and Disembedding: An Analysis of the Oocyte Economy in Contemporary Capitalism

Kathrin Braun

Human oocytes have become a key production factor and an important source of economic gains within an expanding and diversifying fertility industry. A simple Google search yields market research reports on market dynamics, projected growth rates, revenue and future opportunities in the fields of in vitro fertilisation (IVF), egg transfer and egg banking.[1] The retrieval, analysis, storage, management and transfer of human oocytes as well as associated activities of recruitment, counselling, marketing and logistics constitute a booming market that continues to attract capital investment.

Whereas the mainstream literature on bioethics and reproductive medicine has largely focused on the recipients, their desire for a child and their views, expectations, efforts and experiences, critical studies of the oocyte economy, in particular ones by feminist scholars of biopolitics and the bioeconomy, have highlighted the crucial but largely obscured role of women's[2] embodied labour for value creation in the reproductive bioeconomy (Degli Esposti and Pavone 2019; Molas and Perler 2020; Nahman and Weis 2023; Namberger 2016; Perler and Schurr 2020; van de Wiel 2020a; Vertommen, Pavone and Nahman 2021; Waldby 2019). They have drawn attention to the individuals who provide the eggs, their motivations, experiences and views and the embodied labour they invest to make the eggs available, as well as the various mechanisms and strategies used to render women's bodily materials available to regimes of value creation. Above all,

1 Examples include Coherent Market Insights 2021; Future Market Insights 2023; Market Reports World (MRW) 2023.

2 I have chosen to use the term "women" as a generic term in order to highlight the fact that practices and institutions of oocyte procurement are structured by gendered relations of work and exploitation. In doing so, I do not mean to deny that male or nonbinary people may also have the capacity to provide oocytes.

critical analyses have shown how the conditions under which women provide and receive oocytes for IVF treatment are structured by relations of race, class, citizenship, gender and other lines of inequality and domination (Daniels and Heidt-Forsythe 2012; Deomampo 2016; 2019; Namberger 2016; Pande 2021).

This chapter will build on this literature but approach the oocyte economy from a slightly different angle, focusing on its expansionist dynamic and its driving forces and implications. I will argue that in order to better understand this dynamic, we must highlight the role of new economic actors, such as investors, brokering agencies and commercial egg banks, whose interests are increasingly shaping the industry and are mediating "donor"-recipient relations. Drawing on the work of Nancy Fraser and Karl Polanyi, I will argue that at the heart of this expansion is a process of disembedding, rather than one of commodification. Although commodification also occurs, it is an epiphenomenon and not a driving force of disembedding. Disembedding, here, means that economic rationality is increasingly displacing medical rationality in medically assisted reproductive services. However, following Fraser and Polanyi, we can see that this is an inherently contradictory process: medical norms and standards and ideas of donation and altruism, family and parenthood as categories that should remain free of economic rationality are not simply displaced but also utilised economically.

This chapter begins by explaining the background to the growth of the fertility services industry, with a particular focus on oocyte procurement. I then turn to Polanyi's concepts of fictitious commodity and disembedding to describe how oocytes are incorporated into regimes of capitalist accumulation. Section three explains the concepts of commodification and altruism-cum-compensation and gives some background on how the latter plays out in practice. Section four argues that donor altruism, as a legal and discursive construct, is highly compatible with profit-oriented business models to the extent that it caters to customer demand. In this case, non-economic values *as such* are harnessed for economic value production. Section five turns to Fraser's expanded concept of capitalism to provide a theoretical account of this relation. Following Fraser, we can understand the co-existence of commodification and altruism-cum-compensation as a case in point of the interplay of marketised and non-marketised regimes of value creation and the latter as a form of accessing oocytes at almost no cost. In the final section, I take a closer look at the entry of new non-medical intermediary stakeholders into the oocyte economy, such as investors, brokering agencies and commercial egg banks, and show that they have significantly contributed to the erosion of medical rationality in the fertility services sector and the disembedding of the oocyte economy in particular. In the concluding section, I note that we can see a constant tension between medical and economic rationality in the fertility services industry in general and the oocyte economy in particular, with medical rationality belonging to the non-economic conditions of that industry's very possibility while at the same time being constantly undermined by the forces of marketisation.

1. No signs of slowing: the growth of the fertility services industry

Fertility treatments have become a fast-growing business sector. According to the European Society of Human Reproduction and Embryology (ESHRE), the number of fertility treatment cycles[3] carried out has grown by about 5–10 percent per year over the past few years in many developed countries, with no signs of slowing (ESHRE 2022). For the United States, the Society for Assisted Reproductive Technology (SART) reports a steady increase of IVF cycles from 248,086 in 2017 (SART 2023b) to 368,502 in 2021 (SART 2023a). In Europe, the number of fertility treatment cycles rose from 203,225 in 1997 to 1,007,598 in 2018 (Wyns et al. 2022, 3).[4] The number of institutions offering assisted reproductive technology (ART) services rose from 482 in 1997 to 1,422 in 2018 according to the European IVF Monitoring programme (EIM) (ibid., 5).

The vast majority of fertility treatments in the European Union take place in private clinics.[5] According to ESHRE data, in 2015 and 2016 treatments were administered by 275 public and 694 private clinics, but the ratio varied greatly between member states. In Spain, where the highest numbers of treatment cycles with "donor" oocytes are reported, the ratio between pri-

3 Treatment cycles monitored by the ESHRE include intrauterine insemination, IVF and intracytoplasmic sperm injection (ICSI) with or without egg transfer.

4 The ESHRE proudly reported that, as of 2018, "Europe leads the world in ART, initiating approximately 50 % of all reported treatment cycles" (ESHRE 2022).

5 Based on data for 2015 and 2016 reported to the ESHRE and the European Centre for Parliamentary Research and Documentation (ECPRD). Not all member states reported the relevant figures, however.

vate and public was 197 to 41 (fertility europe and ESHRE 2017, 11). In the United States, the majority of IVF clinics are now private, with a growing share owned by private equity groups and only a small minority situated within academic centres (Patrizio et al. 2022). IVF has become big business, attracting investors with its (projected) market and revenue growth. For 2022, the size of the global IVF market was estimated at 23.6 billion United States dollars and is expected to reach 37.4 billion United States dollars by 2030, based on a report by Grand View Research (GVR) (GVR 2023).[6] GVR also reports that Europe dominated the global market with the largest revenue share (37 percent) in 2022, a phenomenon which they attribute inter alia to an increasing number of Americans[7] choosing to travel to the Czech Republic for more cost-effective IVF.

Within the expanding fertility economy, the oocyte economy plays an increasing role. Out of the 1,007,598 treatment cycles reported to the ESHRE in 2018, 80,641 cycles included third-party egg provision[8] (Wyns et al. 2022, 5). In the United States, the annual number of third-party oocyte cycles increased from 10,801 in 2000 to 18,306 in 2010 (Kawwass et al. 2013). Pasquale Patrizio and his co-authors maintain that third-party egg donation cycles represent the most profitable IVF treatment in fertility centres (Patrizio et al. 2022).

But oocyte retrieval is still an invasive, time-consuming, onerous and by no means risk-free procedure that involves hormonal stimulation and surgical intervention. There is a certain risk, however low, of serious or even life-threatening complications, such as severe ovarian hyperstimulation syndrome (OHSS)[9] or ovarian torsion, which may require removal of the ovary. Even if the likelihood of severe complications may be low, it makes oocyte retrieval an invasive intervention into the body by medical means but not for a medical purpose, since neither the "donor's" nor the recipient's life or health

6 Such figures, as Lucy van de Wiel (2020a) notes, vary wildly and the methods they rely on are not transparent.

7 The context suggests that "Americans" refers here to United States Americans and Canadians.

8 The ESHRE, in line with much of the literature, uses the term "egg donation". Since this term is misleading, as explained above, I will speak of egg provision as an activity by women and egg procurement as the ensemble of activities necessary to mobilise, harvest, store and use human eggs for various purposes.

9 Figures on the occurrence of severe OHSS vary greatly. Tober et al. (2023b) cite studies estimating that severe OHSS occurs in roughly 1–10 percent of all ovarian stimulation cycles, whereas the ESHRE (2022) claims that OHSS (though not specifically severe OHSS) "is the most common complication related to ART, with a reported incidence rate of about 0.2 %".

are at stake. Therefore, oocyte retrieval compromises the bodily integrity of the "donor" for the benefit of another person, which contradicts the medical ethical principle of doing no harm. Importantly, the risk of OHSS is higher for younger women and women with a lower body mass index and healthy antral follicle counts (Tober et al. 2023b, 1292). At the same time, this is exactly the group of women who—from the perspective of egg procurement institutions—make the ideal "donor" candidate, since the quantity and quality of eggs they produce are likely to be higher. Moreover, Diane Tober and her team found that the risk of severe OHSS appears to increase according to the number of eggs produced in one cycle and that women who reported severe OHSS on a prior cycle had a significantly higher risk of experiencing severe OHSS on a subsequent one (ibid., 1295). This means that there is a structural incentive for oocyte-procuring actors to use riskier stimulation protocols to retrieve a higher quantity of eggs and an incentive to recruit a group of women who have a higher risk of experiencing severe complications.

In conclusion, oocyte transfer has become a thriving for-profit industry, where the drive for economic growth is at odds with the medical ethical principles of "do no harm" and "put the patient's health first". The expansion of the fertility services industry is therefore based to a significant extent on an invasive practice that aims to render women's bodies and bodily materials available for non-medical purposes.

While many of the public and ethical concerns about oocyte transfer revolve around the issue of commodification and "donor" payments,[10] I argue that we need a broader perspective to understand the expansionist dynamics of the political oocyte economy in contemporary capitalism. Firstly, we see a variety of oocyte procurement regimes, ranging from outright commodification to arrangements couched in terms of gifts, donation and altruism, all of which can be incorporated into capitalist strategies of value creation. Secondly, money does not only enter the sphere of reproductive relations when the egg "donor" is paid; financial incentives are a motivator for a whole range of other players to enter and expand the oocyte economy.

10 On the United States debate on "donor" payments, see Krawiec 2023.

2. Oocytes as fictitious commodities

Critical bioeconomy scholars have long pointed out the futility of trying to draw a clear line between gifts and commodities in relation to the human body and body parts (Almeling 2011, Braun and Schultz 2012, Degli Esposti and Pavone 2019, Høyer 2007, Namberger 2016, Parry 2008). In practice, there are myriad combinations and hybrids of gifts and commodities. Importantly, being a commodity, a gift or, say, an asset or a liability is not an essential quality of things. Rather, economic things can metamorphose through different forms over their lifetime (Braun et al. 2021). My use of the term "form" draws on Marx, who conceptualises form as a historically specific way of organising social relations. In capitalism, dominant forms include commodity, money, value, capital and doubly free labour. The forms that structure capitalist society, as Marx shows, are full of tensions and contradictions, combining use value and exchange value, freedom from serfdom and freedom from the means of subsistence, means of production and means of exploitation, and so on. A form is more than a legal or discursive construct, although it has that dimension too; it is also an institutionalised practice, a "social custom" (Marx 1990, 162) that structures social relations and makes their inherent contradictions and tensions manageable.[11] In this sense, we can understand the altruism-cum-compensation model, which will be explained below, as a specific form. At a conceptual level, we can distinguish it from commodification, even though in practice the two may be intermingled. Understanding altruism-cum-compensation as a specific form, rather than as not-yet-commodification, raises the question of how and why oocyte procurement, when organised through this form, appears as a non-economic process. To better understand how this form operates, I suggest it is useful to turn to the Polanyian concepts of commodity, fictitious commodity and disembedding.

Polanyi (2001 [1944]) understands commodities as goods that have been produced in order to sell them on a market.[12] Importantly, he distinguishes between "genuine" and "fictitious" commodities, with the latter denoting the production factors labour, land and money. Land, for Polanyi, is "only another name for nature" while labour "is only another name for a human ac-

11 On the "analysis of value form" in Marx's theory of capital, see Heinrich 2004a.

12 Polanyi does not depart from Marx on this point, but rather on the distinction between genuine and fictitious commodities.

tivity which goes with life itself" and cannot be detached from the rest of human life (ibid., 75). Another way he puts it is that labour is "the technical term used for human beings" insofar as they are being employed to create economic value (ibid., 79). Land and labour are essential for a capitalist economy and are effectively traded on markets, but they are not *produced* for sale on a market. I would contend that the conceptual distinction between genuine and fictitious commodities ultimately rests on the question of socio-ethical acceptability. When Polanyi says that land and labour *cannot* be produced for sale on a market, this does not mean that it is technically impossible to buy and sell them, or to subject them to market rules, since that is in fact possible. Rather, it means that the consequences of doing so are not acceptable to society. Whether or not it is considered destructive for society to leave masses of people without means of subsistence because their labour power is not in demand on the market is a socio-ethical and political question, not a technical one. Ultimately, the reason behind conceptualising labour as a fictitious commodity is that it is inseparable from the human body and therefore from the human person. When labour is treated like a commodity, the consequences for human life in society are disastrous, as it means that human beings are treated *like* genuine commodities and that human life and social relations are subjected to the rules of the market. Economic activities are then no longer embedded in norms and values of social life. Instead, society becomes subordinate to a disembedded market economy where economic rationality displaces any other social, moral or cultural rationality—including the professional and ethical rationality of medicine.

Critical bioeconomy scholars have used the Polanyian concept of fictitious commodity to capture the status of body parts, bodily materials and living beings that are incorporated into the bioeconomy (Goven and Pavone 2015; Lettow 2014; 2015). If we follow this line of thought, human oocytes can be understood as fictitious commodities: they can be bought and sold on a market and function as essential production factors for a segment of the economy, but as long as they cannot be produced for sale outside the human body in a laboratory, they are fictitious commodities in the Polanyian sense. According to Polanyi, however, the emergence of a disembedded economy has also given rise to countermovements in the form of public policies, safeguards and regulations. These include labour protection laws, minimum wage provisions and social security policies designed to protect society from its most destructive consequences. As regards the fields of biomedicine and reproductive medicine, the "prohibition on making the human body and its parts as such a source of financial gain" (FRA 2025) enshrined in Article 3 of the European Union's Charter of Fundamental Rights and Article 21 of the Council of Europe's Convention on Human Rights and Biomedicine can be considered a protective measure against a disembedded (bio)economy in this sense (Council of Europe 2025).

3. Commodification and altruistic donation: distinctions, co-existence and metamorphoses

It is important to recognise that outright commodification of bodily materials is not the only form that disembedding can take in the bioeconomy. With regard to oocytes, by outright commodification I mean a situation where a woman is officially entitled to offer her oocytes for sale on a market. Under such conditions, oocytes can be retrieved for the overt purpose of being sold by the woman who provides them. Outright commodification means that the woman is the owner of the oocytes even before they are retrieved. But this does not mean that they cease to be fictitious commodities in the Polanyian sense; they are still not produced for sale, but are grown inside the woman's body and cannot be retrieved without intervening in it. It does mean, however, that the woman is entitled to set the price, choose a buyer or cancel the sale. In jurisdictions where there are no politically imposed limitations on such transactions, such as price caps or restrictions on use, we can speak of unfettered outright commodification. Outright commodification means that the oocytes have the form of a commodity from the moment of retrieval, whereas in the altruism-cum-compensation model they take the form of a gift first and then possibly undergo a metamorphosis into a commodity. To be sure, the altruism-cum-donation model does not rule out *all* commodification of oocytes. Depending on the legal framework, formerly "donated" oocytes may become the property of a clinic or an egg bank, who then may decide to offer them for sale to other buyers. Outright commodification only means that the oocytes do not have to metamorphose through the stage of a gift or donation first. Moreover, when outright commodification is allowed in a given jurisdiction, this does not mean that there are no other procurement schemes alongside it, nor that in practice there cannot be combinations and hybrids.

Outright commodification is well established in large parts of the United States (Tober et al. 2023a), where the price of eggs depends to a large extent on mechanisms of supply and demand; eggs for which there is high demand—depending on the providing woman's genetic traits, educational, professional or athletic performance, race, ethnicity or other desired attributes—command higher prices (Deomampo 2019; Levine 2010). In this case, commodification co-evolves with the property rights of both vendors and buyers (e.g. warranty rights or rights to use, destroy or resell the eggs), which are conferred through legislation, court rulings (Lewis 2016) and professional guidelines and regulations. In 2021, the American Society for Reproductive Medicine (ASRM) took another step towards unfettered commodification by abandoning their guidelines on capping egg "donor" compensation (Krawiec 2023).

In Europe and South Africa (Namberger 2016, 52 ff), in contrast, we see various ways in which elements of commodification are combined with elements of the gift relation at the levels of regulation, logistical arrangements, business models, framing and imagination. Nevertheless, the oocyte economy has expanded greatly in these regions even without outright commodification. Framing oocyte provision as a "gift of life" or even "a priceless gift" (ibid., 42) does not rule out monetary incentivisation; it only means that this incentivisation is legally and discursively couched in terms of reimbursement or compensation instead of price. Unlike in the case of outright commodification, where women can negotiate the price for their eggs, the compensation model means that the amount of money she can receive is fixed in advance. Moreover, in the case of outright commodification the woman can decide whether she wishes to sell all the harvested eggs, keep some, destroy some or give them away for free, whereas the donation-cum-compensation model confers this right on a third party, usually the clinic.

Article 12(1) of the European Union Tissue and Cells Directive (2004/23/EC) stipulates that "donors" of cells or tissue, including oocytes, "may receive compensation, which is strictly limited to making good the expenses and inconveniences related to the donation". But in practice, reimbursement for proven expenses has become the exception rather than the rule. Instead, a fixed amount of compensation per "donation" cycle is most common, ranging from 250 euros in Finland to 2,000 euros at some clinics in Belgium (Quaas and Pennings 2018, 1206).[13] In Bulgaria, according to a report by

13 In Spain it is 1,000 euros (Lafuente-Funes 2017) and in Greece 1,200 euros (Bernardo 2022).

the European Data Journalism Network (Bernardo 2022), compensation is equivalent to eleven weeks on the minimum wage, which is the highest amount of compensation relative to the minimum wage in Europe, followed by Greece in second place. In Ukraine, where there are no rules on compensation, there are reports that women can receive outright payment depending on the number of eggs they provide (Baklitskaya and Chodownik 2021). This may *de facto* amount to outright commodification, but not *de jure*, since selling one's oocytes is not officially authorised by law.

Payment according to quantity involves an incentive for the woman to undergo higher hormonal stimulation in order to produce as many eggs as possible. Fixed compensation, by contrast, means that it is the clinic, rather than the woman, that is incentivised to increase hormonal stimulation, as it can obtain a greater number of eggs for the same amount of money. Meanwhile, it creates an incentive for women, especially those with debts and limited earning opportunities, to undergo repeated cycles of "donation".

It should be clear from the previous sections that outright commodification is not the only way that oocytes are inserted into the circuits of capital. Rather, it co-exists alongside, and can be combined with, various versions of the altruism-cum-compensation model. While outright commodification may be increasingly accepted in United States law (Krawiec 2023), it is still constrained in Europe by legal and ethical reservations about the commercialisation of the human body. These reservations are enshrined inter alia in the European Union Charter of Fundamental Rights and the Council of Europe's Convention on Human Rights and Biomedicine. But it should also have become clear that the altruism-cum-compensation model preferred in Europe does not constrain the expansive growth of the oocyte economy.

I therefore suggest giving some more thought to the role that the altruism-cum-compensation model plays in the thriving oocyte economy. What does it do for the oocyte economy that outright commodification cannot do? How can we understand the relation between altruism as a legal and discursive construct and the economic logic that drives the oocyte economy?

4. Altruism and monetary motivation: not so opposed after all

Much of the legal and ethical discourse is preoccupied with the question of "donor" motivation, constructing oocyte provision as ethically problematic only in cases where the motivation of "donors"—not that of clinics—is to make money. If women do it for altruistic reasons, so the assumption goes, it is not ethically problematic because they do it out of their own free will rather than because they are in financial distress and forced to make money. From a business perspective, however, altruistic motives on the part of the "donors" and economic motives on the part of the clinic are not mutually exclusive. On the contrary, donor altruism can actually be a selling point if it aligns with customer preferences, as Krawiec notes:

> At some level, this insistence on the altruistic motives of egg donors is driven by customer demand: donor-agency staff report a belief that fertility customers do not want egg donors who reveal monetary motivations for the desire to donate.
>
> *Krawiec 2009, 1758*

While women may rarely, if ever, undergo egg retrieval without receiving money for it, many customers prefer the idea of receiving a selfless gift instead of purchasing an oocyte (Kroløkke 2013). There may be various reasons behind this preference, among them a desire not to be someone who exploits women who are forced to sell their bodily materials. Another possible reason is a concern that the egg might pass down the "donor's" egoistic personality to the prospective child: Krawiec quotes an egg donor agency director who said that customers "want to know that the person donating is a good person. They want to know that person wasn't doing it for the money" (Krawiec 2009, 1758). Still another reason may be that many prospective parents, even though they may have paid money for IVF which includes an egg transfer, share a culturally entrenched sense that children and family bonds should not be for sale. More specifically, they may want to think that their own parental relationships that they are about to establish are not founded on relations of commodity exchange but on ones of love and care.

If this is so, then the idea of altruism and giving a priceless gift is part of what is being sold; customers pay for a service involving "altruistic donation". Thus, the altruism(-cum-compensation) form benefits the industry by catering to customer demand. To put it more bluntly: the quality of being unsellable is part of what is being sold and the supposed non-economic character of "donor"–recipient relations is incorporated into the economic logic governing the oocyte economy. In the following section, I will argue that Fraser's expanded conception of capitalism is useful for understanding the "imbrications", as she puts it, between these economic and non-economic, marketised and non-marketised relations.

5. The imbrications of marketised and non-marketised relations in the oocyte economy

Following Fraser (2022), we can understand the altruism-cum-compensation model as a case in point of the interplay of marketised and non-marketised regimes of value creation that she sees as a constitutive feature of capitalism. Fraser takes issue with the view of capitalism, articulated inter alia by Georg Lukács, as a system characterised by pervasive commodification and monetisation, where the commodity form colonises all aspects of human life (Fraser 2022, 18). "Commodification", she counters, "is far from universal in capitalist society. On the contrary, where it is present, it depends for its very existence on zones of non-commodification, which capital systematically cannibalizes" (ibid.).

Importantly, she understands capitalism not as a type of economy but a type of society. It is

> a societal order that empowers a profit-driven economy to prey on the extra-economic support it needs to function—wealth expropriated from nature and subject peoples; multiple forms of carework, chronically undervalued when not wholly disavowed; public goods and public powers, which capital both requires and tries to curtail; the energy and creativity of working people.
>
> *ibid., xiv*

Capitalism thus comprises both the capitalist market economy in the narrow sense, structured by class relations, property rights, contract law, commodity production and doubly free labour, and what Fraser terms non-economic conditions for the possibility of a capitalist society. She introduces the conceptual distinction between exploitation and expropriation to denote two different but in her view equally constitutive and interlinked ways of incorporating human capacities into the circuits of capitalist accumulation. Exploitation is mediated through institutions such as the market, property rights and the wage contract, whereas expropriation denotes a method by which capital accesses human capacities, energy, raw materials and other resources cheaply or for free (ibid., 34–35).[14] In the case of oocyte procure-

14 Strictly, it would be more accurate to speak of *a*ppropriation, not *ex*propriation. The term *ex*propriation suggests that the object or capacity being expropriated was previously someone's property. That, however, implicitly construes property as an ahistorical and apolitical condition, rather than one established by legal and political action. Land, for instance, that was appropriated by force and then transformed into the property of the appropriator was not necessarily consid-

ment, we can say that the altruism-cum-compensation model comes close to expropriation in Fraser's sense, making the oocytes and the donors' embodied labour available nearly for free.

Importantly, expropriation operates on an institutional and not an extra-institutional basis. Fraser insists that expropriation is not a lingering remnant from former, precapitalist eras that will sooner or later fade away. Instead, she contends, capitalism structurally relies on expropriation. This structural linkage, in her view, has at least two aspects, an economic and a moral one, both of which are relevant to the oocyte economy. Regarding the economic dimension, she argues that production costs would soar if capital could not freeride on production factors such as the existence of workers and natural resources. Regarding the moral dimension, she follows Polanyi (2001 [1944]) in arguing that markets depend for their very existence on non-marketised social relations. She holds that efforts to totalise marketisation jeopardise non-marketised relations that, however, form the conditions of possibility of capitalist society. These encompass relations of care and social reproduction in a broader sense, including building communities and preserving social bonds and shared horizons of value that underpin social cooperation. In this context, Fraser refers to the Hegelian concept of *Sittlichkeit* as the socio-ethical substratum that makes it possible to sustain social life even in capitalist societies (Fraser 2022, 9).

I suggest that the idea that the sphere of family and parenthood should remain a zone of personalised, non-commodified relationships can be understood as part of this socio-ethical substratum. The same, I would argue, can be said of the medical ethical principle of putting the patient's health first. In the next section, I will therefore take a closer look at the imbrications of economic and medical rationality in the fertility services sector and the forces driving the disembedding of the oocyte economy.

---

ered anyone's property before. For the sake of consistency with Fraser's terminology, however, I will use the term "expropriation" here.

6. New stakeholders and the disembedding of the oocyte economy

I have argued that oocyte "donation" involves an intervention in the body by medical means but not for a medical purpose—and that that intervention is not risk-free. It requires professional medical knowledge to perform the intervention, but its purpose is not to save the life or improve the health of either the "donor" or the recipient. Moreover, performing a non-trivial intervention in the body of one person for the benefit of another violates the medical ethical principles of doing no harm and putting the patient first. From this perspective, medical rationality, understood as a set of professional norms and standards governing knowledge, training and performance as well as values and ethics, forms both a prerequisite for and a constraint on the expansion of the oocyte economy. It is a prerequisite inasmuch as physicians' medical competence and professional integrity, and the confidence that "donors" and recipients have in them, are essential for performing egg retrievals and transfers. However, medical rationality imposes constraints on the oocyte economy inasmuch as it prioritises patient safety over economic gain. It requires physicians to forego treatment options that may be economically attractive but detrimental to patients. To the extent that, in practice, economic rationality displaces medical rationality, we can speak of a disembedding of the oocyte economy. In recent years, this process has been driven in no small part by the entry of new types of stakeholders who are not bound by medical rationality, such as investors, agencies and egg banks.

6.1 Investment firms

Patrizio Pasquale and his co-authors (Patrizio et al. 2022) have shown how private investment firms have increasingly entered the fertility industry in the United States, Australia and New Zealand, fuelling a trend towards economic concentration in the IVF sector and the dominance of large fertility clinic chains. Due to this trend, the authors argue, IVF has not only become big business but transformed from a physician-driven business environment into an investor-driven one. Three types of business models are underpinning economic growth in this for-profit sector:

(a) progressive growth and expansions of physician-owned practices;

(b) private investment firms entering the IVF market through acquisition of existing IVF practices and merging them into networks with physicians remaining employed and becoming shareholders after their "cashout"; and

(c) establishment of new independent IVF clinics, fully financed by investors hiring reproductive endocrinologists to run them profitably under a variety of incentive programme. (Patrizio et al. 2022, 308).

The authors report that in Australia and New Zealand three "mega network companies" now control two-thirds of the region's IVF cycles (ibid., 310). However, they note, this trend has not been accompanied by an increase in live births after IVF. On the contrary: live births have declined, with this decline strongly correlated with economic concentration.

Sometimes, entire fertility chains are sold to even larger chains, as was the case in 2020 with the NMC Eugin Group, which at the time comprised 31 IVF clinics and 34 additional sites across nine countries. It was sold for 430 million euros to German health giant Fresenius Helios, which owns properties in Germany, Spain and Latin America. Large chains are expected to respond to investors rather than patients. The authors describe several mechanisms by which capital accumulation is prioritised over patient health and well-being. These mechanisms include, but are not limited to, encouraging more invasive and costly treatment even when less invasive options are acceptable, aggressively marketing costly but non-validated services such as elective egg freezing to very young women and rejecting patients with a poorer prognosis "unless they can be directed towards third party egg donation cycles, which represent the most profitable IVF treatment in fertility centers" (Patrizio et al. 2022, 310). Large chains have a competitive advantage over academic institutions and are expanding at their expense, which will ultimately mean that institutions that are able to train the next generation of reproductive medicine specialists will die out.

6.2 *Egg brokerage agencies*

Another new type of stakeholder that has proliferated in the ART sector is egg brokerage agencies. Like egg banks, which I discuss in the next section, these agencies can be understood as non-medical "egg intermediaries". Both types of institutions play a part in mediating between egg "donors" and recipients and both exist at a distance from medical accreditation and regulation (Hudson et al. 2020).

Egg brokerage agencies are for-profit organisations that exist outside the realm of professional medicine and are not subject to professional codes of conduct. Katherine Johnson (2017) found that in the United States these organisations are usually staffed and directed by non-medical personnel, reproductive lawyers, family practitioners, previous "donors" and even former modelling agency Chief Executive Officers. They typically set up a website and a "donor" database, recruit "donors", manage the application process and make arrangements between "donors" and recipients. In a study on South Africa, Verena Namberger (2016, 49) found that they may also organise social events for "donors" and coach them on how to fill in the application form and create a personal profile. These profiles form the core of the online databases that are central to the agencies' business model. Egg "donation" agencies can thus be understood as digital platforms (Mejias and Couldry 2019). Digital platforms are intermediaries that collect, process, curate and store data and make it accessible to different types of users. In this case, the platform brings together potential oocyte providers, potential recipients and institutional oocyte buyers such as IVF clinics and, in some cases, research institutions or pharmaceutical companies. Donor agencies do not actually sell oocytes as commodities but generate revenue from creating donor profiles, making them available to other platform users and managing user interactions on the platform. In this sense, donor agencies can be understood as digital platforms that generate revenue in the form of rents from donor profiles as data assets. Following Kean Birch and Fabian Muniesa, we can speak here of a process of assetisation rather than commodification (Birch 2020; Birch and Muniesa 2020). Importantly, platforms are characterised by "network effects" which arise from the fact that the more attractive a platform is, and hence the more revenue it is able to generate, the more users it can win over and the more data it can offer (Birch, Cochrane and Ward 2021; Srnicek 2017). In the case of online donor agencies, this means that the more profiles they have and the more data-rich those profiles are, the more attractive the agency will be to potential customers and the more successful it will be on the market.[15] Analyses of egg "donation" agency websites have shed light on this dynamic and its impli-

15 In other domains, this dynamic has led to processes of economic concentration, with a few big corporations coming to dominate the whole sector. See Kenney and Zysman 2020. However, I could not find any information about whether this is currently happening with donor agencies too.

cations. In her research on the oocyte economy in South Africa, Namberger shows that "donor" profiles, even if they may be formally anonymised, are detailed, carefully curated and highly personalised data assets that offer information on behavioural features, romantic relationships, sexual practices, physical and psychological conditions, genetic traits, hair and eye colour, height, education, talents, religion and more, and often photos of the donor as a child as a way to meet anonymity requirements while still offering customers as much data as possible. Again, these agencies are not bound by medical rationality; staff have usually not taken the Hippocratic oath and professional medical associations cannot sanction any misconduct. Incentives to enrol very young women, for instance, even though the risk of OHSS is higher in this group, and to encourage repeated egg retrieval are not counterbalanced by principles of professional medical ethics.

From another perspective, Jason Keehn and his team (Keehn et al. 2015) looked at the websites of United States egg "donation" agencies and analysed whether they considered medical norms and the risks of oocyte provision. They found that in 2010, 74 percent of websites made no mention of the ASRM ethical guidelines on financial compensation, 41 percent accepted donors aged under 21, 56 percent did not discuss any short-term risks such as OHSS, infection or hospitalisation and 92 percent did not acknowledge any possible risk to future fertility.

6.3 Commercial egg banks

Another type of stakeholder that has newly entered the fertility services sector over the past 15 years or so and also acts as a non-medical intermediary is commercial egg banks (CEBs). The rise of egg banking is closely connected to the technique of vitrification or rapid cooling for oocyte cryopreservation. While oocyte cryopreservation has been used since the 1980s, success rates in terms of live births remained poor for a long time. This changed with the advent of vitrification procedures, which significantly improved success rates and in many respects revolutionised the fertility services industry.

In this context, two new types of practice have emerged, each linked to the formation of a new institutional infrastructure and new business models: a) autologous egg banking, where women freeze and store their own eggs for possible IVF treatment later in life and b) heterologous egg banking, where frozen "donor" eggs are stored for unspecified recipients (CDC

2022; Quaas and Pennings 2018). Autologous egg banking can be subdivided into egg freezing prior to chemotherapy or removal of ovaries, or for other medical reasons, and "social" or "elective" freezing for purposes of fertility preservation for non-medical reasons. Both autologous and heterologous egg banking services are associated with the rise of for-profit institutions that are, once again, shifting the boundaries and power relations between the medical realm and the business sector in favour of the latter.

Lucy van de Wiel (2020a; 2020b) has shown how egg freezing infrastructures in the United States have been expanding due to large financial investments in cryopreservation. Since 2016, she reports, millions of dollars of private equity and venture capital have been invested in egg freezing businesses, often start-ups, followed by strategies of expansion, mergers and acquisitions, as Patrizio et al. also found for the IVF sector in general. Van de Wiel interprets these developments against the backdrop of financial capitalism. What we are seeing, she believes, is a shift towards the financialisation of fertility. She argues that the emergence of financialised egg freezing implies a broader reorganisation of reproductive healthcare, with a focus on fertility preservation and prediction technologies rather than infertility treatment. One key strategy to increase revenue and expand market size in this sector is to target young, presumably fertile women and persuade them to spend a certain amount of money over several years on elective egg freezing in order to preserve their fertility, thereby broadening their range of options for the timing of family and career. It is not infertility treatment that the industry offers but "a state of having options" (van de Wiel 2020b). Targeting fertile women opens up a much bigger market than targeting infertile women. The rise of CEBs is thus expanding the boundaries of the medical realm to the point where they are virtually disappearing.

In addition to freezing and storing services, egg freezing start-ups and companies outside the ART sector have started to market financial products such as subscription plans, fertility loans and fertility insurance in order to lure women, in particular young women, into long-term egg banking. In 2014, Apple and Facebook began offering egg freezing benefits to their employees, and a growing number of companies have since followed suit (van de Wiel 2020a). As van de Wiel points out, these practices actively encourage private indebtedness, another characteristic of financialised capitalism.

In addition to businesses offering autologous egg banking services, commercial "donor" egg banks have become increasingly common. Alexander Quaas and Guido Pennings define a donor egg bank as "a commercial entity that recruits egg donors with the purpose of creating a repository of vitrified oocytes available to prospective recipients of egg donation" (2018, 1205). The first instance of a commercial "donor" egg bank was reported in 2007. Five years later, there were seven such institutions in the United States, and another five years later the number had risen to 16 (Williams et al. 2022). Also in the United States, the percentage of third-party oocyte cycles using oocytes from CEBs instead of oocytes obtained through the clinic's own recruitment scheme increased from 7.7 percent of all reported third-party oocyte cycles in 2016 to 24.2 percent in 2018 (ibid.).

Using CEBs has considerable logistical advantages for IVF clinics: IVF with fresh "donor" eggs is based on a one-to-one model, as Catherine Waldby (2019, 128) explains. Thus, fresh donor cycles are highly personalised transactions involving time-consuming and labour-intensive processes of temporal alignment between the receiving woman's and the providing woman's cycles. Due to these logistical requirements, fresh "donor" eggs can only be used for this one recipient. Cryopreservation in combination with egg banking, in contrast, makes it possible to store eggs that have been harvested from one woman and use them for IVF treatment of multiple recipients at different points in time and in different geographic locations. "The ability to use one batch of donor oocytes", Quaas and Pennings note, "helps to improve access, reduce recipient wait times and costs, and decrease excess embryo storage and wastage" (2018, 30). The shift from a one-to-one to a one-to-many model thus increases the incentive for CEBs to expand and diversify their "donor" pool as much as possible and at the same time to extract as many eggs per "donor" cycle as possible. In the United States, where there are no legal rules on compensation, high amounts of compensation that go beyond ASRM guidelines are one strategy to recruit ever more donors and also to motivate them to undergo egg provision multiple times. According to Quaas and Pennings, recruitment is usually done via websites, and not all of these websites comply with ASRM guidelines. In the absence of a national tracking system, the rise of CEBs could well lead to an increasing number of repeat "donors".

One interesting question in this context is who owns the oocytes once extraction is completed and "compensation" has been paid. "At the moment," Quaas and Pennings note, "CEBs appear to believe that they own the eggs and can decide on their distribution and use" (2018, 1207). As owners, they could also resell them, for instance to other egg banks, to research institutions or to pharmaceutical companies. Whether and to what extent this is already happening is not currently known.

7. Conclusion

IVF has become big business today, and an increasing portion of this business relies on harvesting, screening, storing, dispatching and transferring women's oocytes for other women's fertility treatment. It is a business that relies on medical knowledge but also transgresses medical norms in multiple respects: for instance, invasive and potentially risky interventions in women's bodies in the absence of any medical indication violate the ethical principle of doing no harm. In recent years, the sector has been increasingly dominated by stakeholders from outside the medical profession who are not bound by medical rationality. By medical rationality, I mean the commitment to put the health and well-being of the patient first and above other interests and to make this principle the maxim of one's professional conduct. Medical rationality in this sense is anchored in formal and informal norms and values and is enforced by a variety of institutions, from professional accreditation schemes and codes of conduct to international treaties and conventions. New stakeholders, such as investors, egg brokers and egg banks of various types, are entering what used to be the domain of the medical profession and are reorganising it according to principles of capital accumulation. They have not committed themselves to do no harm and put patients first. Luring people into debt, for instance, for something they may never need is perfectly compatible with economic rationality; whether it is also compatible with medical rationality is not something these stakeholders have to consider. Following Polanyi, we can describe this trend as a process of disembedding the oocyte economy and indeed the ART economy as a whole. It involves structural incentives to displace medical rationality in favour of economic rationality, for instance by using more risky stimulation protocols, specifically recruiting younger "donors" and encouraging repeat "donation". Thus, in the field of ART, actors guided by imperatives of capital accumulation are employing medical knowledge and what remains of medical norms and standards in order to retain trust and attract potential customers while simultaneously eroding the institutional basis of those norms and standards. Following Fraser, we can understand these developments and their implications as contradictory yet institutionalised "imbrications" between the imperative of accumulation and what she terms the non-economic conditions of possibility of capitalist societies. Also following Fraser, we can see that commodification is only part of the story. While women's bodily materials and their embodied labour are integrated into processes of capital accumulation, this does not necessarily take the form of pervasive commodification, but to a large degree occurs through procurement regimes couched in terms of altruism, gifts and compensation. Outright commodification in the form of selling eggs per piece is only one model, mainly found in the United States, while in Europe and South Africa the prevailing model combines monetised incentives with a framing in terms of gifts and altruism. In Fraser's terms, we can speak of a continuum between outright commodification and "expropriation", with altruism-cum-compensation models being located somewhere in the middle, appropriating women's bodily capacities as cheap input into processes that generate revenue and accumulate capital for private clinics and non-medical stakeholders such as investors, agencies and egg banks. Disembedding of the oocyte economy, however, occurs along this entire continuum.

Works Cited

Almeling, Rene (2011). *Sex Cells: The Medical Market for Eggs and Sperm*. Berkeley: University of California Press.

Baklitskaya, Kate, and Magdelena Chodownik (2021). Poor Legal Regulation Threatens Health of Ukraine's Egg Donors. *New Eastern Europe*, 15 March. https://neweasterneurope.eu/2021/03/15/poor-legal-regulation-threatens-health-of-ukraines-egg-donors/.

Bernardo, Ángela (2022). Ten European Countries Pay Egg Donors Anywhere from 250 to 2,000 Euros. *civio: medicamentalia*, 7 March. https://civio.es/medicamentalia/2022/03/07/egg-sperm-donors-financial-compensation-europe/.

Birch, Kean (2020). Technoscience Rent: Toward a Theory of Rentiership for Technoscientific Capitalism. *Science, Technology & Human Values*, 45(1), 3–33.

Birch, Kean, and Fabian Muniesa (2020). *Assetization: Turning Things into Assets in Technoscientific Capitalism*. Cambridge, MA: MIT Press.

Birch, Kean, D.T. Cochrane and Callum Ward (2021). Data as Asset? The Measurement, Governance, and Valuation of Digital Personal Data by Big Tech. *Big Data & Society*, 8(1).

Braun, Kathrin, and Susanne Schultz (2012). Oöcytes for Research: Inspecting the Commercialisation Continuum. *New Genetics and Society*, 31(2), 135–157.

Braun, Veit, Saskia Brill and Alexander Dobeson (2021). The Mutability of Economic Things. *Journal of Cultural Economy,* 14(3), 271–279.

CDC (2022). *2020 Assisted Reproductive Technology Fertility Clinic and National Summary Report.* US Dept of Health and Human Services.

Coherent Market Insights (2021). Ovum Egg Banking Market: Business Growth Factors, Top Manufacturers, Revenue, Demand & Forecast to 2028. *Global Banking & Finance Review,* 10 March. https://www.globalbankingandfinance.com/ovum-egg-banking-market-business-growth-factors-top-manufacturers-revenue-demand-forecast-to-2028/.

Council of Europe (2025). Convention on Human Rights and Biomedicine. https://www.coe.int/de/web/bioethics/oviedo-convention.

Daniels, Cynthia R., and Erin Heidt-Forsythe (2012). Gendered Eugenics and the Problematic of Free Market Reproductive Technologies: Sperm and Egg Donation in the United States. *Signs,* 37(3), 719–747.

Degli Esposti, Sara, and Vincenzo Pavone (2019). Oocyte Provision as a (Quasi) Social Market: Insights from Spain. *Social Science & Medicine,* 234.

Deomampo, Daisy (2016). Race, Nation, and the Production of Intimacy: Transnational Ova Donation in India. *positions: asia critique,* 24(1), 303–332.

Deomampo, Daisy (2019). Racialized Commodities: Race and Value in Human Egg Donation. *Medical Anthropology,* 38(7), 620–633.

ESHRE (2022). *Art Fact Sheet.* https://www.eshre.eu/Data-collection-and-research/Consortia/EIM.

European IVF-Monitoring (EIM) Consortium for the European Society of Human Reproduction and Embryology (ESHRE) (2012). Assisted Reproductive Technology in Europe, 2008: Results Generated from European Registers by ESHRE. *Human Reproduction,* 27(9), 2571–2584.

European IVF-Monitoring (EIM) Consortium for the European Society for Human Reproduction and Embryology (ESHRE) (2017). Assisted Reproductive Technology in Europe, 2013: Results Generated from European Registers by ESHRE. *Human Reproduction,* 32(10), 1957–1973.

fertility europe and ESHRE (2017). A Policy Audit on Fertility. https://fertilityeurope.eu/wp-content/uploads/2018/03/EPAF_FINAL.pdf.

FRA (2025). EU Charter of Fundamental Rights. http://fra.europa.eu/en/eu-charter.

Fraser, Nancy (2022). *Cannibal Capitalism.* London: Verso.

Future Market Insights (2023). In Vitro Fertilization Banking Services Market. https://www.futuremarketinsights.com/reports/in-vitro-fertilization-banking-services-market.

Goven, Joanna, and Vincenzo Pavone (2015). The Bioeconomy as Political Project: A Polanyian Analysis. *Science, Technology & Human Values,* 40(3), 302–337.

GVR (2023). In Vitro Fertilization Market Size to Reach $ 37.4 Billion by 2030. https://www.grandviewresearch.com/press-release/global-ivf-market.

Heinrich, Michael (2004a). Ambivalences of Marx's Critique of Political Economy as Obstacles for the Analysis of Contemporary Capitalism. Paper presented at the Historical Materialism Conference, 10 October, in London, UK.

Heinrich, Michael (2004b). *An Introduction to the Three Volumes of Karl Marx's Capital.* New York: Monthly Review Press.

Høyer, Klaus (2007). Person, Patent and Property: A Critique of the Commodification Hypothesis. *BioSocieties,* 2, 327–348.

Hudson, Nicky, Lorraine Culley, Cathy Herbrand, Vincenzo Pavone, Guido Pennings, Veerle Provoost, Catherine Coveney and Sara Lafuente-Funes (2020). Reframing Egg Donation in Europe: New Regulatory Challenges for a Shifting Landscape. *Health Policy and Technology,* 9(3), 308–313.

Johnson, Katherine M. (2017). The Price of an Egg: Oocyte Donor Compensation in the US Fertility Industry. *New Genetics and Society,* 36(4), 354–374.

Kawwass, Jenniger F., Michael Monsour, Sara Crawford, Dimitry M. Kissin, Donna R. Session, Aniket D. Kulkarni, Denise J. Jamieson and National ART Surveillance System (NASS) Group (2013). Trends and Outcomes for Donor Oocyte Cycles in the United States, 2000–2010. *JAMA,* 17 October, E1–E9.

Keehn, Jason, Eve Howell, Mark V. Sauer and Robert Klitzman (2015). How Agencies Market Egg Donation on the Internet: A Qualitative Study. *Journal of Law, Medicine & Ethics,* 43(3), 610–618.

Kenney, Martin, and John Zysman (2020). The Platform Economy: Restructuring the Space of Capitalist Accumulation. *Cambridge Journal of Regions, Economy and Society,* 13(1), 55–76.

Krawiec, Kimberly D. (2009). A Woman's Worth. *North Carolina Law Review,* 88, 1739–1770.

Krawiec, Kimberly D. (2023). Gametes: Commodification and the Fertility Industry. In Vida Panitch and Elodie Bertrand (eds.). *The Routledge Handbook of Commodification,* 278–289. London: Routledge.

Kroløkke, Charlotte H. (2013). West Is Best: Affective Assemblages and Spanish Oocytes. *European Journal of Women's Studies,* 21(1), 57–71.

Lafuente-Funes, Sara (2017). Egg Donation in the Making: Gender, Selection and (In)visibilities in the Spanish Bioeconomy of Reproduction. In Vincent Pavone and Joanna Goven (eds.). *Bioeconomies,* 253–277. Houndmills, Basingstoke: Palgrave Macmillan.

Lettow, Susanne (2014). *Biookonomie: Die Lebenswissenschaften und die Bewirtschaftung der Körper.* Bielefeld: transcript.

Lettow, Susanne (2015). Biokapitalismus und Inwertsetzung der Körper. *PROKLA,* 45(178), 33–49.

Levine, Aaron D. (2010). Self-Regulation, Compensation, and the Ethical Recruitment of Oocyte Donors. *Hastings Center Report,* 40(2), 2–36.

Lewis, Browne C. (2016). "You Belong to Me": Unscrambling the Legal Ramifications of Recognizing a Property Right in Frozen Human Eggs. *Cleveland State University, Law Faculty Articles and Essays* (Winter), 839.

Market Reports World (MRW) (2023). Global Egg Freezing and Embryo Banking Market New Research Insight Report 2023. https://www.marketreportsworld.com/enquiry/request-sample/24525472.

Marx, Karl (1990). *Capital: A Critique of Political Economy*, vol. 1. London: Penguin Books.

Mejias, Ulises A., and Nick Couldry (2019). Datafication. *Internet Policy Review*, 8(4), 1–10.

Molas, Anna, and Laura Perler (2020). Selecting Women, Taming Bodies? Body Ontologies in Egg Donation Practices in Spain. *Tapuya: Latin American Science, Technology and Society*, 3(1), 396–414.

Nahman, Michal, and Christina Weis (2023). Redefining Bioavailability through Migrant Egg Donors in Spain. *Body & Society*, 29(1), 79–109.

Namberger, Verena (2016). The South African Economy of Egg Donation: Looking at the Bioeconomic Side of Normalization. In Verena Namberger. *Assisted Reproduction across Borders*, 90–102. London: Routledge.

Pande, Amrita (2021). "Mix or Match?" Transnational Fertility Industry and White Desirability. *Medical Anthropology*, 40(4), 335–347.

Parry, Bronwyn (2008). Entangled Exchange: Reconceptualising the Characterisation and Practice of Bodily Commodification. *Geoforum*, 39(3), 1133–1144.

Patrizio, Pasquale, David F. Albertini, Norbert Gleicher and Arthur Caplan (2022). The Changing World of IVF: The Pros and Cons of New Business Models Offering Assisted Reproductive Technologies. *Journal of Assisted Reproduction and Genetics*, 39, 305–313.

Perler, Laura, and Carolin Schurr (2020). Intimate Lives in the Global Bioeconomy: Reproductive Biographies of Mexican Egg Donors. *Body & Society*, 27(3), 3–27.

Polanyi, Karl (2001 [1944]). *The Great Transformation: The Political and Economic Origins of Our Time*. Boston, MA: Beacon Paperback.

Quaas, Alexander M., and Guido Pennings (2018). The Current Status of Oocyte Banks: Domestic and International Perspectives. *Fertility and Sterility*, 110(7), 1203–1208.

SART (2023a). *National Summary Report 2021*. https://www.sartcorsonline.com/rptCSR_PublicMultYear.aspx?reportingYear=2021.

SART (2023b). *National Summary Report 2017*. https://www.sartcorsonline.com/rptCSR_PublicMultYear.aspx?reportingYear=2017.

Srnicek, Nick (2017). *Platform Capitalism*. Malden, MA: Polity Press.

Tober, Diane, Vincenzo Pavone, Sara Lafuente-Funes and Nancy Konvalinka (2023a). Eggonomics: Vitrification and Bioeconomies of Egg Donation in the United States and Spain. *Medical Anthropology Quarterly*, 37(3), 248–263.

Tober, Diane, Kevin Richter, Dougie Zubizarreta and Said Daneshmand (2023b). Egg Donor Self-Reports of Ovarian Hyperstimulation Syndrome: Severity by Trigger Type, Oocytes Retrieved, and Prior History. *Journal of Assisted Reproduction and Genetics*, 40, 1291–1304.

Vertommen, Sigrid, Vincenzo Pavone and Michal Nahman (2021). Global Fertility Chains: An Integrative Political Economy Approach to Understanding the Reproductive Bioeconomy. *Science, Technology, & Human Values*, 47(1), 112–145.

Waldby, Catherine (2019). *The Oocyte Economy: The Changing Meaning of Human Eggs*. Durham, NC: Duke University Press.

Wiel, Lucy van de (2020a). *Freezing Fertility: Oocyte Cryopreservation and the Gender Politics of Aging*. New York: New York University Press.

Wiel, Lucy van de (2020b). The Speculative Turn in IVF: Egg Freezing and the Financialization of Fertility. *New Genetics and Society*, 39(3), 306–326.

Williams, Robert Stan, Dorothy D. Ellis, Elizabeth A. Wilkinson, Joseph M. Kramer, Datta Susmita and David S. Guzik (2022). Factors Affecting Live Birth Rates in Donor Oocytes from Commercial Egg Banks Vs. Program Egg Donors: An Analysis of 40,485 Cycles from the Society for Assisted Reproductive Technology Registry in 2016–2018. *Fertility and Sterility*, 117(2), 339–348.

Wyns, Christine, Christian de Geyter, Carlos Calhaz-Jorge, Markus Simon Kupka, Tatjana Motrenko, Jesper Smeenk, Christina Bergh, Andreas Tandler-Schneider, Ioana Adina Rugescu and Veerle Goossens (2022). ART in Europe, 2018: Results Generated from European Registries by ESHRE. *Human Reproduction Open*, 2022 (3), 1–20.

"My Eggs Belong to Me": Commodification and Property in the Fertility Economy

Rebecca Rahe

"If my uterus 'belongs' to me, then I guess I can sell it," said feminist scholar and activist Maria Mies at the first *Women against Genetic Engineering and Reproductive Technology* conference in West Germany in 1985.[1] Her polemic was directed at supporters of in vitro fertilisation (IVF) and surrogacy who applied "bourgeois notions of property" to the female body (Mies 1986, 118).

Are reproductive technologies merely tools of patriarchal oppression—or might they hold a key to liberating women from the burden of reproduction (cf. Brockskothen et al. 1986)? This ambivalence in feminist assessments of reproductive technologies persists, even though public debate is now dominated by sensationalist news stories about technological advances and their ethical implications, such as a May 2019 report headlined "Children born after uterus transplant" (Bartens 2019).

Over the past 35 years, the use of assisted reproductive technology (ART) has become normalised, with IVF now established as a common method of human reproduction. At the same time, a highly profitable global fertility economy has emerged, growing at a rate of around 9 percent per year (Waldby 2019, 3). For women who can afford it, ART represents a new form of autonomy—they can freely choose, according to the promise, how, when and with whom they procreate, and global markets exist to cater to their desire to have children. For other women, Mies' analysis holds true: they can sell their reproductive capacity, either by providing their labour power as surrogates or by "donating" their eggs in exchange for money. "Donation" is the hegemonic term for the process of extracting human eggs so that they

1 This chapter is a translation of the article: Rahe, Rebecca (2020). "Meine Eizelle gehört mir". Inwertsetzung & Eigentum in der Kinderwunsch-Ökonomie. *PROKLA – Zeitschrift für kritische Sozialwissenschaft* 199 (2), 295–309.

can be artificially inseminated and implanted in a third party's body in the hope that the recipient will become pregnant with the "donated" eggs.

Egg donation involves a series of medical interventions into a woman's reproductive cycle and body, making it "an onerous and risky process, even under the best clinical conditions" (Waldby and Cooper 2008, 60). Women inject themselves with hormones to stimulate egg development. The eggs are then aspirated and removed under general anaesthetic. Using the altruistic-sounding expression "donation" obscures the fact that, in the vast majority of cases, women who provide eggs receive financial compensation (Gupta and Richters 2008, 243). In Germany, egg donation is prohibited under Article 1 (1), and (2) of the Embryo Protection Act (ESchG). It is also banned in Norway,[2] Luxembourg, Lithuania and Switzerland. However, it is permitted in all other European Union countries (Leopoldina 2019, 68).[3]

The "biocapitalist" (Sunder Rajan 2007) fertility economy is based on the commodification of human reproductive materials, which—as Mies pointed out—is primarily achieved by expanding legal categories of property and ownership to parts of the human body. With a specific focus on egg donation, I examine how these categories are applied in German legal discourse and explore how bodily substances become commodified through legal frameworks. I argue that ART provides the necessary technological conditions, while the legal possibility of owning bodily substances provides the political and economic ones. Commodification requires the backing of the law (Gehring 2006, 55)—and as "a social relation that is always already embedded in socially contested structures of domination and inequality" (Buckel 2010, 324); the law is a site of social and political negotiation.

In the first section, I describe the broader context of the commodification of human eggs. The second section outlines the legal debate about ownership of the human body and bodily substances, showing how the application of economic categories to the body has become normalised—including through the legal concept of donating bodily materials. I then propose a theory of egg

2 Since the publication of the original German text in 2020, egg donation has been legalised in Norway.

3 Within the European Union, these legal differences have given rise to the practice of fertility tourism. Generally speaking, women from north-west European countries receive egg donations from women in southern and eastern countries (Czech Republic, Spain, Greece). These cross-border practices can also be observed elsewhere around the globe: for instance, South Africa is the main provider of eggs for the Australian market, Iran for the Middle East, Ecuador for Latin America (Waldby 2019, 89 ff.).

donation as a form of commodification of bodily substances. Through this process, eggs become commodities for which donors charge "rent", developing a new, economic relationship to parts of their own body. I conclude by reflecting on the social and political implications of the commodification of bodily substances within the fertility economy.

1. The fertility economy and egg donation

The development, use, and expansion of bio- and reproductive technologies are not neutral processes; they are embedded in the capitalist mode of production. In biocapitalism (a category to which the fertility economy can be assigned), the convergence of life sciences research, neoliberal regimes of accumulation and the expansion of intellectual property rights has given rise to an industry based on the use and processing of plant, animal, and human bodily materials (Sunder Rajan 2007; cf. Cooper 2014). As a result, human bodies and their parts have been subsumed under the logic of industrial production and "Taylorised"; bodily substances are disaggregated, stored and modified, deployed as discrete units in production processes, and incorporated into the creation of value (Cooper and Waldby 2014, 44). Historically, the use of bodily substances is not new. For instance, the practice of selling parts of corpses for medicinal purposes dates back to the fifteenth century (Lenk 2011, 23). What is distinctive about biocapitalism is the use of bodily substances taken from living individuals. Blood was the first such substance, followed by tissue, organs, cellular components, and DNA. In fields such as plastic surgery and transplant medicine, these substances are directly implanted in other people, while in areas like stem cell research, cloning and pharmaceuticals, they serve as the raw material for experiments and product development (Gehring 2006, 55–56).

The use of reproductive materials such as sperm and eggs can be observed in both research and the fertility economy. There is a close technical interdependence between these two fields, since "surplus" eggs from IVF clinics are often purchased for clinical stem cell research (Gehring 2007, 54 ff.). While the goal of this research is to produce new scientific insights and new medicines, the aim of the fertility economy is to produce children. This shifts medicine's focus from healing existing bodies to producing new ones. In this sense, ART is "neither a curative treatment nor a mere service, but rather productive activity, biotechnical production" (ibid., 56). In both fields, eggs—unlike sperm—are a scarce resource, and their fertility declines with age.

For women who have undergone multiple unsuccessful IVF cycles with their own eggs the next step is often the use of third-party eggs (Waldby 2019, 8, 68). After retrieval, eggs are either directly implanted in a recipient—which requires the women's reproductive cycles to be hormonally synchronised—or frozen using vitrification techniques. This led to the establishment of "egg banks", where eggs are stored and frozen and can then be flexibly thawed, fertilised and implanted as and when required (ibid., 119 ff). This further rationalises and depersonalises the egg transfer process, reinforcing the eggs' character as "things" or "objects". However, egg donation is not solely an external intervention in the body. Eggs must mature before they can be extracted, and that requires an embodied practice on the part of the egg donors, who have to take hormones, modify their lifestyle and undergo medical testing (Namberger 2017, 6).

Egg donation takes place within complex institutional frameworks. As ART has become increasingly established, international markets for reproductive materials and services have emerged (Waldby 2019, 89 ff.). Many people seek ART treatments abroad because they are either banned or unaffordable in their home countries. In effect, these practices turn children into a "project" made possible by economic and technological means. One key factor in choosing a donor is the degree of "match" between donor and recipient—that is, how similar they are (or are deemed to be) in terms of appearance—which helps simulate the ideal of a child that is biologically "own". The geopolitical structure of egg markets is thus shaped by racialising categories and global inequalities (Nahman 2018, 84–85; Waldby 2019, 111). More than half of all ART treatments worldwide take place in Europe, and the sector is rapidly expanding (Cooper and Waldby 2014, 66).

In the United States, there are no legal restrictions on paying egg donors, which has created a market where prices for egg donations vary according to the donors' appearance, education and other attributes (ibid., 57 ff.). In the European Union, by contrast, there is a ban on commercialisation of bodily materials.[4] Only "voluntary and unpaid donation" is permitted, and donors may only "receive compensation" that is "strictly limited to making

4 The principle of non-commercialisation of the human body and its parts is enshrined in Article 3 (2)(c) of the European Union Charter of Fundamental Rights and Article 21 of the European Bioethics Convention.

good the expenses and inconveniences related to the donation" (European Union 2004, Article 12 (1)). The level at which the maximum allowed expenses are set is a crucial structural feature of the European Union oocyte market. Due to economic inequalities within the European Union, the threshold where compensation for egg donation becomes a potential source of income (as opposed to merely covering expenses) varies from place to place, which underscores the connection between socioeconomic precarity and the practice of egg donation (Cooper and Waldby 2014, 74). Compensation ranges from approximately 125 euros (or 200 dollars) per procedure in Romania (Waldby and Cooper 2008, 62) up to a maximum of 1,000 euros in Spain, which accounts for more than half of all egg donation procedures in Europe (Cooper and Waldby 2014, 70 ff.; de Geyter et al. 2020, 4). When asked about their motivations, egg donors primarily cite financial reasons. Egg donation offers an income that can be combined with unpaid care work and other forms of wage labour (Nahman 2018, 88). The emergence of this market for reproductive substances thus reflects a broader reorganisation of biological reproduction in Europe; transnational relations increasingly shape household arrangements at every level of reproductivity and reproduction. Both care work and reproductive capacities have been redistributed within the European Union from south and east to north and west, reflecting and reinforcing Europe's socioeconomic inequalities and entangling "global care chains" with "global fertility chains" (Cooper and Waldby 2014, 72 ff.).

2. Commodification as a process of legal negotiation: do people own their bodies?

The use of bodily substances in the fertility economy therefore allows not only a medical but also a "private economic intervention in the body" (Lettow 2011, 58). In countries where egg donation is practised, donors give contractual consent to eggs being extracted from their bodies, usually in exchange for monetary compensation. This transaction is enabled by a conception of egg donors as owners of their bodily substances, free to dispose of them as they wish. The notion of individuals as owners of their own bodies has been discussed in bioethics since the 1970s (ibid., 58 ff.), while the ownability of the body has been a subject of legal debate in Germany since the 1980s (Schünemann 1985). I argue that this discourse around "ownability" has significantly shaped the process of commodification of the human body, allowing for the creation of new, economic relationships to the self and facilitating the treatment and sale of bodily substances as things external to the body.

In Germany, property is a fundamental institution in both public and civil law. In the former case, it is enshrined in Article 14 of the Basic Law (GG) in the form of a guarantee of property, meanwhile the Civil Code (BGB) operates with a liberal conception of property that emphasises the freedom of the individual: "The owner of a thing may, to the extent that a statute or third-party rights do not conflict with this, deal with the thing at their discretion and exclude others from exerting any influence whatsoever" (Section 903 (1) BGB).[5] This definition describes a relationship of control and disposal between a legal subject and a thing. However, contrary to the slogan "My body belongs to me!", under German law the body is not considered a "thing" (*Sache*) but is inseparably linked to a person (Section 903 BGB; cf. Ring 2016, 489, § 90 BGB Rn. 22). Accordingly, there is broad legal consensus that the human body as such is not ownable (ibid., 489, § 90 BGB Rn. 22, 23; Ellenberger 2019, 70, § 90 BGB Rn. 3).

Within the legal debate, the concept of a "right to one's own body as a particular personality right" (Ring 2016, 490, § 90 BGB Rn. 24) is widely shared (Mössner 2018, § 90 BGB Rn. 15.2). This view extends the notion of *general personality rights* to a legal subject's relationship to their own body (Jickeli et al. 2012, 25, § 90 BGB Rn. 27). At the same time, it relies on the right of ownership, as the legal subject is ascribed "a legal power over their body equivalent to that of an owner in relation to their things" (Ring 2016, 490, § 90 BGB, Rn. 24; Ellenberger 2019, 70, § 90 BGB, Rn. 3). Thus, although the human body is not considered property under civil law, as the body is not a "thing", there is a personality right modelled on property rights, which blurs the boundary between legal subjects and things. While the law maintains a strict division between separate legal subjects, a loophole arises when it comes to a legal subject's relationship to their own body.

The institution of property is more clearly applicable in the legal treatment of bodily parts and substances, since the unequivocal denial of the ownability of the human body does not extend to its parts. German law contains no explicit provisions on the legal status of bodily substances that have been

5 An official English translation of the Civil Code is provided on the German Federal Ministry of Justice website Gesetze-im-Internet.de. Here, the translation of the quoted sentence has been slightly modified.

separated from the body.[6] However, legal discourse generally treats them as potentially ownable things (Busch 2012, 54 ff.).[7] It is assumed that once separated from the body, the *particular personality right* to the body no longer applies and the substance automatically becomes a "thing" as per Section 90 of the Civil Code and hence ownable (Roth 2009, 57). In legal reasoning, this transformation is taken as a given in legal reasoning and ist is rarely explained "why and how the personality rights character of the right to the body shifts into the separated parts having the character of things" (Busch 2012, 58–59). The classification of separated bodily substances as ownable "things" extends the institution of property to the human body, which would give legal subjects the right to freely dispose of their bodily substances and engage in legal transactions with them. According to Petra Gehring, this conceptual shift—even if it has not (yet) entered into law—is

> a remarkable break with tradition [...]. Historically, it would have made no sense for the model of the appropriation and economic circulability of things to be applied to individual embodiment. On the contrary. The new field of application—living human tissue as tradable property—is fundamentally alien to the European legal tradition.
>
> *Gehring 2006, 38–39*

The European legal tradition, as well as the German Basic Law (in which the principle of human dignity is enshrined in the first sentence of the first article), draws on the Kantian idea that people must never be treated as mere means but only ever as ends in themselves (Potthast et al. 2010, 11). The German Constitutional Court regularly refers to this principle, known as the *Objektformel* ("object formula"), when ruling on the legal classification of bodily substances (Herdegen 2019, GG Art. 1 Abs. 1 Rn. 36). According to this principle, any use of bodily substances to generate value would constitute a violation of human dignity as per Article 1 (1) of the Basic Law.

However, the way that bodily substances are used in practice in Germany shows that the *Objektformel* is not consistently applied. Bodily substances "have long been treated as commodities" (Potthast et al. 2010, 9). Products such as medicines and human cells or tissues derived from these substances

6 The provisions of the Transplantation Act (TPG), the Transfusion Act (TFG) and the Stem Cell Act (StZG) only apply to certain specified body parts/bodily substances and people's rights in relation to them.

7 Legal scholar Dörte Busch distinguishes this "purely *in rem* approach" (*rein sachenrechtlicher Ansatz*) from a "personality rights approach" (*persönlichkeitsrechtlicher Ansatz*) and a "refined *in rem* approach" (*fortentwickelter sachenrechtlicher Ansatz*) (Busch 2012, 57 ff.).

may be sold; donated blood can even be used for profit. These transactions are permitted under the Transplantation Act (TPG) and Transfusion Act (TFG) (König 2005, 275, 282; Vor §§ 17, 18 BGB Rn. 1, 35). Nonetheless, direct payment for bodily substances remains prohibited. The same applies to the act of donating, where only financial or in-kind compensation for expenses is allowed (Deutscher Bundestag 1996, 30).

Since Section 8(b) of the Transplantation Act has permitted sperm donation since 2007, there have been calls within the legal debate for the legalisation of egg donation, which has been prohibited by the Embryo Protection Act since 1991. The ban has been widely criticised (Wellenhofer 2017, 45, § 1591 BGB Rn. 45) and seen as violating the property rights of potential egg donors (Radatz 2014, 82 ff.; Reinke 2008, 184 ff.). However, those calling for legislation generally reject a "commercialisation" of egg donation (Kersten 2018, 1253), advocating instead for an egg donation law that "rejects financial remuneration and only allows compensation for expenses" (Radatz 2014, 79). This argument reveals the ambiguities inherent in linking the idea of "donation" to that of monetary compensation. As Jyotsna Agnihotri Gupta and Annemiek Richters argue, it makes a crucial difference whether a transaction in bodily substances involves the exchange of money and hence constitutes a *trade*:

> Although [...] sometimes there seems to be a thin line between an altruistic "gift" (i.e. donation) and "commodity" (i.e. commerce), most transactions in body parts can be characterised (also) as trade, since exchange of money is involved, either directly between the donor and recipient or through a service provider/broker. The term "donation" is often a misnomer for what is actually a market transaction; it imbues it with a higher meaning.
>
> *Gupta and Richters 2008, 243*

This argument suggests that the practice of donation and compensation for expenses does not prevent the emergence of markets and trade in bodily substances. In the European Union, the level at which statutory caps for permissible expenses are set is increasingly determined by market demand and hence by the price at which women are willing to donate their eggs, whereas bioethical considerations have only played a minor role (see Cooper and Waldby 2014, 73).

The tension between rejecting the commercialisation of egg donation and supporting compensation for expenses is typically resolved in the legal debate by deploying the construct of "informed consent". Rooted in a framework of individual rights, this construct obscures social inequalities and compulsions by shifting responsibility to the individual subject. From a neoliberal perspective, the individual subject is supposedly making an autonomous decision and voluntarily consenting to the procedure (Wichterich 2015, 26). The "informed consent" construct is also central to property rights, as it permits not only the exercise of disposal rights but also the transfer of titles of ownership even before the individual has had the opportunity to exercise property rights over the not-yet-separated body parts (Cooper and Waldby 2014, 100). The preconditions for appropriating human bodily substances thus rest on the conception of ownership of human bodily substances, supported by the bioethical construct of informed consent and the formalisation of statutory expense allowances.

In the next section, I develop a theoretical framework to explain how these legal mechanisms have paved the way for the commodification of bodily substances.

3. Eggs as commodities and the collection of rent

Property is historically contingent and must be continuously secured through acts of appropriation and expropriation. In the *Grundrisse*, Marx distinguishes between different forms of property. With regard to "bourgeois property", he remarks that

> *property* thus originally means no more than a human being's relation to his natural conditions of production as belonging to him, as his, as *presupposed* along with *his own being*; relations to them as *natural presuppositions* of his self, which only form, so to speak, his extended body. He actually does not relate to his conditions of production, but rather has a double existence, both subjectively as he himself, and objectively in these natural non-organic conditions of his existence.
>
> *Marx 1973, 415, emphases in original*

According to Marx, the key transition in the development of bourgeois property was that people began to relate to their conditions of production (their labour power, their tools, their materials) as objects external to themselves. Previously, all the things needed for a person's livelihood—tools, clothes, beasts of burden—were conceived as part of their "extended body"; now they were separated from the self. This "separation", Marx says, is "completely posited only in the relation of wage labour and capital" (ibid., 413), whereby those directly involved in production are alienated from the means of production and come to understand their labour power as a commodity that can be sold (Marx 1976, 271). This shift was not a historical given, but emerged through "so-called primitive accumulation" (ibid., 871 ff.).

The more established biocapitalist economies become, the more plausible it becomes to assume a comparable transformation in the subject's relationship to their own bodily substances: rather than taking their embodied existence for granted, they come to perceive their bodies as fragmentable, and relate to them as repositories of extractable, potentially commodifiable components. Commodification of bodily substances is therefore not merely an external intervention into the materiality of the body—a "more effective [...] utilisation of human bodies" (Demirović and Schütt 2015, 8)—but rather produces a historically novel, fragmented, economic understanding of the body and of its relationship to the self—an "interaction between economy, ways of life and body politics" (Lettow 2015, 38).

This economic understanding of the body is evident when egg donors "speak of 'wasting valuable eggs' in each cycle and embed this in the narrative of a resource-efficient body" (Namberger 2017, 6). The commodity form is thereby not only imposed from the outside, but also internalised: donors perceive their eggs as commodities and as a possible source of income, and adopt an economic attitude towards their reproductive cycle in general.

This reflects an extension of the "economic self-relation [...] in line with the model of commodity and vendor" (Lettow 2011, 58). However, this relationship does not neatly fit into the notion of the wage relation, according to which the wage labourer provides their labour power to a third party. In egg donation, a contract is signed to transfer bodily substances. Nonetheless, the notion of egg donation as a new form of wage labour dominates in the feminist debate on reproductive technologies (see Cooper and Waldby 2014).[8]

8 Cooper and Waldby's concept of "clinical labour" (2014) refers to various forms of "tissue donation" under biocapitalism as well as the participation of research subjects in studies that have no or only incidental positive effects for the clinical labourers themselves, but rather subject them to physical and health risks without any welfare safety net. Clinical labour is similar in this respect to other forms of informal and precarious work (ibid., 7 ff.). Cooper and Waldby believe that the work of tissue donors is rendered invisible in the bioethical debate due to a narrow focus on the work of medical staff, and they therefore attempt to highlight the embodied productivity of these clinical labourers (ibid., 100). However, to use Marxist terminology, their understanding of labour appears to rely on a concept of production that treats biological processes themselves as labour, since they situate productivity within those processes (Waldby and Cooper 2008, 59). This reductive vitalism sees the social as biologically grounded, which impedes a critical social analysis (Lettow 2015, 46).

The role of bodily substances in the fertility economy can also be likened to that of soil in agriculture: they function as a raw material in the production process (Franklin and Lock 2003, 8). If the women involved in this process are not equated with nature, and hence viewed as passive victims of totalising exploitation, but rather as active agents who manage their embodied existence to enable the extraction of eggs from their bodies, egg donation can be understood as a form of income generation analogous to charging people rent to work a patch of land.

Rent, in this context, refers to payment made for the right to use something—in this case, the human body—and occurs under specific "institutional conditions, namely property rights" (Zeller 2006, 128) which presuppose the private enclosure of land and the right to exclude people from it (Marx 1981, 752). Based on Marx's concept of "ground rent", Christian Zeller (2006, 127) defines rent as "income that the owner of property rights collects even if they are uninvolved in production", which helps to clarify Marx's labour theory of value: land in itself has no value, as it is not a product of labour (Marx 1981, 772). Yet it is traded as if it did because the ground rent "presents the appearance of the price or value of land" (ibid., 762). Crucially, holding the title to a piece of land makes it possible to exclude other people from using it and to charge them a price—rent—for the right to do so. The land itself is not sold: only the right to use it. This is analogous to the commodity of labour power. It is also similar to the case of the body: personality rights protect a person's body from being freely at the disposal of others, yet individuals can sell rights to make use of it. In the context of ART, this is not the right to use the person's labour power, but rather the right to extract and make use of their eggs. The eggs thereby become commodities. This "becoming-commodity" (Görg 2004, 1501) is "directed not just at the commodity form of products, but rather denotes a multistage process in which resources are first defined or constituted as such, then identified and extracted and finally integrated into the global market" (ibid., 1503). This process is clearly visible in the fertility economy.

4. Conclusion and future work

The new form of commodification of the human body described in this chapter is shaped both by reproductive technologies and the establishment of new legal frameworks. The concept of ownership of human body parts is linked to that of "informed consent", which has paved the way for the commodification of bodily substances. On the European oocyte market, the ban on commercialisation is effectively bypassed through *de facto* payment in the compensation for expenses. Should egg donation be legalised in Germany—a proposal that is gaining traction (Leopoldina 2019; Gassner et al. 2013)—similar dynamics would likely emerge, as the practice would be integrated into the broader European oocyte economy.

These calls for legalisation are part of a broader societal trend in which having children has become a *project*. ART has paved the way for this trend by offering a new degree of planning and control over the process of having a child. Moreover, practices like racialised donor "matching" (see Deomampo's chapter in this volume) and selective genetic screening, which were not discussed in this chapter, have contributed to the conception of an "ideal person" as white and able-bodied gaining social materiality. Building on the legal, political and economic analysis presented here, further research should focus more closely on the consumption side of commodification.

At the same time, pro-natalist groups aim to enshrine a basic right to reproduction in a Reproductive Medicine Act, thus transforming the right to reject state intervention in one's individual reproduction into a right or entitlement to have a child of one's own, which would be realised by all available ART means (Gassner et al. 2013). In this scenario, the fertility economy would become an instrument of a basic right, embedding reproduction even more deeply in the logic of production. Further research is needed to explore the interplay between legal frameworks and the development of reproductive medical technologies.

Works Cited

Bartens, Werner (2019). Kinder kommen nach Gebärmuttertransplantation zur Welt. *Süddeutsche Zeitung*, 23 May. https://www.sueddeutsche.de/gesundheit/tuebingen-gebaermutter-transplantation-unfruchtbarkeit-uterus-1.4459260.

Brockskothen, Michaela, Inge Hehr and Ruth Kühn (1986). *Frauen gegen Gentechnik und Reproduktionstechnik: Dokumentation zum Kongreß vom 19.–21.4.1985 in Bonn*. Cologne: Sozialwissenschaftliche Forschung und Praxis für Frauen.

Buckel, Sonja (2010). Genealogie sozialer Ungleichheit im Recht—Anmerkungen zu Ulrike Davy. *Zeitschrift für Sozialreform*, 56(3), 323–328.

Busch, Dörte (2012). *Eigentum und Verfügungsbefugnisse am menschlichen Körper und seinen Teilen*. Frankfurt: Lang.

Cooper, Melinda (2014). Lebens jenseits der Grenzen: Die Erfindung der Bioökonomie. In Andreas Folkers and Thomas Lemke (eds.). *Biopolitik: Ein Reader*, 468–524. Berlin: Suhrkamp.

Cooper, Melinda, and Catherine Waldby (2014). *Clinical Labor: Tissue Donors and Research Subjects in the Global Bioeconomy*. Durham, NC: Duke University Press.

Demirović, Alex, and Mariana Schütt (2015). Editorial: Biokapitalismus. *PROKLA*, 178(45), 2–9.

Deutscher Bundestag. (1996). Gesetzentwurf der Fraktionen der CDU/CSU, SPD und F.D.P. Entwurf eines Gesetzes über die Spende, Entnahme und Übertragung von Organen (Transplantationsgesetz—TPG). BT-Drucksache 13/4355.

Ellenberger, Jürgen (2019). BGB § 90 Begriff der Sache. In Otto Palandt, Jürgen Ellenberger, Isabell Götz, Christian Grüneberg, Sebastian Herrler, Hartwig Sprau, Walter Weidenkaff, Dietmar Weidlich and Hartmick Wicke. *Bürgerliches Gesetzbuch mit Nebengesetzen* Munich: C. H. Beck.

European Union (2004). Directive 2004/23/EC of the European Parliament and of the Council of 31 March 2004 on Setting Standards of Quality and Safety for the Donation, Procurement, Testing, Processing, Preservation, Storage and Distribution of Human Tissues and Cells. https://eur-lex.europa.eu/legal-content/EN/TXT/HTML/?uri=CELEX:32004L0023.

Franklin, Sarah, and Margaret Lock (2003). Animation and Cessation: The Remaking of Life and Death. In Sarah Franklin and Margaret Lock (eds.). *Remaking Life & Death: Toward an Anthropology of the Biosciences*, 3–22. Santa Fe: School of American Research Press.

Gassner, Ulrich, Josef Franz Lindner, Matthias Krüger, Henning Rosenau, Ulrich Schroth and Jens Kersten (2013). *Fortpflanzungsmedizingesetz: Augsburg-Münchner-Entwurf*. Tübingen: Mohr Siebeck.

Gehring, Petra (2006). *Was ist Biomacht? Vom zweifelhaften Mehrwert des Lebens*. Frankfurt: Campus.

Gehring, Petra (2007). Inwertsetzung der Gattung: Zur Kommerzialisierung der Fortpflanzungsmedizin. In Jochen Taupitz (ed.). *Kommerzialisierung des menschlichen Körpers*, 53–68. Berlin: Springer.

Geyter, Christian de, Carlos Calhaz-Jorge, Markus S. Kupka, Christine Wyns, Edgar Mocanu, Tatjana Motrenko, Giulia Scaravelli, Jesper Smeenk, Snežana Vidaković, Veerle Goossen and the European IVF-Monitoring (EIM) Consortium for the European Society of Human Reproduction and Embryology (ESHRE) (2020). ART in Europe, 2015: Results Generated from European Registries by ESHRE. *Human Reproduction Open*, 1, 1–17.

Görg, Christoph (2004). Inwertsetzung. In Wolfgang Fritz Haug (ed.). *Historisch-Kritisches Wörterbuch des Marxismus*, 6(2), 1501–1506. Hamburg: Argument.

Gupta, Jyotsna Agnihotri, and Annemiek Richters (2008). Embodied Subjects and Fragmented Objects: Women's Bodies, Assisted Reproduction Technologies and the Right to Self-Determination. *Bioethical Inquiry*, 5, 239–249.

Herdegen, Matthias (2019). Die Objektformel. In Roman Herzog, Rupert Scholz, Matthias Herdegen and Hans H. Klein (eds.). *Grundgesetz-Kommentar*. Munich: Beck.

Jickeli, Joachim, Hans-Georg Knothe, Reinhard Singer and Malte Stieper (2012). *J. von Staudingers Kommentar zum Bürgerlichen Gesetzbuch mit Einführungsgesetz und Nebengesetzen: Buch 1*. Berlin: Sellier/De Gruyter.

Kersten, Jens (2018). Regulierungsauftrag für den Staat im Bereich der Fortpflanzungsmedizin. *Neue Zeitschrift für Verwaltungsrecht*, 17, 1248–1254.

König, Peter (2005). Abschnitt 6: Verbotsvorschriften; Abschnitt 7: Straf- und Bußgeldvorschriften; § 18 Organhandel. In Ulrich Schroth, Peter König, Thomas Gutmann and Fuat Oduncu (eds.). *Transplantationsgesetz Kommentar*, 274–323. Munich: Beck.

Leopoldina (2019). *Fortpflanzungsmedizin in Deutschland—für eine zeitgemäße Gesetzgebung*. Halle (Saale): Leopoldina.

Lenk, Christian (2011). Mein Körper—mein Eigentum? *Aus Politik und Zeitgeschichte*, 20–21, 22–27.

Lettow, Susanne (2011). *Biophilosophien: Wissenschaft, Technologie und Geschlecht im philosophischen Diskurs der Gegenwart*. Frankfurt: Campus.

Lettow, Susanne (2015). Biokapitalismus und Inwertsetzung der Körper: Perspektiven der Kritik. *PROKLA*, 178(45), 33–49.

Marx, Karl (1973 [1857–1861]). *Grundrisse: Foundations of the Critique of Political Economy*. https://www.marxists.org/archive/marx/works/1857/grundrisse/index.htm.

Marx, Karl (1976 [1890]). *Capital: Volume I*. London: Penguin.

Marx, Karl (1981 [1894]). *Capital: Volume III*. London: Penguin.

Mies, Maria (1986). Argumente wider den Bio-Krieg. In Michaela Brockskothen, Inge Hehr and Ruth Kühn (eds.). *Frauen gegen Gentechnik und Reproduktionstechnik: Dokumentation zum Kongreß vom 19.–21.4.1985 in Bonn*, 114–118. Cologne: Kölner Volksblatt.

Mössner, Gregor (2018). BGB § 90. Begriff der Sache. a) Lebender Mensch. Randnummer 15–15.2. In Beate Gsell, Wolfgang Krüger, Stephan Lorenz and Christoph Reymann (eds.). *beck-online: Großkommentar zum Zivilrecht*. Munich: Beck.

Nahman, Michal (2018). Migrant Extractability: Centring the Voices of Egg Providers in Cross-Border Reproduction. *Reproductive BioMedicine & Society Online*, 7, 82–90.

Namberger, Verena (2017). Der (re)produktive Körper in der südafrikanischen Ökonomie der Eizellspende. *Open Gender Journal*, 1, 1–15.

Potthast, Thomas, Beate Herrmann and Uta Müller (2010). Einleitung: Ethische, rechtliche und soziale Aspekte der Kommerzialisierung des menschlichen Körpers und seiner Teile. In Thomas Potthast, Beate Herrmann and Uta Müller (eds.). *Wem gehört der menschliche Körper? Ethische, rechtliche und soziale Aspekte der Kommerzialisierung des menschlichen Körpers und seiner Teile*, 9–23. Paderborn: Mentis.

Radatz, Johanna (2014). *Die Eizellspende im europäischen und dänischen Recht*. Frankfurt: Lang.

Reinke, Mathias (2008). *Fortpflanzungsfreiheit und das Verbot der Fremdeizellspende*. Berlin: Duncker & Humblot.

Ring, Gerhard (2016). BGB § 90 Begriff der Sache. In Thomas Heidel, Rainer Hüßtege, Heinz-Peter Mansel and Ulrich Noack (eds.). *Nomos Kommentar BGB: Allgemeiner Teil*, vol. 1, 3rd ed., 485–504. Baden-Baden: Nomos.

Roth, Carsten (2009). *Eigentum an Körperteilen: Rechtsfragen der Kommerzialisierung des menschlichen Körpers*. Berlin: Springer.

Schünemann, Hermann (1985). *Die Rechte am menschlichen Körper*. Frankfurt: Lang.

Sunder Rajan, Kaushik (2007). *Biocapital: The Constitution of Postgenomic Life*. Durham, NC: Duke University Press.

Waldby, Catherine (2019). *The Oocyte Economy: The Changing Meaning of Human Eggs*. Durham, NC: Duke University Press.

Waldby, Catherine, and Melinda Cooper (2008). The Biopolitics of Reproduction—Post-Fordist Biotechnology and Women's Clinical Labour. *Australian Feminist Studies*, 23(55), 57–73.

Wellenhofer, Marina (2017). BGB § 1591. In Franz Jürgen Säcker, Roland Riexecker, Hartmut Oetker and Bettina Limperg (eds.). *Münchener Kommentar zum BGB*, vol. 9, 25–50. Munich: Beck.

Wichterich, Christa (2015). *Sexuelle und reproduktive Rechte*. Berlin: Heinrich-Böll-Stiftung.

Zeller, Christian (2006). Intellektuelle Eigentumsmonopole und die Erzielung von Renten in der globalen Enteignungsökonomie. *Peripherie*, 101/102, 119–146.

Who Has Seized Assisted Reproductive Technologies? The Role of Private Investors in the Fertility Sector[1]

Irina Herb

Over the years, assisted reproductive technologies (ARTs)[2] have evoked various utopian and dystopian visions. At an early stage in their history, Shulamith Firestone famously imagined the ways in which ARTs would support feminist causes by freeing women "from the tyranny of reproduction" (2015 [1970], 185). She called on women to "seize control of human fertility" through ARTs (ibid., 11), hoping that this would not only lead to women's liberation but also to an anti-capitalist revolution. While in Firestone's times the widespread use of ARTs still seemed utopian, fast-forward merely 40 years and they have become an integral part of biological reproduction. Some scholars go as far as to call in vitro fertilisation (IVF)[3] "the new normal of human reproduction" (Kushnir et al. 2022). Similarly, Stanford professor Henry Greely provocatively predicted in *The End of Sex and the Future of Human Reproduction* (2016) that in 30 to 40 years the majority of human pregnancies will be the result of in vitro gametogenesis (IVG).[4] Regardless of how true such predictions turn out to be, current figures show that biological reproduction can no longer be thought of without taking the rapidly increasing role of ARTs into account. For example, in 2023, an estimated ten million

1 I am grateful to Stefanie Graefe, Susanne Lettow, Philipp Köncke, Daniel Kunze, Abibi Stewart and Susanne Schultz for helpful comments on earlier versions of this chapter.

2 According to the American Centre for Disease Control (CDC), ART encompass "all treatments or procedures that include the handling of human eggs or embryos to help achieve a pregnancy". This excludes procedures which only manipulates sperm (e.g. intrauterine inseminations).

3 IVF is a medical technique in which an egg is fertilised in a laboratory. If successful, the embryo is then implanted into a uterus.

4 In vitro gametogenesis (IVG) is a (currently experimental) medical procedure that allows any cell of the body to be reprogrammed in a laboratory to become a gamete (a reproductive cell, i.e. a sperm or an egg). These gametes can then be fertilised and implanted in a uterus. While Japanese researchers have successfully conducted IVG on mice, research with human cells is still ongoing.

babies were born through IVF globally (ESHRE 2023), roughly equivalent to the entire population of Austria. In Spain, about 8 percent of babies born in 2014 were conceived via IVF (Lafuente-Funes 2020, 207) and in Germany in 2021, fertility treatments had increased by about 25 percent within the space of just four years (Deutsches IVF-Register e.V. 2022).

Forty-four years after Firestone's intervention, this chapter revisits the theme of control in the context of biological reproduction. As Judy Wajcman recalled in the 1990s: "Over the last two decades feminists have identified men's monopoly of technology as an important source of their power" (1996 [1991], iii). Against this backdrop, reappropriating reproductive technologies has taken up a central role in some feminist currents. Suchtan struggles for liberation inspired this chapter to ask "in whose hands" ARTs (as a subset of reproductive technologies[5]) lie today. In other words, to reframe Firestone's demand as a question: who is seizing control of ARTs? Research shows that fertility treatments have become deeply integrated into market mechanisms, with ARTs now being "big business around the world" (Patrizio et al. 2022, 305). Yet within these debates, the more concrete question of ownership of ARTs has (with some notable exceptions) receded into the background. Arguably, this reduces transparency (Reddy 2020), creates blind spots regarding crucial economic developments such as financialisation and assetisation (Birch and Tyfield 2012) and limits our ability to discuss control and power over reproductive choices. Informed by Marxist scholars who centre the question of who owns the means of production, this chapter's analysis proceeds from the idea that the question of "property in ARTs"—in analogy to the more common question of "property in the body"—is central to answering feminist questions around control over one's own body and biological reproduction. Against this backdrop, this chapter advocates for putting the question of property in ARTs on the research agenda in order to complement existing literature and debates (section 1).

Crucially, exploring ownership of ART will uncover different trends around the world. For example, in Hungary, Viktor Orbán nationalised

5 Based on work by Martha Gimenez (2018, 188–189), we can distinguish between reproductive technologies designed 1) to control fertility (e.g. contraception, abortifacients); 2) to monitor the genetic features and health of embryos and foetuses and support the provision of prenatal care (e.g. genetic screening, ultrasound scans); 3) to monitor and assist with labour and childbirth (e.g. caesarean sections, anaesthesia); and 4) to treat infertility or preserve fertility (some of which are assisted, in which case we speak of ARTs).

fertility clinics due to their "strategic importance" and announced that IVF treatments would be free for citizens (Doehler 2020). While these kinds of ART-mediated biopolitical state interventions will hopefully receive further attention in future research, this chapter concentrates on another development: the increasing role of asset managers and rich individuals/families in owning, running and making money from ARTs. To illustrate a so far largely neglected shift in the ownership of ARTs, this chapter looks at property in knowledge in the form of patenting and research start-ups as well as fertility clinics in the United States and Germany (section 2).

Based on the finding that ARTs are increasingly owned and controlled by private investors, the concluding section (section 3) presents some initial deliberations on possible implications. Responding to debates on biopolitics in the context of ARTs, a tentative (and equally provocative) question emerges: in the 2000s, scholars discussed whether ARTs have driven a shift from centralised *state* biopolitics towards decentralised *market* mechanisms where consumers' choices come to shape selective biological reproduction (Rose 2006). Now that asset managers and ultra-rich individuals are gaining increasing power, the question may be: are we witnessing another shift towards more centralised forms of control? With reference to a paper title by Carolin Schurr (2016), we may wonder: are we observing a trend "from biopolitics to bioeconomies to *biofinanciers*"?

1. Bringing a neglected dimension of property back in: property in assisted reproductive technologies

To ask about property in ARTs is to revive and build on longstanding feminist concerns. Throughout history, advances in reproductive technologies have entailed struggles over power and control. For example, in the eighteenth century, the development of forceps (a tool to assist with delivery) sparked a "bitter and well documented contest" between female midwives and an emerging male-dominated medical profession "as to who would have control over intervention in the birth process" (Wajcman 1996 [1991], 64; see also Donnison 2025 [1977]). Fast-forward by about 200 years to the (largely white) Californian self-help groups in the 1970s/80s, we find that struggles for control over one's own body was similarly understood as tied to the question of men's privileged position with regard to (reproductive) technologies. Therefore, for the feminist movement, "seizing the means of reproduction", as Michelle Murphy says, included distributing knowledge through health manuals, encouraging photographic diaries of cervical variations, using microscopes to examine one's own menstruation, creating abortion devices with canning jars and aquarium tubing and organising artificial insemination groups (Murphy 2012).

These examples illustrate the kinds of reproductive technologies that 1970s feminists were faced with in their struggles: "taking back control" meant reappropriating knowledge and practices and, at most, attempting to build relatively simple devices. In contrast, from the 1980s onwards, rapid scientific advances in reproductive technologies came to render the processes of human fertility "profoundly manipulable" (ibid. 1) and brought new battlegrounds to the fore. The development of *assisted* reproductive technologies (as a subset of reproductive technologies) posed new challenges and questions: since these technologies are designed to manage egg cells, they generally involve sophisticated and expensive equipment, as well as advanced scientific knowledge. It follows that "seizing the means" to extract eggs and freezing them for later use, for example, cannot be done in a "living room turned into a health clinic", which is how Murphy describes the typical set-up of 1970s self-help groups. Therefore, once the first babies conceived via IVF were born in the United Kingdom and India in 1978, fertility treatments started to become a booming business rather than something undertaken in self-help groups and collective alternative structures. In this context, Laura Mamo recalls how attempts at building "families of choice" (Weston 1991) through alternative and/or queer collectives and practices in the 1970s–1990s came to be increasingly "shaped by and constrained within what had emerged as a biomedicalised menu of technological offerings". In contrast, alternative practices of biological reproduction such as co-parenting, "special uncles" or "bio-dads" receded into the background in the face of technologically mediated options based on principles of buying and selling (Mamo 2018, 26).

As ARTs came to partly escape (queer) feminist attempts at "seizing the means of reproduction", the question of who owns and makes money with these technologies raised itself with fresh force. Yet emerging critical scholarly debates from the late 2000s onwards tended to turn away from the concrete question of ownership and towards the concepts of "work" and "bioeconomies". The term "bioeconomies" sparked important debates about the new ways in which biomaterials have become commodified and integrated into capitalist forms of life (e.g. Cooper and Waldby 2014; Lettow 2015; Pavone and Goven 2017; Namberger 2019). Furthermore, scholars have turned to a critical analysis of the ways egg "donors" and surrogates came to be integrated into logics of capitalist "work" while at the same time being denied this label (e.g. Cooper and Waldby 2014; Namberger 2019; Vora 2019; Vertommen et al. 2022; Deomampo 2016; Rudrappa 2015; Lewis 2019; Wichterich 2018; Pande 2009; 2014).

Since these scholarly debates have centred bodily materials and services as objects of commodification, ARTs as objects of property in their own right have remained under-investigated. The ensuing lack of research on property in ARTs has several implications at a political and analytical level. Analytically, it means that crucial developments in the realm of assisted reproduction have yet to receive appropriate scholarly attention. Most pertinent to this chapter, a focus on commodification and exploitation no longer suffices when value is increasingly extracted through ownership titles in the hands of asset managers and ultra-rich individuals. Accordingly, Kean Birch and David Tyfield have criticised the bioeconomy literature for focusing on the "biomaterials" at the cost of neglecting the role of the firms and asset managers that are gaining increasing power: "the fetishization of the 'bio' has meant that—to different degrees—STS scholars like Waldby, Rose, Rajan, and Cooper have missed an important opportunity to update the understanding of the bioeconomy in light of the financial and economic restructuring of the economy" (2012, 301). While this criticism overlooks at the very least Melinda Cooper's early work on patenting (2008) and does not do justice to her later work on assetisation (Adkins et al. 2020; 2021), Birch and Tyfield's call to "consider the importance of asset-based economic processes (e.g., property, rent, etc.) in any understanding of the bioeconomy" (2012, 301) is well placed and animates the present discussion.

Considering property in ARTs raises a conceptual question: what does it mean to "own" ARTs? It seems fruitful to approach this analogously to a Marxist analysis of ownership of the means of production: the relevant point of ownership is less about the location and proximity of the owner and the owned objects, and more about the power and control the owner holds over value extraction and decision-making. In concrete terms, this will look different for different types of ART. To allow for a finer-grained analysis, a (preliminary) distinction between different aspects of ARTs may help: 1) research/knowledge (e.g. patents/intellectual property, research start-ups); 2) facilities and infrastructure (e.g. fertility clinics, egg banks, fertility agencies); 3) equipment (e.g. IVF equipment, egg freezers); 4) medication and tests (e.g. hormones); 5) information (e.g. platforms and applications which provide information on clinics or available treatments). This chapter focuses on the first two aspects: research/knowledge and fertility clinics.

2. Private investors as an emerging group of property owners in the ART sector

Once we started researching property in ART in capitalist core countries like the United States and Germany, we found that they have to be understood and analysed in the context of broader trends of financialisation and assetisation. Therefore, before we turn to illustrate these developments with regards to patents and fertility clinics (section 3 and 4), this section provides a brief introduction into relevant aspects of assetisation.

Assetisation may be understood as a subset of financialisation: the process of turning "things" like debt, natural resources, housing, roads, education or datasets into property, with the aim of generating and extracting continuous flows of income ("rent") (see for example Birch and Muniesa 2020). The increasing role of assetisation in today's economy is captured by terms like "asset manager capitalism" (Braun 2022).Of particular importance for our context are so-called "real assets" (also "alternative assets"). In contrast to financial products like debt or bonds, these are "real things" like housing and infrastructure). Since the 2007/2008 financial crisis, investors have increasingly embraced "real assets". Crucially, in contrast to financial assets, "real assets" involve direct extraction of continuous income *from people's everyday lives:* investors buy up housing and infrastructure to collect housing rents, payments per unit of electricity used or road toll fees (Christophers 2023, 11–12). To emphasise the ways in which assetisation stretches into the realm of people's everyday lives, Brett Christophers expanded on Braun's "asset management capitalism" and coined the term "asset manager society". He describes the current situation as "a society in which asset managers increasingly own and control our most essential physical systems and frameworks, providing the most basic means of social functioning and reproduction" (ibid., 7).[6]

As scholars have noted, assetisation alters the "very meaning of the concept of property", given that "it is no longer related to a story about productive capital, material machines of production and labour as a single source of profit" (Tellmann et al. 2024, 6). But it also changes who becomes holders of property: Private investors are playing an increasing role in the fertility sector. "Private capital"[7] denotes investments which are handled outside of public stock exchanges such as DAX and NASDAQ. On private markets, private capital buys companies, infrastructure or hospitals which are not listed on public exchanges. The World Economic Forum has observed a "meteoric growth of private markets in recent years" (Ermoline and Kupec 2023) with assets under management doubling in a decade to around 24.4 trillion United States dollars in 2023 (Burke 2024). Private capital is often managed by asset management firms such as Blackstone or Kohlberg Kravis Roberts & Co. Incorporated (KKR), which set up funds in which investors invest. On behalf of the investors, asset managers administer the processes of buying and managing assets such as houses and infrastructure. Investments come from a variety of investors, including institutional investors like pension funds and, increasingly, "ultra-high-net-worth individuals" and "family offices"[8] (Burke 2024). Some of these ultra-rich individuals and families also invest directly in established or emerging companies rather than going through asset managers. When "high-net-worth individuals" directly invest in early-stage (and therefore risky but high-potential) start-ups as "angel investors", they do so in return for partial ownership. Typically, they not only provide initial seed money for the early (and risky) stages of start-up businesses but tend to put money into an idea

6 For a similar line of argument, see Langley 2021, 388; Fine 2020; Christophers and Fine 2020, 20; Martin 2002.

7 Private capital can be broken down into several "asset classes": private equity (investment in non-listed companies or buyouts of public companies), venture capital (investment in emerging or early-stage private companies with high growth potential but also higher risk), private debt (debt investments that are not financed by banks and are not issued or traded in an open market), real estate, infrastructure and natural resources. For the sake of simplicity, this chapter mostly avoids these distinctions, but instead refers to the overall category of private capital.

8 A family office is a privately owned firm that manages investment and wealth planning exclusively for a wealthy family, typically one with at least 50–100 million dollars in investable assets. Its primary purpose is to preserve, grow and transfer the family's wealth across generations, using the family's own financial capital as its foundation.

they like and remain actively involved by offering advice and support (Ganti 2024). In other words, through assetisation, asset management firms and ultra-rich individuals/families gain increasing (partial) ownership of, and therefore control over, the "means of social functioning and reproduction" (Christophers 2023, 7). In other words the fact that the fertility sector is mainly backed by private capital, rather than being listed on stock markets, has implications for who is able to hold property titles: while public stock exchanges are, more or less, accessible to anyone, "private markets" are more exclusive. With some regional variations, minimum investments into private capital funds tend to range somewhere between 250,000 and several million United States dollars, thereby constraining ownership titles to ultra-rich individuals/families and institutional investors.

The trend of private capital permeating into ever more areas of life has been fruitfully researched with regard to healthcare (e.g. Borsa et al. 2023), housing (e.g. Christophers 2023), education (e.g. Milyaeva and Neyland 2020), unemployment (e.g. Williams 2020) and biotechnologies (e.g. Cooper 2008; Birch and Tyfield 2012; Birch 2016; Roy 2020). The specific case of fertility and pregnancy, in contrast, has so far been neglected in the emerging body of literature. The following two sections draw together the (slim) body of existing knowledge/research regarding ARTs and fertility clinics in the United States, and supplement it with original findings concerning Germany.

3. Property in knowledge of assisted biological reproduction

The assetisation of knowledge in the bioeconomy more generally has been widely acknowledged (e.g. Birch and Tyfield 2012; Birch and Muniesa 2020; Kang 2020). Already in 2008, Cooper argued that the 1980s saw a "new academic personage", the "scientistrepreneur", emerge: academics and venture capitalists came together "to commercialize the results of public research", and the "importance of patent rights" within that process "cannot be overstated" (2008, 27).

A similar trend can be observed with regards to property in ART knowledge more narrowly. According to Cyranoski et al. (2023a; 2023b), early developments of ARTs in the 1970s typically took place in academic settings. Patient needs, scientific advancements and academic recognition seem to have been the driving force of research endeavours. Early ARTs like IVF were therefore developed with "little attention to patent or commercial gain" (2023a, 14), which meant that IVF/ICSI procedures were based on shared technologies and spread quickly around the world. The authors diagnose a "shifting ART landscape" (ibid., 15) from the 1980s onwards, with changes gaining particular momentum in the 2000s: patenting started to shape research on ART, with the number of ART-related patent claims jumping to hundreds per year. Against this backdrop, Cyranoski et al. claim that research on new ARTs, such as IVG (in vitro gametogenesis), will hit the market in a transformed property regime—one in which biotech entrepreneurs' and pharmaceutical companies' search for the next business opportunity will drive the direction of research. In this context, academics themselves are pushed towards patenting and commercialising their inventions: "Scientists often actively pursue commercial opportunities related to their discoveries, and, if they do not, university technology licensing offices encourage them to do so" (ibid., 15).

The rising role of property in ART knowledge since the 1980s leads Cyranoski et al. to ask: "Who will own the next generation of assisted reproductive technologies?" (2023b). Drawing on the examples of the companies Dioseve, Ivy Natal, Houjou, Gameto and Conception Biosciences, they show how current research facilities are more and more backed by private capital. For instance, Gameto is a United States–based start-up active in the areas of egg freezing, infertility and disease research. After initial research conducted at Harvard Medical School, Gameto was founded as a biotechnology company in 2020, raising 3 million dollars in seed capital. Investors included notable angel investors Dan Rose (previously involved with Facebook and chair of the venture capital firm Coatue), Brian Armstrong (CEO of cryptocurrency platform Coinbase) and Jack Abraham (associated with the conservative Thiel Foundation). In 2022, Gameto raised another 23 million dollars (Gameto 2022). This time, various asset management firms (all specialised in venture capital) participated, including Lux Capital (which claims to "turn sci-fi into sci-fact"), as well as wealthy individuals.. Since 2022, Gameto has not only licensed patents from Harvard University (Regalado 2023) but also applied for several new patents (Justia 2023). To mention another example, Conception Biosciences was founded in 2017 by entrepreneur Matt Krisiloff to research IVG technologies. Since its initial seed funding round in 2020, it has been able to raise 38 million dollars in venture capital (PitchBook 2023). Similarly to Gameto, the backers include asset management firms as well as wealthy individuals, such as heavyweight tech investors Jaan Tallinn

(Skype co-founder) and Sam Altman (former president of Y Combinator and current OpenAI CEO) (Regalado 2021). In November 2021, Conception Biosciences filed 154 patent claims (Cyranoski et al. 2023a).

When research facilities like Gameto and Biosciences are backed by private capital, emerging knowledge is also subjected to (varying degrees of) control by investors, who have an interest in extracting profits from patent claims. For example, Jorge Contreras reports that asset management firms have asserted patents against new findings even in cases where the research facility which produced the original knowledge had ceased operations (Contreras 2021). Looking at the assetisation of knowledge furthermore shows the increasing role of ultra-rich individuals in partially owning—and therefore to a certain degree controlling—research start-ups and patents. In this context, recalling the above-mentioned struggles between midwives and the emerging male-dominated medical profession in the seventeenth century, twenty-first-century developments may have to be discussed in terms of new ways of removing knowledge from those receiving treatment.

4. Property in fertility clinics in the United States and Germany[9]

Scattered across several academic disciplines, research on the assetisation of fertility clinics in the United States has recently started to pick up. Publications by Pasquale Patrizio and colleagues, Rajesh Reddy and Lucy van de Wiel all point to a rising role of private capital in the fertility clinic sector.

Patrizio and colleagues observe a "changing world of IVF", where the treatment of fertility "that began as an academic, innovative, research activity" has become a commercial service and thus "big business" (2022, 305). They report that the United States fertility treatment industry grew to 8 billion United States dollars (gross revenues) in 2022, while the global fertility services market is estimated to have exceeded 20 billion dollars in 2021, growing at a compound annual growth rate of almost 9 percent (ibid., 307). With regards to the question of who owns and runs these clinics, they outline how in the United States "the majority of IVF clinics are private" while only a "small minority of data-reporting clinics (< 15 %) are currently

9 Some parts of the research on Germany have previously been published in two blog posts. I am very grateful to Zelda Wenner, whose research was tremendously helpful.

within academic centers" (ibid., 306). From Patrizio et al., we learn that private owners include individuals, groups of physicians and private capital groups.

Reddy's article adds further information on the last of these three categories, by focusing on the role of private capital in obstetrics and gynaecology practices in the United States more broadly. He finds that "private equity has evolved into a major force in health care" (2020, 1217), with fertility treatments being an "especially lucrative market" which attracts an ever-greater amount of private capital funding. The market tripled in size between 2009 and 2018 to a total value of 624 million United States dollars (ibid., 1218).

Lucy van de Wiel's research complements Reddy's insights by focusing on IVF and egg freezing facilities in the United States. She shows that egg freezing technologies and start-ups have attracted millions of dollars in private capital since 2016 (ibid., 312). Furthermore drawing on examples of fertility companies which are run by private capital, she concludes that financialisation plays a "pivotal role in fertility (preservation)" (2020, 306).

Given that existing publications on the assetisation of fertility treatments focus mostly on the United States, the impression may arise that such trends are confined to that country alone. It therefore seems fruitful to expand the debate by looking at another country. Germany is an interesting case given that it is one of the top three European Union member states by number of fertility treatments (Wyns et al. 2022) but, to the best of our knowledge, no research has yet been conducted on who owns and makes money from fertility clinics. In contrast to the United States, fertility treatments such as "egg donation" and surrogacy are illegal, and private capital investments are less advanced rendering Germany an interesting case. To shed light on the case of Germany, we rely on secondary and primary research. The latter includes the collection of information from fertility clinics' websites, registry entries, press releases and business reports, as well as conducting interviews with four German experts from the reproductive sector as part of the project *Property in the Human Body in the Context of Transnational Economies of Reproduction*, which is part of the Collaborative Research Centre TRR 294 "Structural Change of Property."[10]

As outlined by Denise Lehner-Renken (2020), research on reproductive technologies such as IVF was conducted at a number of German universi-

10 See https://sfb294-eigentum.de/en/subprojects/eigentum-am-menschlichen-korper-im-kontext-transnationaler-reproduktionsokonomien/.

ties (Erlangen, Kiel, Lübeck, Bonn) between the 1950s and 1980s. In 1981, the first private fertility clinic opened, which mainly offered heterologous insemination ("sperm donation"). When Germany's first IVF-conceived baby was born in 1982, the path was paved for further reproductive interventions, and the founding of fertility clinics and research bodies rapidly accelerated. A handful of university-based clinics and research institutes became established players in the field but, inspired by private research and treatment facilities in the United States and United Kingdom, more and more professionals left public institutions to found private facilities. In 1982, all five of the fertility centres in Germany were based at universities, generating a sales volume of 3.7 million Deutsche Mark (about 2 million euros). By 1990, the number of centres had increased tenfold, and 30 percent were already being run as small-scale businesses by doctors (*niedergelassene Ärzt*innen*), generating a sales volume of 36.7 million Deutsche Mark. Of today's roughly 150 fertility clinics, many were founded by doctors during the 1990s and 2000s as small-scale businesses. Similar to other medical professions in Germany, these practices operate for profit, but their small to medium size limits their market power.

More recently, it has been possible to observe a slow but steady shift in the landscape of fertility clinics in Germany. More and more clinics are bought up and incorporated into large chains. As some of our interviewees noted, one reason for this shift is that some of the founders are now ready to retire. While it used to be commonplace—and reportedly also preferred—for doctors to hand over their clinics to the next generation of medical professionals, members of the current new generation are rarely able to afford to buy clinics off retiring colleagues. The gap tends to be filled by larger corporations and asset management firms. Following the changing ownership of the Spanish fertility clinic Luarmia serves as a prototypical example of this development: Luarmia was founded by two doctors in the 1990s. In 2010, the private capital firm ProA Capital bought the clinic for 75 million euros. Just four years later, it sold Luarmia for 143 million euros—more than twice what it paid—to NMC, a stock-listed healthcare group based in the United Arab Emirates. Luarmia was restructured and became part of the Eugin Group. In line with trends of transnationalisation, at this point the Eugin Group held shares in clinics in the United States, Spain, Brazil, Italy, Sweden, Denmark, Argentina, Colombia and Lithuania. In 2021, the German company Fresenius Helios bought the Eugin Group for 430 million euros. Fresenius Helios now owned not only several fertility clinics, but also fertility information channels, including a 24-hour hotline for intended parents and Pineapp Fertility, which provides information on fertility clinics and treatments. In other words: it is not just ARTs that are privately owned; information on fertility treatments, which consumers likely assume comes from scientists or "neutral" sources, is increasingly also provided by private companies. In late 2023, Fresenius sold the Eugin Group—which at that point comprised 69 clinics in eleven countries—to KKR and GED Capital in a deal worth up to 500 million euros. KKR is a United States–based global investment firm which handles 497 billion United States dollars of private capital investments (KKR 2024). In line with the trend of monopolisation, this deal expanded KKR's sizeable investment in the fertility sector. For example, in January 2023, it was involved in what was then the largest fertility clinic acquisition, when it purchased another group of fertility clinics, IVIRMA, for 3.25 billion United States dollars (Shinkman 2023).

The role of asset management firms in the German fertility sector is also apparent when we look at the three large chains amedes, TFP and Next Fertility, all of which are backed by private capital. For example, Goldman Sachs Asset Management and AXA IM Alts acquired the amedes Group from another asset management firm (Antin Infrastructure Partners) in 2021 (OMERS 2021). AXA IM reported that "the investment gave us access to their 75+ laboratories and specialty medicine sites, supporting sectors ranging from fertility medicine to rheumatology and oncology" (AXA 2024). NextClinics financed its expansion into the fertility sector by cooperating with the United States–based Oaktree Capital Management, one of the world's largest investment groups. With the help of this financial backing—225 million euros was invested in Europe in 2019—NextClinics became, in its own words, "a top 3 ART provider in Europe with 15 IVF clinics and sites in 8 countries across the continent [...] in less than two years" (NEXTCLINICS 2020).

To conclude, despite some variations, trends towards assetisation of fertility clinics that scholars have observed in the United States can also be found in Germany. While the German fertility sector was primarily built up by doctors who founded clinics as small-scale businesses, we are currently witnessing a changing landscape in which asset management firms gain an increasing role in acquiring fertility clinics. In this context, examples like KKR illustrate trends towards a more centralised and transnational reproductive market. It is noteworthy that at this point in time, national and international private capital is more dominant in buying up clinics than stock-listed companies which reflects the above-outlined developments around assetisation and private capital. In short, while we lack precise figures due to opaque, fast-changing ownership structures, we can conclude that German fertility clinics are rarely owned publicly, but rather are often owned by doctors as small-scale businesses or, increasingly, by asset managers and investors.

5. Concluding deliberations: from biopolitics to bioeconomies to "biofinanciers"?

This chapter has sought to complement recent research on ARTs by considering property in such technologies. Focusing on the United States and Germany, we drew together initial findings on how asset management firms and ultra-rich individuals and families are increasingly owning, running and making money from ART research and fertility clinics.

Given that research on private capital in the context of reproductive technologies is only at an early stage, we lack "a clear understanding of the effects of private equity on national health care costs" (Reddy 2020, 1219). Some initial findings include the fact that assetisation has gone hand in hand with trends of monopolisation and transnationalisation (as illustrated by the examples given above). Transnationalisation allows fertility conglomerates to circumvent state regulations and taxes and exploit currency differences and cheap labour power. For instance: "egg donation" is illegal in Germany, but German fertility corporations can simply cater to German patients at their clinics in neighbouring European countries. Furthermore, Reddy has noted that private capital firms tend to end their financial involvement in medical facilities within three to seven years, which encourages short-term growth plans and may generally clash with the necessity of long-term planning in the health sector to ensure quality and safety (ibid., 1219). It has also been reported that private-capital-owned practices use different strategies to increase revenue, including overprovision of services. Patrizio and colleagues note that large investors' incentives are not aligned with medical ethics. Rather, they are motivated to obtain returns on their investments—"profits, and not patients, emerge as a principal priority" (2022, 310)—which may encourage doctors to spend less time with patients and recommend more (or more expensive) treatments or non-validated tests. Patrizio and colleagues note that in Australia and Aotearoa (New Zealand) "three mega network companies control two-thirds of the region's IVF cycles" and that live births (referred to as "baby take home rate") "have been declining in strong correlation with increasing monopolization of IVF and, in parallel, declining patient satisfaction, while costs [for intended parents] have been increasing" (ibid., 310).

Beyond such potential implications at the level of patient care, this chapter has been driven by an interest in a more structural question of control in the context of biological reproduction. Here, it seems appropriate to cycle all the way back to the example of Shulamith Firestone, who was so very enthusiastic about ARTs and even saw advanced technologies as a necessary prerequisite for women's liberation (2015 [1970], 186). In her view, ARTs not only had the potential to free women "from the tyranny of reproduction" (ibid., 185) but, in freeing women from their biology, would also threaten the capitalist system, thereby creating the conditions for a revolution that would, ideally, usher in communism (ibid., 186). However, looking at who owns ARTs today, 44 years after the publication of Firestone's *The Dialectic of Sex*, the picture bears little resemblance to her idea that women would seize control of human fertility through ARTs. It also bears little resemblance to the 1970s women's self-help groups, which sought to reappropriate knowledge and practices. Rather than women-controlled ARTs which abolish the biological family and capitalism, we are currently witnessing the rise of private investors which are generally overwhelmingly male (see for example Lerner et al. 2021). Current developments in the ART context thus appear to show parallels with the above-discussed struggles over male-dominated reproductive technologies in the 18th century. These developments merit further discussion, in which it will be crucial to attend to how the nature of private capital restricts ownership titles to the ultra-rich and so adds another layer of exclusion.

Next to such mechanisms of exclusion, the "colonisation" (Christophers 2023, 18) or "enclosure" (Tellmann et al. 2024, 3) which Christophers and Tellmann et al. have diagnosed for the general trend of assetisation, requires us to update our analyses of control and choice in the ART context. We may find some initial insights in work on assetisation more generally. For example, recent assetisation scholarship has stressed how assets not only come with "distinct modes of ownership" but also distinct modes of *control* (Birch and Muniesa 2020, 6). To quote Braun: "In this world of private capital, asset managers forfeit the exit option in exchange for full ownership rights. Their power is clearly based on control" (2022, 631–632). A remark by Preqin, an investment data company specialised in "real assets", is telling in this regard:

> Compared to public markets, private capital fund managers typically take a more active role in the management of the companies and assets in which they invest. They will often contribute to business strategy and can play a part in directly managing assets.
>
> *Preqin 2024*

Against this backdrop, at least two factors need to be taken into account in future analyses. Firstly, market forces render certain fertility biographies more profitable than others. Given asset managers' and rich individuals' interests in maximising future revenues, we may expect that the availability of certain fertility treatments over others will be at least partially shaped by financial incentives. In this context, van de Wiel's research underscores that asset managers enter the ART market with the stated aim of changing it to increase profits. With regards to the United States, she outlines how investors follow the vision of shifting the fertility market towards proactive, technologically mediated management: while ARTs used to be primarily (albeit never exclusively) employed to treat infertility, the new vision widens the target group considerably to include anyone who might want children in the future. In this context, fertility companies "aggressively market proactive fertility management" (2020, 312), including fertility check-ups, data-driven estimations of future reproductive chances and egg freezing, thereby targeting people who are not currently infertile. Laura Perler's work on Spain (2021; 2022) shows that "proactive management" goes hand in hand with what some may uncritically understand as "quality management". In line with van de Wiel's findings, investors envision the purpose of ARTs as going beyond the treatment of infertility to include helping intended parents to select genetic traits so they can conceive what is perceived as "healthy children". The idea is that sex should be for fun, while conception should occur in fertility clinics to ensure the "best possible outcomes" (Perler 2022). Secondly, investments are not free of ideological motivations. For example, it has been shown that angel investors are not merely driven by profit interests, but invest in companies that they personally like (Ganti 2024). While this chapter has made some tentative observations about investors' political affiliations, more systematic research is needed, especially with regards to "new eugenics" (Obasogie 2018; Athanasiou and Darnovsky 2018).

Crucially, fertility is arguably not just yet another sphere of social reproduction, which becomes subjugated under the logics of capital. Rather, the assetisation of ARTs has potential implications for fundamental questions of biological reproduction: which reproductive choices are available or unavailable? And *to whom* are they (un)available? Which genes get to be reproduced? How will aggressive marketing influence reproductive choices? In this context, this chapter may contribute to debates which emerged in the early 2000s on the changing nature of biopolitical power (e.g. Rose 2001; Rabinow and Rose 2006; Rose 2006; Braun 2007). Against the backdrop of advancements in biotechnologies and neoliberal governance, Rose (2001, 2006) and Rabinow and Rose (2006) argued that biopolitical power no longer operates primarily at the level of populations, as Foucault described it, but now increasingly targets life at the molecular, genetic, and individual level: Until the 1970s, the central actors that intervened in biological reproduction to shape future populations in Europe and the United States tended to be (albeit never exclusively) states. With the integration of reproductive technologies into market mechanisms from the 1980s onwards, individuals were increasingly encouraged to take responsibility for managing their own biology and that of their children by participating in market-mediated biotechnological interventions. Therefore, reproductive choice became more and more structured by decentralised market forces, even if biopolitical state projects were never entirely replaced (see e.g. Schurr 2016; Schultz 2011). In these conditions, individuals operate as consumers in bioeconomies which offer a variety of options, including the option to select embryos according to sex, phenotype and (dis)ability, or to postpone pregnancy by egg freezing. At the same time, their choices are constrained by market mechanisms, including the price or societal/economic consequences of different options. Carolin Schurr (2016) encapsulated these shifts in the pointed title she chose for her essay "From Biopolitics to Bioeconomies". More than 20 years after Rose's initial publications, this chapter's finding that assetisation may represent a centralisation of power in the hands of financial actors calls for an exploration of whether we are faced with new mechanisms and holders of biopolitical power. In other words, we may tentatively (or provocatively) wonder whether such shifts away from more centralised forms of biopolitical state interventions towards decentralised market mechanisms could again be complemented by more centralised forms of control—this time exerted by asset managers and ultra-rich individuals. In other words, we may in future observe a trend "from biopolitics to bioeconomies to *biofinanciers*."

Works Cited

Adkins, Lisa, Martijn Konings and Melinda Cooper (2020). *The Asset Economy: Property Ownership and the New Logic of Inequality*. Medford: Polity Press.

Adkins, Lisa, Melinda Cooper and Martijn Konings (2021). The Asset Economy: Conceptualizing New Logics of Inequality. *Distinktion: Journal of Social Theory*, 23(1), 15–32.

Athanasiou, Tom, and Marcy Darnovsky (2018). The Genome as Commons. In Osagie K. Obasogie and Marcy Darnovsky (eds.). *Beyond Bioethics: Toward a New Biopolitics*, 158–162. Berkeley: University of California Press.

AXA Investment Managers. *Investing in Global Health: AXA Investment Managers*. Accessed October 2024. https://alts.axa-im.com/investment-expertise/private-equity-and-infrastructure/healthcare.

Birch, Kean (2016). Rethinking Value in the Bio-Economy: Finance, Assetization, and the Management of Value. *Science, Technology, & Human Values*, 42(3), 460–490.

Birch, Kean, and David Tyfield (2012). Theorizing the Bioeconomy. *Science, Technology, & Human Values*, 38(3), 299–327.

Birch, Kean, and Fabian Muniesa (eds.) (2020). *Assetization: Turning Things into Assets in Technoscientific Capitalism*. Cambridge, MA: MIT Press.

Borsa, Alexander, Geronimo Bejarano, Moriah Ellen and Joseph Dov Bruch (2023). Evaluating Trends in Private Equity Ownership and Impacts on Health Outcomes, Costs, and Quality: Systematic Review. *BMJ*, 382, e075244.

Braun, Benjamin (2022). Exit, Control, and Politics: Structural Power and Corporate Governance under Asset Manager Capitalism. *Politics & Society*, 50(4), 630–654.

Braun, Bruce (2007). Biopolitics and the Molecularization of Life. *cultural geographies*, 14(1), 6–28.

Burke, Ryan (2024). *Are You Harnessing the Growth and Resilience of Private Capital?* Accessed October 2024. https://www.ey.com/en_gl/insights/private-business/are-you-harnessing-the-growth-and-resilience-of-private-capital.

Christophers, Brett (2023). *Our Lives in Their Portfolios: Why Asset Managers Own the World*. London: Verso.

Christophers, Brett, and Ben Fine (2020). The Value of Financialization and the Financialization of Value. In Philip Mader, Daniel Mertens and Natascha van der Zwan (eds.). *The Routledge International Handbook of Financialization*, 19–30. London: Routledge.

Contreras, Jorge L. (2021). Patent Reality Checks: Eliminating Patents on Fake, Impossible and Other Inoperative Inventions. *Journal of the Patent and Trademark Office Society*, 102. https://papers.ssrn.com/sol3/papers.cfm?abstract_id=3872710.

Cooper, Melinda (2008). *Life as Surplus: Biotechnology and Capitalism in the Neoliberal Era*. Seattle: University of Washington Press.

Cooper, Melinda, and Catherine Waldby (2014). *Clinical Labor: Tissue Donors and Research Subjects in the Global Bioeconomy*. Durham, NC: Duke University Press.

Cyranoski, David, Jorge L. Contreras and Victoria T. Carrington (2023a). Intellectual Property and Assisted Reproductive Technology. *Nature Biotechnology*, 41(1), 14–20.

Cyranoski, David, Jorge L. Contreras and Victoria T. Carrington (2023b). Who Will Own the Next Generation of Assisted Reproductive Technologies? *Springer Nature Research Communities*, 19 January. https://communities.springernature.com/posts/who-will-own-the-next-generation-of-assisted-reproductive-technologies.

Deomampo, Daisy (2016). *Transnational Reproduction: Race, Kinship and Commercial Surrogacy in India*. New York: New York University Press.

Deutsches IVF-Register e.V. (2022). Jahrbuch 2021. *Journal für Reproduktionsmedizin und Endokrinologie*, 19(4).

Doehler, Austin (2020). The "Strategic" Reason for Hungary's Free Fertility Plan. *Balkan Insight*, 17 February. https://balkaninsight.com/2020/02/17/the-strategic-reason-for-hungarys-free-fertility-plan/.

Donnison, Jean (2025 [1977]). *Midwives and Medical Men: A History of the Struggle for the Control of Childbirth*. London: Routledge.

Ermoline, Pavel, and Blazej Kupec (2023). Investors Are Increasingly Attracted to Private Markets. Why? *World Economic Forum*. Accessed October 2024. https://www.weforum.org/agenda/2023/12/private-markets-investors/.

ESHRE (2023). *ART Fact Sheet*. Accessed October 2024. https://www.eshre.eu/Europe/Factsheets-and-infographics.

Fine, Ben (2020). Framing Social Reproduction in the Age of Financialisation. In Ana Cordeiro Santos and Nuno Teles (eds.). *Financialisation in the European Periphery: Work and Social Reproduction in Portugal*. London: Routledge. Preprint version available at http://iippe.org/wp-content/uploads/2018/12/sroverviewben.pdf.

Firestone, Shulamith (2015 [1970]). *The Dialectics of Sex: The Case for Feminist Revolution*. London: Verso.

Fresenius (2020). Fresenius Helios erwirbt führenden Anbieter von Reproduktionsmedizin. *Fresenius*. Accessed October 2024. https://www.fresenius.com/de/node/5160.

Gameto (2022). Gameto Raises $ 23M to Redefine Reproductive Longevity with Reprogrammed Ovarian Cells. *PR Newswire*. Accessed October 2024. https://www.prnewswire.com/news-releases/gameto-raises-23m-to-redefine-reproductive-longevity-with-reprogrammed-ovarian-cells-301456850.html.

Ganti, Akhilesh (2024). Angel Investor: Definition and How It Works. *Investopia*. Accessed October 2024. https://www.investopedia.com/terms/a/angelinvestor.asp.

Gimenez, Martha (2018). *Marx, Women, and Capitalist Social Reproduction: Marxist Feminist Essays*. Chicago: Haymarket Books.

Greely, Henry T. (2016). *The End of Sex and the Future of Human Reproduction*. Cambridge, MA: Harvard University Press.

Justia (2023). Patents Assigned to Gameto. *JUSTIA*. Accessed October 2024. https://patents.justia.com/assignee/gameto-inc.

Kang, Hyo Yoon (2020). Patents as Assets: Intellectual Property Rights as Market Subjects and Objects. In Kean Birch and Fabian Muniesa (eds.). *Assetization: Turning Things into Assets in Technoscientific Capitalism*, 45–74. Cambridge, MA: MIT Press.

KKR (2024). KKR. What Will We Accomplish, Together? *KKR*. Accessed October 2024. https://www.kkr.com/.

Kushnir, Vitaly A., Gary D. Smith and Eli Y. Adashi (2022). The Future of IVF: The New Normal in Human Reproduction. *Reproductive Sciences*, 29(3), 849–856.

Lafuente-Funes, Sara (2020). Shall We Stop Talking about Egg Donation? Transference of Reproductive Capacity in the Spanish Bioeconomy. *BioSocieties*, 15(2), 207–225.

Langley, Paul (2021). Assets and Assetization in Financialized Capitalism. *Review of International Political Economy*, 28(2), 382–393.

Lehner-Renken, Denise (2020). Zwischen Markt und Moral: Reproduktionsmedizin und ihre Akteure in der Bundesrepublik der 1980er-Jahre. *Zeithistorische Forschungen/Studies in Contemporary History*, 17, 308–334.

Lerner, Josh, Rahat Dewan, Jake Ledbetter and Alex Billias (2021). *Knight Diversity of Asset Managers Research Series: Industry: A Study of Ownership Diversity and Performance in the Asset Management Industry*. https://knightfoundation.org/wp-content/uploads/2021/12/KDAM_Industry_2021.pdf.

Lettow, Susanne (2015). Biokapitalismus und Inwertsetzung der Körper: Perspektiven der Kritik. *PROKLA*, 45(178), 33–49.

Lewis, Sophie (2019). *Full Surrogacy Now: Feminism against Family*. London: Verso.

Mamo, Laura (2018). Queering Reproduction in Transnational Bio-Economies. *Reproductive BioMedicine & Society Online*, 7, 24–32.

Martin, Randy (2002). *Financialization of Daily Life*. Philadelphia: Temple University Press.

Milyaeva, Sveta, and Daniel Neyland (2020). English Higher Education: From a Public Good to a Public Asset. In Kean Birch and Fabian Muniesa (eds.). *Assetization: Turning Things into Assets in Technoscientific Capitalism*, 261–286. Cambridge, MA: MIT Press.

Murphy, Michelle (2012). *Seizing the Means of Reproduction: Entanglements of Feminism, Health, and Technoscience*. Durham, NC: Duke University Press.

Namberger, Verena (2019). *The Reproductive Body at Work: The South African Bioeconomy of Egg Donation*. Abingdon: Routledge.

Next Clinics (2019). Nextclinics baut Position in Europa weiter aus Führung im Bereich künstlicher Befruchtung angestrebt. *Next Clinics*. Accessed October 2024. https://www.next-clinics.com/de/reports/nextclinics-baut-position-in-europa-weiter-aus-fuehrung-im-bereich-kuenstlicher-befruchtung-angestrebt/.

Obasogie, Osagie K. (2018). The Eugenics Legacy of the Nobelist Who Fathered IVF. In Osagie K. Obasogie and Marcy Darnovsky (eds.). *Beyond Bioethics: Toward a New Biopolitics*, 73–77. Oakland: University of California Press.

Obasogie, Osagie K., and Marcy Darnovsky (eds.) (2018). *Beyond Bioethics: Toward a New Biopolitics*. Oakland: University of California Press.

OMERS (2021). OMERS Infrastructure announces investment in amedes, a leading laboratory services provider. *OMERS Infrastructure*. Accessed October 2024. https://www.omersinfrastructure.com/news/omers-goldman-sachs-asset-management-axa-im-alts-sign-agreement-to-purchase.

Pande, Amrita (2009). "It May Be Her Eggs but It's My Blood": Surrogates and Everyday Forms of Kinship in India. *Qualitative Sociology*, 32(4), 379–397.

Pande, Amrita (2014). *Wombs in Labor: Transnational Commercial Surrogacy in India*. New York: Columbia University Press.

Patrizio, Pasquale, David F Albertini, Norbert Gleicher and Arthur Caplan (2022). The Changing World of IVF: The Pros and Cons of New Business Models Offering Assisted Reproductive Technologies. *Journal of Assisted Reproduction and Genetics*, 39(2), 305–313.

Pavone, Vincenzo, and Joanna Goven (eds.) (2017). *Bioeconomies: Life, Technology, and Capital in the 21st Century*. Basingstoke: Palgrave Macmillan.

Perler, Laura (2021). Selektive assistierte Reproduktion. *Gen-ethischer Informationsdienst*, 259, 34–36.

Perler, Laura (2022). *Die Verheißung des Gesunden Kindes: Eine Analyse der spanischen Eizellenspendeökonomie*. Doctoral thesis, University of St Gallen. https://boris.unibe.ch/165846/1/Die_Verheissung_gesundes_Kind_Laura_Perler_2021-ohneAnhang_Komprimiert.pdf.

PitchBook (2023). *Conception PitchBook*. Accessed October 2024. https://pitchbook.com/profiles/company/265222-81#overview.

Preqin (2024). What Is Private Capital? Accessed October 2024. https://www.preqin.com/academy/lesson-2-private-capital/what-is-private-capital.

Reddy, Rajesh (2020). Private Equity Investments in Women's Health and Obstetrics and Gynecology Practices. *Obstetrics and Gynecology*, 136(6), 1217–1220.

Regalado, Antonio (2021). How Silicon Valley Hatched a Plan to Turn Blood into Human Eggs. *MIT Technology Review*. Accessed October 2024. https://www.technologyreview.com/2021/10/28/1038172/conception-eggs-reproduction-vitro-gametogenesis/.

Regalado, Antonio (2022). This Biotech CEO Decided to Take Her Own (Fertility) Medicine. *MIT Technology Review*. Accessed October 2024. https://www.technologyreview.com/2023/10/16/1081670/gameto-biotech-ceo-fertility-experiment/.

Rabinow, Paul and Nikolas Rose (2006). Biopower Today. *BioSocieties*, 1(2), 195–217.

Rose, Nikolas (2001). The Politics of Life Itself. *Theory, Culture & Society*, 18(6), 1–30.

Rose, Nikolas (2006). *The Politics of Life Itself: Biomedicine, Power and Subjectivity in the Twenty-First Century*. Princeton: Princeton University Press.

Roy, Victor (2020). A Crisis for Cures? Tracing Assetization and Value in Biomedical Innovation. In Kean Birch and Fabian Muniesa (eds.). *Assetization: Turning Things into Assets in Technoscientific Capitalism*, 97–124. Cambridge, MA: MIT Press.

Rudrappa, Sharmila (2015). *Discounted Life: The Price of Global Surrogacy in India*. New York: New York University Press.

Schultz, Susanne (2011). New Biopolitics? The Articulation of Demographic Aims and Gender Policies in International Population Programs. In Kathrin Braun (ed.). *Between Self-Determination and Social Technology: Medicine, Biopolitics and the New Techniques of Procedural Management*, 239–270. Bielefeld: Transcript.

Schurr, Carolin (2016). From Biopolitics to Bioeconomies: The ART of (Re-)Producing White Futures in Mexico's Surrogacy Market. *Environment and Plan D*, 35(2), 241–262.

Shinkman, Ron (2023). $ 3.25B: World's Largest Ever Fertility Clinic Acquisition Approved after Almost One Year. *Inside Reproductive Health*. Accessed October 2024. https://www.fertilitybridge.com/news-articles/digest01262023.

Tellmann, Ute, Veit Braun and Barbara Brandl (2024). The Challenges of Assets: Anatomy of an Economic Form. *Economy and Society*, 53(1), 1–14.

Vertommen, Sigrid, Vincenzo Pavone and Michal Nahman (2022). Global Fertility Chains: An Integrative Political Economy Approach to Understanding the Reproductive Bioeconomy. *Science, Technology, & Human Values*, 47(1), 112–145.

Vora, Kalindi (2019). After the Housewife: Surrogacy, Labour and Human Reproduction. *Radical Philosophy*, 204 (Spring), 42–46.

Wajcman, Judy (1996 [1991]). *Feminism Confronts Technology*. Philadelphia: Pennsylvania State University Press.

Waldby, Catherine, and Melinda Cooper (2008). The Biopolitics of Reproduction: Post-Fordist Biotechnology and Women's Clinical Labour. *Australian Feminist Studies*, 23(55), 57–73.

Weston, Kath (1991). *Families We Choose: Lesbians, Gays, Kinship*. New York: Columbia University Press.

Wichterich, Christa (2018). Zur transnationalen Rekonfiguration von (Re-)Produktion durch Leihmutterschaft: Biopolitiken, Reproduktionsindustrie und Subjektweisen. In Katharina Pühl and Birgit Sauer (eds.). *Kapitalismuskritische Gesellschaftsanalyse: Queerfeminstische Positionen*, 93–112. Münster: Westfälisches Dampfboot.

Wiel, Lucy van de (2020). The Speculative Turn in IVF: Egg Freezing and the Financialization of Fertility. *New Genetics and Society*, 39(3), 306–326.

Williams, James W. (2020). Recidivists, Rough Sleepers, and the Unemployed as Financial Assets: Social Impact Bonds and the Creation of New Markets in Social Services. In Kean Birch and Fabian Muniesa (eds.). *Assetization: Turning Things into Assets in Technoscientific Capitalism*, 287–312. Cambridge, MA: MIT Press.

Wong, Julia Carrie (2017). Meet the Rightwing Power Players Lurking beneath Silicon Valley's Liberal Facade. *The Guardian*. Accessed October 2024. https://www.theguardian.com/technology/2017/feb/10/silicon-valley-right-wing-donald-trump-peter-thiel.

Wyns, Christine, C. De Geyter, C. Calhaz-Jorge, M. S. Kupka, T. Motrenko, J. Smeenk, C Bergh, A. Tandler-Schneider, I. A. Rugescu and V. Goossens (2022). ART in Europe, 2018: Results Generated from European Registries by ESHRE. *Human Reproduction Open*, 2022 (3), hoac022.

II
Contested Objects of Property

> Usually the Asians are really rare and hard to come by. Chinese, Japanese, Korean, Vietnamese. Those types of Asians. And Caucasians. Those are the most popular. That's usually the biggest factor when recipients are deciding what egg donor they choose. So of course we are trying to recruit more for those populations because those are the ones that are going to be bought—as bad as that sounds! But then because we're in Hawai'i, there are a lot more local people; so mixed, less educated people, those are the ones that are volunteering. There's a lot more donors that apply in that demographic, but the other ones, like the Asians and Caucasians, are rarer to come in, and they are more popular, so their eggs are more sought after. So if a full Chinese donor came in today, there would be like five families immediately signing up! There's waiting lists for them!

Jacquelyn's comments vividly illustrate the ways in which reproductive tissues become racialised and commodified. Jacquelyn's racial categorisations distinguish between "Asians" and "local people". Many people I interviewed understood the first category as including Chinese, Japanese and Korean and the second as a diverse group of ethnicities, including people of Native Hawai'ian, Filipino, Samoan and other Asian/Pacific Islander backgrounds, as well as people of mixed race or mixed Asian backgrounds. While some of my interlocutors might have used "Asian" to describe any person with some Asian heritage, Jacquelyn's statements indicate she uses the term to refer exclusively to people with a "full" Asian background, a category that carries economic value in the market in gametes. As Jacquelyn discussed HCR's efforts to recruit more strongly for populations that are more likely to be purchased, she highlighted the significance of market supply and demand in egg procurement and the commodification of gametes.

Jacquelyn's comments raise several questions that are central to this chapter, relating to race, identity and commodification in gamete donation: how do donor coordinators and other medical providers construct, value and commodify race? What role do market pressures play in categorising and constructing racial boundaries? And how might donors and recipients themselves reify or respond to such characterisations? In this chapter, I examine the intertwined processes of racialisation and commodification in order to elucidate the ways in which race becomes commodified as a resource for family-making. Put differently, how does racial identity become constructed as an inheritable form of property within a broader system of racial capitalism? My goal is to show the ways in which actors involved in egg donation construct, market and categorise race with respect to particular desires for family formation. Race materialises in various ways within egg donation among diverse actors, who construct race along a spectrum,

Purchasing Race: Commodifying "Asian" Eggs in Assisted Reproduction

Daisy Deomampo

In early 2017, I met with Jacquelyn Liu in her office at the Honolulu Centre for Reproduction (HCR), a busy fertility clinic in the heart of Hawai'i's biggest city.[1,2] HCR offers a range of assisted reproductive technologies (ARTs), including in vitro fertilisation, intracytoplasmic sperm injection and preimplantation genetic screening and diagnosis, but I was most interested in Jacquelyn's role managing the clinic's in-house egg donor programme. A college-educated Chinese American raised in Hawai'i, Jacquelyn had been coordinating the programme for several years, and had unique insight into the factors that influence supply and demand of donors of different racial/ethnic backgrounds.[3]

Typically, Jacquelyn speaks quickly and to the point, but she hesitated when I asked her about egg donors' ethnic backgrounds. "When the donors come in—well, it's also driven by what kind of recipients there are. There's a lot of—how do I say this? There are certain [she paused] ethnicities [she paused again] that are more popular than others." "Which ones?" I inquired. She answered:

1 Material in this chapter was adapted from the 2019 article "Racialized Commodities: Race and Value in Human Egg Donation", published in *Medical Anthropology*.

2 All names of individuals and organisations have been changed to protect confidentiality.

3 Understandings of the terms "race" and "ethnicity" are subjective and remain contested in lay and academic literature. While "race" may refer to biological or genetic notions, "ethnicity" is often seen as grounded in language, culture and ancestry rather than biology (Fenton 1999). Yet the distinctions between the two terms are often blurred and authors have challenged this binary distinction, contending that biological referents are never fully absent from notions of ethnicity, as physical markers such as skin colour have been used to imply social and cultural differences between groups (Smaje 2000). Thus, because of the fluidity and overlapping nature of the terms, I link race/ethnicity together throughout the chapter.

at times reinforcing its biogenetic status and at others deemphasising it. Race, I argue, emerges in often-opposing ways in the commodification of gametes, the construction of property and the formation of families.

As increasing numbers of people access ART procedures, stereotypes about race and ethnicity continue to influence ideas and perceptions about those who use ARTs to build their families. While social scientists have made important contributions to the literature on minority experiences with assisted reproduction in the United Kingdom (Nordqvist 2012; Culley et al. 2013; Hudson and Culley 2014), research on ethnic minority experiences of infertility and ART use in the United States is scarce (exceptions include Bell 2014; Quiroga 2007; Inhorn et al. 2009; Inhorn et al. 2021). At the same time, Asian Americans' experiences of infertility and gamete donation remain largely underexplored, despite their being the fastest-growing minority group in the country (Hoeffel et al. 2012). Moreover, studies have shown that Asian women are most likely to pursue oocyte donation in the United States (Shapiro et al. 2016), and in 2014, Asian American and Pacific Islander women had the highest rates of ART utilisation (Dieke et al. 2017).

In this context, I am particularly interested in how human eggs function as commodities, capital and forms of property—and how this informs understandings of race and racial identity as properties to be acquired. Historically, the human body and its parts have been seen as exceptional in property law, in that the commercialisation of the human body and bodily parts is an obvious slight to human dignity. But the fertility industry and the stem cell research enterprise have created the conditions for human eggs to attain market value—a process that depends on the ability to "obtain possession and control from women and transfer possession and control to others, including women who hope to become pregnant, embryologists, and researchers" (Ikemoto 2009, 777). As legal scholar Lisa Ikemoto contends, the medical and commercial practices of egg donation enable the physical transfer of control, while the legal and normative context converts eggs into capital. Following the 1990 California Supreme Court case *Moore v. The Regents of the University of California*, the ethical focus moved to how this transfer occurs and whether companies and clinics attained proper informed consent. In other words, as Ikemoto writes, "the question of whether anyone can own human tissue is no longer regarded as an ethical issue" (ibid., 779). Moreover, the very act of defining human eggs as objects of value, things that can be bought and sold, highlights how women's labour in egg extraction produces something of value—in other words, egg extraction counts as labour which confers a property right (Dickenson 2001).

Thus, while human eggs clearly function as commodities within the reproductive marketplace—that is, they are extracted, valued and traded for economic exchange—they also invite characterisation as a form of property, a "thing" to be owned. Here, it is worth noting that egg donation functions as a key ART that is used to reinforce dominant cultural notions of kinship and inheritance, in which *racial identity* becomes an inheritable characteristic or asset—in other words, an object of property that can be valued and commodified. As legal scholar Cheryl Harris (1993) argues, the notions of racial identity and property are profoundly interrelated. Whiteness in particular evolved into a form of property that became the foundation of racialised privilege—an identity or attribute that confers status and societal benefits. If, as Donna Dickenson (1997) argues, we might think of property as a set of relationships among persons with respect to things (rather than as an object or thing in itself), imagining racial identity as inheritable genetic property helps make sense of racialised value creation and commodification in the context of egg donation among "Asian" donors. In the reproductive marketplace, I argue that notions of property and commodification are deeply intertwined, as such property relations depend on market forces and unequal power relations of capital accumulation, which commodify specific human traits and privilege particular racialised egg donors.

In this chapter, I explore racialisation processes in the context of Asian American egg donation, highlighting intersections between ideas about race, reproduction, property and market value. Diverse Asian identities become racialised in various ways, including as a tool for family formation, as a proxy for shared ancestry and similar phenotype and as a marker of blood "purity". Further, I examine how reproductive medicine structures a market in racialised gametes, illustrating the importance of understanding how biogenetic and social ideas about race are created and valued in the context of in vitro fertilisation (IVF) and gamete donation. I begin by describing the methods and broader research study on which this chapter is based. I then turn to place this discussion within the context of egg procurement in the United States, which enables my analysis of the various ways in which donor coordinators, recipients and other actors construct race along a spectrum. As I discuss, research participants alternately reify and deemphasise the genetic and biological status of race, all the while illustrating how actors commodify race as a resource for family-making. Finally, I examine how eggs come to be constructed as a form of racial property to be acquired or lost, with consequences for thinking about the relationship between structural racism, racial capitalism and notions of "appropriate" families.

1. Methods

This chapter is based on ethnographic research conducted between 2016 and 2022 and is part of a larger project that investigates how diverse Asian American groups experience social and cultural issues related to egg donation. Data for this chapter derive from 28 interviews with 19 medical providers, clinic staff and egg donor programme coordinators, whose understandings of how race is constructed, categorised and marketed within fertility clinics are the focus of this chapter. I also incorporate analyses of textual sources including organisational websites and printed materials; I focused on selecting marketing materials produced by major medical associations, fertility clinics and egg donor agencies, health advocacy organisations and pharmaceutical companies. I also draw on intended parents' comments on online blogs and forums as key sites through which to access frank conversations about race that do not happen in other spheres. Following Boellstorff and colleagues, I draw on the "principle of care" when considering how to analyse this data; as a result, given the sensitivity of the topics discussed, I avoid using direct quotes in particularly delicate scenarios, opting instead to pull back to a more abstract level of analysis (Boellstorff et al. 2012). I analysed these diverse data using an inductive methodology in which the categories for coding and theoretical insights emerge from the data. I obtained ethical clearance to conduct this research from the Institutional Review Board at Fordham University.

The three metropolitan areas where my fieldwork took place have highly diverse Asian populations. New York and Los Angeles encompass the two largest Asian populations in the United States, with 1.1 million and 484,000 Asian residents, respectively, while Honolulu has the highest number of Asians as a proportion of the population (62 percent). The precise makeup of the Asian populations varies between the regions; 71 percent of Japanese in the United States and 66 percent of Filipinos live in the West, while 30 percent of South Asians, 26 percent of Chinese and 21 percent of Koreans live in the Northeast (Hoeffel et al. 2012). I conducted research in each of these regions over multiple periods between 2016 and 2022. I also conducted ongoing phone interviews with egg donor programme coordinators during this time. Field research in each of these places uncovered a complex calculus of factors—including the cost and availability of and ideas about genetic inheritance and identity—that shape understandings of race in the context of egg donation. Given their different demographic profiles, each of these places provides an excellent case study of egg donation among Asian Americans, offering a critical opportunity to investigate the various ways in which eggs become racialised commodities.

2. Egg procurement in the United States: creating racial commodities

The process of transferring reproductive biomaterial from one body to another involves a series of hormonal injections that cause the ovaries to produce multiple mature eggs in one menstrual cycle. The eggs are then surgically removed from the ovaries with the goal of eventually developing embryos with sperm from an intended parent or donor and transferring fertilised embryos to the person hoping to become pregnant, who may be the intended parent or a surrogate. In 2020, fresh or frozen eggs were used in more than 24,000 IVF cycles (approximately 7 percent of all cycles) (Centers for Disease Control and Prevention 2022). Egg donation has become an important aspect of the ART industry, as infertile couples, same-sex couples and single individuals who do not have or cannot use their own eggs and sperm rely on "donated" eggs to conceive children. Egg donation is now entrenched in the broader suite of ART procedures that have led to parenthood for millions of people around the world.

Embedded in egg donation are not only intensive medical procedures but also social and cultural expectations regarding race. In the public imagination, eggs are vital, bodily substances through which people construct and inherit racial and social identities (Thompson 2009), and egg donation offers a key opportunity to explore perceptions about the inheritance of racial identity from donor to offspring (Hudson 2015). Yet they also reflect distinct cultural, social and biological meanings. For instance, in the context of gestational surrogacy in India, ART consumers expressed conflicting ideas about class, race and nation in the process of selecting an egg donor. While many intended parents, for example, seek eggs from donors of similar racial background, others select donors from distinct backgrounds, as in the case of a white United States father who opted for an Indian egg donor because of his abiding interest in Hinduism (Deomampo 2016a). Such racial preferences not only assume that cultural and religious identities can be genetically transferred, but also influence demand in the international market, making eggs a racialised property-as-commodity to be obtained and purchased.

Here, it is critical to note that the commodification of racialised eggs converts them into a form of property—a thing to be exchanged, acquired, bought and sold. In other words, commodification processes in commercial assisted reproductive practices always overlap with notions of property; eggs come into existence as property through the performance of relationships between persons and things (Grubb 1998). Embedded in this process is the reproductive labour needed to extract eggs from women's bodies and trade them on the marketplace—transforming eggs into things to be owned and things to which people have rights through contractual relations. Here, notions of property and commodity are deeply intertwined. As I will discuss later in this chapter, the commodification (and thus "propertisation") of eggs also enables people to purchase race—including ideas about race, phenotype, heritage and purity.

Indeed, race is perhaps the most salient feature in gamete donation, and is a primary trait used to recruit and select egg and sperm providers (Almeling 2011; Roberts 2011; Thompson 2009). For instance, sociologist Lauren Jade Martin found that almost three-quarters of Craigslist posts for egg donors in New York City specify race or ethnicity (Martin 2017, 155). Moreover, in the contemporary United States, notions of race and ethnicity structure scarcity and demand in the market in gametes. While egg agencies and sperm banks strive for diversity in race, ethnicity, religion and other donor characteristics, many agencies encounter difficulty in recruiting Asian American donors, among others. These donors, as a result, are viewed as particularly scarce and "valuable", with many sperm banks and egg donor agencies offering increased compensation for such precious biomaterial (Almeling 2011). Increasing demand for eggs from particular racialised bodies and disputes over what is considered "appropriate" compensation for egg donors led to a federal lawsuit in 2015, in which a group of women claimed that industry guidelines regarding compensation amounted to illegal price-fixing (Lewin 2015). In 2016, the American Society for Reproductive Medicine (ASRM) settled the case and removed all language pertaining to donor compensation guidelines or caps from the industry guidelines at issue. Some have argued that the removal of the compensation guidelines had a limited impact on prices, claiming they did not increase substantially in the years following the lawsuit (Sanders 2022). In practice, however, I found that many doctors, donors and agencies acknowledged enormous variability in compensation, particularly among egg donors who knew that their eggs were in high demand, signalling potential changes in public attitudes towards the commodification of race within reproductive practices.

Media coverage spotlights the intersections of commodification and race in the context of egg donation, indicating that reliance on racial classification in assisted reproduction only seems to be intensifying (Bodenner 2017). The *Los Angeles Times* reported that Asian women command around 10,000 to 20,000 dollars for their eggs, well above the amount ASRM previously recommended, especially "if a donor is 100 % Chinese [and] highly intelligent with a degree in math, for example" (Li 2012). Similarly, in 2017 an ad placed in the Massachusetts Institute of Technology student newspaper read:

> We are a couple seeking an Asian egg donor to help build our family. You should be near the top of your class, and preferably have some outstanding achievements and awards. We prefer Asian race, such as Chinese, Japanese, Korean, Vietnamese […]. About us: we are a highly educated couple, but we are unable to have children due to infertility of the woman. The man is a highly accomplished scientist-mathematician and businessman, the woman has a good PhD-level university degree. The man is of European race, woman is Chinese.

I found similar ads in college newspapers and on egg donor sites dating as far back as 2010.

While the ART market clearly naturalises the marketing and commodification of eggs based on race, such practices may serve to solidify racial categories in troubling ways. In her study of race, consumption and "ethnically correct" dolls, Elizabeth Chin noted, "The commodification of race and the introduction of racialised commodities have not erased the color line so much as they have replaced it with lines of color, an array of products intended for minority consumers" (Chin 2001, 154). While there are numerous naturalised assumptions at the heart of the ART market surrounding racial commodification, in this chapter I explore the ways in which reproductive actors construct and acquire race in the context of a neoliberal market economy. A market-based approach to understanding race is fundamental to analyses of family formation, particularly in the ART industry (Rich 2020). As prospective parents turn to egg or sperm donation, surrogacy and other ART services to build their families, we must pay close attention to the relationship between race and market forces. In a context in which parents are compelled to acquire donor traits such as eye colour and height, as well as intelligence, education and career aspirations,[4] race emerges at the top of the heap for many prospective parents.

3. Commodification of racialised eggs: histories and regulation

Racial considerations are especially critical when considering American society's naturalised assumptions about race in the context of histories in which racialised peoples were commodified. The early United States economy was organised on the principle of racial commodification: slavery was based on a process of racialisation and racial formation that ensured the availability of forced labour to develop the agricultural economy of the United States. Likewise, Asian and Latino workers were racialised in order to exploit and undervalue their labour (Hernandez-Lopez 2008). Racialised populations who were subject to commodifying and exploitative forces have long played a significant role in the formation of United States histories and economies. Yet the racial commodification that exists in egg markets—whether explicit or implied—requires further examination. Currently no clear law or regulation prohibits individuals from selling or acquiring racially marked material for reproductive purposes. Within this context, I focus on the practices of clinics, egg providers and ART consumers as they participate in market exchanges involving racialised reproductive substances.

Reproductive market exchanges unfold in distinct national contexts. Spain, for example, is at the forefront of egg procurement in Europe. In contrast to other European countries that prohibit egg donation, or permit it without compensation, clinics in Spain have monetised the process so that donors receive compensation for "pain and suffering" or "reasonable expenses". But while white egg donors are highly sought after, compensation remains the same regardless of racial background (Marre et al. 2017). In the United States, on the other hand, no such limit to compensation exists, resulting in a thriving market in eggs. As Ikemoto has noted, eggs are a "vital commodity of the [US] fertility industry" (2009, 776). Yet the market value

4 For example, one donor questionnaire asks prospective donors to imagine what they will be doing in five years.

of eggs also depends on the differential valuation of social identities such as race and class; as ethicist Laurie Zoloth, quoted in the *Los Angeles Times*, noted, "the fact that we think of these gametes as having particular worth depending on race and class is really one of the starkest examples of how capitalism has entered the market in human parts" (Li 2012).

Below I elucidate the entwined racialisation processes and market exchanges inherent in gamete donation in the United States context. While several scholars have examined the role that race, ethnicity and skin tone play in the context of ARTs (Bell 2014; Thompson 2009; Deomampo 2016b; Harrison 2016; Speier 2016), a deeper analysis is needed of the ways in which race materialises, becomes commodified and is consequently converted into a form of property. Clearly, race has become more than a reproductive resource (Roberts 2016); it is a marketised resource that can be purchased and consequently acquired as a form of property. Not only might race—an idea that the ART industry embeds in eggs themselves—be something to be acquired, but so, too, might certain racialised notions such as phenotype, ancestry and purity. While scholars have attended to the ways in which third-party reproduction affects labour markets and reproductive labour (Rudrappa 2014; Pande 2014; Cooper and Waldby 2014; Teman 2010), as I will show in this chapter, egg donation offers a unique case study within which to understand how eggs become racialised commodities and forms of property.

4. Racialising reproductive tissues

How do consumers, donor coordinators and other actors racialise reproductive tissues? I organise this section thematically to identify various strategies that are central to the process of racialisation. These strategies include using race as a tool for family formation, matching phenotype and approximating shared ancestry; relying on race as a proxy for racial "purity"; and shifting attitudes towards race in response to market pressures. Taken together, these themes illustrate the diverse ways in which eggs are racialised.

4.1 Race as a tool for family formation, matching phenotype and approximating ancestry

The racialisation of eggs depends on the simultaneous, intertwined processes of reifying race as genetic and framing ART use as a tool for family formation. Family formation provides a compassionate rationalisation for ART use: to meet a profoundly felt human need to nurture and form families (Thompson 2005). The frame of family formation serves to conceal potentially troubling commercial aspects of ART use by emphasising individual choices made, rather than the choices offered (Ikemoto 2009). By focusing on individual decision-making, the language of family formation invokes public sympathy; it also makes it difficult to criticise the pursuit of families through assisted reproduction, even when certain practices raise concerns around justice, inequality and compensation, particularly with respect to the treatment of egg donors and surrogates.

Family formation rhetoric may serve to mask ART use and reinforce the biogenetic family norm; it may also reinforce the single-race family norm. This is achieved through various norms and practices, ranging from explicit searches for donors with a particular racial background or specific blood type, to searches for phenotypic matching with the intended mother. These framing narratives naturalise ART use and its relation to commercial practices intended to facilitate procurement of human eggs, thus making eggs a vital commodity of the ART industry. Here, donor coordinators, or "matchers" as Tessa Moll (2019) calls them, occupy critical positions in shaping racial imaginaries of clients, as they are privy to frank conversations about race in the formation of families.

Margaret Zhou, for instance, observed how individual decision-making and desire for single-race families influenced her clients' donor egg choices. A Chinese immigrant to the United States, Margaret worked in a fertility clinic in the north-east for many years, where she observed numerous Asian couples unable to find Asian egg donors. As she explained, they had "no choice but to use Caucasian donors [...] that's how my motivation started". She founded a boutique egg donor agency specialising in Asian egg donation a little over a decade ago. Margaret described the most important characteristics that her clients seek in an egg donor:

> Obviously cultural background is pretty important. For example, you might think Chinese people and Japanese people look similar, but a Japanese couple will prefer a Japanese donor over a Chinese donor. So the cultural background is important [...]. I think for Asian people,

it's kind of natural. They want that their offspring is close to their ancestor, where they're coming from. I think it's pretty common understanding for Asian people.

Margaret shifts between discussing cultural background and similar phenotype. Her comments imply that a desire for "closeness" to ancestry may very well mean a desire for similar appearance. But ancestry and "culture" may also indicate more than simply phenotypic matching. Margaret's comments reflect the ways in which human eggs take on racialised reproductive meanings, where a donor's "cultural background" stands in for people who "look similar", and seeking "shared ancestry" normalises the phenotypic preferences of ART clients. Such phenotypic preferences emerge as racialised properties that can be acquired to indicate shared ancestry. Egg donor programme coordinators such as Margaret continue to reinforce the perceived connections between genetics, ancestry and reproductive tissues in the context of egg donation.

4.2 Race and notions of purity

Such efforts to manufacture "closeness" in families often overlap with notions of purity. Because commercial egg donation is prohibited in Japan, infertile couples often travel abroad in search of donor eggs. Sam Yamada, a Japanese national, came to the United States in the early 2000s to start an egg donor agency focused on Asian egg donation, viewing such medical tourism as a primary market. He told me that clients frequently sought donors who were "100 percent" Japanese or Chinese. Like Jacquelyn's clients, similar phenotype did not suffice for his clients. As Sam explained, blood type carries a great deal of significance in Japan, where schoolchildren begin learning about blood group inheritance as early as age six. He attributed intended parents' interest in donors' blood type to their desire to maintain secrecy or delay disclosure about egg donation to their children. Here, the process of creating the single-race family is embedded in substance, as "closeness" becomes inscribed in blood and prospective parents seek a racially "pure" Japanese donor. For these Japanese clients, racial/ethnic identities overlap with attachments to particular notions of blood and racial purity.[5] Attach-

5 See Robertson 2012 for a discussion of cultural meanings attached to blood in Japan. See also Kahn 2000 on how religious identity and notions of purity may parallel Japanese notions of identity, blood and racial purity.

ments to notions of purity serve not only to perpetuate biological notions of race, but also to reinforce the discomfort with mixture. Mixture and purity exist in tension with one another; purity is "not a simple matter; it exist[s] in a precarious relationship with mixture" (Wade 2017, 28). The tensions between mixture and purity become particularly salient in the context of egg donation, where the prospect of maintaining illusions of racial purity determines the market value of commodified eggs.

While Margaret, too, acknowledged that her clients may look for donors of specific racial/ethnic backgrounds, notions of similarity come to the fore in the process of helping them select gametes:

> Couples are also looking for similar physical features with themselves. Not all couples are planning to disclose to their future children that they are from an egg donor. I'm pretty sure there are some couples that probably would keep this a secret. So some people look for blood tests, similar blood type, similar physical features. So the children are more similar to themselves.

But while searches for donors with "similar physical features" or blood type may not always explicitly refer to race, they often imply a desire for specific racial qualities in a donor. They conflate culture, genetics and race in the racialisation of gametes, in the service of reinforcing the assumed cultural norm of the single-race family.

4.3 Race and market pressures

Whether they result from demand for explicit racial matches, for blood type matches or for similar phenotype, market pressures dictate how agencies recruit donors. Margaret explained that Chinese clients had increased in recent years and that demand for Chinese donors had as well. But as "full" Chinese donors are scarce, Margaret acknowledged that some clients are willing to compromise: "They do accept Korean and Japanese donors, but they can be equally difficult to find. And for Chinese to accept a Filipino [donor] might be even more difficult, because there is a significant difference in physical character." Margaret's comments reflect broader practices of creating agency-specific standards of racial categorisation and identification. In this case, agencies make up their own rules for how Asian (or Chinese or Filipino) is categorised, taking for granted the existence of essential differences in physical character between different racial/ethnic groups, despite the fact that race has no biological or essentialised foundation.[6]

Recipients, however, do not always share such categorisations, and they sometimes question the fixed categories that agencies present. One member of an online forum for infertile couples and individuals wrote of her struggles seeking an egg donor who matched her racial background and blood type. She explained how difficult it was to find a donor as a "100% Chinese" woman; as she searched egg donor databases, she eventually came to realise that she bears a strong physical resemblance to many Filipino donors. While she acknowledged that she is now strongly considering Filipino donors, she also admitted an internal conflict between the desire to maintain ancestral "purity" and the wish to start a family without delay. The contrast between Margaret's comments and the poster's dilemma over what kind of donor to choose illustrates the complexity of egg donor selection. Matchers' practices of categorising gametes through racialising processes may serve to reinforce biological, essentialised notions of race. Matchers operate based on what they believe patients desire; in this way, their role is similar to that of a gatekeeper who controls access to information. However, matchers' ideas about how recipients value race in gamete selection can misalign with what patients actually want. Given that much of matchers' work of recruiting, sorting, categorising and recommending certain kinds of donors to prospective parents occurs behind the scenes, matchers' decisions still determine the worth of eggs; they may also result in a failure to serve recipients.

The forum member's comments reveal that the experience of egg donation can force prospective parents to confront some of their implicit beliefs, challenging their prior assumptions about a desire for "closeness" and "similarity". Recipients find themselves working out their racial assumptions as they go along, sometimes questioning the importance of similarity in their family-making plans. As one forum member pointed out, there is great diversity within China and throughout the Asian diaspora; thus, it would not

6 Such practices may also be connected to class-related concerns among Asian ethnic groups; the Philippine national economy is much smaller than that of China or Japan, and beliefs about the relationship between class, income and health may influence decisions around egg donation. However, Filipinos in the United States have the second-highest median income among the United States Asian population (Pew Research Center 2017), which should caution us not to make overly simplistic conclusions regarding race and class among Asians pursuing egg donation.

be surprising to encounter a Filipina who resembles a Chinese woman. For many recipients, attention to phenotype (i.e. "closeness" or "similarity") is an articulation of race, which becomes embedded in the market-driven selection of donors. As recipients consider their options for gametes, race configures in specific, though not necessarily consistent, ways.

The online poster's search for a donor who looked like her was, according to one doctor in Hawai'i, typical of recipients of mixed Asian backgrounds. Blood and genes matter little: "People look for 'like–like' [phenotype] when they can," as another doctor explained. Seeking a donor of a specified racial mix does not always "work", he claimed, because "in Hawai'i, we often don't know what that [mix] really is. A lot of people don't really know exactly what they are and there is no objective genetic marker to say what this means. Here, it's about a picture, in terms of what's acceptable by society or by their families." Again, phenotypic similarity emerges as a primary concern; as Charis Thompson (2009) found in her work on skin tone and the visibility of race on reproductive bodies, a donor's visible, bodily features become a site for the racialisation of eggs to occur. In the context of Hawai'i, the most ethnically diverse United States state, where nearly one in four residents identifies as mixed-race, doctors and donor recipients seem to accept that race does not embed in genes or blood. Hawai'ian prospective parents will even seek donors of a different background than their own in order to create a particular kind of "mixed-race" child, reflecting positive associations in Hawai'i with *hapa* identity, which refers to a person who is considered half-Asian and half-white. In any case, as doctors and matchers explained, recipients scrutinise donor profiles for certain visible traits, with the promise of inheritable phenotypic and skin colour characteristics, among other features.

The doctor's statement that "here, it's about a picture" is significant on two levels. First, the picture signifies the visible clues that recipients and coordinators consider when looking for a match. Second, the picture references the importance of "closeness", of "like–like" outcomes of a single-race family. Scrutinising donor photos is similar to how actors might scrutinise assumptions about where likeness originates. Yet in an industry in which donor selection is market-driven, phenotype becomes an indication of race, something to evaluate and select when considering egg donors.

These findings indicate the diverse ways in which the commodification of eggs is entangled with race. Prospective parents' motivations for selecting a gamete donor and the ideas about race that accompany them are wide-ranging, reflecting both the commodification of biological race and the normalisation of racially blended families. However, the close entanglement of eggs with race highlights how commodification processes render eggs as objects to be purchased, exchanged and owned, which through the diverse practices of racialisation described here become isolated as commodified objects, or forms of property to be acquired in the formation of families. As I discuss in the following section, this process has significant implications for how race itself becomes construed as a biological object.

5. Re-biologising race

Donor coordinators, psychologists and medical doctors expressed diverse stances on the heritability of race and other traits. While many acknowledged the importance of racial marketing in egg donation, they also understood that traits such as musical talent and Scholastic Assessment Test (SAT) scores are not, scientifically speaking, heritable qualities (Martin 2014b). Several doctors I spoke with were sensitive to the contradictions inherent in the marketing of race in gamete donation. Many providers are aware that the eggs they sell do not carry inherent racial qualities; these providers instead focus on offering their clients a gene pool that has strong chances of passing on particular racialised characteristics.

For instance, Dr Carla de León, a reproductive endocrinologist in Honolulu, said she focuses on donors' "face armature" and its similarity to the recipients', rather than race, to determine which donors would make "good matches". Yet facial structure reflects racialised phenotypes. Thus, race remains central to "good matches". Dr de León acknowledged that she sells gametes: "You have to be able to sell a commodity. It *has* to be sellable." Although she puts "facial armature" above racial identity, she acknowledged that her clinic attaches increased value to eggs from certain racialised bodies (e.g. "full" Asian, "100 percent Japanese") in the market in gametes.

Other doctors I spoke with aimed to convince people of the unpredictability of reproduction, and so persuade them that seeking donors of particular ethnic backgrounds might not be necessary. Dr Andrea Cohen, an infertility specialist who worked with Jacquelyn at HCR, often encountered patients who searched for egg providers of specific racial backgrounds. She sought to broaden their considerations of other factors, such as health status or responsiveness to drug protocol, which affected pregnancy success rates:

> Race is definitely a priority. I have a patient who is 100 percent Japanese. She wants as close to 100 percent Japanese as possible. So she found somebody who is not 100 percent Japanese but she really looks very Japanese and she's nearly 100 percent Japanese and she really wanted this particular girl. And I reviewed her records and I thought that they were troubling in the sense that she cycled previously and it didn't go that well and I thought that she wasn't an ideal donor. So I said, "I reviewed the records of this donor, there are definitely some red flags, maybe you should look into somebody else before you go ahead with this donor." But she said, "There's nobody else, so we're going to proceed with that donor," even though she understands that it's not ideal. So I think that [patients are] willing to compromise in other areas maybe, but in ethnicity less so. Like I think that if it were me, I'd rather just pick someone else. But there's just not that many [Japanese donors], so she's willing to proceed with that donor.

Dr Cohen did not explicitly deny the heritability of race, but instead chose to emphasise the importance of clinical factors that correlate with pregnancy outcomes and "just picking someone else" in order to maximise the probability of a successful pregnancy. In this case, her efforts to encourage her patient to consider the clinical variables for success failed to convince the patient to change her mind. Dr Cohen emphasised the possibility of disappointing the patients' hopes, but she also had a financial stake in raising the chances of pregnancy. ART clinics publish their success rates, and a failed cycle would lower the marketability of Dr Cohen's services. Yet, although doctors might deemphasise the importance of, or relationship between, genetics and race, Dr Cohen's quote sheds light on the entanglement of race and commodification; clinics and medical providers still aim to attract consumers in order to sell a desired commodity. Put another way: good clinical care might also be considered "good business" in the context of assisted reproduction.

Several doctors I spoke with sought to challenge prevailing popular ideas regarding genetics and racial inheritance, preferring to emphasise broader notions of genetics that go beyond individual donor characteristics and focus on broader gene pools. For example, Dr Joan Wolff, a clinical psychologist at a prominent fertility clinic in New York, sought to combat certain myths among her patients. She referenced the emotional pain of recipients who might prefer to reproduce with their own eggs and pointed out that the DNA in the sperm and eggs that are needed to build a baby comes not from the individuals who provide them, but from their respective gene pools. When meeting recipients, she explains that genetic possibilities are like a lottery: "Think of a lottery ticket. How many numbers are on a lottery ticket? In New York State there are 59 numbers with ten panels. Think of all the combinations! Yet week after week no one wins. It's about the gene pool." She clarified that she tells clients, "Your egg is a cup dipped into three trillion possible DNA combinations. People then start to look at eggs and sperm a little differently."

A pamphlet by the company Freedom Fertility Pharmacy, entitled "Oocyte Donation", put it similarly: "Consider the donor's gene pool, not her genes" (Birrittieri et al. n.d.). It noted that many recipients believe that a donor with certain characteristics and achievements (e.g. high SAT scores, advanced degrees) will increase their child's chances to attend Harvard, but "even if a donor is a fabulous dancer, a terrific tennis player or loves horseback riding, that doesn't mean she would pass on those attributes to your child; she may in fact pass on her grandfather's talent for math puzzles instead" (ibid.). This pamphlet ultimately reinforces genetic heritability, although it warns recipients that they cannot predict which traits donors will pass on, and that these traits may include ones the donors themselves do not possess.

Race emerges in the pamphlet in coded ways. Regarding "matching", it says:

> If the recipients come from fair-eyed gene pools, the donor should also. If the recipients come from very tall, thin gene pools, and want a tall, thin child, the donor should come from a tall, thin gene pool, too. That way, if genetics are passed on that were not expressed in the donor (and therefore not similar to the recipient either) the child will still look like "family." Think about whether the donor and members of her family might blend into a photo of your extended family.
>
> *ibid.*

A match in phenotype serves as code not only for a match in race, but also a match in family (Moll 2019). Jacquelyn of HCR put it similarly: "A lot of people have told me that they want the baby to fit into their family. So they don't want somebody to look at their family and think, 'Wow, that baby doesn't really look like them.' They really just want to fit into society and how people think. It's kind of what everybody wants." Even as agencies might avoid explicitly naming race, they reinforce the heritability of racially associated physical characteristics, such as eye colour, physical build and height, and the importance of single-race families. Racial constructs continue to play a central role in the choices offered in egg donation.

This promise of choice leads couples to egg or sperm donation, as opposed to embryo donation, for example, in which prospective parents elect to "adopt" frozen embryos that were created with eggs and sperm from another couple. When I asked how often embryo donation occurs at HCR, Jacquelyn replied,

> Not that much. People don't really want to take the embryos because they want the options. Because people come in and they usually have an idea of what they want. They come in and they specifically want only this ethnicity or this educational background—those are the two most popular things that they ask for. And if you can't match that then it becomes even harder to find an embryo that matches, and it's going to take forever.

Consumer demand is of clear importance in the fertility industry; the ability to select particular characteristics through egg donation profoundly affects the market value and desirability of donor eggs (over donated embryos) for many recipients.

Jacquelyn described Hawai'i's unique demographic population as a selling point for her clinic:

> We have patients that come here specifically seeking certain ethnicities. Like we have people coming from the mainland looking for Asians or Hawai'ian egg donors. They just randomly call us and say, "I've been looking for this for a long time and I would think that Hawai'i has a lot of Asians," so that's why they're calling. And if they're coming here, our patients—recipients—are already those people who are looking for specific ethnicities.

As Jacquelyn noted, the egg donation market is not limited by geography, and consumer demand is not locally bound. Sociologists have shown how local and state-level factors—such as state insurance coverage, regulation and other "ecological factors"—influence the mobility of supply and demand in the egg donation market (Johnson 2017). Others have critically analysed the various factors that influence intended parents' decisions to travel abroad in order to access ARTs (Speier 2016; Inhorn 2015), as well as within the United States in order to bypass state-level restrictions or in search of eggs or sperm from donors of particular racial backgrounds (Martin 2014a). However, as Jacquelyn made clear, any analysis of the mobility of supply and demand in egg markets requires an explicit consideration of racialisation processes that occur in a context in which biocommodities are valued and exchanged.

6. Race as property

The diverse ways in which eggs reflect the broader workings of race in the United States offer insight into how eggs are used to facilitate connection through the practices described above. But while eggs assume unique value as biocommodities, they also come to be constructed as a form of racial property that can be acquired or lost. In the absence of robust federal measures to regulate egg donation, legal disputes illustrate how race becomes a form of property in assisted reproduction.

The case of Jennifer Cramblett is particularly instructive as it resonates with broader racial logics in the United States. In 2014, Cramblett, who is white, filed a "wrongful birth" and "breach of warranty" lawsuit before the Illinois District Court, alleging that the Midwest Sperm Bank erroneously used sperm from a Black rather than a white donor, leading Cramblett to suffer "personal injuries, medical expenses, pain, suffering, emotional distress, and other economic and non-economic losses, and will do so in the future" (*Cramblett v. Midwest Sperm Bank*, cited in Ehlers 2021, 515). The case highlights how the reproduction of certain kinds of people is valued while that of others is devalued. Formally speaking, policy and guidelines for ART practice are "colourblind". However, it is race—articulated via skin tone and other racialised characteristics—that makes visible any legal "mistakes" that occur. These cases are often publicised in a sensational manner in the media, emphasising the "unnaturalness" of the families that were created as a result of these mistakes and raising the spectre of the racially mismatched family. But these cases also highlight the broader workings of race in the United States, offering insight into how eggs and sperm are called on to facilitate connection, and in some cases, loss, "where loss denotes the fact or process of something being taken away or the deprivation of something of value" (Ehlers 2021, 515). *Cramblett* illustrates how notions of value, because they differentiate unequally along racial lines, reinforce race-based hierarchies and the privileging of whiteness, which ultimately reinforces the inequities of racial capitalism.

As Nadine Ehlers shows, this case offers insight into how loss is related to property (as a material or immaterial possession or attribute) within a broader system of racial capitalism. While a parallel, race-based tiered market does not exist to the same degree in sperm donation as it does in egg donation, *Cramblett* illustrates how racial norms become self-evident through legal cases, which hold significant implications for how race attains meaning and value in egg donation. In other words, Ehlers asks how

> race, value, and property [inter-articulate] in *Cramblett* through notions of biogenetic relations and familial whiteness; [...] how do these ideas travel through to *investments in life*—and its continuation—*as a form of racial property* (for some); and what can this tell us about broader workings of structural racism and the role of biomedicine (and law) within these operations?
>
> *ibid., 515*

The *Cramblett* case holds critical implications for understandings of race in the context of Asian American egg donation. As Ehlers argues, race stands in for affinity in assisted reproduction, where genetic inheritability is intimately associated with racial identity. The idea of substantiating affinity ties via race emerges clearly through what scholars have called "resemblance talk" (Becker et al. 2005). Cramblett, for example, stated that she intentionally chose a "blond-haired, blue-eyed" sperm donor who would closely resemble her partner. Clearly, assisted reproduction works to buttress ontologies of kinship and inheritance that reinforce race as an inheritable genetic property. Achieving the "white genetic tie is an extremely valuable attribute entitling [...] a privileged status" (Roberts 1997, 269).

Here, Ehlers's notion of property encompasses multiple meanings. On the one hand, race itself is viewed as property, in the sense that "whiteness" itself can be a "treasured property" (Harris 1993, 1713) that can be used to maintain control or privilege. But in the context of assisted reproduction, the ART industry clearly constructs race as a genetic resource, something that can be inherited and affords biogenetic affinity, in the sense that "kinship has a colour" (Lenhardt 2017, 2075). This also taps into longstanding ideas of kinship that assume monoracial family formation (Rich 2020). While Ehlers examines these concepts in the context of sperm donation, I extend Ehlers's analysis to egg donation, as racial identity is embedded in the egg that can be purchased and possessed as property—marking the egg cell itself as a "propertised" biomaterial. These multiple meanings of property reveal the ever-shifting ways in which race, identity and genetics overlap.

Cramblett shows the stakes associated with and the visibility of racial reproduction—as well as what happens "when white reproduction fails" (Fielder 2020, 14). While others have argued that gamete donation reinforces the "negative relation of blackness", wherein IVF mix-ups such as Cramblett's highlight the "costs of blackness" (Ehlers 2021, 520–521), what do these legal mix-ups mean for understandings of race beyond a black/white binary? In other words, what do current practices of egg donation reveal about Asian racialisation? While whiteness has historically been constructed as property (Harris 1993), Asian egg donation, too, serves to structure and limit kinship. Eggs racialised as Asian become especially valued for their perceived capacity to pass on particular racial identities, marking Asian racial identities as a unique commodity—or a form of property. Ultimately, even when white reproduction is not centred, the concept of biogenetic affinity is strengthened all the same, leading to further stratification along racial lines. Reproduction, here, is always already intimately tied to the reproduction of relations of capital accumulation. As Ehlers writes, "Race, property, and value are inextricably linked in the overarching operations of racial capitalism" (2021, 525). This case, in a brutal twist on stratified reproduction, highlights how it is not the sperm donor or other parent who is deemed unfit, but the child who is viewed as the cause of "personal injury [...] economic and non-economic losses". Here, what is clear are the ways in which the broader workings of structural racism and racial capitalism bleed into notions of "appropriate" families. Cramblett's case illustrates all too well how the pursuit of racialised eggs in the ART market reinforces the notion that race is an object that can be paid for, acquired and used as a marker of prestige and identity.

7. The promise of race?

As I have argued, human eggs are racialised in various ways in order to convert them into key commodities of the fertility industry. Perhaps one of the biggest dangers that the racialisation of gametes in the ART market poses to racial equality is that providers offer the promise of race as genetically inheritable, in both explicit and implicit ways. As I have shown, egg donor programmes and fertility clinics make discretionary decisions regarding how to define and categorise race. Yet this process of racialisation has consequences: it "makes" race real in a concrete way, applying racial labels to egg tissues and donors, despite the fact that geneticists agree that race has no biological basis. While some ART consumers may have never been persuaded that race is not biological, the persistence of the logic of blood and racial purity nonetheless has pernicious effects. These actions have important systemic, structural and political implications beyond the realm of individual choice. The desire for a "pure" Japanese egg donor, for instance, may reflect and reinforce dangerous beliefs about Japanese identity and nationalism based in blood (Robertson 2012). It also reveals how Harris's concept of "whiteness as property" has ramifications for thinking about how value attaches to "Asian" eggs—not just whiteness. Notions of purity and racial identity become commodified forms of property—a dangerous precedent, as notions of blood and purity have long been central to xenophobia and racial discrimination against minority groups in the United States.

Race is re-instantiated as a biogenetic category in various ways, and the intertwined medical and commercial practices of egg procurement described above effectively convert racialised eggs into commodities, or forms of property that can be purchased. However, as I have shown, these practices rely on processes of racialisation that often appear and disappear from view. Even when race seems absent, it remains as a commodified presence. Egg donation, as others have argued, represents a kind of neo-eugenics (Daniels and Heidt-Forsythe 2012), but here I call attention to the links between neo-eugenic practices and capitalist motivations. Marketing and matching practices in egg donation perpetuate stratified norms of race and class, creating hierarchies of value based on notions of purity and market demand. The data described in this chapter reveal the ways in which racialised human traits are believed to be transmitted genetically through human eggs; such beliefs, I contend, are a historical characteristic of the eugenics movement and buttressed by consumer-driven demand and fertility industry practices. As the very substance through which racial inheritance is imagined, racialised eggs are at the centre of this neo-eugenics.

Analysis of the intersection of race, property and capitalism provides a more nuanced discussion that helps us understand how ARTs are employed in what anthropologist Duana Fullwiley (2014) called the "contemporary synthesis", which mixes old concepts such as that of "pure human 'types'" with new approaches aimed at democratic inclusion, multicultural diversity and anti-racism. This new synthesis, Fullwiley argued, merges ideas about human biological difference that are both race- and population-based, yet conflated. In doing so, it simultaneously reinvigorates old ideas of racial types *and* possesses the potential to normalise multiracial families. This synthesis, I would add, must be considered within a framework of late capitalism, in which race is mobilised in diverse and contradictory ways to give eggs racialised meaning and capital value.

In addition to the ethical implications of the use of race and racial classification in assisted reproduction, we are left to consider what these examples mean for racial and reproductive justice. On the one hand, increasing attention to the demand for better options for "under-represented ethnicities" in gamete donation reflect calls for increased equity and representation in healthcare. Yet such calls seem to overlap with—and, indeed, rely on—the acceptance of race as biological, as it is configured through phenotype, appearance, blood, gene pools and individual genetics. As I have illustrated, the marketplace values attached to human eggs reflect particular racialised fantasies and kinship preferences. The ways in which race lives on in these vital substances reproduce old ideas of race *and* hold important implications for notions of justice, inheritance and identity.

Works Cited

Almeling, Rene (2011). *Sex Cells: The Medical Market for Eggs and Sperm*. Berkeley: University of California Press.

Becker, Gay, Anneliese Butler and Robert D. Nachtigall (2005). Resemblance Talk: A Challenge for Parents Whose Children Were Conceived with Donor Gametes in the US. *Social Science & Medicine*, 61(6), 1300–1309.

Bell, Ann V. (2014). *Misconception: Social Class and Infertility in America*. New Brunswick: Rutgers University Press.

Birrittieri, Cara, Mary M. Fusillo and Georgia Witkin (n.d.). Oocyte Donation. Freedom Fertility Pharmacy.

Bodenner, Chris (2017). Debating the Ethics of Egg Donation. *The Atlantic,* 26 January. https://www.theatlantic.com/health/archive/2017/01/egg-donation/622581/.

Boellstorff, Tom, Bonnie Nardi, Celia Pearce and T. L. Taylor (2012). *Ethnography and Virtual Worlds: A Handbook of Method*. Princeton: Princeton University Press.

Centers for Disease Control and Prevention (2022). 2020 Assisted Reproductive Technology Fertility Clinic and National Summary Report. US Dept of Health and Human Services.

Chin, Elizabeth (2001). *Purchasing Power: Black Kids and American Consumer Culture*. Minneapolis: University of Minnesota Press.

Cooper, Melinda, and Catherine Waldby (2014). *Clinical Labor: Tissue Donors and Research Subjects in the Global Bioeconomy*. Durham, NC: Duke University Press.

Culley, Lorraine, Nicky Hudson and Frances Rapport (2013). Assisted Conception and South Asian Communities in the UK: Public Perceptions of the Use of Donor Gametes in Infertility Treatment. *Human Fertility*, 16(1), 48–53.

Daniels, Cynthia R., and Erin Heidt-Forsythe (2012). Gendered Eugenics and the Problematic of Free Market Reproductive Technologies: Sperm and Egg Donation in the United States. *Signs*, 37(3), 719–747.

Deomampo, Daisy (2016a). Race, Nation, and the Production of Intimacy: Transnational Ova Donation in India. *positions: asia critique*, 24(1), 303–332.

Deomampo, Daisy (2016b). *Transnational Reproduction: Race, Kinship, and Commercial Surrogacy in India*. New York: New York University Press.

Deomampo, Daisy (2019). Racialized Commodities: Race and Value in Human Egg Donation. *Medical Anthropology*, 38(7), 620–633.

Dickenson, Donna (1997). *Property, Women and Politics: Subjects or Objects?* New Brunswick: Rutgers University Press.

Dickenson, Donna (2001). Property and Women's Alienation from Their Own Reproductive Labor. *Bioethics*, 15(3), 205–217.

Dieke, Ada C., Yujia Zhang, Dmitry M. Kissin, Wanda D. Barfield and Sheree L. Boulet (2017). Disparities in Assisted Reproductive Technology Utilization by Race and Ethnicity, United States, 2014: A Commentary. *Journal of Women's Health*, 26(6), 605–608.

Ehlers, Nadine (2021). Life's Continuation: Repro-Tech, Biogenetic Affinity, and Racial Capitalism. *BioSocieties*, 16, 514–529.

Fenton, Steve (1999). *Ethnicity: Racism, Class and Culture*. Lanham, MD: Rowman & Littlefield.

Fielder, Brigitte (2020). *Relative Races: Genealogies of Interracial Kinship in Nineteenth-Century America*. Durham, NC: Duke University Press.

Fullwiley, Duana (2014). The "Contemporary Synthesis": When Politically Inclusive Genomic Science Relies on Biological Notions of Race. *Isis*, 105(4), 803–814.

Grubb, Andrew (1998). "I, Me, Mine": Bodies, Parts and Property. *Medical Law International*, 3(4), 299–317.

Harris, Cheryl I. (1993). Whiteness as Property. *Harvard Law Review*, 106(8), 1707–1791.

Harrison, Laura (2016). *Brown Bodies, White Babies: The Politics of Cross-Racial Surrogacy*. New York: New York University Press.

Hernandez-Lopez, Ernesto (2008). Global Migrations and Imagined Citizenship: Examples from Slavery, Chinese Exclusion, and When Questioning Birthright Citizenship. *Texas Wesleyan Law Review*, 14, 255–288.

Hoeffel, Elizabeth M., Sonya Rastogi, Myoung Ouk Kim, and Hasan Shahid (2012). The Asian Population: 2010. United States Census Bureau.

Hudson, Nicky (2015). Gamete Donation and "Race". In *eLS*, 1–5. Chichester: John Wiley & Sons.

Hudson, Nicky, and Lorraine Culley (2014). Infertility, Gamete Donation and Relatedness in British South Asian Communities. In Tabitha Freeman, Susanna Graham, Fatemeh Ebtehaj and, Martin Richards (eds.). *Relatedness in Assisted Reproduction: Families, Origins and Identities*, 232–250. Cambridge: Cambridge University Press.

Ikemoto, Lisa C. (2009). Eggs as Capital: Human Egg Procurement in the Fertility Industry and the Stem Cell Research Enterprise. *Signs*, 34(4), 763–781.

Inhorn, Marcia C. (2015). *Cosmopolitan Conceptions: IVF Sojourns in Global Dubai*. Durham, NC: Duke University Press.

Inhorn, Marcia C., Rosario Ceballo, and Robert Nachtigall (2009). Marginalized, Invisible, and Unwanted: American Minority Struggles with Infertility and Assisted Conception. In Lorraine Culley, Nicky Hudson and Floor van Rooij (eds.). *Marginalized Reproduction: Ethnicity, Infertility and Reproductive Technologies*, 181–197. London: Earthscan.

Inhorn, Marcia C., Ruoxi Yu, and Pasquale Patrizio (2021). Upholding Success: Asian Americans, Egg Freezing, and the Fertility Paradox. *Medical Anthropology*, 40(1), 3–19.

Johnson, Katherine M. (2017). The Price of an Egg: Oocyte Donor Compensation in the US Fertility Industry. *New Genetics and Society*, 36(4), 354–374.

Kahn, Susan (2000). *Reproducing Jews: A Cultural Account of Assisted Conception in Israel.* Durham, NC: Duke University Press.

Lenhardt, R. A. (2017). The Color of Kinship. *Iowa Law Review*, 102(5), 2071–2107.

Lewin, Tamar (2015). Egg Donors Challenge Pay Rates, Saying They Shortchange Women. *New York Times*, 16 October. https://www.nytimes.com/2015/10/17/us/egg-donors-challenge-pay-rates-saying-they-shortchange-women.html.

Li, Shan (2012). Asian Women Command Premium Prices for Egg Donation in U.S. *Los Angeles Times*, 4 May. https://www.latimes.com/health/la-xpm-2012-may-04-la-fi-egg-donation-20120504-story.html.

Marre, Diana, Beatriz San Román, and Diana Guerra (2017). On Reproductive Work in Spain: Transnational Adoption, Egg Donation, Surrogacy. *Medical Anthropology*, 37(2), 158–173.

Martin, Lauren Jade (2014a). *Reproductive Tourism in the United States: Creating Family in the Mother Country*. New York: Routledge.

Martin, Lauren Jade (2014b). The World's Not Ready for This: Globalizing Selective Technologies. *Science, Technology & Human Values*, 39(3), 432–455.

Martin, Lauren Jade (2017). "They Don't Just Take a Random Egg": Egg Selection in the United States. In Ayo Wahlberg and Tine Gammeltoft (eds.). *Selective Reproduction in the 21st Century*, 151–170. Cham: Palgrave Macmillan.

Moll, Tessa (2019). Making a Match: Curating Race in South African Gamete Donation. *Medical Anthropology*, 38(7), 588–602.

Nordqvist, Petra (2012). "I Don't Want Us to Stand Out More than We Already Do": Lesbian Couples Negotiating Family Connections in Donor Conception. *Sexualities*, 15(5–6), 644–661.

Pande, Amrita (2014). *Wombs in Labor: Transnational Commercial Surrogacy in India*. New York: Columbia University Press.

Pew Research Center (2017). Key Facts about Asian Americans, a Diverse and Growing Population. https://www.pewresearch.org/short-reads/2021/04/29/key-facts-about-asian-americans/.

Quiroga, Seline Szkupinski (2007). Blood Is Thicker than Water: Policing Donor Insemination and the Reproduction of Whiteness. *Hypatia*, 22(2), 141–160.

Rich, Camille Gear (2020). Contracting Our Way to Inequality: Race, Reproductive Freedom and the Quest for the Perfect Child. *Minnesota Law Review*, 104(5), 2375–2469.

Roberts, Dorothy (1997). *Killing the Black Body: Race, Reproduction and the Meaning of Liberty*. New York: Pantheon Books.

Roberts, Dorothy (2011). *Fatal Invention: How Science, Politics, and Big Business Re-Create Race in the Twenty-First Century*. New York: New Press.

Roberts, Elizabeth F. S. (2016). Resources and Race: Assisted Reproduction in Ecuador. *Reproductive BioMedicine & Society Online*, 2, 47–53.

Robertson, Jennifer (2012). Hemato-Nationalism: The Past, Present, and Future of "Japanese Blood". *Medical Anthropology*, 31(2), 93–112.

Rudrappa, Sharmila (2014). Mother India: Outsourcing Labor to Indian Surrogates. In Sayantani DasGupta and Shamita Das DasGupta (eds.). *Globalization and Transnational Surrogacy in India: Outsourcing Life*, 240–271. New York: Lexington Books.

Sanders, Bailey K. (2022). Setting the Price of Fertility: Egg Donor Compensation Following Famakahi v. American Society for Reproductive Medicine. *Houston Journal of Health Law & Policy*, 22.

Shapiro, A., D. H. Barad, S. Darmon, D. Albertini, N. Gleicher, and V. A. Kushnir (2016). Racial and Ethnic Disparities in the Use of Third-Party Art in the U.S. *Fertility and Sterility*, 106(3), e108–e109.

Smaje, Chris (2000). A Place for Race? Medical Sociology and the Critique of Racial Ideology. In Simon J. Williams, Jonathan Gabe, and Michael Calnan (eds.). *Health, Medicine and Society: Key Theories, Future Agendas*, 67–86. London: Routledge.

Speier, Amy (2016). *Fertility Holidays: IVF Tourism and the Reproduction of Whiteness*. New York: New York University Press.

Teman, Elly (2010). *Birthing a Mother: The Surrogate Body and the Pregnant Self*. Berkeley: University of California Press.

Thompson, Charis (2005). *Making Parents: The Ontological Choreography of Reproductive Technologies*. Cambridge: MIT Press.

Thompson, Charis (2009). Skin Tone and the Persistence of Biological Race in Egg Donation for Assisted Reproduction. In Evelyn Nakano Glenn (ed.). *Shades of Difference: Why Skin Color Matters*, 131–147. Stanford: Stanford University Press..

Wade, Peter (2017). *Degrees of Mixture, Degrees of Freedom: Genomics, Multiculturalism, and Race in Latin America*. Durham, NC: Duke University Press.

Who Owns What Remains in the Cryotanks? Turning Sperm, Eggs and Embryos into Reproductive Materials and Duties in the Spanish Context

Sara Lafuente-Funes

Previous studies on assisted reproduction have largely focused on investigating the experiences of reproductive patients and the motivations of donors[1], or on how to find broader frameworks in which to situate reproductive bioeconomies and their third-party arrangements[2] (e.g. Franklin 1997; Thompson 2005; Almeling 2011). They have looked at whether the transfers of reproductive materials took commercial form or could be understood in terms of donations or gift-giving, motivated by altruism, economic interests or both (e.g. Orobitg et al. 2013; Waldby 2019; Jociles Rubio 2020). Studies focusing on embryos as property have largely been prompted by conflicts of interest in particular cases where disagreements about the use of the embryos arose between their supposed "owners"; such cases are usually linked to divorce or the death of one or both of the previously intended parents (e.g. Dolgin 1996; Farnós Amorós 2007). However, some aspects of these processes remain unexplored. Looking at how regulations define who owns embryos and gametes, and who can decide what to do with them once they are in the laboratory or the cryobank, remains an important question for the social and political sciences. Spain is a particularly interesting case study, as it has a large market that has received less scholarly attention than those in the United States of America and the United Kingdom. In this chapter I will explore the regulations that govern what people can and cannot do with their reproductive material in Spain and how these regulations frame and construct this

---

1 This chapter presents findings from the research project *Suspended Life: Exploring Cryopreservation Practices in Contemporary Societies*, funded by the European Research Council (Grant Agreement number: 788196).

2 "Third party" as in reference to reproductive treatments using egg, sperm, embryos or gestation not from the woman or couple aiming to be parents, but rather form *third parties*. That is, in reference to what is commonly referred to as egg, sperm or embryo donations and surrogacy.

material, the people it comes from and the markets formed around it. I argue that they are moulded by heteronormative and gendered ideals of family-making rooted in moral (conservative) concerns that undermine women's reproductive autonomy, and that they extend logics of (scientific) productivity and capital accumulation. This has helped a market to develop around reproductive material in Spain. At the same time, it has created the problem of unused tissue accumulating, which professionals frequently identify as one of the major complications that the current regulations cause for the clinics.

1. Introductory considerations

1.1 The Spanish reproductive landscape

Spain has a very strong reproductive market. As well as being the European leader for egg donation treatments, it is also one of the main destinations for reproductive travel (Wyns et al. 2021) and use of assisted reproduction and third-party eggs among its population is substantially higher than in other parts of the world. The use of assisted reproductive technologies (ARTs) is linked to around 9.3 percent of all births in Spain (Seiz et al. 2023), and approximately four in ten babies born from in vitro fertilisation (IVF) come from third-party eggs, most of which are transferred from donors to recipients in the private sector. Spain has a very strong private sector that accounts for around 70 percent of all healthcare units dedicated to assisted reproduction, according to the most recent data registered by the Spanish National Commission on Assisted Human Reproduction. The country also has relatively broad public coverage compared with other countries in the region: the right to use ARTs[3] is recognised within the public sector for mixed-sex and same-sex couples and single people as long as they have a uterus to carry the embryo to term.[4] However, public-sector resources are limited, which makes it difficult for many to access these treatments unless they go private (Pérez Milán 2011). There is also an age limit of 40 in most cases (42 in some

3 Including several attempts at artificial insemination with or without a sperm donor, and IVF with or without a sperm donor. In certain cases, that involves PGD (with a medical diagnosis), cryopreservation of surplus embryos and cryopreservation of eggs for people with certain illnesses (such as cancer patients undergoing chemotherapy treatment).

4 Surrogacy is not allowed in Spain.

regions since 2022). Overall, Spain has more clinics and has carried out more assisted reproduction treatments in recent years than countries with larger populations such as Germany, France and Italy (Wyns et al. 2021). Looking at the Spanish reproductive market is of interest, because its market model is certainly putting pressure on others in the region (Danish Council of Ethics 2013) and because this industry is responsible for an increasing number of births in Europe, both inside and outside Spain.

For years, the main topic discussed in relation to Spain has been egg donation (e.g. Kroløkke 2014; Molas 2021; Perler 2022). Even though this is still a pressing topic and an interesting area to study, looking at the broader picture helps to better capture what has made it easier for a market around eggs to grow in this context, compared with other countries working under the same European Union directives. One key aspect is to understand the ways in which regulations present reproductive materials, their potential uses and what can legitimately be done with them and by whom, for example in relation to selling, donating or discarding these materials.

The development of technologies enabling eggs to be extracted from bodies and the confirmation, following the birth of Louise Brown in 1978, that fertilisation leading to successful pregnancies could take place in a laboratory setting introduced two new entities that needed to be routinely managed (and preserved) in clinics' laboratories: eggs and embryos. The expansion of assisted reproduction also saw a greater amount of sperm being stored in these laboratories. In conjunction with the increasing use of cryopreservation technologies for storing reproductive materials, this created a need to regulate and organise their management, storage and associated practices—and encouraged an image of these cells as "autonomous" (Lie 2012).

Another problem that has accompanied the boom in assisted reproduction and the markets formed around it has been the accumulation of embryos or, what in Spanish law is labelled as pre-embryos[5] (Laws 45/2003 and 14/2006; Reguera Cabezas and Cayón-de las Cuevas 2021). Since the introduction of vitrification (a fast-freezing technique with very good success rates) in the last decade, the extent of cryopreservation in Spanish reproductive clinics has grown immensely (Lafuente-Funes 2023), which has further exacerbated this problem. As of 31 December 2021, clinics in Spain had 371,626 oocytes and 777,679 embryos stored in their cryopreservation tanks.

5 The law defines the fertilised eggs as pre-embryos until day 14 after fertilisation (Law 14/2006, 5).

In this context, and since eggs and embryos can be extracted from bodies and moved to laboratories and storage facilities, the state's regulatory role is extending into new areas. Careful analysis is needed to understand how this is affecting reproductive justice and the expansion of reproductive markets. Looking at what may (and may not) be done with these cells by donors, patients or clinics is therefore of great importance. I am interested here in studying how particular demarcations—what is a gamete or how are embryos defined, when are they eligible for reproductive use or for research, when can they be discarded?—are settled by regulations determining who can decide all these things about the biological material once it is in the cryotanks. Over the course of this chapter, I will trace the history of the relevant Spanish regulations on ARTs—from the first one, adopted in 1988, to an important but short-lived 2003 regulation, to the current one from 2006.

1.2 Reproductive bio-objects and property relations

> "Things are not born as property, as critical studies of property have pointed out time and again, they are made property."
>
> *Braun, 2024*

In this section, I will analyse Spanish regulations with a particular focus on how they frame and construct gametes and embryos in culturally specific ways that, by reference to these cells' potential reproductive capacities and the duties that supposedly arise with them, set out the conditions in which they may be stored, transferred or discarded. Following Klaus Hoeyer's (2007) suggestion that we should take seriously the role of moral concerns in the construction of these types of bio-objects and the markets around them, I will show how moral (patriarchal) concerns are embedded in defining and stabilising these cells, particularly eggs and embryos, as objects that should have an end use—preferably reproductive—and that require a certain level of protection in law for their recipients and providers. I will also show how this makes it easier for these cells to enter circuits of market interchange that draw in and incorporate both moral and economic interests, and how this has eased the path for the cells to be commodified to some degree by market logics (which are interlinked with, and not opposed to, moral ones). These logics coexist with rhetorical denials or disavowals of those self-same logics, and alongside many other processes that make commodification possible under anti-commodification rules, such as the current European Union directives on tissue donation and Spanish regulations on ARTs.

Commodification looms large in current processes of making reproductive cells and materials matter within Spanish reproductive markets, both as something that is actually happening and as an image of the market that needs to be avoided.[6] Accordingly, we might understand commodification as "transformation of body parts into objects that can be exchanged and capitalized" (Hauskeller and Beltrame 2015). However, and following Hoeyer's review of the literature on commodification, I wish to avoid subsuming my argument into the "commodification hypothesis" (Hoeyer 2007): I take commodification not to be the end but rather the starting point of analysis, or as *a sign showing that analysis is needed*.[7] I recognise the intense efforts institutions make to keep reproductive cells "un-commodified" and on the side of *gifts*, but I also find that commodification does take place in the context analysed here in part precisely *in virtue of* those efforts. I contend that much of what happens around assisted reproduction in Spain involves processes of commodification (through active denials of it), even if this is not the whole story. Rather, it is the tip of a much larger iceberg made up of forms of capitalisation that are not easily understood in terms of commodification vs decommodification (Hoeyer 2007; Hauskeller and Beltrame 2015). Feminist studies on ARTs (e.g. Thompson 2005; Franklin 2013; Almeling 2011) have shown that the ways that commodities, subjects and markets are constructed have much to do with moral concerns and with the reproduction of social, cultural and gender norms.

Furthermore, I look at how Spanish law turns reproductive material into something that can be owned and treats it as a part of (partially new) property regimes that delineate its use. I do so in order "to appreciate what biotechnology and the socio-cultural significance of the body do to capitalism and its property structures" (Hoeyer 2007). Exploring the ways in which current (and past) regulations *make these cells into* something that can be owned may help to shed light on how these reproductive markets grow and are entangled in the reproduction of a particular social order.

6 By "an image of the market that needs to be dispelled", I am referring to the repeated instances in which regulations and institutional/corporate discourses engage in a narrative of altruism (see Lafuente-Funes 2017; Molas and Whittaker 2021).

7 As Nikolas Rose (2007) once said with reference to medicalisation.

Understanding reproductive cells as bio-objects helps me to "think-with" (Haraway 2016), as this concept "stresses the point that boundaries around 'the living' are not stable and that there is what we may call a potential openness in processes of bio-objectification and bio-identification through which such boundaries are drawn" (Holmberg et al. 2011, 742). Bio-objectification is defined by Holmberg et al. (ibid., 740) as a "process wherein life-forms or living entities are first made into objects, become possible, through scientific labor and its associated technologies", so that they can later be "attributed with specific identities". Regulations are also key tools in turning things into bio-objects in this context and in setting the boundaries of what they are (and are expected to be, to entail, etc.). I therefore look at the space that Spanish law demarcates for sperm, eggs and embryos as bio-objects—and hence as something separated from, independent of, the bodies and biographies in which they originated—and consider how they are understood as a somehow independent entity that can be *owned* but to which something is also *owed*, as will be shown below, particularly so in the case of women and *their* cells.

Oftentimes, ownership is thought of as a relation "between a person of agency and unlimited rights, on the one hand, and a passive object with no rights, on the other" (Hoeyer 2007, 334). But reality tends to be much more complex. As has frequently been argued (e.g. Siegrist 2007), property does not mean total power of disposal, but rather depends on a variety of social conditions. Thus, the relational aspect of property, along with a less stable definition of owner and owned, is key to thinking with ownership and property regimes. There are a number of studies reminding us of how common it used to be to understand property as coming with both freedoms and obligations, and of the extent to which this is still relevant today (Hoeyer 2007; Braun 2024). By looking at how these entities are described and, up to a certain point, "made property" (ibid.), we can learn much about the ways in which reproductive markets develop and what types of ideas or ideologies they reproduce. I understand property relations here as "historically and culturally specific forms of power" (Hoeyer 2007, 333) and ownership as loaded with ambiguities. It is through the lens of this ambiguity that I seek to understand current forms of owning and owing to sperm, eggs and embryos under Spanish assisted reproduction regulations.

2. Three laws regulating assisted reproduction in Spain: 1988, 2003, and 2006

Sociopolitical, religious and moral controversies,[8] along with potential lobbying from an ever-growing industry,[9] have shaped how embryos, eggs and sperm are defined in Spanish law and the things that may legitimately be done with them. All regulations on ARTs since the first one, adopted in 1988, have stated what pre-embryos are and how they differ from embryos-in-the-body (or those once gestation has begun). The regulations of 2003 and 2006 dealt with the problem of pre-embryo accumulation using two different and politically charged strategies. These regulations delimit the use, storage and exchange of gametes, establishing an asymmetry between sperm on the one side, and eggs and pre-embryos on the other.

2.1 Defining pre-embryos, setting the framework for assisted reproduction: the 1988 law

The first regulation on assisted reproduction was signed into law in 1988 by President Felipe González from the socialist party Partido Socialista Obrero Español (PSOE). This law understands life as starting at gestation—a demarcation that made assisted reproduction possible or at least easier in moral and sociopolitical terms within a mostly Catholic country. Embryological development is said to be "moving through uncertainty", as it is not until gestation has proven successful that "the biological reality that an embryo is" can be confirmed (Law 35/1988). Precisely because of this, the law uses the terms "pre-embryos" (*preembriones*) and "embryological materials" (*material embriológico*) and says that these things need to be regulated—but not as strictly as they would if they had already been implanted:

8 This did not take the form of open or public debates about assisted reproduction, as the issue has never been a topic of broad public debate, but rather tensions relating to other topics, such as access to abortion, the "right to life" posited in anti-choice discourse and struggles for sexual and reproductive rights more generally.

9 The main body that issues regulatory recommendations is the Spanish National Commission on Assisted Human Reproduction, which is made up of professionals, experts and political representatives. A significant proportion of its members also work in the reproductive industry, which may open up opportunities for lobbying.

> Taking into account that in vitro fertilisation and cryopreservation facilitate the availability of gametes and fertilised oocytes, and not only to perform the techniques of assisted reproduction for the persons who provide them or for others, but also for diverse manipulations of a diagnostic, therapeutic or industrial (pharmaceutical) nature, it is evident that the embryological materials cannot be used in a voluntary or uncontrolled manner, and that their availability, traffic,[10] uses and transport must be regulated and authorised.
>
> *ibid., 33374*

These provisions can be seen as a way of turning pre-embryos into "matters of concern" (Latour 2004): entities that need to be protected, but that can be used in ways that make space for assisted reproduction to take place and for an industry to develop. In this sense, it is important to note that a positive view of the technologies as "scientific advancement" prevails in the law. This view is mixed with a certain pride in Spain's biomedical industry, which had by then already helped around 2,000 babies to be born. This industry was regulated so that it could expand, while at the same time restrictions were put in place to control what happened with these new *in vitro* entities, the pre-embryos, which the law permitted to be kept frozen for a maximum of five years.

2.2 The early problem of accumulation and the conservative turn in ART regulation: the 2003 law

Even though the law of 1988 established a time cap of five years for the cryopreservation of pre-embryos, it did not "specify what should be the fate of cryopreserved pre-embryos that have not been transferred" (Law 45/2003, 41459). Discarding the embryos was not seen as an option here, due to the idea of protecting the cells and most probably also to culturally and religiously driven views that framed it as problematic to discard embryos. Thus, in 2003, when the conservative Partido Popular (PP) was in power, a new law was adopted that was intended to address the problem of embryo accumulation, but with a more restrictive and conservative agenda. This regulation starts on a similar note of enthusiasm regarding the role of ARTs, which it says have contributed to "solving in a far more efficient manner the infertility problems of many couples" (ibid.). Nonetheless, due

10 Spanish original word "tráfico", which mostly translates to "traffic", although in this context might mean both legal and illegal circulation, it remains not fully clear.

to what is seen as a *natural* asynchronism in scientific and regulatory developments, the change in the law is seen as necessary, as "the passage of time has revealed the existence of certain limitations in the regulation, which have given rise to situations of certain legal uncertainty and problems of considerable ethical and health-related significance". Ethical significance here is linked to an understanding of pre-embryos as particular entities in need of care and protection, which in turn is linked to a conservative view of conception that is common in the Partido Popular.[11] Among the problems this regulation aimed to solve, the most important was "the accumulation of a large number of surplus human pre-embryos, the fate of which has yet to be determined".

This new regulation, signed by Spain's then president, José María Aznar (PP), was meant to fill this legal void. That included imposing more restrictions on the use of technologies. The law offered two main solutions to the problems that it identified. The first solution was focused on finding a use for the embryos that had already been frozen, in which case reproduction was encouraged, although the option of donating embryos for research was also allowed. The second solution was directed at lowering the production of surplus embryos in subsequent treatments by limiting the number of eggs that could be extracted from each woman per cycle to three. On top of this limitation, the law established that if excess pre-embryos were created in exceptional cases, they could be cryopreserved for as long as the woman was considered to be in her fertile years so that these pre-embryos "can be transferred to her in later attempts". Patients were required to sign a "commitment of responsibility for their cryopreserved pre-embryos", in which they had to "give their consent so that, in the event that the cryopreserved pre-embryos are not transferred to them within the established period of time, they will be donated for reproductive purposes as the only alternative".

As can be seen, this law had a pro-natalist undertone that also enforced greater protection of pre-embryos. It stipulated that pre-embryos were to be used for reproductive projects, narrowing women's range of possible choices:

11 Ten years later, the PP tried to change the law on voluntary interruption of pregnancy based on the same idea of "protecting the life of the conceived", shifting the focus from gestation to conception, limiting regulators' capacity to distinguish between embryo and pre-embryo. This bill was not approved, and the minister who tried to push it forward had to resign, in part due to the vigorous opposition from the feminist movement on the streets, but possibly also due to less visible lobbying from the reproductive industry.

in cases where pre-embryos were created, women were supposed to either transfer them to their own bodies or donate them to others. The regulation understood pre-embryos as entities that should not only be "protected" but also used for reproduction, as is evident in the requirement to sign the above-mentioned "commitment of responsibility". Pre-embryos were apparently seen as occupying a position somewhere between a potential human life and reproductive capacity. I use the idea of capacity here as the "ability to perform, yield, or withstand" (Flexner 1993).[12] As long as these entities were seen as potential human lives, their "production" was to be controlled, and only allowed if their final use was regulated to ensure their reproductive capacity was indeed encouraged to develop, through the morally charged "commitment of responsibility" that patients were required to sign. This regulation focused less on what people are allowed to do with the cells and more on what people owe to the cells they have produced.

2.3 Replacing the short-lived 2003 regulation: the industry-friendly law of 2006

Less than three years after the restrictive regulation was passed, José Luis Rodríguez Zapatero (PSOE) signed the new and current law regulating ARTs' use in Spain. This is the law that has regulated the ART industry over the last 17 years and has made it possible for the industry to thrive. It was adopted in the mid-2000s, following years of much hype at international and national level about the possibilities linked to research on embryos, which explains the law's relative openness towards research, although in practice research on embryos has remained limited in Spain.

The 2006 regulation on assisted reproduction removed the limit of three eggs per treatment, presenting this limitation as contrary to women's reproductive autonomy (since it restricted the potential success of women undergoing those treatments). Even though the law presented itself as clearly different from the previous one in this respect, it did inherit certain other as-

12 I have here used the *Random House Dictionary* to introduce the concept of capacity, although I started using it in the context of reproduction in a previous piece entitled "Shall We Stop Talking about Egg Donation? Transference of Reproductive Capacity in the Spanish Bioeconomy" published in *BioSocieties* (Lafuente-Funes, 2020). I use the idea of reproductive capacity to point to the ability to (reproductively) perform, yield or withstand reproduction.

pects and sought to address some of the same concerns. In particular, it defended "the need to respond to the problem of the fate of excess pre-embryos" (Law 14/2006, 4). The five-year time cap was removed, but the regulation established a set of possible fates for sperm, ovarian tissue, oocytes and pre-embryos, as well as defining who can make decisions about them and until what point. It allows four options for all these categories of cells, although for oocytes and pre-embryos specific restrictions and particular routes apply, which make the first option the easiest and the last the most difficult to exercise:

1. Use by the woman herself[13] or her spouse
2. Donation for reproductive purposes
3. Donation for research purposes
4. Cessation of storage, without any other use

The regulation privileges using these cells for oneself, and makes it very difficult to have the storage of eggs and pre-embryos stopped (that can be done more easily for sperm and ovarian tissue). Having eggs and embryos stored and then used by the same woman who provided them or her spouse means that the cells are still understood as part of a particular reproductive biography—something that belongs to this person or couple. Once using the cells for one's own reproduction is off the table, the cells become something else—separated and somehow autonomous from the original person (a shift made possible by the combination of technologies used for extraction and maintenance and the surrounding regulatory framework). In this case, people can either donate to other couples/women for reproductive purposes or donate for research. Donating to other patients is only possible if the woman was younger than 35 at the time of ova extraction.[14]

13 When the law says "the woman herself", it is referring to the woman from whom the egg has been extracted, if that is the patient herself, or the woman who is the recipient of a donation. Egg donors donate their material, and from that moment on it is legally detached from them. Clinics act as "temporary owners" of the material until they transfer it to a patient. From the moment a patient receives a donation, the material is considered as much hers as if the eggs had come from her own ovaries. There is therefore no separate explanation of how she makes decisions about cells from her own ovaries or ones that came from a third party, as the procedure is the same in both cases.

14 This refers to the age of the woman from whom the eggs were extracted, whether that be the patient herself or a donor.

Deciding to donate these cells either for reproductive or research purposes implies recognising them as independent from the body and person they originally came from, as well as from the reproductive project they were thought to be part of, and identifying in them a—what I call their (re)productive capacity—that can be transferred (to other bodies, freezers, etc.). Discarding eggs or embryos is made quite difficult by this regulation. This is the case even though the regulation inherits from the last one the rationale of a need to find a solution to the problem of accumulation of excess pre-embryos. Discarding the cells is not presented as a choice, since "in the case of cryopreserved pre-embryos and oocytes, this last option will only be applicable once the maximum conservation period established in this law has expired without any of the options mentioned in the previous sections having been taken".

But what is the time limit for keeping pre-embryos and oocytes in the freezers? According to the law, it is "women's fertile years"—a concept that is in general difficult to grasp, but even more so in the context of using cryopreserved material. In order to solve this problem, the regulation established that women or couples who want to discard their embryos need to provide a "favourable verdict by independent specialists outside the corresponding centre to the effect that the recipient does not meet the clinical requirements for the use of the assisted reproduction technology".

This means that women or couples cannot choose for themselves to discard the eggs or pre-embryos stored under their names, as this is made into a medical decision. The continuity of these cells is not linked to the women's willingness to become pregnant. Rather, before they can terminate the cryopreservation of these cells, they have to present proof, from at least two independent doctors, that they do not meet the clinical requirements for a pregnancy. That is, the willingness or unwillingness of a woman to become pregnant is considered irrelevant. Of course, she will not be forced to have the embryos transferred into her body, but nor can she choose to thaw and discard pre-embryos and eggs. This forces her to either use them herself, keep on storing them (which tends to involve paying storage fees) or donate them to other women or couples, if they meet the requirements, or to research.

These reproductive cells (eggs or pre-embryos) are not conceived of here as part of a particular body or biography, but rather as independent entities with a role of their own. The law understands this role in terms of the cells' (re)productive capacity—and as imposing certain *duties* on their owners. These include a duty not to discard the cells, a duty to make use of their *capacities*, whether for reproductive or productive processes (pregnancies or research), and a duty to "not let [them] die" (Friedrich and Höhne 2014; see also Radin and Kowal 2017; Lemke 2023). These cells are no longer (or not only) seen as an extension of the woman's body or biography, and are conceived as needing to be protected by the state from the fate of being wasted or discarded.

The underlying logic is that if these women *can* use their material, they *should*, and that discarding the cells is the least desirable option—though it is unclear *for whom* it is undesirable, or why. It is in this sense that I think a certain pro-natalist ideology can be noted even in the current regulation, albeit in a softer form than in the law of 2003. This regulation has a patronising undertone that positions the law as needing to act as guardian of the cells rather than of the adults (protecting the "children" the cells could potentially develop into). Women are not fully allowed to decide what to do with cells that came from their bodies or were expected to be transferred to them (in the case of egg donation) and that need (willing) bodies in order to develop. They are seen as owners of the cells (whether because those cells came from their bodies or were donated to them) inasmuch as they need to make decisions about them and can use them to get pregnant. But they have no right to decide to stop having the cells stored, nor are they allowed to donate them to someone they know. I speak here of an anti-choice, pro-natalist ideology because women and couples are encouraged to use their cells or donate them to (anonymised) third parties and discouraged from discarding them, and because the cells are bound up with reproductive duties. This pro-natalist ideology is accompanied by an entrepreneurial, scientific and industry-friendly rationale that also facilitates research. Above all, what we witness is a regulation that does not recognise the right of women to make certain decisions about *their* reproductive cells; in that sense, the state locates itself and medical practitioners as guardians of the eggs and embryos, stationed above the women themselves.

Even though the law explicitly makes it possible to donate for research purposes and even though this is the preferred option of many of the women or couples that have stored embryos, a lack of resources and permits along with a shift in research agendas has meant that the number of actual projects working with embryos is less than the number of embryos stored "for research". On top of this, the far greater expansion of the Spanish fertility industry compared with that of the research sector has made these cells much more valued for their reproductive capacities than their research applications. Clinics are increasingly finding ways to discourage women from choosing to donate their eggs or embryos for research, such as making them pay the storage fees until a research project is found, which might take several years or not happen at all. The way in which donation for reproductive use is regulated in the law is also industry-friendly, as can be seen in the fact that more relational logics, such as allowing donation of the surplus cells to a friend or acquaintance, are not allowed, while industry-driven options like anonymous donations are facilitated. This makes the reproductive material available for clinics to develop treatments and therefore facilitates its commercialisation, even if indirectly.

Although the cap on egg extraction set by the 2003 law is described in the 2006 law as contrary to "reproductive autonomy",[15] there is no further discussion of this autonomy. In particular, there is no consideration of the possibility of discarding oocytes and pre-embryos, and this is never presented as a woman's choice. The same happens with the idea of sharing the surplus cells with a friend or acquaintance: it is not seen as part of the woman's reproductive autonomy but as something that needs to be forbidden by law. The cells are here understood as something that can be owned until a certain point, coming with freedoms (to use, to store, etc.) and obligations (to maintain, to decide on future use, etc.) but also several limitations in regard to what the person who initially intended to use the cells for reproduction can decide to do with them. The law also establishes a clear-cut distinction between sperm and eggs. Sperm's reproductive potential is recognised as something that can be owned or donated to others, but sperm can also be discarded. Eggs and pre-embryos can be *owned* (in the sense that they can be stored, used or donated anonymously) but come with obligations: ideally, they are there to be used, either for reproduction or for research, and the woman or couple cannot choose to stop having them conserved. Frozen eggs and pre-embryos not only become things that can be owned, but also things to which something is *owed*—an extension of (feminised) reproductive duties.

15 The cap limiting retrieval to only three eggs per cycle was taken out of the law, as it was seen as limiting the utility of assisted reproduction and diminishing women's chances of getting pregnant. It could therefore be said that the law protects reproductive autonomy, but only for women who want to reproduce.

3. A duty to (re)produce: clinics as custodians of sperm, eggs and embryos

The way the current regulation on assisted reproduction in Spain deals with the fact that eggs and embryos leave bodies is by understanding them as something that needs to be managed and that, until a certain point, can be *owned* and should be *used*—something that has to be safeguarded for the sake of its *owners* and their right to *use* it, or that can be transferred so that others can own and use it. That leaves a great deal of space for clinics to locate the cells here or there, exercising a sort of "custodial" role. The cells are, as explained above, made into property inasmuch as they are understood as possessing a certain reproductive capacity that brings with it certain duties. These duties are culturally tied to the idea of being able to reproduce and to the (conservative) duty imposed on women to do so (using either their own or other people's genetic material).

The relations that the law establishes by delineating what can be done with these cells and by whom can be understood, at least in part, as "manifestations of a power matrix granting some persons legitimate entitlements that others do not possess" (Hoeyer 2007, 334). On this anthropological understanding, property is not only seen as coming with both freedoms and obligations, but also as something that is further complicated in the case of body products by ethical and moral concerns. The laws on assisted reproduction presented above see gametes and embryos as coming with freedoms (to use, to store, to exchange) and obligations (to use, to keep, to not discard unless certain conditions are met). This makes sense as long as the cells are understood as isolated entities and no longer as part of someone's identity, biography or body. Looking at the freedoms and obligations that come with storing eggs and embryos gives us an insight into what this particular society is thinking, and reinforcing through the law, with regard to kinship, family-making and reproduction more broadly.[16]

The management of sperm occupies the least space in the regulation and seems to entail the fewest obligations—unless it is used in the creation of an embryo, in which case (unless it has been provided through a private, clini-

16 Even though the expression "intended parent" is not present in the law, the logic underlying it is that owning an embryo is linked to an intention to have it transferred at some point. This logic applies equally to embryos resulting from eggs that came from the patient and those resulting from donor eggs.

cally driven, anonymised donation) it would entail paternity, and all the duties that come with it, if a child is born as a result. But before any of this happens, sperm is seen as something that the person from whom it comes *owns*. This might be linked to the fact that sperm has always already left the body—and thus there is nothing that "new" to its existing outside the body, albeit now in laboratories and cryotanks and for longer periods. In this sense, the main "new" thing is the possibility of donating it, which is clearly delimited in the law through compulsory anonymity. In those cases, the embryos that come into existence using donor sperm will, in the case of a heterosexual couple, be equally understood as belonging to the man in the relationship, or to the female partner if a lesbian couple is recognised as undergoing the reproductive process together.[17] Therefore, men[18] not only have the right to discard their material if they no longer want to keep it or use it, but they also have a say on what to do with the embryos created with it (or with sperm donated to them).[19] Discarding sperm is uncontroversial, as it is understood as "just" a gamete: providers and recipients are allowed to use it, donate it or discard it. But sperm nonetheless marks the ownership of an embryo, just as an egg does.

Curiously, eggs are not seen by this regulation as "just" gametes in the same sense. They are directly, and without any particular controversy, explanation or discussion, equated with pre-embryos in the 2006 regulation. This introduces an imbalance in the way the regulation understands "male" and "female" gametes, which in turn leads to differences in the right to discard one versus the other. This is particularly problematic now, more than 15 years later, when the consolidation of fertility preservation treatments is linked to a growing accumulation of egg cells in cryobanks. This undermines women's capacity to freely choose their (non-)reproductive options in a similar way to men—an imbalance that has historically been linked to how bodies work

17 At times this is linked to them being married, at others it is delimited by their expressed intention to be part of the process from the beginning of treatment.

18 Even though trans women can also donate, freeze and do IVF with their sperm and trans men can donate or freeze their eggs, I use the more reductionist term "men" here, and will in the following use the language of male and female gametes. I do so because I believe that the different way that sperm and eggs are treated in the Spanish regulation is rooted in gender inequalities linked to sperm being most commonly (and symbolically) associated with cis men and eggs with cis women.

19 For instance, if a woman wants to discard the embryos because she does not want to become pregnant with them or to donate them, she would need her (current or ex) partner's signature to discard the embryos—even though they would need her body to develop.

but is now reinforced by the law which restricts the use of technology, thus extending the social mandate of motherhood by legal and technical means.

Eggs and pre-embryos are understood as entities that belong to or can be owned by the woman or couple from whom they were first retrieved or by others (either clinics or recipients), but whose use none of the owners are fully free to decide. Accordingly, understanding these cells as property in a classical sense, i.e. as something that comes with both freedoms and duties, has allowed me to recognise that the cells are made into specially protected bio-objects. While in Germany embryos are highly regulated according to the principle of protection, but have also been defined by Bettina Bock von Wülfingen (2012) as bio-objects inasmuch as they are "fruits of love", I contend that in the Spanish case eggs and embryos could be defined as bio-objects that are also seen as needing protection but involve highly gendered (re)productive properties and duties. The law views these cells as embodying reproductive capacities that come with certain duties as well as certain freedoms—the freedom to use them to try to become pregnant either now or at some later point, and the duty to keep them stored until a reproductive or research use has been found for them.

The egg or embryo invested with a (re)productive duty does not create as much concern in relation to maintaining genetic ties or lineages. On the contrary, the cells are there to be used, to fulfil a (re)productive purpose—no matter for *whom*, provided the anonymity requirement is met if they are donated.[20] First and foremost, the spirit of the 2006 regulation is linked to enhancing the use of these cells for *reproductive* purposes, but opening enough space for the cells to become *productive* by being used for research. To justify the scientific use of eggs and embryos, the law relies on the idea of them being pre-embryos (as explained by the first regulation of 1988) and thus not yet entirely embryos. This second option is not straightforward, since even if the cells are donated for research it is very difficult to actually secure permits for research projects on embryos, on top of the difficulties of finding funding for research in Spain, and so most cells donated for research end up in the freezers for very long or indefinite periods.

20 *Whose* reproductive purpose does matter in the sense that the way these markets are constructed tends to facilitate the reproduction of certain (whiter, wealthier) people rather than others, as studies around stratification of reproduction have long shown. The point I want to make here is that this pro-natalist undertone is not necessarily linked to genetic reproduction, but to reproduction as such.

While we can find pro-natalist and anti-choice undertones in the three laws on ARTs (in line with the pro-natalist and anti-choice regulation on abortion, mentioned in a footnote above, that was in force during the same period, from around 1985 onwards), a different rationale is to be found in the 2010 regulation on voluntary interruption of pregnancy, which was also signed by President Zapatero.[21] This, once again, shows how sociopolitical tensions and debates get entangled in the ways that women's rights are presented and made real through particular regulations, and calls our attention to how these rights are indirectly restricted when regulating things that (at least in Spain) are less politicised or open to public debate than access to abortion, such as ART use. If we were to understand eggs and embryos as extensions of women's bodies and broader biographies based on a similar rationale to that of the law on abortion, prohibiting women from discarding their material out of choice would be seen as contrary to their reproductive autonomy and their recognised right to freely choose whether or not to become mothers. Something in the way the ART regulation is presented, and the way that both gametes and embryos have been made to matter in Spanish reproductive markets, has meant this is not the case. Even though forbidding a woman from discarding an embryo-in-utero is not the same as forbidding her from doing the same if the embryo is outside the body, there are still pressing questions regarding reproductive autonomy in the way the regulation intervenes in these decision-making processes. This might be related to the way in which gametes and eggs are understood as just extensions of the body or as body parts, but rather as entities that can be possessed and exchanged once outside the body. Or in other words, in order to regulate the use, storage and potential discarding of gametes and embryos, the law first needed to separate these tissues from the bodies they came from, both symbolically and physically, by making them into property and moral objects. Only by understanding these cells in isolation from the bodies and biographies they were once entangled with (either physically, emotionally or logistically) can the regulation forbid a woman or a couple from discarding them. That is, the fact that the egg or the embryo was first frozen so that a particular woman could have it transferred into her uterus does not come with a right to stop having it stored if she changes her mind about the originally intended use. In that sense, the technologically gener-

21 It is important to note that this second law was passed in a different period, when the socialists had more power overall in the Parliament.

ated disentanglement between body and cells is reinforced by the law, both for donors (who lose their ownership) and for women using their own eggs or receiving donor eggs. The law positions itself as better qualified to decide the cells' fates than the women they came from or the couple who originally provided them with the plan of having a baby, and so designates the clinics as intermediate, custodial owners.

In practice, the 2006 regulation seems to have created, firstly, ideal conditions for an ever-expanding industry fuelled by egg, sperm and increasingly also embryo donation programmes and, secondly, an ever-growing problem of accumulation of both eggs and embryos, as their owners seem to be resisting the *duty* to either use them themselves or find another use for them. Accumulation happens if people donate embryos for research but no research is actually conducted,[22] if people do not know what to do with their material and keep storing it or if they stop updating the clinics about their whereabouts. The latter two possibilities appear to be fairly frequent occurrences (Reguera Cabezas and Cayón-de las Cuevas 2021). In these cases, it is interesting to see how this reproductive material can move from being a reproductive or productive potentiality to a potential *liability*.

Going back to the idea of commodification, and taking up Hoeyer's (2007) reflections on how an excessive focus on it as the main explanatory force in the ART industry might overlook the power of moral concerns, I think two main points apply. Firstly, in the Spanish case the bio-objectification of eggs and embryos in terms of *(re)productive duties* opens up a space between a person's reproductive biography and their reproductive material. This makes it possible or easier to see this material as "independent" and interchangeable. In an industry context, this might have eased the path to the cells becoming commodified. Even when the cells are extracted for a person's own use, they are already conceived of as potentially ending in circuits of exchange. If these entities were identified as extensions of bodies, biographies or body parts, the questions asked about them would probably have more to do with people's reproductive autonomy than with (legitimate or illegitimate) forms

22 Even though Spain has adopted a regulation that appears to remove obstacles to research on embryos and so might be expected to boost it, the reality seems to be that those pre-embryos donated for research very rarely end up in research projects. This is either, as already mentioned, due to difficulties securing funding for research projects, or due to bureaucratic barriers to gaining the informed consent needed to actually use the cells. Thus, most pre-embryos "donated for research" end up adding to the accumulation problem so often mentioned by professionals from the clinics, who struggle to keep on storing increasing numbers of pre-embryos with unclear fates.

of exchange. Furthermore, allowing de-personalised exchange in the handling of this reproductive material, such as that encouraged by compulsory anonymity, in a context of great expansion of the private sector allows clinics to be positioned as custodians, giving them a central role in the reorganisation and management of, and decisions about, the use of the reproductive material. This role makes it easier for sperm, eggs and pre-embryos to fuel an industry whose success rate with patients' own material has proven to be very low.

4. Conclusions

In this chapter I have shown how the first regulation of 1988 introduced the term "pre-embryos" for IVF embryos until day 14 after fertilisation, which—in the context of a Catholic country—made it easier to extract cells and keep them cryopreserved, as it helped to counter understandings of the cells as "lives" in need of protection. This law established a time limit of five years for the embryos to be kept in freezers, although it did not explicitly specify what was to be done with them after that period. As this provision was not, or not automatically, assumed to mean that after this time the pre-embryos were to be taken out of the tanks, a problem of accumulation arose in the first decade after this regulation was adopted, since professionals were not sure what to do with the cells after the five-year period had elapsed. The subsequent law of 2003 was interested in reducing the number of embryos stored, mainly due to religious and conservative ideals that problematised the creation of surplus embryos whose fate was unclear. By limiting the number of eggs that could be extracted from a woman per cycle, the law aimed to reduce the number of excess embryos—although it also reduced women's chances of actually achieving a pregnancy at all. This regulation, which drew much more on conservative ideology than the other two, lasted only three years, and constituted a barrier to the clinics continuing their business model. Finally, the last and current regulation on ARTs, adopted in 2006, created ideal conditions for a reproductive market to thrive, fuelled by the reproductive capacity of donated reproductive material. Much of this material comes from donors who came to the clinics for the purpose of donating, although the way the regulation is written also enables clinics to access eggs and embryos from patients who no longer want to get pregnant using their own material. This last point is one of the topics I have explored in this chapter, along with the fact that this regulation also encourages eggs and embryos to be donated for research—even though research has not thrived to the same degree as the fertility industry. The current regulation, while encouraging patients to donate their reproductive material, makes it rather difficult for women or couples to decide to stop the cryopreservation of their material. It instead places that decision in the hands of "experts" or "doctors", introducing an anti-choice spirit to the regulation that implies that if a woman has material frozen, the ideal scenario is for her to use it. This has the extreme consequence that she is not allowed to discard her material unless two independent professionals agree that she does not meet the conditions to use it. In practice, what this regulation allows is for all that surplus material to end up belonging to the clinics in a "custodian" role, in which they are responsible for transferring the material to other patients via paid treatments.

The way the current regulation sets the rules of what can happen with gametes and embryos makes it easier to understand them as part of the making of a property regime rather than as a regulation of one's own body or biography. The fact that the cells are "produced" and extracted opens up a space for their resignification, and the regulations use that space to build a type of ownership that comes with both freedoms to use the cells (under particular circumstances) and with duties. These freedoms and duties are, as seen above, very different depending on whether we are talking about sperm, eggs or embryos: sperm comes with more freedoms and eggs and embryos with more duties. Moreover, some subjects are more bound by the duties than others, and this is one area where we see gender and economic inequalities shaping this market. It is important to note that those storing sperm are freer to decide what to do with their reproductive material (for instance, they are allowed to discard it whenever they want) than those storing eggs. While sperm is seen as "just" a gamete, eggs are understood similarly to embryos, with both framed as deserving protection. They can accordingly be seen as property of their *owners*—which allows the owners to make use of their capacities but also imposes certain duties. The freedoms and obligations that come with sperm, eggs and embryos are thus not equally distributed but follow a heteronormative and highly gendered pattern, thanks to a combination of moral and economic concerns that have combined to create this particular market model.

It is clear that in a Catholic country that was just emerging from a very long dictatorship, the introduction of IVF must have been very shocking to many people, and lawmakers had to be mindful of tensions stemming from the recent past and the moral norms that the dictatorship imposed. It is also true that the 1980s were years of intense resignification of old concepts, and that reproductive freedom and the changing significance of motherhood were one of the key battlegrounds during those years—something that probably eased the way for flexible regulations (Alkorta 2003). Thus, the tensions we can see in the ways that embryos, pre-embryos and gametes are understood in different regulations are to be expected, but the consequence of facilitating an industry to grow around reproductive desires is more surprising. The regulations can be understood as trying to achieve a balance between more conservative and religiously based ideas about embryos and more industry/science-driven ideas about reproductive markets and biomedical research. This balance has allowed enough space for the industry to thrive while maintaining protections on certain matters of moral concern. Accordingly, following Klaus Hoeyer's reading of Nikolas Rose, it is interesting to see that "in some instances a ban on commodification indicates not a protection of the poor but an ambition to protect perceptions and symbols held by a majority" (Hoeyer 2007, 343). Moral arguments are also used in the Spanish regulation to argue for a ban on commodification (along similar lines to European Union directives). But at the same time, this regulation has made it easy for private clinics to gain access to reproductive material at very low cost or even for free. Indeed, allowing clinics to use the surplus material of previous patients means that patients can end up paying the clinic for the privilege of producing embryos that the clinic then gets to use for commercialised treatments—thus granting them access to material without requiring them to invest money, as in the case of egg or sperm donation. The key aim seems not to be to ban profit-making in the reproductive industry, but rather to prevent women from having the full power of decision over what to do with their reproductive material (e.g. whether to make profit from it, to give it as a gift to someone they know or to simply discard it). Thus, in the case of the Spanish regulation, moral and economic concerns have worked together in the framing of reproductive material as a particular type of property object, proving once again that capitalist logics are often as much economically as morally driven (something that has long been pointed out in feminist economic theories; on the Spanish context see Pérez Orozco 2022) and how ownership tends to be ambiguous, since "you may own things that you are not allowed to use, sell or destroy, and you may be entitled to use things you do not own" (Hoeyer 2007, 334).

Works Cited

Alkorta Idiakez, I. (2003). Los derechos reproductivos de las españolas: En especial, las técnicas de reproducción asistida. *DS: Derecho y Salud*, 11(2), 165–178.

Almeling, Rene (2011). *Sex Cells: The Medical Market for Eggs and Sperm*. Berkeley: University of California Press.

Bock von Wülfingen, Bettina (2012). The Fruit of Love: The German IVF-Embryo Turning from Abject into Bio-Object. En Niki Vermeulen, Sakari Tamminen and Andrew Webster (eds.). *Bio-Objects: Life in the 21st Century*, 137–150. Farnham: Ashgate.

Braun, Veit (2024). *At the End of Property: Patents, Plants and the Crisis of Propertisation*. Bristol: Bristol University Press.

Danish Council of Ethics (2013). *International Trade in Human Eggs, Surrogacy and Organs*. Copenhagen: Danish Council of Ethics.

Dolgin, Janet L. (1996). The "Intent" of Reproduction: Reproductive Technologies and the Parent–Child Bond. *Connecticut Law Review*, 26, 1261–1314.

Farnós Amorós, Esther (2007). ¿De quién son los embriones? Crisis de pareja y revocación del consentimiento a la reproducción asistida. *InDret*, 1.

Flexner, Stuart Berg (1993). Capacity. In Random House Webster's Unabridged Dictionary, 2nd ed. New York: Random House.

Franklin, Sarah (1997). *Embodied Progress: A Cultural Account of Assisted Conception*. London: Routledge.

Franklin, Sarah (2013). *Biological Relatives: IVF, Stem Cells and the Future of Kinship*. Durham, NC: Duke University Press.

Friedrich, Alexander, and Stefan Höhne (2014). Frischeregime: Biopolitik im Zeitalter der kryogenen Kultur. *Glocalism: Journal of Culture, Politics and Innovation*, 1–2, 1–44.

García Torres, Miriam, and Ruth Caravantes Vidriales (2023). "Yo soy porque las otras están": Investigación sobre el papel y el impacto del movimiento de mujeres y feminista en el reconocimiento de derechos y el avance de la Agenda 2030 en el Estado español. https://civicrm.calala.org/wp-content/uploads/2023/10/Resumen-ejecutivo-Investigacion-sobre-el-aporte-del-movimiento-de-mujeres-en-el-avance-de-los-derechos-humanos.pdf.

Haraway, Donna J. (2016). *Staying with the Trouble: Making Kin in the Chthulucene*. Durham, NC: Duke University Press.

Hauskeller, Christine, and Lorenzo Beltrame (2015). Hybrid Practices in Cord Blood Banking: Rethinking the Commodification of Human Tissues in the Bioeconomy. *New Genetics and Society*, 35(3), 228–245.

Hoeyer, Klaus (2007). Person, Patent and Property: A Critique of the Commodification Hypothesis. *BioSocieties*, 2, 327–348.

Holmberg, Tora, Nete Schwennesen and Andrew Webster (2011). Bio-Objects and the Bio-Objectification Process. *Croatian Medical Journal*, 52(6), 740.

Jociles Rubio, Maribel (2020). "Supongo que si hubiera tenido pasta, no lo habría hecho": motivaciones par donar óvulos e ideología del altruismo. In Ana María Rivas Rivas and

Consuelo Álvarez Plaza (eds.). *Etnografía de los mercados reproductivos actores, instituciones y legislaciones*, 35–93. Valencia: Tirant lo Blanch.

Kroløkke, Charlotte (2014). Eggs and Euros: A Feminist Perspective on Reproductive Travel from Denmark to Spain. *IJFAB: International Journal of Feminist Approaches to Bioethics*, 7(2), 144–163.

Lafuente-Funes, Sara (2017). Egg Donation in the Making: Gender, Selection and (In)visibilities in the Spanish Bioeconomy of Reproduction. In Vincenzo Pavone and Joanna Goven (eds.):). *Bioeconomies: Life, Technology, and Capital in the 21st Century*, 253–277. Cham: Palgrave Macmillan.

Lafuente-Funes, Sara (2020). Shall We Stop Talking about Egg Donation? Transference of Reproductive Capacity in the Spanish Bioeconomy. *BioSocieties*, 15, 207–225.

Lafuente-Funes, Sara (2023). The Role of Vitrification in Spanish Reproductive Labs: A Cryo-Revolution Led by Strategic Freezing. *Science, Technology, & Human Values*, 48(4), 752–776.

Lafuente-Funes, Sara (2024). "Being Useful, I Think It's the Result of a Sick Society": Critical Reflections on Reproductive Politics and Markets by Women Freezing Their Eggs in Spain. *BioSocieties* (online first). https://doi.org/10.1057/s41292-023-00321-y.

Latour, Bruno (2004). Why Has Critique Run Out of Steam? From Matters of Fact to Matters of Concern. *Critical Inquiry*, 30, 225–247.

Lemke, Thomas (2023). Welcome to Whenever: Exploring Suspended Life in Cryopreservation Practices. *Science, Technology, & Human Values*, 48(4), 700–726.

Lie, Merete (2012). Reproductive Images: The Autonomous Cell. *Science as Culture*, 21(4), 475–496.

Molas, Anna (2021). Taming Egg Donors: The Production of the Egg Donation Bioeconomy in Spain. Unpublished PhD thesis, Monash University.

Molas, Anna, and Andrea Whittaker (2021). Beyond the Making of Altruism: Branding and Identity in Egg Donation Websites in Spain. *BioSocieties*, 17, 320–346.

Orobitg, Gemma, Joan Bestard and Carles Salazar (2013). El cuerpo (re) productivo: interés económico y altruismo social en las experiencias de un grupo de mujeres donantes de óvulos. *Revista Andaluza de Antropologia*, 5, 91–104.

Pérez Milán, Federico (2011). La reproducción asistida en el medio sanitario público. In Roberto Matorras Weinig (ed.). *Libro Blanco Sociosanitario "La infertilidad en España: situación actual y perspectivas"*. Madrid: Imago Concept.

Pérez Orozco, Amaia (2022). *The Feminist Subversion of the Economy: Contributions for Life against Capital*. Brooklyn: Common Notions.

Perler, Laura (2022). *Selektioniertes Leben: Eine feministische Perspektive auf die Eizellenspende*. Münster: Edition Assemblage.

Radin, Joanna, and Emma Kowal (eds.) (2017). *Cryopolitics: Frozen Life in a Melting World*. Cambridge, MA: MIT Press.

Reguera Cabezas, Marta, and Joaquín Cayón-de las Cuevas (2021). Deseados pero abandonados: el incierto destino de los embriones criopreservados. *Revista de Bioética y Derecho: Perspectivas bioéticas*, 53, 139–157.

Rose, Nikolas (2007). Beyond Medicalisation. *Lancet*, 369(9562), 700–702.

Seiz, Marta, Tatïana Eremenko and Leire Salazar (2023). *Socioeconomic Differences in Access to and Use of Medically Assisted Reproduction (MAR) in a Context of Increasing Childlessness*. Seville: European Commission. JRC Working Papers Series on Social Classes in the Digital Age, JRC132097.

Siegrist, Hannes (2007) Die Propertisierung von Gesellschaft und Kultur. Konstruktion und Institutionalisierung des Eigentums in der Moderne. In Hannes Siegrist (ed.). *Entgrenzung des Eigentums in modernen Gesellschaften und Rechtskulturen*, 1–52. Leipzig: Leipziger Universitätsverlag.

Thompson, Charis (2005). *Making Parents: The Ontological Choreography of Reproductive Technologies*. Cambridge, MA: MIT Press.

Waldby, Catherine (2019). *The Oocyte Economy*. Durham, NC: Duke University Press.

Wyns, Christine, Christian de Geyter, Carlos Calhaz-Jorge, Markus Simon Kupka, Tatjana Motrenko, Jesper Smeenk, Christina Bergh, Andreas Tandler-Schneider, Ioana Adina Rugescu, Snezana Vidakovic and Veerle Goossens (2021). ART in Europe, 2017: Results Generated from European Registries by ESHRE. *Human Reproduction Open*, 3.

Liquid Gold: The Monetisation of Breastmilk

Katherine Carroll and Charlotte Kroløkke

> The healthiest nutrition for the newborn baby is breastmilk, and breastfeeding positively affects a range of health factors related to the mother as well as the child.
> *Danish Health Authority (2022)*

The reproductive body has become a goldmine of usable bits (Kroløkke 2018). What may be considered bodily waste, excess, vacant, or simply extractable reproductive material has, fuelled by scientific and technological progress and a growing fertility market, contributed to an emerging relationship between the body, commerce, and the production of biovalue (Mitchell and Waldby 2006). Breastmilk is a maternal reproductive fluid produced after birth that is tailor-made for sustaining a newborn infant. The hormones of the pregnant body enable the development of breast tissue specifically for lactation. A hormonal cascade triggers the production of breastmilk once the baby and placenta are delivered by the labouring body. Thanks to the labours of breastfeeding and/or the use of a breast pump, a mother's lactation can be maintained over weeks, months or years following the birth of a baby. It is at this point of extraction of breastmilk from the mother's body that a separate product is readied for entry into monetised circuits of exchange (Prouse 2021; Carter and Reyes-Foster 2020, 51).

In this chapter, we explore the ways in which breastmilk is made into an exchangeable commodity in the Danish context. We argue that the Danish state and national and international health organisations play a critical role in how breastmilk is first disentangled from a provider's body and then comes to be understood as not only intervening in and enhancing human lives but also as being something exchangeable. We examine the webs of relations that collectively sustain donor breastmilk's passage from providers' homes to technology-rich human milk banks and maternity wards in hospitals, supported by the Danish welfare state, national health policy, health promotion discourses and ideals of motherhood. Accordingly, we join Boyer (2010), Swanson (2014) and Carroll (2014) in arguing that breastmilk—like other reproductive substances—has been transformed into a bankable and mobile fluid by technologies of pumping, freezing, pasteurisation and screening. Moreover, by applying the heuristic of bio-objectification (Metzler and Webster 2011) we situate donor milk as collective commodity suspended in webs of relations and discourses that seek both to enhance maternal and infant health and to disrupt understandings of milk as the property of individual mothers or infants.

Against this backdrop, in this chapter we ask how Danish health authorities, private companies and other relevant organisations have conferred on breastmilk the status of property that can be owned and sold by lactating mothers. While at the same time we examine the role of these organisations in fostering the universalist Danish welfare goals of creating a shared resource that can be redistributed to enhance the health of some of the most vulnerable Danish citizens: premature infants. We argue that the propertisation of breastmilk must be situated within webs of relations between the breastfeeding mothers, their reproductive bodies, babies, imagined recipients, technologies and the Danish welfare and healthcare sectors. We begin by outlining previous feminist theories of reproductive labour, breastfeeding and breastmilk banking, before turning to our chosen empirical material and discussing how in the Danish context breastmilk can be understood as a form of property akin to bio-objects, which not only enhances human life but disrupts boundaries and identities as a result of its circulation, exchange and relations to the state, healthcare organisations, medical associations, milk banks and infants (including those of other mothers).

1. A short history of breastfeeding and milk banking: feminist perspectives

The growth in both state support and markets for breastmilk has historically strengthened the demand for, and exchange and monetisation of, donor breastmilk among various actors. Before examining this collective propertisation in contemporary Danish culture, it is important to understand the wider historical and technological shifts that surround breastmilk feeding and through which the separation, storage and transfer of breastmilk products between providers and recipients have long been established. In this section, we therefore first discuss breast milk feeding before providing a brief account of milk banking as an essential institutional element in the propertisation of breastmilk.

1.1 Breastmilk feeding

Breastmilk for infant feeding has not always enjoyed as much prominence as it does today. The early 1900s saw the medicalisation of infant feeding thanks to the development of commercial bovine milk formulas, as breastmilk substitutes were supported by the growth in technologies for bovine milk pasteurisation and refrigeration. In the post–World War II years, it was a majority view in the United States that bottle feeding was superior to breastfeeding (Swanson 2014, 178) and a way of achieving "enhanced autonomy for affluent women in their maternal bodies" (Blum 1999, 31). But in the late twentieth and early twenty-first centuries, growing public health support for breastfeeding, continued medicalisation of breastfeeding and maternalist organising and activism around women-centred maternity care and autonomy over breastfeeding, have contributed to breastfeeding being viewed today in many Western societies as an essential part of maternity (Blum 1999; Swanson 2014; Wolf 2011).

In contemporary Denmark, breastmilk—frequently referred to as "maternal milk"—is firmly positioned as "the best food for newborn nutrition" (Boquien 2018). According to the Danish Paediatric Society (n.d.), the composition of breastmilk precisely satisfies nutritional requirements for infants up to six months of age. Echoing this, the Danish Health Authority (2022) recommends that new mothers breastfeed exclusively until six months of age and then continue to breastfeed after the introduction of solid food up till the age of two. Scientific reports are cited explaining that breastmilk's composition adjusts according to the baby's gender and age and the environment's unique pathological demands (Danish Paediatric Society n.d.). It is also speculated that breastmilk has other qualities. For example, in Danish media reports, like in other high-income countries, breastfeeding is associated with higher intelligence and hence with a stronger likelihood that the child will end up with a high level of education and income. While the research supposedly showing this correlation has been contested or found to have been misreported due to the media's cursory interpretations of scientific papers (Wolf 2011), Danish media coverage supports the idea that breastmilk is not only good for the baby but also good for the mother and the welfare state, as breastfed children are believed to have fewer illnesses and breastfeeding mothers are viewed as generally healthier (Sahin 2015). Breastfeeding is depicted as having a range of positive qualities that go beyond its immediate nutritional aims and also including benefits for the economy and overall population health (Fentiman 2010).

1.2 Milk banking

Over the last decades, paediatricians' collective interest in infant feeding has grown (Fentiman 2010; Wolf 2001). This has influenced both individual practitioners' advice to mothers and their collective professional lobbying of the government regarding public health and health promotion guidelines on infant feeding. It has also created demand for human milk. The public health advice to exclusively feed infants on breastmilk for the first six months of life has added to the demand for breastmilk. This is particularly acute in the neonatal infant care sector, where scientists have repeatedly endorsed the benefit of exclusive human milk feeding for fragile babies in neonatal intensive care units (NICUs) (Herrmann and Carroll 2014), which is regarded as a form of "medical therapy" (Meek and Noble 2022). Since the historic "low point" of breastfeeding in the middle of the last century, the milk banking sector has undergone slow but steady growth internationally—initially as a middle-class maternalist project, before becoming the medicalised affair we witness today (Swanson 2014).

Technological developments (e.g. the breast pump, pasteurisation, freezers, cold-chain storage) have also contributed to the growing milk banking sector and have been crucial in assisting with the extraction of breastmilk from the maternal body and the sharing of extracorporeal breastmilk across geographical and temporal divides. Notably, the breast pump (invented in the United States back in 1854) can be understood as a low-tech device that has greatly affected how maternity is understood today (Courage 2022; Layne 2009). These technological developments were later supported by advancements in serological screening of donors and bacterial testing of breastmilk. Doctors' immaterial labour, such as calculating individual doses and prescribing donor milk for each hospitalised baby (Mol and Mesman 1996; Carroll 2014), position donated banked milk as a "safe" option for infant feeding and as a product that can be marketed and sold by milk banks at a cost recovery rate to NICUs. Danish state-owned milk banks operate on a monetised but not-for-profit basis rather than as a free market (Phillips 2011).

The sharing of bodily tissue and fluids must also be understood as a cornerstone of the welfare state. As noted in Richard Titmuss's (1970) classic *The Gift Relationship* altruistic blood donation and banking systems are classic examples of state-supported redistributive welfare systems based on in-kind giving to others in need. Applied to the tissue economy more broadly, "the sharing of human tissues can be a powerful expression of communal solidarity and civil empathy" (Mitchell and Waldby 2006, 8). But other forms of exchange in the tissue economy often follow pathways of power and wealth and run along racialised and classed lines (ibid), and breastmilk is no exception. Human milk and, with it, the labour of the lactating woman herself have long been viewed as tradable commodities. Examples include the payment of destitute women to supply milk through the embodied act of wet nursing, America's history of wet nursing by African slaves and, in contemporary times, the additional payments given to gestational surrogates for providing breastmilk or breastfeeding as contracted labour (Smith 2020). Ethical concerns have also been raised about for-profit milk banks and biotech companies paying women to provide expressed milk. These concerns include the impact that breastmilk provision has on ensuring milk supply for the providers' own children—a concern that was not extended historically to enslaved and destitute women (Wolf 2001; Swanson 2014; Newman and Nahman 2022).

1.3 Feminist perspectives

The separation of gift and commodity described by Titmuss in his comparative study of post–World War II blood banking in the United States of America and United Kingdom has been both celebrated and criticised. Contra the gift/commodity dichotomy, attention has been drawn to the commodification of unpaid altruistic donations in the processing of banked blood, milk and assorted human tissues (Swanson 2014). Feminist scholars have argued that "voluntary" exchanges are not free of exploitative labour nor free of the market itself (Newman and Nahman 2022). It is important to make visible the many practices of women's material labour that are relegated to the private sphere and play a crucial role in (re)production. Julie Smith (2020), drawing on Marilyn Waring's classic work *If Women Counted*, has long decried the invisibility and devaluation of women's contribution as producers of breastmilk to both the infant food sector and infants' healthcare. She argues that women's economic contribution through breastfeeding needs to be taken into account, including the costs to women such as the time they expend on breastfeeding (ibid., 213). On an international scale, with growing markets for extracorporeal human milk in Scandinavia, North America and South Asia, there is obfuscation of and dependence on breastmilk-as-property and the often-unwaged labour of women (Newman and Nahman 2022, 1972).

Accordingly, feminist scholars argue for the significance of the sociotechnical processes enacted by women in making milk and then separating it from their bodies so that it can enter the value chain of human milk commodification as property (Carroll 2015c; Newman and Nahman 2022). On this view, breastmilk gains value throughout the processes of its extraction, industrialisation, promotion, commodification and consumption (Mitchell and Waldby 2006). Thus, whether or not a donor is compensated, and whether or not the recipient pays for the milk, human milk has already been turned into property, as it has already entered into wider discourses of human milk's valorisation and monetisation by the state and public health campaigns (Fentiman 2010; Swanson 2014, 196).

However, feminist scholars also note that sharing breastmilk is about more than just economic factors. Just as altruistic blood donation and banking systems are imagined, across different cultural contexts, to strengthen the solidarity of a nation (Titmuss 1970), so too does breastmilk provision create (and threaten) bonds between women who are united in their desire for maternity yet perhaps separated by their ability to breastfeed infants (Carroll 2015a; 2015b; Oreg 2023). While the use of donor milk rather than infant formula in NICUs is due to the need to prevent necrotising enterocolitis—a potentially deadly and costly disease—in premature infants (Carroll and Herrmann 2013), the use of donor milk also happens to align with the broader "breast is best" infant feeding ideology surrounding motherhood and can thus enhance a sense that one is doing motherhood "right" by avoiding infant formula in favour of human milk (Carroll 2015a). Despite this, for some mothers with a child in the NICU donor milk feeding poses a significant threat to their sense of motherhood due to a perceived transgression of the idealised exclusive relationship between mother and infant, most commonly portrayed as involving a dyadic infant feeding bond between a breastfeeding mother and child (Carroll 2015a; 2015b). Thus, breastmilk provision may challenge forms of kinship, while gaining value throughout the processes of its extraction, industrialisation, promotion, commodification and consumption (Mitchell and Waldby 2006) and at the same time being understood as an act of maternal care (Swanson 2014; Carroll 2015c).

Below, we set out a feminist framework to highlight the ways that breastmilk, as an alienable substance that can be owned and shared between women and families, is situated within a history of breastfeeding, "doing" motherhood, technological developments, medicalisation and material culture and gets spoken into existence in recognisably gendered ways. Although we focus here on the Danish milk banking sector,[1] we are aware of the diverse historical, cultural and contemporary modes of sharing breastmilk, and the relations that were/are formed, strengthened, coerced and sometimes threatened and thwarted through the diverse practices of cross-nursing (Carroll 2015a; Falls 2017; Shaw 2007), enslaved or paid wet nursing, expressing milk for milk donation to human milk banks and sharing expressed milk informally between families.

2. An empirical analysis: The situation in Denmark

The establishment of milk banks in Scandinavia can be traced back to the late 1930s and 1940s, when new findings on the benefits of breastmilk were combined with a focus on child health and the later development of the milk pump (see also Borring et al. 2018). In Denmark, milk banking currently takes place at three separate public, state-owned milk banks (locations: Copenhagen, Aarhus, Aalborg). Danish guidelines recommend that breastmilk provision should start during the first eight to ten weeks post-partum, due to the higher levels of protein in the milk in that period. Prior to donating, the provider must have a minimum daily excess of 200 millilitres milk. She must also undergo a blood test and have a telephone consultation with a member of the milk bank staff. One milk bank stipulates that providers may only donate if they are healthy. Breastmilk can be picked up at the

1 An archive of varied materials was built up to provide data for this study: information materials from two Danish milk banks (the "*kvindemælkecentralen*" at Hvidovre Hospital and the "*mælkekøkkenet*" at Skejby Hospital), contemporary Danish health materials and campaigns calling for women to breastfeed (time period: 2022–2023) and mainstream Danish media content from a range of different sources (time period: 2014–2023).

provider's home address. While only available to state-owned hospitals, the sale price for one litre of milk is anywhere between 1,000 and 1,700 Danish krone (approximately 135 to 230 euros), depending on the level of protein. Meanwhile, the mothers providing the milk currently receive 196 Danish krone (26 euros) per litre of milk provided (Borring et al. 2018, 101–102). The human milk bank must recover the costs of serological screening, pasteurisation and the milk bank staff's material labour (Carroll 2014), but the price differential between the purchase and sale is also a clear example of how those producing the materials are assigned the least value and consequently receive the least money (Newman and Nahman 2022).

The analysis presented here is based on information materials, conversations with the head of the milk bank unit at Hvidovre Hospital and an archive of Danish news reporting (print and TV) on breastmilk provision. This archive was created using sources from digital databases (such as InfoMedia, search terms: "brystmælk", "modermælk", "brystmælk donation", "kvindemælk"; time period: 2014–2023). Referring to information materials and Danish news coverage reveals the ways that breastmilk provision is articulated by a range of actors. Consequently, unlike the ethnographic study carried out by Borring et al. (2018), our work focuses heavily on the ways that breastmilk provision is presented by welfare state institutions (information materials and campaigns) and in media coverage. Accordingly, we view information materials and health campaigns as playing a vital role in creating demand for expressed breastmilk, due to public health and medical experts endorsing the value of human milk for both infants and women (Fentiman 2010; Walters et al. 2019).

Based on our empirical archive, we identified two main analytical threads to focus on. The first addresses the ways in which breastmilk provision in Denmark is framed as both "gift-giving" and "labour". The second centres on how in the Danish context breastmilk transitions from "maternal milk" to "banked milk", and re-emerges in media representations of "happy recipients". In our final discussion, we return to feminist scholarship and look at the ways that the propertisation of breastmilk—understood here as existing within a web of relations that cut across different sectors and domains—can be conceived.

2.1 Breastmilk provision as gift-giving and labour

A brief televised report on Hvidovre Hospital milk bank, titled "Lucrative business: make 196 DKK per litre of breastmilk", begins by stating that each year 4,000 babies are born prematurely in Denmark. The "milkman" (*mælkemanden*) (the worker who picks up breastmilk at the providers' homes, described by the show in gendered terms) and a breastmilk provider who makes the difference "between life and death". In this televised account, a picture of a premature infant resting on the mother's breast and weighing little more than a litre of milk is combined with narratives of women donating breastmilk.

Building on recent ethnographic work conducted in Indian milk banks that critiques the invisibility of the value created by human labour in the production of breastmilk, in this thread of our analysis we show how value accrues along the chain of trading when scientific techniques are applied to the procurement of breastmilk from women's bodies (Newman and Nahman 2022). Like Newman and Nahman, we argue that we should go beyond dualistic framings of gift/commodity, and instead position commodity and gift as co-constitutive in the process.

In the Danish context, monetary payment is continually intermixed with the desire, encouraged by public health campaigns, to help premature infants. Breastmilk provision is articulated as a chance to help ill, weak and premature infants, who are visualised by photos of colourful lunchboxes and white toddlers with blue eyes. Providing these babies with breastmilk is also, however, framed as an act of self-care. We learn on one website, for instance, that breastfeeding helps women to maintain their own health (Brødsgaard 2020). This is echoed in Danish campaigns and institutional materials that present breastfeeding as an opportunity for women to continue living healthy lives. In this formulation, healthy lives are understood as lives free of alcohol, caffeine and smoking. As noted in one information resource: "We only accept milk from women who are non-smokers and are not taking any type of medication" (Hvidovre Hospital 2024).

Breastfeeding and providing breastmilk to the milk bank are also framed as a profitable line of business for some Danish women who easily produce excess milk. An article titled "Milked herself to a record: Sisser made half a million on her breastmilk" introduces a narrative along these lines. We learn in the article that Sisser Weinreich has made as much as 460,000 Danish krone (approximately 62,000 euros) from selling her breastmilk (Lindberg

2015). The mother of seven may, according to the article, have broken a world record by donating an astounding 4,308 litres of milk to Hvidovre Hospital. Weinreich recounts that she began donating her breastmilk to the milk bank back in the 1980s at a rate of about four litres a day and that her milk production increased when listening to Mozart or looking at photos of flowers—"it really made the milk flow". She positions breastmilk donation within idealised notions of relaxation and nursing. Weinreich's three daughters have likewise donated breastmilk, making her speculate that the talent might be genetic (ibid.).

While Weinreich's own narrative and that of the article and accompanying video, despite the headline ("Sisser made half a million on her breastmilk"), situate this significant income within an altruistic discursive frame, payment is made very explicit in Hvidovre Hospital's recruitment materials: "Will you sell your breastmilk?" a brochure for Hvidovre Hospital milk bank titled "Information on the sale of breastmilk" bluntly asks. Unlike in Norway and Australia, for example, where payment is prohibited, in this recruitment brochure—which features a picture of a woman using a breast pump (figure 1)—monetary payment is mentioned upfront. Later on, it is specified that this payment is "taxable income", but the rest of the brochure consists of practical information: how the milk is picked up, what milk is preferred (the answer: milk from during the first eight to ten weeks, due to the protein content) and how the payment is recorded. Potential providers must, as already noted, have a daily surplus of at least 200 millilitres. The brochure also stresses that this is a chance to "help other children". In this way, practical matters (when and how to become a breastmilk provider) and a discourse of "helping children" overshadow the potential monetary compensation as well as notions of where the milk comes from and who it belongs to. Unlike egg donation, which has prompted concerns that compensation may lead to women's bodies being exploited, at no point is breastmilk provision seen as remotely problematic. Because monetary compensation appears just above the words "Will you sell your breastmilk?" (figure 1) and the context of helping premature infants, it is normalised as a form of payment for the labour that goes into pumping and, additionally, as an act of altruism. As a consequence, monetary compensation and altruism go hand in hand in the Danish brochure.

---

2 Retrieved from https://www.hvidovrehospital.dk/undersoegelse-og-behandling/find-undersoegelse-og-behandling/Sider/Vil-du-saelge-din-modermaelk-24071.aspx.

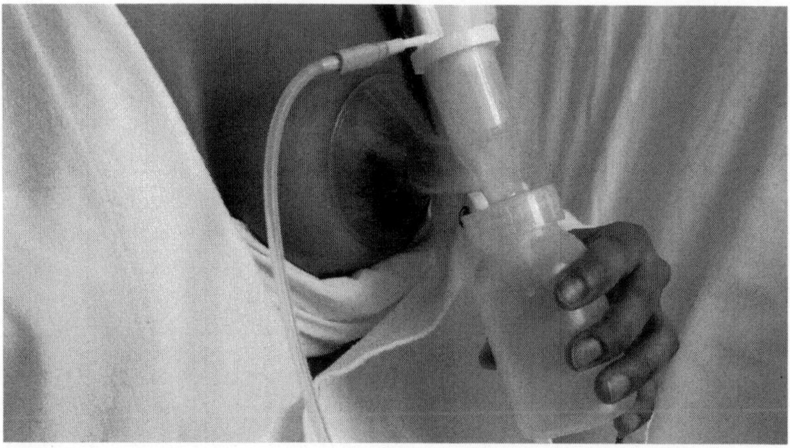

Figure 1: photo from a recruitment brochure published on Hvidovre Hospital's website. It shows a white hospital gown, an empty pump and a woman's breast, presumably belonging to a younger woman.[2]

As already noted in feminist scholarship on reproductive technologies, the discourse of "giving a gift" is a dominant narrative (Almeling 2011; Gunnarson and Svenaeus 2012; Kroløkke 2014; Pollock 2003; Roberts 2012). This is also the case in the Danish context, where cultural discourses around altruism have guided legislative practices and ethical debates (Kroløkke et al. 2020). Bronwyn Parry (2007, 1140) believes that compensation discourse is also, however, used as cover for a "collective squeamishness" about money changing hands between different and differently positioned reproductive actors. This squeamishness is frequently located at the beginning of the value chain, at the point where women create value through their work of producing and extracting milk.

Although in Denmark the hospital pays for the banked milk, the hospitalised babies receive donated milk for free. But while it may seem like a kind of gift from the perspective of a recipient family, and therefore has the effect of positioning women as "donors", there is a strong tendency, as described earlier, to normalise the "sale" and "labour" aspect of milk donation. To acknowledge this paradox, the term "providers" is used throughout this chapter. In addition to justifying breastmilk provision on the grounds that it meets the needs of vulnerable infants, the brochure also says that breastfeeding reduces the risk of certain breast and ovarian cancers, among other diseases. It thus justifies donation as a way for women to reap the wider benefits associated with breastfeeding. When gift-giving becomes the preferred metaphor, reproductive providers' bodies are positioned as legitimately constructed for someone else's desires and needs (Pollock 2003; Raymond 1993) in addition to their own. Moreover, as we have seen, the rhetoric of altruism draws upon cultural notions of dignity and integrity (Kroløkke et al. 2020).

Having discussed the ways that breastmilk provision is framed in Denmark as forms of both gift-giving and labour, we will now turn to the construction of "happy recipients".

3. From "maternal milk" to "banked milk": the construction of "happy" and "vulnerable recipients"

Like all other foods,
it is preferable for women's milk to be enjoyed fresh.
Petersen (1983, 19)

In this section, we argue that the separation of milk from the provider and the processing of the breastmilk are essential to the ways that breastmilk is made to "naturally" flow between provider and recipient bodies. Moreover, the rhetorical and visual move from provider bodies to preterm infants makes breastmilk provision a lifesaving choice.

While the term "mother's milk" (*modermælk*) is the preferred label in many of the materials, it is sometimes replaced as "donor milk" (*donormælk*). With regard to the processes of pumping, freezing and banking—which Høyer and Olejaz (2011) also refer to as "purification work"– the term "donor milk" serves to more aptly illustrate how breastmilk becomes, as we argue, a type of property. Kara Swanson (2014, 4) observes with regard to "body banking" in general, though the point also applies to breastmilk banking in particular, that "at the origins of the transformation of the body into a source of harvestable property, *bank* was chosen as a metaphor for understanding body product exchange. This term [was] borrowed from financial banking and [is] redolent with implications for markets and cash flows". Banking of body products has been chiefly supported by the collective action of medical societies seeking to advance professional goals and patient care by having body products available for use to treat a patient as and when they are needed (ibid., 13).

Despite lofty goals of improved care, the development of successful body banks was also reliant on the mundane technologies of refrigeration and cold storage (ibid., 5). Ninety years later, the banking metaphor still persists. It continues to govern our thoughts and encourages us to think about body products—blood, sperm, bones, cells, milk and more—in terms of money and markets (ibid., 6). This persistence across the decades has, of course, not been without controversy about whether or not body products should be bought or sold (ibid., 8). But the term "bank" was not always used for milk banks. Before it became established, the terms "milk station" and "milk bureau" were used in the United States of America. The former made reference to other concurrent campaigns to deliver safe cow's milk to the urban poor, the latter to public improvement agencies such as the Children's Welfare Bureau, which administered breastmilk stations (ibid., 162). Similarly, the milk bank at Skejby Hospital (Aarhus) in Denmark was formerly known as the "milk kitchen" (*mælkekøkkenet*). In each case, milk as property was controlled by the medical profession so that it could be used for their purposes, and the terms "bureau and station maintained the focus on this medically directed goal rather than on the treatment of human milk as a market commodity" (ibid., 162–163).

In the case of Denmark, the move from "mother's milk" (*modermælk*) to "donated milk" (*donormælk*) is intertwined with the emergence of breastmilk as a form of "excess" milk. We saw this earlier in the example of Sisser Weinreich, who is said to have produced an excess of 4,308 litres of milk. It is similarly present in the story of Mette, who reportedly had a freezer full of breastmilk and decided it would be a shame to "throw it out" (Askgaard 2014). But "excess" does not occur naturally as a precursor to a property object that becomes monetised. To ask a potential provider to position milk as exceeding their infant's needs requires engaging with women's own understandings of their milk supply and their infants' needs. This is something many not-for-profit milk banks take seriously as an ethical practice: for example, they do not allow providers to enrol too close to the birth of an infant, when a mother's milk supply is still variable, or to deliberately create "oversupply" through additional pumping of milk simply in order to be able to donate "the excess". In Denmark, providers must, as previously noted, produce an excess of at least 200 ml a day to be eligible, but how this 200 millilitres excess is defined or determined is not made clear. This attention to the ethics of the production of "excess" milk contrasts with some less scrupulous milk banking operations, which work with poorer communities to produce excess for the purposes of donation by "turning women's understandings of their own bountiful supply of milk into a sense of 'waste'" and then encouraging them to turn their milk into a monetised, commodifiable substance (Newman and Nahman 2020, 1980).

Interestingly, in the Danish empirical material, the notions of "vulnerable recipients" and "lifesaving breastmilk" are rhetorically central. The milk bank itself goes from being understood as a bank ("the milk bank" (*mælkebank*), Aarhus University Hospital) to becoming a type of provider "hub" ("the women's milk central" (*mælkecentralen*), Hvidovre Hospital). The practice of providing other women with breastmilk is thus institutionalised and encouraged by a range of rhetorical frameworks. The work underpinning these bodily exchanges is mostly undertaken within the domestic sphere, as frequently visualised by pictures of refrigerators, sofas, toys and living rooms, which makes breastmilk provision appear natural and even innate—and potentially also disguises the work that goes into it. This becomes even more salient when, in the Danish case, vulnerable recipients take centre stage in images of vulnerable white premature twin infants (Aalborg University Hospital 2021).

In short, our Danish example is reminiscent of studies done in the United States of America, where breastmilk provision is presented as a naturalised caring practice and, by combining it with personal stories about "naturally" flowing breastmilk (somehow the breast pump and all the other material and immaterial labour are invisible), the work that goes into collecting, pouring and freezing breastmilk becomes naturalised as well. Accordingly, when "women's milk" changes status and becomes "banked milk", it turns into a disembodied and anonymised nutritional substance that emerges out of the milk bank (and not from the breastmilk provider herself) and "naturally" flows towards a diverse group of "happy" recipients. Our empirical material reveals how images of vulnerable white infant recipients affectively call on other women/mothers to act. As a slogan by Aalborg University Hospital puts it: "Your excess breastmilk can save lives!" (Aalborg University Hospital 2021).

4. Conclusion

In this chapter, we have discussed how breastmilk provision comes to be understood as a form of property that is shared within a web of relations. Rather than "merely" becoming valued individual property thanks to the technological innovations within the human milk bank, the propertisation of breastmilk emerges *materially* in the relationships between the developing maternal body and her labour, the foetus and the pumping and storage technologies as well as *discursively* within a set of conventional cultural discourses perpetuated by the Danish welfare state that relate to good motherhood and public health as a form of welfare provision by and for the Danish state. Banked breastmilk is positioned as a lifesaving fluid, the best nutrition a baby can get, a shared substance, a Danish form of sisterly solidarity, an act of self-care, pure love (in a bottle) and—once it is frozen and banked—a mobile nutritional substance.

One thing that is of note in the Danish context, and which transcends the gift/commodity dichotomy, is that the paid donation of breastmilk to a human milk bank is cast as an act of care not only towards others (Newman and Nahman 2022) but towards the milk provider herself (Carroll 2015c, 184). Likewise, the use of provider milk is an act of twofold care directed towards both the recipient infant and their mother, who is enabled to provide lifesaving care and enact the ideal of good motherhood by using provider milk if she cannot give her own breastmilk to her premature infant.

In the Danish case of "banked milk", breastmilk is reformulated as a lifesaving tool, available as a form of nutrition—not only for the anonymous (blonde and blue-eyed) infant, but also, because breastfeeding is viewed as having a set of redeeming qualities for the provider herself. The media material reveals the ways that breastmilk provision, within the context of the welfare state, is framed to unite Danish women around a naturalised desire to enact good Danish motherhood. Meanwhile, the Danish healthcare authorities, in their efforts to promote breastmilk, naturalise the notion that "breast is best" (as evidenced in the introductory quote). In our archive of Danish material, breastmilk turns into a mobile substance, so that breastmilk provision is positioned as similar to blood donation (Valentine 2005) and is culturally constituted as circulating within an imagined community of likeminded providers and recipients. It is in this context that breastmilk provision escapes any criticism about payment and instead becomes an altruistic labour of "pure love".

Works Cited

Aalborg University Hospital (2021). Your Excess Milk Can Save Lives! Facebook post, 12 January. https://www.facebook.com/AalborgUH/posts/din-overskydende moderm%C3%A6lk-kan-redde-livtvillingepigerne-her-er-for-tidligt-f%C3%B8dt/10159428087933092/.

Almeling, Rene (2011). *Sex Cells: The Medical Market for Eggs and Sperm*. Berkeley: University of California Press.

Askgaard, Sofie W. (2014). Mette donerer modermælk: Det er fantastisk at hjælpe andre babyer. *Vores Børn*, 11 December. https://www.alt.dk/boern/mette-donerer-modermaelk-det-er-fantastisk-at-hjaelpe-andre-babyer.

Blum, Linda M. (1999). *At the Breast: Ideologies of Breastfeeding and Motherhood in the Contemporary United States*. Boston: Beacon Press.

Boquien, Clair-Yves (2018). Human Milk: An Ideal Food for Nutrition of Preterm Newborn. *Frontiers in Pediatrics*, 16(6), 295–304.

Borring, Julie, Ditte S. Hansen, Mie S. Dam and Mette N. Svendsen (2018). Fra modermælk til donormælk: Forhandlinger af mælk, individ og velfærdskollektiv. *Tidsskrift for Forskning i Sygdom og Samfund*, 29, 99–119.

Boyer, Klaus (2010). Of Care and Commodities: Breast Milk and the New Politics of Mobile Biosubstances. *Progress in Human Geography*, 34(1), 5–20.

Brødsgaard, Anne (2020). Du kan sælge din modermælk. https://sundhedsplejersken.dk/mad/amning-faa-den-til-at-lykkes/du-kan-salge-din-modermalk/.

Carroll, Katherine (2014). Body Dirt or Liquid Gold? How the "Safety" of Donated Breast Milk Is Constructed for Use in Neonatal Intensive Care. *Social Studies of Science*, 44(3), 466–485.

Carroll, Katherine (2015a). The Milk of Human Kinship: Donated Breastmilk in Neonatal Intensive Care. In Charlotte Kroløkke, Lene Myong, Stine Willum Adrian and Tine Tjørnhøj-Thomsen (eds.). *Critical Kinship Studies*, 15–33. London: Rowman & Littlefield.

Carroll, Katherine (2015b). Representing Ethnographic Data through the Epistolary Form: A Correspondence between a Breastmilk Donor and Recipient. *Qualitative Inquiry*, 21(8), 686–695.

Carroll, Katherine (2015c). Breastmilk Donation as Care Work. In Tanya Cassidy and Abdullahi El Tom (eds.). *Ethnographies of Breastfeeding*, 173–186. London: Bloomsbury.

Carroll, Katherine, and Kenneth Herrmann (2013). The Cost of Using Donor Human Milk in the NICU to Achieve an Exclusively Human Milk Diet through 32 Weeks Postmenstrual Age. *Breastfeeding Medicine*, 8(3), 286–290.

Carter, Shannon K., and Beatriz M. Reyes-Foster (2020). *Sharing Milk: Intimacy, Materiality and Bio-Communities of Practice*. Bristol: Bristol University Press.

Courage, Katherine. H (2022). The Sucky History of the Breast Pump. *Smithsonian Magazine*, 12 September. https://www.smithsonianmag.com/innovation/sucky-history-of-the-breast-pump-180980653/.

Danish Health Authority (2022). Amning. https://www.sst.dk/da/Borger/En-sund-hverdag/Kost,-motion-og-hygiejne/Anbefalinger-om-kost/Mad-til-spaed–og-smaaboern.

Danish Paediatric Society (n.d.) Enternal ernæring til præmature nyfødte. https://paediatri.dk/images/dokumenter/Retningslinjer_2019/Enteral_ern%C3%A6ring_.pdf.

Falls, Susan (2017). *White Gold: Stories of Breastmilk Sharing*. Lincoln, NE: University of Nebraska Press.

Fentiman, Linda C. (2010). Marketing Mother's Milk: The Commodification of Breastfeeding and the New Markets for Breast Milk and Infant Formulas. *Nevada Law Journal*, 10(1), Article 3.

Gunnarson, Martin, and Fredrik Svenaeus (eds.). (2012). *Exchanging Organs, Tissues, and Cells in the 21st Century.* Södertörn: Södertörn Högskola.

Herrmann, Kenneth, and Katherine Carroll (2014). An Exclusively Human Milk Diet Reduces Necrotising Enterocolitis. *Breastfeeding Medicine*, 9(4), 185–190.

Høyer, Klaus, and Maria Olejaz (2011). Kroppen politiske økonomi: Om grænsedragningen mellem person, krop og vare i medicinske udveksklingssystemet. *Kuluturstudier*, 2(2), 157–177.

Hvidovre Hospital (2024). Kvindemælkcentralen. https://www.hvidovrehospital.dk/praktisk-information/faciliteter/Sider/Kvindemaelkcentralen.aspx.

Kroløkke, Charlotte (2014). West Is Best: Affective Assemblages and Spanish Oöcytes. *European Journal of Women's Studies*, 21(1), 57–71.

Kroløkke, Charlotte (2018). *Global Fluids: The Cultural Politics of Reproductive Waste and Value.* New York: Berghahn Books.

Kroløkke, Charlotte, Thomas Søbirk Petersen, Janne Rothmar Herrmann, Anna Sofie Bach, Stine W. Adrian, Rune Klingenberg and Michael Nebeling Petersem (2020). *The Cryopolitics of Reproduction on Ice: A New Scandinavian Ice Age*. Bingley: Emerald Group Publishing.

Layne, Linda L (2009). The Home Pregnancy Test: A Feminist Technology? *Women's Studies Quarterly*, 37(1/2), 61–79.

Lindberg, Helle (2015). "Malkede" sig til rekord: Sisser tjente en halv million på sin modermælk. *TV2 News*, 28 March. https://nyheder.tv2.dk/2015-03-28-malkede-sig-til-rekord-sisser-tjente-en-halv-million-paa-sin-modermaelk.

Meek, Joan Y., and Lawrence Noble (2022). Policy Statement: Breastfeeding and the Use of Human Milk. *Paediatrics*, 150(1), e2022057988.

Metzler, Ingrid, and Andrew Webster (2011). Bio-Objects and Their Boundaries: Governing Matters at the Intersection of Society, Politics, and Science. *Croatian Medical Journal*, 52(5), 648–650.

Mitchell, Robert, and Catherine Waldby (2006). *Tissue Economies: Blood, Organs, and Cell Lines in Late Capitalism.* Durham, NC: Duke University Press.

Mol, Annemarie, and Jessica Mesman (1996). Neonatal Food and the Politics of Theory: Some Questions of Method. *Social Studies of Science*, 26(2), 419–444.

Newman, Susan, and Michal Nahman (2022). Nurture Commodified? An Investigation into Commercial Human Milk Supply Chains. *Review of International Political Economy*, 29(6), 1967–1986.

Oreg, Ayelet (2023). Written on Milk: Exploring Messages Written on Donated Human-Milk Bags. *Medical Humanities* (online first). https://doi.org/10.1136/medhum-2022-012608.

Parry, Bronwyn (2007). Entangled Exchange: Reconceptualising the Characterization and Practice of Bodily Commodification. *Geoforum*, 39, 1133–1144.

Phillips, Anne (2011). It's My Body and I'll Do What I Like with It: Bodies as Objects and Property. *Political Theory*, 39(6), 724–748.

Pollock, Anne (2003). Complicating Power in High-Tech Reproduction: Narratives of Anonymous Paid Egg Donors. *Journal of Medical Humanities*, 24(3/4), 241–263.

Prouse, Carolyn (2021). Mining Liquid Gold: The Lively, Contested Terrain of Human Milk Valuations. *Environment and Planning A: Economy and Space*, 53(5), 958–976.

Raymond, Janice (1993). *Women as Wombs: Reproductive Technologies and the Battle over Women's Freedom*. San Francisco: HarperSanFrancisco.

Roberts, Elizabeth F. S (2012). *God's Laboratory: Assisted Reproduction in the Andes*. Oakland, CA: University of California Press.

Sahin, Sultan (2015). Derfor giver amning højere intelligens. *Berlingske Tidende*, 8 June. https://www.berlingske.dk/det-sunde-liv/derfor-giver-amning-hoejere-intelligens.

Shaw, Rhonda (2007). Cross-Nursing, Ethics, and Giving Breast Milk in the Contemporary Context. *Women's Studies International Forum*, 30(5), 439–450.

Smith, Julie (2020). Making Mothers' Milk Count. In Margunn Bjørnholt and Ailsa McKay (eds.). *On Marilyn Waring: New Advances in Feminist Economics*, 213–228. Bradford, ON: Demeter Press.

Swanson, Kara W. (2014). *Banking on the Body: The Market in Blood, Milk, and Sperm in Modern America*. Cambridge, MA: Harvard University Press.

Titmuss, Richard M. (1970). *The Gift Relationship: From Human Blood to Social Policy*. London: Allen & Unwin.

Valentine, Kylie (2005). Citizenship, Identity, Blood Donation. *Body & Society*, 11(2), 113–128.

Waldby, Catherine, and Melinda Cooper (2010). From Reproductive Work to Regenerative Labour: The Female Body and the Stem Cell Industries. *Feminist Theory*, 11(1), 3–22.

Waldby, Catherine, Ian Kerridge, Margaret Boulos and Katherine Carroll (2013). From Altruism to Monetisation: Australian Women's Ideas about Money, Ethics and Research Eggs. *Social Science & Medicine*, 94, 34–42.

Walters, Dylan T., Linh T. H. Phan and Roger Mathisen (2019). The Cost of Not Breastfeeding: Global Results from a New Tool. *Health Policy Plan*, 34(6), 407–417.

Wolf, Jacqueline (2001). *Don't Kill Your Baby: Public Health and the Decline of Breastfeeding in the Nineteenth and Twentieth Centuries*. Columbus, OH: Ohio State University Press.

Wolf, Jacqueline (2011). *Is Breast Best? Taking on the Breastfeeding Experts and the New High Stakes of Motherhood*. New York: New York University Press.

III
Conceptualising Property, Propertisation and Moral Economies

Subordination, Surrogacy and the Body: Feminist Perspectives on Locke's Individualism and His Conception of "Property in the Person"

Janice Richardson

How is it that surrogates are able to do things that are romanticised as priceless yet are often treated as subordinate, while having little ability to negotiate their payments or their working conditions? It is as if there were only two images of the pain and effort involved in such pregnancies. Surrogates' efforts must either fit within a feudal image, in which everyone had a fixed role from birth, associated with their status; or within capitalism, in which such activity must be classified as "work", and must fit within images of "cis men's work" to have value. Surrogates understandably say that they should be paid for their pain, effort and the risks to their health when they undertake surrogacy. In a market society, the value of such effort is viewed as its price and commodified accordingly.

Many are understandably disturbed by the commodification of gestation, to the extent that it can be commercialised. For example, Elizabeth Anderson argued that commercial surrogacy "constitutes the unconscionable commodification of children and of women's reproductive capacities" (Anderson 1990, 71). This concern is situated within a more general change in society that has accompanied the rise of neoliberalism, in which more human abilities and attributes have come to be treated as objects of commodification. However, as Amrita Pande (2014, 92–93) highlights in her study of Indian surrogates, it is surely exploitative to tell desperately poor women that they should "not be greedy". The voices of women who work as surrogates, particularly in the Global South, certainly need to be heard. It also goes without saying that it would be a better world if they did not need to undertake commercial surrogacy as it stands, given its potential risks to health that are both physical and mental in nature.

In this chapter, I consider some of the theoretical questions that are raised in discussions about commercial surrogacy in relation to John Locke, in particular his conception of "property in the person" and his associated image of the individual. Locke's position is still relevant because of his continuing influence on liberalism and neoliberalism. As the feminist philosopher of history of political thought Janet Coleman (2005) details, Locke's conception of the individual occupies a transitional position between the medieval image of a person as having a God-given, fixed place within a hierarchy on the one hand and the modern individual on the other, a shift that is associated with the historical transition from one mode of production to another, from feudalism to capitalism. I show how Locke's individualism is problematic for thinking about surrogacy.

As Coleman (ibid.) demonstrates, Locke's argument, which is based upon our *duty* to God to keep ourselves alive and was employed to justify private property, would later, in a more secular society, end up forming the basis of a right-wing libertarian claim that the rich have *rights* over the fruits of their labour (Nozick 1974). It is this attitude to rights to private property, along with associated neoliberal views of the individual (who is characterised as having free will to consent to sometimes dangerous working conditions, irrespective of her poverty), that Veronika Siegl (2023, chapter 7) detects at play in some of the attitudes to surrogates today.

I have divided this chapter into two parts. In the first, I explain Locke's justification of private property based on the notion of "property in the person", pausing at what I term "feminist staging posts" to add commentary as I progress with this close reading. At these staging posts, I will depart from my textual outline of Locke's chapter "Of Property" in the *Second Treatise of Government* to examine feminist arguments that are relevant to his text and to draw out the arguments that are relevant to surrogacy. The feminist interventions that I discuss at the staging posts can be briefly explained. Firstly, I note that when Locke asks at what point private property first comes into being, he briefly considers whether it could be at the point when a man digests some acorns he has picked. Our "acorn-loving man" (as I will call him) is situated in the state of nature (i.e. envisaged as occurring before sovereignty and laws). It is unusual to concentrate on Locke's passing mention of digestion, which is quickly dismissed. However, I use it to make a brief observation about some attitudes to surrogacy: the resistance to the idea that gestation within the body could be viewed as work at all, such that it would give rise to any sorts of rights to payment. I briefly turn to the analysis by Sophie Lewis (2021) and consider her response to this argument and the way it is associated with the claim that pregnancy is somehow a "natural resource".

After this brief staging post, I then return to my outline of Locke's "Of Property", picking up at the point when he dismisses the idea that acorns became the property of the man in the state of nature when he digested them and instead decides that they actually became his property when he first worked on them by picking them. At the second staging post, I consider what is entailed in the work of surrogacy, drawing on Verena Namberger's (2019) analysis of what is entailed in the work of egg donation. This is useful because she is attentive to areas of work that often fall from view, including the emotional labour that women often have to perform in any workplace but that went unacknowledged in the absence of feminist interventions (see also Hochschild 2023; Siegl 2023, chapters 5 and 6).

I then return to Locke's text to consider the famous paragraph 28 of "Of Property", in which he introduces the figure of the servant. Locke argues that the acorn-loving man has a right to the products of his servant's labour. At the final feminist staging post, I turn to Carole Pateman (1988; 2002; Pateman and Mills 2007; 2010) and her important argument that subordination (which was enforced by law in feudal times) came to be both perpetuated and managed through contracts in modernity. Importantly, she highlights that this subordination involves not only the obedience of subjects to their sovereign and the obedience of workers to their employers, but also, in the heyday of patriarchy, the obedience of wives to their husbands, a contract to which many political theorists were blind at the time she was originally writing. I consider Pateman's concern that such contracts undermine the possibility of developing a participatory democracy, since they train workers to obey. Consequently, they do not expect to have a say in the workplace and do not develop the skills necessary for participatory democracy, such as public speaking. I discuss this in the context of the extremely weak position of surrogates today.

In the second part, I further problematise Locke's view of private property by examining the way that his political (and legal) fiction of property in the person is associated with his characterisation of what it is to be an individual. I highlight the problems with Locke's conception of the individual by comparing his framework with that of his contemporary Benedictus de Spinoza, the central philosopher of the Radical Enlightenment (Israel 2001). I then illustrate how our interactions (with other people and with things in the world) are better understood by substituting Locke's framework with that of Spinoza. In particular, I firstly demonstrate how this substitution provides a more coherent and useful image of human beings than is provided by Locke's individualism; and secondly how we can envisage surrogacy more productively by employing Spinoza's ontology. I argue that Spinoza provides a conceptual framework that includes an analysis of selfhood, which has the properties that Namberger (2019) claimed are required for thinking about egg donation, and which I argue are also useful for conceptualising surrogacy.

1. Locke's justification of private property

1.1 Introducing the "acorn-loving man" in the state of nature

Locke says that we have a right to preserve our own lives in a state of nature, a state without a sovereign and laws. Christianity is central to Locke's arguments. For Locke, suicide is morally wrong because God *made us* and so the decision as to when we die should be up to him, as our maker (Locke 2003 [1689], chapter 2 § 6). The arguments that Locke makes in chapter 5 of the *Second Treatise*, "Of Property", draw on this view. It follows that we should not allow ourselves to starve to death while we wait for everyone to give us permission to eat what God provided for us in nature. This is the case even though Locke argues from the Bible that God gave the earth to all mankind in common. So, the question arises for Locke: how can private property be justified? He envisages an individual man in a state of nature picking up, boiling and eating acorns and then asks when the acorns become his private property. Locke poses this question as follows:

> He that is nourished by the acorns he picked up under an oak, or the apples he gathered from the trees in the wood, has certainly appropriated them to himself. Nobody can deny but the nourishment is his. I ask then, when did they begin to be his? when he digested? or when he ate? or when he boiled? or when he brought them home? or when he picked them up?
>
> *ibid., chapter 5 § 28*

Feminist staging post 1: work and the insides and outsides of human bodies

By asking, "when did they begin to be his? when he digested? or when he ate?", Locke contemplates, at least for a moment, the idea that something occurring within the body could be viewed as the point when the man in the state of nature starts to have private property rights over the acorns. While

I do not want to stretch this analogy, especially as surrogacy does not produce property rights *per se*, I want to use Locke's reference to the inside of the body to consider the strangeness, for some, of thinking about what happens within the body as producing any sort of rights.

Recall that, against feminists like Anderson who worry about the commodification of pregnancy, there are feminists who argue that surrogacy should be viewed as work. This is based on the argument that surrogates' pain and the risks to their health should be rewarded and that payment is therefore appropriate in our capitalist society. Indeed, it is unlikely that there would be sufficient surrogates to meet demand if they were not paid (see Pande 2014, 69). As I will discuss below in section 1.3, gestation is no longer simply associated with the marriage contract. It now takes place as part of an employment contract. At this first staging post, I only wish to address two issues. First, the point that a child is not the property of anyone in law and, second, the idea that surrogacy could not fit within our idea of work because it takes place within the body.

The first point is straightforward. What is at stake in surrogacy may appear to be about selling a newborn, but this is not what happens in law. What are acquired are the rights and obligations involved in raising the child (see, for example, Wilkinson 2004, chapter 8). Secondly, the idea that what happens within the body cannot be viewed as work—which in the context of my reading of Locke would mean that rights could not be acquired at the time when the man digests the acorn—is discussed by Lewis (2021). Lewis makes a striking claim with reference to Bini Adamczak's proposed term "circlusion" as the (active) antonym of penetration, designating the same process but from the opposite perspective. Circlusion, as Lewis explains, entails active "enfolding, sucking and—yes—*gestating*" (ibid., 81, emphasis in the original). Lewis comments:

> Failure to fully appreciate the ubiquitous reality of circlusion results in a thoroughgoing analytic femmephobia and means that, unlike the voice-boxes of call-center workers, the muscles of athletes, or the eyeballs of those on a smartphone-assembly line, it is assumed that the "inside of a woman's body" cannot work: it can only be defiled, exposed and ceded.
> *ibid., 81*

Lewis's analysis of the work that is carried out by a gestating cis woman or a pregnant trans or non-binary person aims to overturn the image of the pregnant body as merely a passive vessel. The idea of pregnant bodies as passive rather than working hard in ways that entail "sweat and blood" is an image that stems from ancient Greek patriarchs but is still promoted by popular pictures of foetuses from medical scans. For example, there are striking images of foetuses that are portrayed as if they are completely independent of the mother's uterus.[1]

While Lewis's argument against characterising pregnancy as passive is a good one, part of what is at play when people are horrified by the idea of viewing pregnancy and, indeed, caring as work is the teleological and misogynist notion that reproduction is natural and so should go unpaid. There are further examples of this attitude to women that can serve to illustrate my point. For example, in my paper on negligence claims in so-called "wrongful birth" cases (Richardson 2011), I trace this attitude among some members of the United Kingdom judiciary and certain commentators. Wrongful birth cases arise when doctors negligently perform sterilisation operations. Suppose a couple have sex assuming that contraception is not needed, and this results in the birth of a child.[2] Some judges and commentators, trying to avoid the defendant having to pay the usual damages for this negligence in the United Kingdom, have taken the attitude that having children is "what women are for"; that it is natural; and that they want it really.

Just as it may have initially surprised people to think of surrogacy, which takes place within the body, as work, a similar shock accompanied the Wages for Housework movement, which started in 1972 and exposed another refusal to see what has been classed as "women's work" as "real work" rather than as a natural resource. This refusal is also based on a division between the inside and outside, this time with regard to the home, stemming from the point at which industrialisation shifted some work to outside the home.

Part of women's struggles has been to get decent pay; to move away from being characterised as "dependent" on a male wage, with their own work going unacknowledged. As I will discuss further, in the context of Pateman's analysis, this concern is not simply about pay but about the ability to have a

1 For a critique of such "art books", see Stormer 2008; the topic is also discussed in Richardson 2023, 77–78.

2 Note that these "wrongful birth" legal cases differ substantially from "wrongful life" legal cases. The facts of wrongful life cases "usually involve a claim where a child has been born with a (severe) disability and, if not for the medical negligence (e.g. failure to diagnose a condition of the foetus) the parents would have had a choice of lawfully terminating the pregnancy". This argument has been rejected by the courts on the policy grounds that it would "devalue the worth of lives" and "discriminate against persons with disabilities" (Kyriakakis et al. 2019, 157). See, for example, the judgment of Kirby J. in Harriton v. Stephens (2006) HCA 15 [110].

voice in decisions that affect your everyday life. In this regard, it is useful to consider the way that there is a politics around the meaning of "dependency", given that men's dependency on "women's work" within the home is ignored (Fraser and Gordon 1994). Against this backdrop, Lewis situates surrogacy in the context of broader work when she employs the term "surrogate" to draw out stark issues of race and class (in ways that challenge the supposed naturalness of practices in relation to birth). In doing so, she undermines the distinction between the inside and the outside of both the home and the body. She says,

> "surrogate" more than "reproductive" or "feminized" might be a word that proves useful [...] in bringing together the millions of precarious workers and/or migrant workers labouring today as cleaners, nannies, butlers, assistants, cooks, and sexual assistants in First World homes, whose service is figured as dirtied by commerce, in contrast with the supposedly "free" or "natural" love-acts of an angelic white bourgeois femininity it in fact makes possible.
>
> *Lewis 2021, 56*

Prior to this staging post, I stopped at the point at which Locke was trying to decide when his man in a state of nature became the proud owner of the acorns. I paused my close reading of Locke to consider and reject arguments that surrogates could not be viewed as working because what they do is internal to the body, drawing from Lewis (ibid.). I will now return to Locke and see how he develops his influential story about the origins of private property.

1.2 Returning to Locke's story: work is viewed as creating private property

In the last section, I paused at the point in the text when Locke asks when private property arises in a state of nature. Locke then answers his own question: our acorn-loving man gains private property rights over the acorns when he picks them. It is his labour in doing so that gives rise to these rights. Locke says,

> It is plain, if the first gathering [of the acorns] made them not his, nothing else could. That labour put a distinction between them and common: that added something to them more than nature, the common mother of all, had done; and so they became his private right.
>
> *Locke 2003 [1689], chapter 5 § 28*

Locke's concept of "property in the person" has been subject to much critique (see for example Pateman 2002); this idea is sometimes referred to as "self-ownership" (Cohen 1995) or is said to give rise to "possessive individualism" (Macpherson 1962) in political thought, as will be discussed below at staging post 2 and then again at staging post 3 (when the servant appears). Locke says,

> Though the earth, and all inferior creatures, be common to all men, yet every man has a property in his own person: this nobody has any right to but himself. The labour of his body, and the work of his hands, we may say, are properly his. Whatsoever then he removes out of the state that nature hath provided, and left it in, he hath mixed his labour with, and joined to it something that is his own, and thereby makes it his property.
>
> *Locke 2003 [1689], chapter 5 § 27*

Here, Locke makes the clear link between gaining private property rights (which are rights to property against other people's claims) and "the labour of his body and the work of his hands" (ibid.).

Locke considers our relationship to others in his provisos concerning the use of private property. The duty to God to preserve others (provided it does not undermine our own survival) is dealt with by employing the provisos that, when we take something from nature, there is "enough, and as good, left in common for others" (ibid., chapter 5 § 27) and that we do not allow it to spoil or destroy it (ibid. § 31). As Crawford Brough Macpherson demonstrates, Locke then undermines these two provisos. Locke (ibid. § 41) argues that enclosing and working on the land adds value to it such that "several nations of the Americans" are "rich in land and poor in the comforts of life" compared with the English poor.[3] Regarding the second proviso, money does not spoil and so, for Locke, conversion of food to money eliminates the problems caused by this proviso of not allowing food to rot.

Feminist staging post 2: the work entailed in surrogacy

In order to think about the work of surrogacy in detail, I will draw on a similar analysis of egg donation made by Namberger (2019). Namberger's observations are made in the context of her analysis of the South African bioeconomy of egg donation, which is usually required for gestational surrogacy today. She provides examples of activities that constitute egg donors' work that I

3 For arguments that Locke's claims about land were employed to justify colonial exploitation and the British Enclosure Acts of 1750–1860, which were framed in the language of colonialism, see Murray 2022 and Griffin 2023 respectively. Commoners were deprived of their land rights, e.g. the rights to gather the wood or hunt animals (Thompson 1977).

will adapt to a consideration of surrogacy. Her analysis is useful in that she highlights activities that easily go unrecognised because they involve work that occurs inside the body, as discussed at the first staging post. Her examples include women's labour in oocyte cultivation *in vivo*, the injections that are required daily, along with other medical procedures, the monitoring of food intake to ensure it includes fresh fruit and vegetables and restrictions such as prohibitions on alcohol, drugs and sex. She includes the medical risks that come with the work as well as all the bureaucracy involved in applying for it. This list of the donors' work, which takes between two to four weeks, therefore shares some features with the more onerous work of surrogacy. Applying Namberger's approach, surrogates' work includes not only the pain and suffering of pregnancy and birth, but also everything that is done from the start of the process: the interactions with the intended parents and the emotional labour involved in surrogacy; all the medical procedures and associated risks, such as daily injections and monitoring; the constraints regarding eating well and avoiding alcohol and sex. If the work done to get the job in the first place is included, then it also involves the initial interviews and psychological evaluations.

I will focus further on one of these areas. Surrogates' work, like that of egg donors, involves emotional labour. It has taken time for feminist arguments that managing feelings in the workplace—a skill associated with women—should be recognised as work (see Hochschild 2023) to gain acceptance. As part of their work, surrogates employ social skills to deal with the intended parents, who may be supportive or anxious, along with agents who may seek to manipulate them. These interactions may vary internationally. For example, Pande (2014, 167) shows how the bargaining power of Indian surrogates can be undermined if they feel the need to reassure the intended parents that their motives are, at least in part, based on wanting to help infertile women. This may well be a source of satisfaction. However, as Pande comments, when discussing how the clinic uses the image of worker and mother as a disciplinary tool:

> The clinic employs the rhetoric of "good motherhood" to restrain surrogates as workers, and the rhetoric of "good workerhood" to contain them as "mothers". While a good worker is professional, a good mother is expected [...] not to be business minded, and to refrain from negotiating the wages involved.
>
> *ibid.*

This lies in stark contrast with the situation in Russia, where some surrogates were clear that they would not undergo such medical risk and the pain involved in surrogacy without payment. Siegl describes how "doing it business-style" is encouraged by the agents, who stand between the surrogate and intended parents, discouraging their interactions and positioning the intended parents, their paying clients, as vulnerable. Surrogates are encouraged to "align" their own feelings in order to control any maternal feelings about the foetus, as illustrated in detail by Siegl (2023, chapters 4 and 5).

Sometimes the birth seems to be handled so badly that it poses a risk to the surrogates' mental or physical health, which would be very different if surrogates had more power. This includes the overuse of caesarean sections. Another example is provided by Pande (2014, 183), who describes a case in which the intended parents left with the child while the surrogate was still unconscious after a difficult birth. The surrogate did not want to keep the child but felt, understandably, that she was not shown respect. When surrogacy is considered through the lens of employment, such a foreseeable risk to mental health could constitute the basis of a negligence claim against employers in some common law jurisdictions. Intended parents are highly motivated to keep in touch during the pregnancy. They may then feel pressure to leave with the child immediately after the birth, based on the—usually unjustified—worry that the surrogate may want to keep the child. However, some surrogates and intended parents are able to handle this well, so there are clearly better practices. Further, some surrogates and intended parents are able to maintain their relationship, sending letters and photographs on birthdays for example. As Lewis (2021, chapter 6) suggests, these relationships point to the possibility of creating new kinship relationships, a situation that becomes more likely if surrogates are able to increase their control over their working conditions. I will refer back to this point in the next section when I position the surrogacy contract as historically having elements of both employment and marriage contracts.

1.3 Returning to Locke: the sudden appearance of a servant

Locke makes an important addition to his argument when he introduces the figure of a servant into the state of nature in § 28:

> Thus the grass my horse has bit; the turfs my servant has cut; and the ore I have digged in any place, where I have a right to them in common with others; become my property, without the assignation or consent of any body. The labour that was mine, removing them out of that common state they were in, hath fixed my property in them.
>
> *Locke 2003 [1689], 112 § 28*

At this point, the individual is no longer alone but is envisaged as owning the labour power (the capacity to work) of a servant. This formulation is used to justify the master being treated as the owner of what his servant produces.

Feminist staging point 3: Carole Pateman on "property in the person" and contracts

Pateman (1988) analyses Locke's above-quoted argument from § 28 in ways that add a critical discussion to Macpherson's Marxist reading of Locke. While Pateman does not focus on Macpherson directly, citing him only once in *The Sexual Contract* (ibid., 81), I think that her important feminist intervention can best be understood by first explaining Macpherson's position. When considering Locke, Macpherson draws together two rather different contracts: Locke's story of the emergence of the social contract (which is a fictional contract imagined in political thought) and actual employment contracts. Employment contracts emerged with the transition from feudalism (in which an unequal status was expressed in law) to a capitalist mode of production. In capitalism, everyone was viewed as having the same legal rights, but workers no longer had access to the land and therefore needed to sell their ability to work for a wage in order to survive.

In Locke's story of the social contract, he envisages a move from the state of nature (i.e. a society without laws) to a state with a sovereign who enforces laws. It is understood to be fictional. Locke is telling his readers that society runs as if this social contract had occurred. The social contract is envisaged as an agreement by the people to *obey* the sovereign in exchange for the benefits of living in a society with laws. Macpherson compares this with actually existing employment contracts to demonstrate how they have a similar structure. Both entail the need for obedience in the historically weaker party. This arises through the fictional exchange of "property in the person".

It is worth considering the meaning of "property in the person" in detail. Macpherson discusses the image of a "possessive individual" who is envisaged as owning his or her ability to work as if it were a type of property that can be exchanged for a wage. In practice, this type of "property in the person" is not like eggs or other substances that can be removed from the body.

In Macpherson's Marxist analysis, workers are envisaged as agreeing to obey their employers, just as subjects are envisaged as obeying their sovereign through contractual exchange of the fictional "property in the person". What may appear as an equal contractual exchange of things creates and governs relations of subordination in modernity.

Pateman (ibid.) argues that, in their description of the transition from feudalism to capitalism, political theorists such as Macpherson were blind to another contract with the same structure: the marriage contract. This governed the relationship between husband and wife and was particularly oppressive during the time of the doctrine of coverture when married women, just like employees ("servants"), could not leave their place of work and were clearly treated as subordinate. Pateman describes the heyday of these oppressive marriage contracts as occurring between 1840 and the 1970s in the West (Pateman and Mills 2010, 113–114). However, there is still a hangover from women's historical position in marriage worldwide, as illustrated by economist Linda Scott's 2020 remarks about the "*Double X Economy*":

> The crux of the Double X Economy's plight is its burden of servitude; so called "obligations" at home penalize women in the workplace and increase their personal economic risk. Women in every country work as many total hours (or even more than) men, but because females carry the burden of unpaid household labour, they have fewer hours to devote to paid work, as well as to leisure time. Men can work longer hours—and garner the economic benefits—because women are serving them at home.
>
> *Scott 2020, 22*

In the case of surrogacy, women's obedience straddles two contracts. It arises through duties to obey in employment contracts and also historically in marriage contracts, under which women were expected to bear children. If surrogates achieved a radically greater voice, the implications of such a change could affect both areas of life, not only improving their terms and conditions but also radically changing how kinship is acted out and understood, as mentioned in the last section. Pateman's analysis of contracts highlights her further argument in favour of a radical shift to a participatory democracy. Importantly, she asks how we can have democracy in the *polis* when workers (in and out of the home) neither expect to have a voice in their everyday lives, nor gain the skills necessary for such a participatory democracy to function.

2. Feminist readings of Locke's individualism

In order to understand the relationship between surrogacy and subordination it is useful to consider Locke's image of the individual. I will first draw from Janet Coleman, whose analysis is important in that it brings together two areas of Locke's thought that are usually kept separate in scholarship: the *Second Treatise of Government* (Locke 2003 [1689]), already discussed in part one, and *An Essay concerning Human Understanding* (Locke 1997 [1689]).[4] After explaining Coleman's analysis below, I turn to Spinoza to demonstrate how his ontology is more compelling than Locke's as a way of understanding ourselves. I also argue that Spinoza offers more resources for conceptualising surrogacy, in that his framework fulfils Namberger's theoretical requirements for understanding egg donation, which, I further argue, can be extended to our understanding of surrogacy.

To explain Coleman's historically informed analyses of Locke's concept of the individual, it is useful to start with a quotation and then unpack what is at stake in relation to surrogacy:

> Today there is a tendency to identify the self with the body more directly than it ever could be so conceived in pre-modern discourse. But what Locke seems to mean by self-ownership, property in one's own person, always entails obligations beyond that self, and one's own person is equated with the obligation to maintain one's very life and thereby one's identity in time. Locke made this much clearer in his *Essay Concerning Human Understanding* where he expressed the view that while everything each of us thinks has its origin outside us, when things are grasped or mentally appropriated or laboured on by each individual, they become, through reflection, our own inalienable and subjective thoughts.
>
> *Coleman 2005, 135*

Coleman describes how Locke's analysis of property in the person in the *Second Treatise* has its *counterpart* in his *An Essay concerning Human Understanding* ("*Essay*"). In the *Essay*, Locke describes how we work upon other people's ideas to make them our own, in a way that is comparable to the process by which we make acorns our own property by working on them—specifically,

4 For my outline of Coleman's position on conceptions of the self in Locke and Spinoza and how it relates to Étienne Balibar's "Lockean Concepts: A Philosophical and Philological Glossary" (Balibar 2013), see Richardson 2020, 155–156. I draw on some of my earlier arguments regarding Coleman in this section in order to apply my analysis of selfhood in Locke and Spinoza to the question of surrogacy. To the best of my knowledge, Coleman and Balibar do not discuss each other's work. Coleman's research is on ancient and medieval political philosophy while Balibar's is situated within Marxism and continental philosophy.

by picking them. So Locke envisages a mental appropriation of others' ideas (envisaged as outside our selves) just as he describes a physical appropriation of acorns in the *Second Treatise*. As a result of these appropriations, we fulfil our duty to God to stay alive. This was already explained in part one with regard to the appropriation of food. Coleman detects a comparable duty to God to continue to live mentally, i.e. to maintain the same identity as a person over time. In a more complex move, there is an additional stage involved in continuing to live mentally, aside from the appropriation of others' ideas. Coleman says,

> In asserting in the *Second Treatise* that man already has a property in his own person to which nobody has any right but himself, Locke seems to be arguing that to remain a person into the future, to stay alive and be a person in one's own eyes, self-consciously, *in foro interno*, one is obliged through the activity of appropriation, *mental and physical*, to extend one's own independent personality into the world in present and future time and then bring it back in, as it were, through consciousness "owning" its own acts.
>
> *ibid., 136*

Locke's individuals carry out two comparable tasks, both of which he believes can be viewed as work: (a) they think about (i.e. work upon and thereby appropriate) others' ideas that are external to them as individuals; and (b) they act upon the external world, for example by appropriating acorns that they then also "own", as discussed in part one. In the above passage, Coleman highlights an additional Lockean claim concerning identity: by reflecting on both (a) and (b) Locke's individuals are able to remember their *own* development through "consciousness 'owning' its *own* acts" (ibid.). This memory (of their work appropriating ideas and acorns) allows individuals to secure their identity over time.

As Coleman (ibid.) explains, there is a second reason why individuals' ability to secure their identity over time is important to Locke, aside from the fact that it is linked to our duty to God to survive mentally as well as physically. For Locke, as a Christian, it was also important to understand how we maintain our identity over time because this continuity of identity is relevant to what happens to us come Judgement Day. It is relevant to whether we are to be saved or damned that we are responsible for *our own thoughts and* actions. Locke illustrates this argument by envisaging the Day Man and the Night Man, long before Robert Louis Stevenson's (2006 [1886]) *The Strange Case of Dr Jekyll and Mr Hyde*. Locke (1997 [1689]) imagined two consciousnesses within the same body. One consciousness, referred to as "the Day Man", is good and the other, "the Night Man", is bad. If the Day Man is unable to reflect upon and remember his thoughts and actions during the time his body was taken over by the Night Man, then he would not be responsible for these acts on Judgement Day. This is because it is the *memory* of our appropriation of things (such as food) and of others' ideas that gives us our continued identity and "ownership" of our actions over time. The Night Man's appropriations of acorns or his darker deeds and thoughts are therefore not part of the Day Man's identity.

Locke's ideas on internalising food and ideas as part of self-ownership are far more individualistic than earlier images of selfhood, as Coleman (2005) demonstrates. This individualism is problematic when it comes to conceptualising struggles over surrogacy contracts and their terms and conditions (see, for example, Siegl 2023, chapters 5 and 6). I would also add that Locke's emphasis on the individual depends upon a clear divide between inside and outside that is inconsistent with trying to think of pregnancy, where a body is gradually becoming two bodies. This problem is discussed in different contexts by Christine Battersby (1998). In the next section, I will explain why I find Spinoza's conception of selfhood more compelling as a way of thinking about surrogacy and how it satisfies Namberger's (2019) ideas of what is required conceptually to think about surrogacy.

2.1 Spinoza contra Locke

Drawing from Spinoza's *Ethics* (1985 [1677]),[5] I will now return to Locke's acorn-loving man, discussed in part one, to explain what is happening from a Spinozist perspective. Spinoza would term my picking and eating acorns a "joyful encounter", i.e. an interaction with the acorn that improves my powers of acting because nutritious food improves my ability to thrive and survive—in contrast to, say, a snake bite, which decreases my powers of acting and is associated with sadness. In the same way, my encounters with ideas that provide me with an adequate understanding of the world produce

5 Passages from Spinoza's (1985b) Ethics (E) will be referred to by means of the following standard abbreviations: initial numerals stand for part/book numbers, "a" for "axiom", "c" for "corollary", "p" for "proposition", "s" for "scholium", "lem" for "lemma", "pref" for "preface" and "app" for "appendix"; "d" stands for either "definition" (when it appears immediately to the right of the part of the book) or "demonstration" (in all other cases), "da" for "definition of the affects". Hence, "E 1d7" is the seventh definition of part 1 and "E 1p16d" is the demonstration of proposition 16 of part 1.

joy because they increase my powers of acting. Learning that acorns should be boiled before eating them and how to avoid snakes are examples. Note that to understand any interaction gives us joy in itself. This is in addition to the fact that we are then able to be more active (rather than merely passive) when it comes to selecting food and avoiding snakes.

For Spinoza, the more that we (including surrogates) learn about the world, the more active we can be. He describes this as increasing our "powers of acting". This is central to his *Ethics*. Given that, as individuals, we have little power compared with the whole of nature, we need to combine with others to increase our powers of acting. While other people are important in this regard (*E* 4p18s), we can combine to form "singular things" with anything at all.

Compare this conceptual framework with Locke's conception of the individual, as discussed above. Locke's image is of a separate individual, whom he envisages as collecting and working on others' ideas (which are external to that individual) to make these ideas their own. The individual's thought is envisaged as split off from others, just as Locke's acorn-loving man initially picks acorns in solitude. When Spinoza envisages such activities, he characterises us as what Étienne Balibar (1997) later termed "trans-individuals". For Spinoza, as trans-individuals, we think in concert with others. When doing so, we can be envisaged as forming a greater entity (or "singular thing") rather than as acting purely as an individual human being (*E* 2d7). Similarly, Spinoza describes bodies as comprised of parts that act together as a singular thing to have an effect on the world. For example, we combine to become a "singular thing" and have an effect on the world when we pull on a rope together to move a stone. In this example, the rope would be included as part of the singular thing. Similarly, we can also *think together* to address a problem such as exploitation or subordination (associated with a failure to have a voice in our everyday lives). We thrive when we are more able to form "singular things" in combination with others because we gain their strength and insights at the same time as they gain ours. Spinoza's *Ethics* is in part an analysis of what undermines our attempts to combine in this way and how to overcome these problems.

What is at stake is not the Lockean duty to God to survive and to maintain our identity over time through the memory of our *appropriation* of ideas and things through work. Instead, for Spinoza, the same acts and thoughts go beyond simply maintaining ourselves. As human beings, we thrive by increasing our understanding. Importantly, we do this best by thinking together, and so anything that undermines our ability to do so is a serious problem and, for Spinoza, unethical. Some ideas systematically impair the ability of any society, organisation or group (i.e. any nested singular thing of which we are a part) to survive and thrive. Spinoza uses the example of superstitious beliefs that weaken the ability of both individuals and societies. Superstitions prompt us to think that everything can be explained by God's will. This systematically undermines us because such ideas appear to answer all our questions so that no further enquiry is necessary, blocking curiosity and scientific analysis. For example, if snakes are evil and created by God for some ineffable reason, then there is no need to enquire further about how their venom interacts with our bodies.

Given the central importance of our ability to think in concert to improve our lives, I have argued elsewhere from a Spinozist position that systematic subordination of any group of people within a culture also systematically weakens its ability to thrive (Richardson 2023, 65–66). To put it bluntly, I may have fun oppressing people, as a tyrant, yet still die of a disease that could have been prevented by the insights of those who are subordinated, had they received a better education and access to a laboratory and been listened to with respect rather than belittled or ignored.

How does Spinoza's *Ethics* make a difference to the way that we think about commercial surrogacy? Drawing from Locke, surrogates can be viewed as workers. However, Locke's further move, which Pateman has attacked, is the fiction of property in the person as a commodity, which, she argues, forms the basis of relationships based upon subordination. In the workplace, including the surrogacy hostel, this entails being told what to do rather than having a say in your everyday life. The fact that this applies to most workers does not mean these arguments should not be raised in the context of surrogacy for a couple of reasons. First, surrogates have sometimes lacked established rights, such as the need for a safe system of work that considers concerns about mental as well as physical harm.[6] While workplace injuries may not be new, the ways in which they occur (for example, the risks involved

6 Siegl (chapter 7) highlights references to surrogates' individual free will to agree to their workplace conditions. These are exactly the same arguments that were employed in the 19th-century English courts to prevent workers from claiming against employers for negligence. See Smith v. Baker (1891) AC 325, in which the British House of Lords finally recognised that workers were pressured by poverty to work in dangerous conditions, rejecting the existing defence of "voluntary assumption of risk".

in giving birth, which can be mental and physical) are new in the context of work. Additionally, and unique to surrogacy, there would be radical implications for the development of new kinship ties if surrogates were able to better control their working conditions, as explored by Lewis (2021) and discussed in part one.

By contrast with Locke, Spinoza did not employ the idea of property in the person and so did not consider our bodies as anything other than "ourselves", expressed through the "attribute of extension" (bodies) compared with "the attribute of thought" (minds). This means that the alienation that is involved in thinking of our bodies' abilities as if they were commodities that we own is better conceptualised in Spinoza's framework. To view one's abilities as a commodity and to feel alienated from one's body as a result would constitute what Spinoza terms an "inadequate idea": a mistaken view that is associated with sad passions. The emotion associated with this idea is important, as it is a warning sign that something is wrong, that our powers of acting are being undermined. Such situations can be rectified, in this case through political thought and action, when we understand their causes.

From a Spinozist perspective, all the physical interactions outlined earlier that form part of surrogacy can increase or decrease commercial surrogates' powers of acting. At the same time, surrogates' experiences are expressed mentally through ideas as well as physically through the body. This involves drawing on earlier knowledge, cultural ideas about pregnancy and surrogacy and other ideas and images that the surrogates create together. Whereas Locke describes picking acorns in terms of "work", Spinoza does not use the term "work" when he describes our encounters with food or ideas. His conceptual framework of trans-individuals has no split between work outside and inside the body. Like all parts of nature, everyone, including surrogates, tries to increase their powers of acting. They do so not as powerless individuals, but by combining with others to share both knowledge and bodily action.

As discussed earlier, Namberger reflects on the ontology she considers useful for framing the problems that she raises regarding the position of egg donors. She calls for a theoretical position that satisfies a number of criteria. Firstly, it should undermine the idea of a Cartesian mind/body split and the view of the mind as superior to the body (Namberger 2019, 105). Secondly, it should allow us to conceptualise our ability to join with others, not simply human beings but also both animals and technological entities. Finally, she describes the "core" of her book as dealing with "the question of how to think the 'working body' in the context of egg donation without reverting to the body as an organic whole infused with vitality" (ibid., 88).

Spinoza's ontology satisfies all of these criteria. In particular, Spinoza argues against (his contemporary) Descartes's conception of a mind/body split and provides an alternative conceptual framework in which a human being is fully expressed by both mind and body. As discussed, Spinoza also envisages us as joining with anything (e.g. human, animal or technological) that can increase our powers of acting to form a singular thing (*E* 2d7) at the time at which they are acting in concert. Spinoza provides a better way of conceptualising both pregnancy, which it does not make sense to think of in terms of an individual that is cut off from others, and human relationships themselves. This allows us to consider what can facilitate surrogates to join together to increase their powers of acting.

3. Conclusion

In the absence of a radical change in society, the romanticism about anything associated with women's bodies characterises motherhood and care work as priceless in a way that perpetuates their being treated, in reality, as worthless. This is demeaning to those who want or need to derive greater financial security from these forms of work and is associated with a misogynist teleology according to which sex and pregnancy are "what women are for". Pateman's political critique of all work contracts and the way that they undermine the possibility of a participatory democracy may seem far removed from the concerns of those engaged in a struggle over basic medical care and safety. However, it should not be forgotten in daily struggles over control of workplace activities.

While Locke's argument that work creates private property rights can be used to support a claim that surrogates should be paid for their efforts because it is work, there are problems with employing his conceptual framework. In the first section, I examined Locke's influential argument that private property arises through work, and that this originally needed to occur in a state of nature (i.e. a state without laws) based on our duty to God not to starve while we gained the consent from others to gather food. At the first staging post, I drew on Lewis's (2021) argument against the difficulties of imagining a woman's uterus as capable of "work". I compared this with judges' attitudes in so-called "wrongful birth" cases and the earlier shock elicited by the Wages for Housework movement. At the second staging post, I adapted Namberger's (2019) analysis of what constitutes the work of egg donors in order to consider surrogates' work. This work includes managing emotions, such as the way that surrogates themselves are encouraged to try to manage their own emotions as well as those of others, and the potentially demeaning treatment by clinics and fraught relations with intended parents (Pande 2014, chapter 7; Siegl 2023, chapter 4).

Finally, I turned to Pateman's analysis of how, in modernity, subordination is managed through contracts (historically, that included marriage contracts as well as employment contracts). Comparing these contracts with Locke's social contract allows us to recognise that surrogacy now spans two different historical contracts in which women have been and often still are subordinate, both as workers and as women. Pateman's aim of creating a participatory democracy opens up the radical possibilities of changes to kinship if surrogates gain a greater say in their lives, including control over the surrogacy process itself.

In the second part, I critiqued Locke's image of the individual. Drawing on Coleman's analysis, which situates Locke's ideas within the history of political thought, I explained why Locke's image of the individual is not useful for thinking about the position of surrogates. Finally, I drew out what is problematic in his individualism by illustrating how his contemporary Spinoza produced an entirely different ontology. I explained how Spinoza's ontology fulfils the criteria that Namberger (2019) views as necessary for conceptualising the process of egg donation and that I argue are also necessary for thinking about surrogacy itself.

Works Cited

Anderson, Elizabeth (1990). The Ethical Limitations of the Market. *Economics and Philosophy*, 6(2), 179.

Balibar, Étienne (1997). *Spinoza: From Individuality to Transindividuality*. Delft: Eburon.

Balibar, Étienne (2013). Lockean Concepts: A Philosophical and Philological Glossary. In Stella Sandford (ed.). *Identity and Difference: John Locke and the Invention of Consciousness*, 71–124. London: Verso.

Battersby, Christine (1998). *The Phenomenal Woman: Feminist Metaphysics and the Patterns of Identity*. London: Routledge.

Cohen, Gerald Allan (1995). *Self-Ownership, Freedom, and Equality*. Cambridge: Cambridge University Press.

Coleman, Janet (2005). Pre-Modern Property and Self-Ownership before and after Locke: Or, When Did Common Decency Become a Private Rather than a Public Virtue? *European Journal of Political Theory*, 4(2), 125–145.

Fraser, Nancy, and Linda Gordon (1994). A Genealogy of Dependency: Tracing a Keyword of the U.S. Welfare State. *Signs: Journal of Women in Culture and Society*, 19(2), 309–336.

Griffin, Carl J. (2023). Enclosure as Internal Colonisation: The Subaltern Commoner, Terra Nullius and the Settling of England's "Wastes". *Transactions of the Royal Historical Society*, 1 (December), 95–120.

Hochschild, Arlie Russell (2023). The Managed Heart. In Amy Wharton (ed.). *Working in America*, 5th ed., 40–48. London: Routledge.

Israel, Jonathan Irvine (2001). *Radical Enlightenment: Philosophy and the Making of Modernity, 1650–1750*. Oxford: Oxford University Press.

Kyriakakis, Joanna, Tina Popa, Francine Rochford, Natalia Szablewska, Xiaobo Zhao, Jason Taliadoros, Darren O'Donovan and Lowell Bautista (2019). *Contemporary Australian Tort Law*. Cambridge: Cambridge University Press.

Lewis, Sophie (2021). *Full Surrogacy Now: Feminism against Family*. London: Verso Books.

Locke, John (1997 [1689]). *An Essay concerning Human Understanding*, edited by R. S. Woolhouse. Harmondsworth: Penguin.

Locke, John (2003 [1689]). Second Treatise. In *Two Treatises of Government: And a Letter concerning Toleration*, edited by Ian Shapiro, 100–209. New Haven, CN: Yale University Press.

Macpherson, Crawford Brough (1962). *The Political Theory of Possessive Individualism: Hobbes to Locke*. Oxford: Clarendon.

Murray, Calum (2010). John Locke's Theory of Property, and the Dispossession of Indigenous Peoples in the Settler-Colony. *American Indian Law Journal*, 10(1), 1–12.

Namberger, Verena (2019). *The Reproductive Body at Work: The South African Bioeconomy of Egg Donation*. Abingdon: Routledge.

Nozick, Robert (1974). *Anarchy, State and Utopia*. New York: Basic Books.

Pande, Amrita (2014). *Wombs in Labor: Transnational Commercial Surrogacy in India*. New York: Columbia University Press.

Pateman, Carole (1988). *The Sexual Contract*. Cambridge: Polity.

Pateman, Carole (2002). Self-Ownership and Property in the Person: Democratization and a Tale of Two Concepts. *Journal of Political Philosophy*, 10(1), 20–53.

Pateman, Carole, and Charles W. Mills (2007). *Contract and Domination*. Cambridge: Polity.

Pateman, Carole, and Charles W. Mills (2010). Contract Theory and Global Change: The Intersections of Gender, Race and Class. In Anna G. Jónasdóttir, Valerie Bryson and Kathleen B. Jones (eds.). *Sexuality, Gender and Power: Intersectional and Transnational Perspectives*, 113–126. London: Routledge.

Richardson, Janice (2011). The Concept of Harm in Actions for Wrongful Birth: Nature and Pre-Modern Views of Women. *Australian Feminist Law Journal*, 35(1), 127–143.

Richardson, Janice (2020). Spinoza's Conception of Personal and Political Change: A Feminist Perspective. *Law and Critique*, 31(2), 145–162.

Richardson, Janice (2023). *Law, Selfhood and Feminist Philosophy: Monstrous Aberrations*. London: Routledge.

Scott, Linda (2020). *The Double X Economy: The Epic Potential of Empowering Women*. London: Faber & Faber.

Siegl, Veronika (2023). *Intimate Strangers: Commercial Surrogacy in Russia and Ukraine and the Making of Truth*. Ithaca, NY: Cornell University Press.

Spinoza, Benedictus de (1985 [1677]). *Ethics*. In *The Collected Works of Spinoza*, edited and translated by Edwin M. Curley, vol. 1, 408–617. Princeton: Princeton University Press.

Stevenson, Robert Louis (2006 [1886]). *The Strange Case of Dr Jekyll and Mr Hyde*. London: Penguin.

Stormer, Nathan (2008). Looking in Wonder: Prenatal Sublimity and the Commonplace "Life". *Signs: Journal of Women in Culture and Society*, 33(3), 647–673.

Thompson, Edward Palmer (1977). *Whigs and Hunters: The Origin of the Black Act*. Harmondsworth: Penguin.

Wilkinson, Stephen (2004). *Bodies for Sale: Ethics and Exploitation in the Human Body Trade*. London: Routledge.

Beyond the Lockean Paradigm: Property and Propertisation in the Reproductive Economy

Susanne Lettow

While critical analyses of the reproductive economy have made extensive use of the concepts of labour, value and accumulation and the production/reproduction distinction, discussions of property and propertisation are largely absent in this branch of scholarship. In contrast, concepts of property and (self-)ownership are widely deployed within bioethical debates. The question of whether and if so to what extent the human body, embryos or gametes can be regarded as property has been discussed in bioethics ever since the emergence of the reproductive economy in the late 1970s. Despite this focus on property, the property relations and processes of propertisation that shape this economy remain largely undertheorised. Moreover, the focus on property in the body actually seems to obscure the socioeconomic property relations that structure the reproductive economy and to contribute to the propertisation of bodily materials and reproductive practices. The latter occurs because the very notion of property in the body has helped to establish the idea that bodily materials and services can be sold and bought on markets—regardless of whether this is affirmed or problematised within bioethical arguments.[1] As Melinda Cooper and Catherine Waldby have succinctly put it, bioethics can be understood as "a crucial component of the normative and legal infrastructure regulating the political economy of the life sciences, even when [it] assumes a principal opposition to the body's commodification" (Cooper and Waldby 2014, 14).

1 In my book *Biophilosophien. Wissenschaft, Technologie und Geschlecht im philosophischen Diskurs der Gegenwart* (Lettow 2011), I argue that bioethics—despite political and ethical differences among bioethicists, and despite the fact that bioethical arguments in the German context usually make reference to Kant's concept of dignity rather than Locke's concept of property in the person—is marked by structural epistemological shortcomings. On the differences and overlaps between Kantian and Lockean approaches, see ibid., 71 ff.

However, given the virtual absence of theoretical reflections on the concept of property in critical research on the reproductive economy, I think that a critique of the specific conception of property in the body that circulates in bioethical discourse is a valuable starting point for developing a more complex understanding of property and propertisation in that economy. In this chapter, I therefore build on criticisms that have been formulated in feminist political theory, in particular by Rosalind Pollack Petchesky, Anne Phillips and Donna Dickenson. As these and other authors have stressed, the bioethical notion of property in the body draws on Locke's idea of property in the person in an anachronistic way. Through this transposition of Locke's idea into a present-day context that would have been technologically, economically, politically and ethically unthinkable for Locke, bioethics conceals the "startling rupture with tradition" that has occurred in biomedicine, in which "the living human material" is constituted as "marketable property" (Gehring 2006, 39). Accordingly, my focus in this chapter is not on Locke's own theory of property but rather on bioethical adaptations of that theory or of what Petchesky calls the "Lockean paradigm" (1995, 388).[2] Although I take Petchesky's, Phillips's and Dickenson's problematisations of the Lockean paradigm in bioethics as crucial starting points for my attempt to conceptualise property and propertisation in the reproductive economy, I think that two shortcomings of the Lockean paradigm need to be addressed in more detail in light of the current expansionist dynamic of the reproductive economy—a dynamic which is driven by technical innovations that allow for further fragmentation of reproductive processes, by increasing economic growth rates and by a constant reorganisation of global fertility chains according to territorialised technical, economic and political constraints and possibilities.[3] Firstly, the Lockean paradigm cannot account for the entanglement of different objects of property along global fertility

2 For a detailed discussion of Locke's theory of property, see Janice Richardson's chapter in this volume.

3 Sigrid Vertommen, Vincenzo Pavone and Michal Nahman have proposed using the concept of global fertility chains to develop an "integrative political economy framework" for understanding the reproductive bioeconomy. They understand global fertility chains as "a nexus of *intraconnected* practices, operations, and transactions among firms, states, and households through which a particular reproductive service (such as egg provision or surrogacy), commodity (such as a baby, stem cell line, regenerative drug, or therapy) or data are produced, distributed and consumed across the globe" (2022, 119–120). On the constant restructuring of the territorialised global reproductive economy, see also König and Jacobson 2023. On the impact of financialisation, see Kathrin Braun's and Irina Herb's chapters in this volume.

chains and the multiple—technological, economic, juridical, cultural and affective—dimensions that co-constitute these property objects and the interlinkages between them, because it focuses on single objects and the individuals who own them. Secondly, in order to analyse the current dynamics of the reproductive economy, it is crucial to conceptualise processes of propertisation, that is, the fact that in conjunction with the emergence of new property objects social relations "as a whole or partially are interpreted and institutionalised as property relations" (Siegrist 2006, 32).

I discuss these two shortcomings in more detail in the first part of the chapter. I then explore some theoretical alternatives that allow them to be addressed. In the second part, I discuss Dickenson's turn to the bundle theory of property.[4] I argue that this is a helpful move if the bundle theory is not understood in a narrow juridical way but rearticulated in praxeological terms. In this context, I draw on Benda-Beckmann et al.'s interpretation of the bundle theory as an analytical tool which, in my view, helps us to grasp the complex entanglements of property objects and subjects in global fertility chains. In this context, I also discuss the extent to which critical new materialist theories provide important insights by challenging the idea of the object as a single passive thing upon which human subjects exert their free will.[5]

In the third part, I then look at Hegel's theory of property, in particular his understanding of private property as a mode of social interaction that is embedded in a wider context of social relations or "ethical life" (*Sittlichkeit*). Referring once again to Dickenson, who turns to Hegel to overcome the overtly individualistic notion of property that prevails in bioethical discourse, I argue that Hegel's theory of ethical life, as formulated in the second part of the *Philosophy of Right*, provides a launching pad for a critical understanding of propertisation. Hegel's reflections on the ethicalisation of property in and through the family, civil society and the state can be read

4 According to the bundle theory, property consists in a bundle of rights or "sticks": for example, the right of use, the right of exclusion, the right of disposal, the right of alienation. This theory is opposed to the Blackstonian idea that property consists in the right of full disposal over an object. The bundle theory was initially formulated in the early twentieth century by W. N. Hohfeld. It was further developed in the 1960s by Anthony M. Honoré, who distinguishes between eleven types of rights in the bundle. The bundle theory of property began to gain increasing attention and influence in United States jurisprudence in the 1960s (Stepanians 2005). Although it is widely regarded as a theoretical alternative to Blackstonian understandings of property, both approaches share certain central assumptions (see Olsen 2019, 19).

5 On critical perspectives within the heterogeneous field of new materialism, see Lettow 2017.

as a theoretical articulation of the modern order of property that is marked by the structural but contested division of these spheres.[6] With regard to notions of new enclosures and ongoing original accumulation that have been fruitfully adapted in critical scholarship on the bioeconomy, and the reproductive economy in particular, I argue that a perspective inspired by a critical rereading of Hegel's theory of ethical life helps to overcome reductionist understandings of processes of propertisation. In contrast to understandings of propertisation that articulate it merely as an "expansion" of the social forms of private property, commodity production or capital accumulation, I think that it is crucial to conceive of propertisation as a multidirectional process. This means that the ways in which the family as a social institution is constantly transformed and restabilised, as well as the ways in which the state and supranational political regulation shape the reproductive economy, need to be regarded as constitutive elements of processes of propertisation.[7] A critique of propertisation, it follows, thus cannot content itself with denouncing encroachments on the family sphere resulting from the logic of private property, commodification and capital accumulation, but rather needs to scrutinise the manner in which the whole modern property order, based on the nexus between family, civil society and state, is involved in and reshaped by the dynamic of the reproductive economy. Such a view, I argue, not only avoids overtly economistic notions of propertisation but also challenges the conservatism that comes along with criticisms of propertisation, commodification or new enclosures that romanticise the family sphere that these processes encroach upon, portraying it as a static domain or *terra nullius*.

I conclude that conceptualising property and propertisation in ways that go beyond the Lockean paradigm is crucial for studying the dynamics of the contemporary reproductive economy. A property-based approach that is not embedded in the Lockean paradigm, I argue, can better analyse the formation, circulation and consumption of new bio-objects in the context of global

6 Nancy Fraser (2022) introduced the concept of boundary struggles to highlight that the structural division between the family or private household, the market economy characterised by commodity production and exchange (what Hegel calls "civil society") and the modern state is not fixed but contested. As a consequence, the boundaries shift over time. On the fragile character of Hegel's structural divisions, see also Hutchings 2017.

7 On the role of family law within the reproductive economy, see Susanne Schultz's chapter in this volume.

fertility chains as well as the intersectional relations of power and inequality that these processes are both shape and are shaped by.

1. The Lockean paradigm in bioethics and its critics

References to Locke's theory of property have been ubiquitous in bioethical debates about property in the body or bodily materials (such as genetic material or eggs) ever since the inception of bioethics in the second half of the twentieth century. In particular, Locke's idea that "every man has a property in his own person" (Locke 1988 [1689], *Second Treatise,* § 27) has been widely used either to defend or to problematise the commercialisation of the body. Tristam H. Engelhardt, for example, gives an argument that clearly affirms the notion that bodily materials are alienable goods that can be exchanged on markets, claiming that

> next to one's own body, the sperm, ova, zygotes, and fetuses one produces are most primordially one's own. They are the extension of and fruit of one's own body. They are one's own to dispose of until they take possession of themselves as conscious entities, until one gives them a special standing in a community, or until one transfers one's rights in them to another.
>
> *Engelhardt 1986, 219*

In his view, the commercial alienation of these materials is thus unproblematic and should be restricted only by an individual's autonomy.[8] In addition to Locke's notion of property in the person, Engelhardt also refers to Locke's labour theory of property. Locke argued that

> whatever he [the person who is regarded as having property in himself] removes out of the state that nature hath provided, and left it in, he hath mixed his labour with, and joined to it something that is his own, and thereby makes it his property.
>
> *Locke 1988 [1689], Second Treatise, § 27*

8 See also, for example, Andrews (1986) who likewise advocates a "property approach" to bodily materials. Her argument is that individual autonomy is only secured if property rights in the body are granted. She therefore makes clear that she is arguing for property rights in one's own body, and does not see the body as such as a property object—a position that would, she argues, amount to a justification of slavery. On the repercussions of slavery in the reproductive economy and analyses of biocapitalism, see Penelope Deutscher's chapter in this volume.

This argument is often invoked in bioethical discussions about who exactly should be regarded as the owner of materials that are derived from the body.[9]

However, these adaptations of Locke's theory of property—whether they advocate for or seek to restrict commercialisation—conflate seventeenth-century and present-day contexts, and reformulate some of his core ideas in ways that are not made explicit. Critical analyses have repeatedly shown that Locke is often used in bioethics in ways that significantly depart from his original ideas. As Phillips observes, Locke did not think of property in the person "as implying property in the body, and certainly not as conveying the absolute right to do what one wished with one's body and bodily parts" (Phillips 2011, 726). He conceived of the body as belonging to God, not as an object of arbitrary disposal. In a similar vein, Dickenson stresses that Locke was making an argument about moral agency, not about the physical body, when he spoke of property in the person, "since we do not labour to create our bodies" (Dickenson 2017, 11). It follows that "neo-liberals who claim a Lockean basis for the argument that we own our bodies unreservedly are misinterpreting proper Lockean liberalism rather badly" (ibid., 38). That is because the classical liberal understanding of autonomy or self-determination presupposes the integrity of the body, and does not envision its commodification.[10]

Although contemporary rearticulations of Locke's concept of property thus certainly need to be distinguished from Locke's own thought and scrutinised as intellectual constellations in their own right, they can also be understood as adaptations and rearticulations of what Erik J. Olsen calls the "classical liberal paradigm of private property" (Olsen 2022, 111). This paradigm emerged in the seventeenth and eighteenth centuries when

> thinkers like Grotius, Pufendorf, Locke, Hume and Blackstone [...] converged in their answers to the question of the true nature of property even though they came to these an-

9 See also the paradigmatic case *Moore v. Regents of the University of California*. In 1990, the Supreme Court of the United States ruled that John Moore did not have property rights in the cancer cells of his body, of which his physician had taken samples without his knowledge in order to develop a cell line that was later commercialised.

10 On this point, see also Gehring 2006 and Richardson's chapter in this volume. Neoliberalism as an economic doctrine was formulated in the twentieth century by members of the Chicago School and Friedrich August von Hayek in opposition to Keynesianism. It informed policies of privatisation and deregulation in many parts of the world from the late 1970s on. While neoliberalism as an economic doctrine and political project builds on the tradition of liberal political theory, and in particular on thinkers such as Locke, it is not identical with this tradition.

swers from different and sometimes fundamentally disparate political and philosophical standpoints.

Olsen 2022, 2

William Blackstone's theoretical rearticulation of property as "sole and despotic dominion which one man claims and exercises over the external things of the world, in total exclusion of the right of any other individual in the universe" (Blackstone 1753, cited in Olsen 2022, 114) was especially crucial for the formation of the liberal paradigm, which, as Olsen stresses, "has proven to be remarkably adaptable and durable" (2022, 20) over the centuries. This paradigm encompasses not only the property theories formulated in the context of social contract theory but also Kant's and Hegel's criticisms and modifications.[11] In the twentieth century, it was a central reference point for neoclassical, neoliberal and libertarian approaches, through which it made its way into bioethics.[12]

The Lockean paradigm in bioethics can be characterised by reference to the four axioms that Olsen regards as constitutive of the liberal paradigm broadly conceived, which

involve[s] a possessive relationship between a potential property owner and an object, an emphasis on material things, the association of true property with private property for individuals, and presumptively exclusive ownership.

Olsen 2019, 6

The bioethical notion of property in the body or in bodily materials conforms to all four axioms. Firstly, property is reduced to a relation between a subject and an object. Secondly, bodily materials are regarded as "things" that can be removed from the body, stored, circulated and worked upon. Thirdly and fourthly, these "things" are regarded as private property that is (almost) exclusively owned by individuals.

Feminist theorists have criticised these axioms in detail, in particular the focus on the subject/object distinction and on the ownership of material

11 Although Kant, in contrast to Locke, emphasised that the relation between a subject and an object of property is mediated through law, he "also joined with Locke and the other thinkers of the early modern project of creation [of property theory] in seeking to reduce property to exclusive, private ownership of external things" (Olsen 2022, 18). On Hegel's rearticulation of Locke's possessive individualism, see Lettow 2024.

12 On neoliberal and libertarian rearticulations of Locke's notion of property in the person in terms of self-ownership, see Pateman 2002. On the concept of self-ownership in bioethics, see Gehring 2006 and Lanphier 2021.

things. In her seminal essay "The Body as Property: A Feminist Re-Vision", Petchesky argues that interpretations of the idea of property in the person "in terms of a Lockean paradigm", according to which it "signifies radical individualism, instrumentalism, and a dualism between the body as commodity and the 'person' as transactor", tend to "reify the idea of property itself" (Petchesky 1995, 388). Such interpretations stick to a narrow, historically and culturally specific idea of property while ignoring both the variety of meanings of property in different societies, in particular noncapitalist ones, and the alternative meanings of property that have emerged in the context of emancipatory social movements.[13] According to Petchesky, feminists should abandon the Lockean paradigm and the restricted understanding of social life contained within it in order to develop a more politicised understanding of "self-propriety, bodily integrity and rights" (ibid., 394). This, she suggests, should be framed in the "language of social need and common ownership" (ibid.) of the communal resources that form the socioeconomic foundation for reproductive freedom.[14]

While Petchesky only touches in passing on the reproductive economy and its commercialisation of bodily materials, Phillips and Dickenson have addressed these issues explicitly in their critiques of the Lockean paradigm in bioethics.

According to Phillips, the "distinction [...] between owner and that which is owned: between 'me' and this 'thing' that is my body" (Phillips 2011, 728) is particularly misleading, because "we do not just 'have' our bodies. In an important sense, we 'are' them" (ibid., 729). Framing the body as a property object also obscures the ways in which bodies are disciplined within the reproductive economy, particularly in the surrogacy industry,[15] so that "thinking of one's body as distinct from oneself is a difficult accomplishment, and not easy to sustain" (ibid., 730).[16] The political-ethical conclusion that Phillips draws from this criticism is that markets in bodies or bodily ma-

13 Petchesky refers to the seventeenth-century Levellers and to the Black feminism of the nineteenth and twentieth centuries.

14 Similar arguments are made by reproductive justice theorists and activists. See Schultz's and Elizabeth Lanphier's chapters in this volume.

15 In her seminal study *Wombs in Labour: Transnational Commercial Surrogacy in India* (2014) Amrita Pande showed how surrogates' everyday routines were managed and disciplined by the clinics, for example through dietary regimes and restrictions on sexual activity, but also how the surrogates developed strategies to subvert these disciplinary regimes. See also Wichterich 2018.

16 Critical research on the reproductive economy has shown how processes of objectification operate on a variety of levels, from the disciplining of surrogates through to the technical and juridical

terials such as eggs should be rejected because they "depend on background inequalities", in particular socioeconomic inequalities between those who sell and those who buy bodily materials (ibid., 737). In contrast, more traditional labour markets, Phillips argues, at least partly rely on differences in skills and knowledge. In her view, they can be justified on this ground because skills and knowledge can be acquired and are—in principle—available to everyone. Phillips thus formulates a clear critique of the commercialisation of the body and calls for processes of marketisation to be curbed. However, she does not analyse the ongoing processes of propertisation, primary valorisation and accumulation that shape the global reproductive economy on an increasing scale.[17]

Dickenson, on the other hand, starts from the recognition that "human biomaterials extracted from the body enter into research and commerce as objects—not only in more commodified economies such as the USA but increasingly on a global level" (Dickenson 2017, 6). In light of this ongoing objectification of the body, she seeks to distinguish between problematic and non-problematic aspects of the notion of property in the body. In this context, she refers to the bundle theory of property and distinguishes different "sticks" of the bundle of rights "that we most need in order to protect ourselves from the enclosure of the body" (ibid., 13). Although Dickenson criticises "overtly simplistic liberal" (ibid., 12) arguments, she does not fully reject the notion of property in the body, but rather aims for a more nuanced understanding.

> Just as our ancestors merely demanded rights of use over the commons, rather than powers of complete alienation such as gift or sale, so too can we comfortably make do with a limited number of sticks from the bundle.
>
> *ibid., 13*

Rather than viewing the body as an object of property over which we have a Blackstonian "sole and despotic dominion", it makes more sense, Dickenson argues, to "disaggregate" property rights; those needed to confront the objectification of the body "will certainly include protection against unauthorized taking, but we might also want to debate rights of conditional gift, income and management over our tissue and gene sequences" (ibid., 13).

---

procedures of disentangling reproductive materials from the body. See Pande 2014 and Cooper and Waldby 2014.

17 I discuss normative critiques of commercialisation/marketisation with reference to Fraser's Polanyian understanding of marketisation in Lettow 2015.

Property, proponents of the bundle theory argue, cannot be reduced to a single subject–object relation, but comprises various rights, such as the rights to access, use, exclude others from and alienate a certain property object. Accordingly, Dickenson suggests reformulating the "no-property rule" according to which the body cannot be a legal object of property by distinguishing between different rights relating to the body. As a consequence, she can argue for the right to exclude others from using one's bodily materials and at the same time reject the right to alienate and sell one's own bodily materials. Her position is not opposed to the Lockean paradigm and the idea of property in the body but rather a refinement of it, and a proposal for how economies of bodily materials can be regulated. "Lockean liberalism", Dickenson contends, has "an important contribution to make to the philosophical and legal resources we need to defend ourselves from the 'new enclosures'" (ibid., 38).

However, Dickenson's understanding of Lockean liberalism is clearly anti-neoliberal, insofar as she opposes the commercialisation of the body. In theoretical respects, her positive reference to Locke is mediated through her adaptation of Hegel's theory of property.[18] Hegel is interesting for Dickenson because he introduces "a societally rather than individually centred model of property [...] that suggests *collective* mechanisms for governance of the new biotechnologies" (ibid., 49). Hegel's theory of property is inspired by an intersubjective turn, even if he starts his discussion of property by focusing on the relation between persons and things. His full argument for private property in the first part of the *Philosophy of Right* depends, as David James puts it, "on his account of the alienation of property" (James 2022, 101), and the notion of "a relation between two persons mediated by things" (ibid., 101–102). The practice of exchange and the legal form of the contract in which two property owners recognise each other as equals are key to this. However, Hegel does not content himself with this basic idea, but further develops his intersubjective theory of property in the second part of the *Philosophy of Right*, where he introduces the distinction between family, civil society and the state. According to Dickenson, for Hegel "contract is merely a necessary but preliminary stage among many, in terms of social relations and mutual recognition" (ibid., 51). In contrast to the individualism

18 Dickenson also refers to the Marxist feminist concept of reproductive labour in this context. On the role of reproductive labour and the conceptual challenges that arise from adapting this concept to analyse the reproductive economy, see Schultz's chapter in this volume.

of the Lockean paradigm, Dickenson's turn to Hegel is indeed helpful for developing a critical understanding of property and propertisation in the reproductive economy. So too is her use of the bundle theory, which likewise challenges the idea of property as a simple subject-object relation even if her approach remains bound to the idea of property in the body. In the next section I will therefore discuss her two moves in more detail and make some suggestions for how they can be further developed in ways that go beyond the Lockean paradigm.

2. Beyond the Lockean paradigm I: towards an analysis of multidimensional and entangled property objects

Although Dickenson's reference to the bundle theory of property remains within the confines of the liberal paradigm, I think that the bundle theory can provide important insights for understanding property and propertisation in the reproductive economy, because it helps us to differentiate between the various entangled property objects and dimensions of property that are at stake in practices such as egg donation or surrogacy and in the reproductive economy at large. However, in order to make critical use of the bundle theory, it is crucial to replace the narrow focus on rights with a broader perspective that also encompasses societal relations and practices and the objects entangled with them. Accordingly, Franz von Benda-Beckmann, Keebet von Benda-Beckmann and Melanie Wiber have translated the bundle theory into an "analytical framework" (Benda-Beckmann et al. 2006, 14) for studying social property arrangements across different societies and historical periods. They start from a social-anthropological understanding of property that highlights "the ways in which the relations between society's members with respect to valuables are given form and significance" (ibid., 14). On this ground, they distinguish between different dimensions or "layers" of property, namely "cultural ideas and ideologies, […] legal institutions and […] actual social relationships and social practices" (ibid., 15). This focus on the different "layers" of property—what in this volume we call "dimensions" of property—decentres the focus on the legal aspects of property, though these still remain crucial. Or to put it the other way round, in Benda-Beckmann et al.'s view property objects cannot be reduced to legal objects but are also shaped by social practices and cultural processes.

Nevertheless, Benda-Beckmann et al. refer to the bundle of rights in order to pluralise the ideas of both the property object and the property subject. The metaphor of the bundle, they claim, makes it possible "first, to characterize the specific rights bundled in one property object, and second to characterize the different kinds of property held by one social unit" (ibid., 15). Accordingly, the notion of a simple subject–object relation is replaced by an understanding of the property object being shaped by multiple relations and of the subject relating to multiple objects at the same time. This is an interesting move with regard to analysing the reproductive economy, because it means, firstly, that different legal rights and claims that are "bundled" in one object, such as an oocyte or embryo, can be analysed according to the ways in which they converge, conflict or are contested.[19] Secondly, different property rights and claims that co-constitute a "social unit" such as a fertility clinic or an egg bank can be addressed and analysed. In addition, if we take Benda-Beckmann et al.'s argument about the different "layers" of property objects seriously, we can see that the multiple relations between property objects and subjects that are at stake are not merely legal. In contrast to the bioethical discourse on property in the body and the idea of a sovereign subject that deliberately disposes over the body as object, this theoretical perspective thus accounts for the fact that the property objects that circulate within the global reproductive economy are multidimensional; that is, they simultaneously function as economic, legal, technological, cultural and affective objects. Accordingly, these objects—such as eggs, sperm, embryos, data, knowledge, equipment and technical infrastructures, clinics, agencies, egg banks and the enterprises and consortia to which they belong—must be regarded as existing in the plural and within specific constellations. It therefore seems more appropriate to speak of multidimensional property assemblages than of single property objects.

The notion of "assemblages" that has been widely used in research inspired by actor–network theory should, however, not be understood as flattening social hierarchies and differences but as a conceptual tool for exploring sociotechnical arrangements, their global entanglements and their situatedness within complex structures of multiple power and domination relations. Verena Namberger has taken the notion in this direction in her analysis of the South African fertility industry and the various forms of work that are required for this industry to function. Her key argument is "that

19 See Stefanie Graefe's and Sara Lafuente-Funes's chapters in this volume.

the global circulation of subjects, bodily tissue, technologies and expertise within the bioeconomy of egg donation rests on human labour in various, somewhat less obvious ways" (Namberger 2019, 219), including the work needed for the production of technical equipment and medical supplies, and that needed for the shipping and transport of reproductive materials. This argument also holds with regard to property relations, which, viewed through this lens, appear to be complex assemblages of overlapping legal, ideological and everyday understandings and relations of property, which connect things, apparatuses, ideas and actors. As Sigrid Vertommen, Vincenzo Pavone and Michal Nahman stress, such assemblages should not be understood in the sense of Bruno Latour's "symmetric anthropology" or in a way that ignores structural differences between the "agencies" of human and non-human actors and downplays relations of power and domination (Vertommen et al. 2022, 121). On the contrary, global fertility chains and the reproductive economy at large are obviously structured by multiple inequalities and a highly uneven distribution of power. Vertommen et al. therefore deploy commodity chain analysis to highlight the importance of analysing how property assemblages entangle multiple objects and subjects. In particular, they suggest analysing, firstly, the "structure of inputs and outputs which refers to the various 'nodes' involved in the production of a finished commodity" (ibid., 120); secondly, the uneven global geographies that this structure is both based on and reshapes; and, thirdly, the role of states and political regulation. This is certainly at odds with the focus on subject–object relations that prevails in the Lockean paradigm in bioethics.

By implication, the pluralisation of the "object" also complicates the notion of the property subject, which can no longer be conceived of as having full disposal over the things it owns. In contrast, agency in the global reproductive economy needs to be understood as "distributed" in several respects. First of all, in contrast to the rhetorics of choice, reproductive freedom and free will, the agency of all social actors that are involved in global fertility chains needs to be understood as situated and structured by specific economic and discursive constellations, including the bioethical discourse and the political-ethical discourse around altruism. Secondly, if the materiality of property objects is taken into account, agency is revealed to be distributed in another sense too. As Namberger puts it, bodily materials often "kic[k] back" (2019, 105). For example,

> despite high-tech equipment and advanced medicine, and regardless of how healthily donors try to live, there is no guarantee that they will produce viable oocytes. Nor is it predictable whether the fertilised oocytes will then grow into regular blastocysts in the lab, not to mention the chances that the insertion of one or two of them will eventually result in a pregnancy.
>
> *ibid.*

The whole reproductive economy builds on the fact that the generative capacities of bodies have their own momentum, so that, on the one hand, reproduction can be technically "assisted" but not controlled while, on the other, medical risk and unintended consequences can never be fully excluded.[20] Technological innovations such as cryopreservation, uterus transplantation or artificial uteruses are, to a large extent, driven by this structural problem: an "imperative of 'improvement' that has […] been refocused at the level of reproductive substance itself, now of course the object of a level of surveillance, management and handling that is unprecedented in human history" (Franklin 2014, 50).

In theoretical respects, actor–network theory and new materialism thus provide important insights into the materiality and agency of the "objects" of the reproductive economy. At the same time, many authors, including Namberger, have distanced themselves from vitalist approaches that conceive of bodily materials or embryos as productive or even labouring subjects, that is, as "actors" on an equal footing with human individuals or social actors, on the grounds that such approaches neglect structural differences between the activity of non-human materials and human modes of action and downplay differences and power relations within human societies.[21] In addition, feminist authors have repeatedly criticised the construction of the embryo as a person or autonomous subject—a construction particularly prominent within anti-abortion and pro-life discourses—because it ignores the specific relation between the embryo and the pregnant person and tends to downplay the rights of the latter. Accordingly, references to actor–network theory and new materialism only make sense if they are reconceptualised in terms of a critical praxeological materialism that takes the turn to materiality and the specific dynamics of the non-human world seriously without subscribing

20 On this point, see Braun's chapter in this volume.

21 For critiques of vitalist notions in critical research on the bioeconomy, see Schultz and Braun 2012, Birch 2017 and Lettow 2015.

to ontological, scientistic and posthumanist narratives.[22] This means that while it is helpful to acknowledge that social relations and human agency are always mediated through technological apparatuses and infrastructures, other living creatures and non-living materials, all of which assert their own dynamics and temporalities, there is no need to subscribe to the thesis that the "agency" of these entities cannot be ontologically distinguished from that of humans.

Largely in line with this criticism, Margaret Davies, explicitly suggests reconceptualising property in new materialist terms. According to Davies, the notion of owning or possessing is profoundly altered if human–non-human interrelations are taken into account. Rather than ownership being a matter of disposing over a thing—or an assemblage of things—she sees it as an interactive process that alters both the "human" and the "non-human" side of the process, both the "subjects" and the "objects". In the words of Patricia Williams, we could, for example, "say not that we own gold, but that a luminous golden spirit owns us" (Williams 1987, 433, cited in Davies 2016, 49). This means that the object is not a mere thing that is detached from its owner, but affects the owner in both material and phantasmatic ways. This, I think, is certainly true for bio-objects such as gametes and embryos that are laden with a wide range of personal and sociocultural expectations, beliefs and imaginings about life and death, kinship and family, the transmission of property, and property and social belonging in general.

With regard to the reproductive economy, this perspective is especially fruitful for understanding how the emergence of new property objects and object constellations in global fertility chains shapes and alters the materiality of bodies, sociotechnical infrastructures and modes of social interaction and subjectivities. With regard to the Lockean paradigm, this means that the property object can no longer be conceived of as a completely fungible thing over which a "sole and despotic dominion" (Blackstone 1753, cited in Olsen 2022, 4) can be exercised. On the contrary, both property objects and subjects are formed in and through sociomaterial relationships. "Reorienting

22 As I have argued elsewhere, new materialism is a heterogeneous field in which ontological and more or less praxeological positions coexist. I have also argued that the related problems of ontology, epistemology and anthropology—respectively: vitalism, scientism and posthumanism—have a much longer history and have already posed challenges for the tradition of historical materialism, which means that a critical materialism should draw on some positions of both kinds while rejecting others (Lettow 2017).

the justifications for property away from the self-owning individual towards the connections between humans, and between the human and non-human world," as Davies puts it, "results in an idea of property and an idea of the human subject that is never prior to these relationships" (2016, 53).

To sum up, understanding the bundle theory of property in terms of multiple practices and layers or dimensions of property subverts the subject–object distinction that is a constitutive feature of the liberal paradigm of property. In addition, such an understanding goes beyond the critique of the objectification of the body that has been formulated in critical approaches to the Lockean paradigm in bioethics, such as those of Petchesky, Phillips and Dickenson. Instead of problematising the reduction of the lived body to the status of a "mere" thing, a praxeological understanding of the bundle theory shifts our perspective towards critical analyses of how multiple material-semiotic objects are formed within the global reproductive economy, of how these objects are entangled or interlinked and of how they circulate in the context of multiple overlapping relations of power and inequality. As a result, the idea of a subject that freely disposes over objects as things is undermined and replaced by the notion of distributed and situated agency of multiple subjects that shape and are shaped by global fertility chains.

3. Beyond the Lockean paradigm II: towards a multidirectional understanding of propertisation

As Benda-Beckmann et al. highlight, "property relationships and property practices" are always "embedded" within a broader set of social relations (2006, 30). This means that "property ideologies, legal institutions and concretised property relations are all part of wider contexts that form the condition under which social interaction takes place" (ibid.). Indeed, the very concept of propertisation presupposes that not all social relations within a given society are property relations. According to Hannes Siegrist, a major theoretical advantage of the concept of propertisation is that it draws attention to "the interdependence between processes of propertisation and other basic processes of social, cultural, juridical, economic and political change" (Siegrist 2006, 38). This is crucial for critical analyses of the global reproductive economy, which is closely connected to changing relations of reproduction and family formation, technoscientific developments and transformations of the dominant regime of capitalist accumulation. Propertisation, it follows, can only be analysed and understood if the dynamics of non-propertised social relations are taken into account.

In a similar vein, Dickenson has argued that society "is not 'contract all the way down'" (Dickenson 2017, 51–52) by drawing on Hegel's critique of social contract theory in his *Philosophy of Right*. Hegel's critique starts from the "abstract" concept of property according to which, firstly, the right to private property is foundational for an individual being able to constitute themselves as a "person" and, secondly, this right presupposes a contractual form in which two individuals mutually recognise themselves as legal subjects. In the second part of the *Philosophy of Right*, Hegel then discusses how the "abstract" concept of private property becomes "actual" (*wirklich*) in the context of what he calls "ethical life" (*Sittlichkeit*), that is, the social totality that is structured by the divisions between the family, civil society and the state.[23] As Dickenson stresses, Hegel's theory of property is designed to overcome the liberal paradigm's individualist perspective, and explores the role of private property within the modern social order. However, she does not engage with his theoretical articulation of the nexus between family, civil society and the state despite highlighting the relevance of the state both in Hegel's theory and with regard to political regulation of the reproductive economy.

Hegel's theory of ethical life—that is, of the complex social structure in which property actually functions—provides crucial foundations for developing a multidirectional understanding of propertisation and overcoming the theoretical pitfalls of the metaphors of expansion or capitalist land grabs (*kapitalistische Landnahmen*) that are widely used in critical analyses of propertisation, commodification and ongoing original accumulation.[24] These metaphors portray propertisation as a one-dimensional process, and neglect the dynamic processes and transformations of the family (or modern systems of kinship and alliance) and the state that actively drive, contribute to and structure processes of propertisation. Hegel's theory of the family is, of course, dated and highly problematic with regard to gender, race and class, insofar as he presents a highly idealised picture of the bourgeois-patriarchal European mode of relatedness that he regards as superior to all other forms of kinship. However, his reflections on the family as part of

23 For a more detailed analysis of Hegel's political economy of the family and correlations between his articulations of kinship, race and reproduction, see Lettow 2021 and 2024.

24 For a detailed discussion of this branch of scholarship, see Schultz's chapter in this volume.

ethical life shed light on the constitutive role that the apparatus of family and state plays for the modern order of property. Hegel discusses the specific form of *familial* property and the importance of the supra-generational transmission of property through inheritance. In addition, he shows that the family plays a constitutive role for what he calls "civil society", that is, an economy that is shaped by division of labour and commodity production and in which private property is the dominant form of property.[25] The family, as Hegel makes clear, is a social arrangement on which civil society hinges, or a mode of subsistence that is simultaneously undermined by civil society and necessary for its functioning. The state, on the other hand, is a political structure that is geared towards stabilising the family–civil society nexus and mediating its contradictions. What is important here is that in Hegel's theory of ethical life, the family and the state cannot be viewed as being prior to the political economy of civil society, nor as mere "background conditions" on which the dynamics of this economy depend.[26] Rather, he regards them as co-constitutive.

Accordingly, social transformations of family and kinship relations, processes of political regulation and processes by which new property objects are formed in the context of the global reproductive economy must be seen as interrelated. Propertisation is thus not a form of what Jürgen Habermas once called the colonisation of the lifeworld, and certainly it does not spring solely from an internal logic of commodity production and private property. It is also driven and mediated by practices and dynamics in the domains of family and state. That means, for example, that processes which are geared towards stabilising the social apparatus of the family through the use of reproductive technologies and discourses around the sociocultural meaning of genetically related "children of one's own" need to be understood as part of processes of propertisation.[27] These processes are overdetermined by the precarious and contradictory political economy of the family that, despite wide-rang-

25 On Hegel's reception of political economy and his "economic" understanding of civil society, see Lettow 2024.

26 According to Fraser, Hegel's notion of ethical life designates "the socio-ethical substance" that brings forth and sustains human subjects and "in which they move" (Fraser 2022, 9). The activities that uphold this socio-ethical substance are what Fraser terms the "background conditions" of commodity production. On Fraser's analysis of disembedding and her concept of boundary struggles, see Braun's chapter in this volume. For a critical discussion of Fraser's critique of marketisation, see Lettow 2015.

27 On this point see also Schultz's chapter in this volume.

ing transformations that this social apparatus has undergone since the early nineteenth century, remains a central socioeconomic institution in modern societies. The same is true for processes that are geared towards a pluralisation of family forms through the use of reproductive technologies and the emancipatory demands of queer and trans people. A multidirectional understanding of propertisation reveals that the tensions between these (partly highly traditional, partly emancipatory) family-focused perspectives on the one hand and perspectives that focus on intersectional relations of power and exploitation in the capitalist, profit-oriented reproductive industry on the other are better understood in socio-theoretical rather than moral terms, with a focus on the structural significance of the family in modern society. Sophie Lewis, who argues that the family "functions as capitalism's base unit" (Lewis 2022, 6), correctly highlights that the social apparatus of the family is part of the modern order of property, that is, the nexus of family–civil society–state. Even if her idea that surrogacy can promote postcapitalist perspectives seems too optimistic,[28] her recognition that struggles over queering the structure of the family and over the form of the family itself contribute to processes of propertisation or the development of perspectives of de-propertisation that seek to overcome the proprietary form of the nuclear family is of crucial importance in the present context.

This has important political and ethical implications for the critique of propertisation in the context of the reproductive economy. A multidirectional understanding of propertisation avoids the conservatism that can accompany criticisms that address the expansionist dynamics of capitalist accumulation, private property and commodity production in an imperial language that construes the practices and social structures on which "expansion" works as passive, amorphous terrains and renders their specific dynamics, power relations and contestations invisible. This can make it seem as though previous social forms and arrangements through which procreation and reproduction have been organised are simply overridden by forces that are alien to these practices and structures, so that, as Susanne Schultz highlights in her critique of conservative anti-surrogacy positions, women are treated as mere victims.[29] This kind of critique neglects the fact that the procreation and generation of children has always been mediated

---

28 Again, see Schultz's chapter in this volume.

29 See Schultz's chapter in this volume, which refers in this context to groups such as Stop Surrogacy Now and the German section of Terre des Femmes. In the global context, the ban on surrogacy

through economic and political processes. A multidirectional understanding of propertisation, in contrast, centres the interlinkages between familial, sexual and reproductive relations, state or political regulation (for example, through population, health or employment policies) and the economic dynamics that operate in and beyond the reproductive economy.

At the same time, it is crucial to focus on the specific economic dynamics by which procreative and reproductive processes are integrated into processes of capitalist accumulation in the reproductive economy. A central aspect here is the constitution of new property objects such as sperm, eggs or cryopreserved embryos. Their transformation into discrete things that can be owned and that circulate in and through global fertility chains is frequently analysed in terms of extraction and resourcification. Sarah Franklin and Margaret Lock, for example, have said that the economic processes of the global fertility industry "are driven by a form of extraction that involves isolating and mobilizing the primary reproductive agency of specific body parts" (Franklin and Lock 2003, 8). I believe we can gain a deeper understanding of this process by referring to Christoph Görg's notion of primary valorisation as a multistage process. According to Görg, primary valorisation is a complex process "in which resources are first defined or construed, identified and extracted and finally integrated into the world market. At each of these stages, the subsumption to capitalist relations of production is associated with sometimes considerable conflicts" (Görg 2004, 1502). Although Görg mobilises Marx's notion of the "real subsumption" of practices and procedures under capitalist imperatives, his explanation of primary valorisation goes far beyond the one-dimensional metaphors of subsumption and capitalist land grabs. Instead, he focuses on the multiple processes through which materials or material capacities are transformed into resources prior to their formal integration into processes of capitalist accumulation and the world market. Görg's account coheres with the focus on the entanglement of multiple and multidimensional property objects that, as I explained in the previous section, is key to a critical analysis of global fertility chains. The notion of primary valorisation as a multistage process helps us to understand that the formation of new property objects that circulate within the capitalist economy involves redefinitions, extractions and transformations of materials and practices on different levels. With regard to the primary

issued by the Hindu nationalist Indian government in 2015 is a prominent example of a right-wing prohibitionism that seeks to protect traditional, heteronormative forms of family.

valorisation of reproductive capacities and materials, it reveals that this is not a "merely" economic process: that is, one confined solely to the sphere of the economy. Rather, processes of primary valorisation include cultural redefinitions of kinship and belonging, of reproductive capacities or the lack thereof, of the body and bodily integrity, and of labour; the introduction of new technological procedures; and of course legal and political redefinitions of what counts as a "true" property object.

The notion of primary valorisation as a multistage process thus draws attention to the role of the state and political regulation. Legal norms around the usage of reproductive technologies are certainly the most obvious ways in which states and supranational bodies, for example the European Union, shape the reproductive economy and establish frameworks for processes of propertisation. However, other policy fields, such as health or family policy, also impact on the concrete form that the reproductive economy takes in specific geopolitical contexts, and the same holds for science and innovation policy and industrial policy more generally. What this shows is that the political regulation of the reproductive economy is much more complex than the opposition between banning and legalising practices such as egg donation and surrogacy that often dominates the public discussion. Taking political regulation into account may become even more important in the near future, in light of a "global process of reconfiguration in the forms and modalities of state action [...] fraught with geopolitical tensions and accompanied by a profound crisis of liberal reason" (Alami and Dixon 2023, 73).

4. Conclusion

In this chapter, I have argued that the Lockean paradigm that prevails in bioethics and the related notion of property in the body are not well suited for analysing the property relations and processes of propertisation that shape the global reproductive economy. Based on criticisms raised by Petchesky, Phillips and Dickenson, I have further explored two of Dickenson's suggestions, namely the use of the bundle theory and the use of Hegel's critique of social contract theory. Both theoretical perspectives, I have argued, can and should be expanded beyond Dickenson's account in order to conceptualise property and propertisation in the reproductive economy in ways that move past the Lockean paradigm. In particular, this would allow us to conceptualise the entanglement of multiple property objects in global fertility chains, and the multidimensional character of these objects. I have also argued that the turn to Hegel's articulation of the modern order of property in his theory of ethical life is helpful for overcoming economistic understandings and conservative criticisms of propertisation. Analysing the global reproductive economy through the lens of property and propertisation, I conclude, can reveal a complex picture of the ways in which this economy develops on the basis of multiple relations of power and inequality. A precondition for this, however, is an understanding of property and propertisation that goes beyond the Lockean paradigm.

Works Cited

Alami, Ilias, and Adam D. Dixon (2023). Uneven and Combined State Capitalism. *Economy and Space*, 55(1), 72–99.

Andrews, Lori B. (1986). My Body, My Property. *Hastings Center Report*, 16(5), 28–38.

Benda-Beckmann, Franz von, Keebet von Benda-Beckmann and Melanie G. Wiber (2006). The Properties of Property. In Franz von Benda-Beckmann, Keebet von Benda-Beckmann and Melanie G. Wiber (eds.). *Changing Properties of Property*, 1–39. New York: Berghahn.

Birch, Kean (2017). The Problem of Bio-Concepts: Biopolitics, Bio-Economy and the Political Economy of Nothing. *Cultural Studies of Science Education*, 12(4), 915–927.

Cooper, Melinda, and Catherine Waldby (2014). *Clinical Labour: Tissue Donors and Research Subjects in the Global Bioeconomy*. Durham, NC: Duke University Press.

Davies, Margaret (2016). Material Subjects and Vital Objects—Prefiguring Property and Rights for an Entangled World. *Australian Journal of Human Rights*, 22(2), 37–60.

Dickenson, Donna (2014). Alternatives to a Corporate Commons: Biobanking, Genetics and Property in the Body. In Imogen Goold, Kate Greasely, Jonathan Herring and Loane Skene (eds.). *Persons, Parts and Property: How Should We Regulate Human Tissue in the 21st Century?*, 177–196. Oxford: Hart Publishing.

Dickenson, Donna (2017). *Property in the Body: Feminist Perspectives*. Cambridge: Cambridge University Press.

Engelhardt, Tristam H. (1986). *The Foundations of Bioethics*. New York: Oxford University Press.

Franklin, Sarah (2014). *Biological Relatives: IVF, Stem Cells, and the Future of Kinship*. Durham, NC: Duke University Press.

Franklin, Sarah, and Margaret Lock (2003). Animation and Cessation. In Sarah Franklin and Margaret Lock (eds.). *Remaking Life and Death: Toward an Anthropology of the Biosciences*, 3–22. Santa Fe: School of American Research Press.

Fraser, Nancy (2022). *Cannibal Capitalism: How Our System Is Devouring Democracy, Care, and the Planet—and What We Can Do about It*. London: Verso.

Gehring, Petra (2006). *Was ist Biomacht? Vom zweifelhaften Mehrwert des Lebens*. Frankfurt: Campus.

Görg, Christoph (2004). Inwertsetzung. In Wolfgang Fritz Haug (ed.). *Historisch-kritisches Wörterbuch des Marxismus*, vol. 6.2, 1501–1506. Hamburg: Argument.

Hutchings, Kimberly (2017). Living the Contradictions: Wives, Husbands and Children in Hegel's *Elements of the Philosophy of Right*. In David James (ed.). *Hegel's Elements of the Philosophy of Right*, 97–115. Cambridge: Cambridge University Press.

James, David (2022). *Property and Its Forms in Classical German Philosophy*. Cambridge: Cambridge University Press.

König, Annika, and Heather Jacobson (2023). Reprowebs: A Conceptual Approach to Elasticity in the Global Assisted Reproduction Industry. *BioSocieties*, 18(1), 174–196.

Lanphier, Elizabeth (2021). A Problem of Self-Ownership for Reproductive Justice. *Cambridge Quarterly of Healthcare Ethics*, 30, 312–327.

Lettow, Susanne (2011). *Biophilosophien: Wissenschaft, Technologie und Geschlecht im philosophischen Diskurs der Gegenwart*. Frankfurt: Campus.

Lettow, Susanne (2015). Biokapitalismus und Inwertsetzung der Körper: Perspektiven der Kritik. *PROKLA*, 1(45), 33–49.

Lettow, Susanne (2017). Turning the Turn: New Materialism, Historical Materialism and Critical Theory. *Thesis Eleven*, 140(1), 106–121.

Lettow, Susanne (2021). Re-Articulating Genealogy: Hegel on Kinship, Race and Reproduction. *Hegel Bulletin*, 42(2), 256–276.

Lettow, Susanne (2024). Hegel and the Political Economy of the Family: Property, Subsistence, Labor. *Graduate Faculty Philosophy Journal*, 44(1–2), 171–194.

Lewis, Sophie (2022). *Abolish the Family: A Manifesto for Care and Liberation*. London: Verso.

Locke, John (1988 [1689]). *Two Treatises on Government*. Cambridge: Cambridge University Press.

Namberger, Verena (2019). *The Reproductive Body at Work: The South Africa Bioeconomy of Egg Donation*. London: Routledge.

Olsen, Erik J. (2022). The Early Modern "Creation" of Property and Its Enduring Influence. *Journal of Political Theory*, 21(1), 111–133.

Pande, Amrita (2014). *Wombs in Labour: Transnational Commercial Surrogacy in India*. New York: Columbia University Press.

Pateman, Carol (2002). Self-Ownership and Property in the Person: Democratization and a Tale of Two Concepts. *Journal of Political Philosophy*, (10)1, 20–53.

Petchesky, Rosalind Pollack (1995). The Body as Property: A Feminist Re-Vision. In Faye Ginsburg and Rayna Rapp (eds.). *Conceiving the New World Order: The Global Politics of Reproduction*, 387–406. Berkeley: University of California Press.

Phillips, Anne (2011). It's My Body and I'll Do What I Like with It: Bodies as Objects and Property. *Political Theory*, 39(6), 724–748.

Richardson, Janice (2010). Feminism, Property in the Person and Concepts of Self. *British Journal of Politics and International Relations*, 12, 56–71.

Schultz, Susanne, and Kathrin Braun (2012). Der bioökonomische Zugriff auf Körpermaterialien: Eine politische Positionssuche am Beispiel der Forschung mit Eizellen. In Susanne Lettow (ed.). *Bioökonomie: Die Lebenswissenschaften und die Bewirtschaftung der Körper*, 61–84. Bielefeld: transcript.

Siegrist, Hannes (2006). Die Propertisierung von Gesellschaft und Kultur: Konstruktion und Institutionalisierung des Eigentums in der Moderne. *Comparativ*, 16(5–6), 9–52.

Stepanians, Markus (2005). Die angelsächsische Diskussion: Eigentum zwischen "Ding" und "Bündel". In Andreas Eckl and Bernd Ludwig (eds.). *Was ist Eigentum? Philosophische Positionen von Platon bis Habermas*, 232–245. Munich: C. H. Beck.

Vertommen, Sigrid, Vincenzo Pavone and Michal Nahman (2022). An Integrative Political Economy Approach to Understanding the Reproductive Bioeconomy. *Science, Technology and Human Values*, 47(1), 112–145.

Wichterich, Christa (2018). Zur transnationalen Rekonfiguration von (Re-)Produktion durch Leihmutterschaft: Biopolitiken, Reproduktionsindustrie und Subjektweisen. In Birgit Sauer and Katharina Pühl (eds.). *Kapitalismuskritische Gesellschaftsanalyse: Queer-feministische Positionen*, 93–113. Münster: Westfälisches Dampfboot.

Altruism and (De-)Propertisation: On the Moral Economy of Egg Donation[1]

Stefanie Graefe

In modern societies, there is consensus that human eggs cannot be sold in the same way as cars, toothbrushes or loaves of bread. Our basic intuition (which is also reflected in law: see Rebecca Rahe's chapter in this volume) is that the human body should not be treated as a thing that can be traded on markets and assigned a price according to the interplay of supply and demand. That intuition extends to the human gametes that are used in the context of assisted reproductive technology (ART). Sperm and eggs are highly sensitive materials closely bound up with notions of intimacy, family, gender, kinship and generational continuity, as well as the ideals of the "good life".

It is therefore significant that in ART contexts, the "stuff humans are made of" becomes something "[economically] valuable" (*wertvoll*) (Gehring 2006, 35) and the reproductive body a "commodity that can be bartered, sold or stolen in divisible and alienable parts" (Scheper-Hughes 2001, 1; cf. Kunow 2015). Technologically assisted reproduction is a globally expanding growth sector (Herb and Wenner 2023; van de Wiel 2020; Vertommen et al. 2022), whose profits are harvested by an increasingly complex array of private actors, including fertility clinics, gamete banks and agencies (König and Jacobson 2023; cf. Kathrin Braun's chapter in this volume). It is predicted that the ART sector will grow to a total global value of 45 billion United States dollars in 2025 (Aderaldo et al. 2023).

1 As will become clear over the course of this chapter, there are various reasons to be critical of the term "donation", and so strictly speaking it (and all related terms) should always be placed in quotation marks. However, both for the sake of readability and because I am concerned with the construct of altruistic donation as a social (and not a moral) phenomenon, I shall refrain from doing so here.

There is clearly considerable normative tension between the *de facto* marketisation of reproductive bodily substances and the widespread moral unease about commercialisation of bodies and bodily substances. Attempts have been made to defuse this tension through legal regulation. With regard to egg transfer,[2] which is the primary focus of this chapter, a central role is played by the normative-juridical construct of "altruistic donation". For instance, legislators in Spain, the leading European provider of egg transfers (see Degli Esposti and Pavone 2019; Hudson et al. 2020), and analysed in the empirical study on which this chapter is based, have defined the provision of eggs as a voluntary and altruistic act, in line with the relevant European Union directive (EU 2004). Accordingly, although donors can receive financial compensation for any costs and loss of income incurred as a result of the transfer, no other economic incentives for egg donation are permitted, in order to prevent it from assuming a "lucrative or commercial character" (Law 14/2006).[3]

When framed as reimbursement of expenses, payment for egg donation counts neither as the proceeds of a sale nor as a wage for (clinical) labour (Cooper and Waldby 2014). In Spain, egg donations are made anonymously, mainly in private clinics that are increasingly owned by multinational companies and/or ultra-rich individuals (cf. Herb's chapter in this volume). The current cap on donors' compensation is set at around 1,200 euros per egg retrieval, slightly above the minimum monthly wage (Tober et al. 2023, 252). Demand for eggs in Spain comes from both domestic and international sources, including Germany, where egg transfers remain prohibited.

Characterising egg transfer as altruistic donation, and thereby positioning it within a non-economic or "moral" sphere (Degli Esposti and Pavone 2019), accommodates the consensus that bodies and bodily substances are not things that can be owned. However, this "moralisation" appears to have no categorical limiting effect on the expansion of the reproductive econ-

2 Sara Lafuente-Funes has drawn attention to the fact that it is not just eggs that are transferred in the egg transfer process but also "reproductive capacity", which she characterises as a "concept that facilitates our understanding of the socio-technical practices in which eggs are currently entangled, signified, and made sense of" (Lafuente-Funes 2020, 207; cf. also her chapter in this volume).

3 https://www.boe.es/eli/es/l/2006/05/26/14/con.

omy.[4] In light of this, I am interested here[5] in how the *economisation*[6] of bodily substances and reproductive medical infrastructure in the context of the global ART economy relates, both conceptually and in everyday practice, to the *moralisation* of gamete provision as "altruistic donation". I focus on relevant findings from a qualitative empirical study conducted as part of the Collaborative Research Centre "Structural Change of Property".[7] For the study, people involved in the egg transfer process (donors, recipients, professionals) in Spain and Germany were interviewed about their experiences with, and views on, egg transfer.

In light of this volume's focus, our empirical findings are particularly relevant insofar as they reveal practices of "doing"[8] or "undoing" property: that is, ways of (not) thematising or (de)problematising property relations. As we shall see in the main part of the chapter, there were certain characteristic differences between the various interviewee groups' interpretive schemas. At the same time, one general overarching finding was that none of them spontaneously discussed egg transfer in terms of property. In fact, our interviewees often explicitly deproblematised the aspect of propertisation. Since the construct of altruistic donation, by contrast, played a central role in the interviewees' narratives, I argue that it should be understood as an important driver of the economisation, and hence also the propertisation, of bodily substances and infrastructures in ART contexts.

The chapter begins with some theoretical reflections on the relation between property, economisation and donations of (reproductive) bodily substances (1). Building on these reflections, I then present relevant empirical

---

4 See on this topic also Tober and Pavone 2018. They compare Spain (as a more strictly regulated egg donation market) and the United States (as a more liberalised one) and find that in both countries, despite considerable differences in donor selection, marketing channels and the level of "compensation" paid, a discursive framing of egg transfer as "altruistic" is combined with a steadily growing egg donation market that is essentially based on exploiting the reproductive "labour" of precarised young women.

5 This chapter is based not just on my own work and analysis, but also that of my current and former colleagues Irina Herb, Merle Heusmann and Zelda Wenner, to whom I am very grateful. I would also like to thank Lea Kolling and Klara Morfeld for their constructive support during the early phases of the project.

6 As explained further below, "economisation" is understood here as an umbrella term for propertisation and commodification.

7 See https://sfb294-eigentum.de/en/, and especially https://sfb294-eigentum.de/en/subprojects/eigentum-am-menschlichen-korper-im-kontext-transnationaler-reproduktionsokonomien/.

8 On the sociological concept of "doing", see for instance Gildemeister 2019, 411.

findings on the ways those involved in the egg transfer process interpret and "moralise" their (property-related) practices and experiences (2). Finally, I bring together the conceptual reflections and empirical insights in order to sketch the contours of the "moral economy" of egg donation (3).

1. Property in ART contexts: theoretical reflections

In transnational ART economies, sperm and eggs are transformed into marketisable entities, or in short: they are commodified (Castree 2003). Commodification in turn presupposes that the relevant objects can be owned, that is, that they can be *property*, which raises the question of the relation between commodification and propertisation (1.1). Propertisation can be understood as both an objective and a subjective process. This chapter focuses on the subjective dimension. In the next subsection, I outline the conceptual relationship between property and subjectivity (1.2). I then discuss certain peculiarities of the relation between body, property and subjectivity in the context of *bodily* donations (1.3). Building on that discussion, I critically reflect on the construct of bodily *donation* and its supposed opposition to the practices of commodity exchange that dominate in capitalist societies (1.4) and on the moral dualism between economic and altruistic motivations that is central to both juridical and scholarly understandings of egg donation (1.5).

1.1 Propertisation, commodification, economisation

Generally speaking, property can be described as a relation in which one or more *subjects* are able to dispose of one or more *objects* and possess certain rights to use or transfer those objects (Carruthers and Ariovich 2004). In capitalist societies, rights, uses and forms of transfer that enable profit generation are particularly significant—something that presupposes the transformation of things into commodities. Processes of commodification in turn presuppose processes of propertisation in the sense of an "assignation of legal title to a named individual, group or institution [that] gives more-or-less exclusive rights of the owner to dispose of that which is named by the title" (Castree 2003, 279; cf. Davies 1999, 329). However, the ability to dispose profitably of goods or resources is not always dependent on explicit property titles; "*functional equivalents* of property" can substitute for them (Reitz et al. 2023, 267, emphasis in original). In the ART context, that happens when donors provide consent to the transfer of their gametes, and thereby transfer extensive usage rights and opportunities for profit to clinics without the eggs or sperm becoming the clinics' property (see Rahe's chapter). Conversely, not every property object is also commodified; commodification is a possible and often probable consequence of propertisation, but not a necessary one.

Sociologists have long noted the growing importance in modern times of property in general, and processes of propertisation in particular. Hannes Siegrist has observed an expansion in the scope of property rights since the late twentieth century (Siegrist 2006). We are witnessing an expansion and valorisation of private property rights, accompanied by "the cultural construction and mediation of property-related concepts, symbols, systems of meaning and knowledge, [...] social norms, role scripts, forms of habitus, routines and guiding ideals" (ibid., 31). Propertisation, then, is not merely a legal or economic matter but a broader social process. It holds significance both for the production and distribution of goods, resources and wealth and for people's self-relations, intersubjective practices and normative orientations. Propertisation is, moreover, not just a *condition* for commodification, but also one of its possible *effects*: specifically, in cases where the transformation of former non-commodities into commodities helps to expand private rights of disposal, which can in turn accelerate processes of commodification.

In short, propertisation and commodification are not the same, but they are often mutually reinforcing. Together, they enable an *economisation* of formerly non-economic domains (cf. Köhler 2019), such as human reproduction. Accordingly, an examination of the ways in which actors involved in the ART economy "do property" raises the question of whether, and if so to what extent, reproductive bodily substances are experienced and conceived as property objects and/or as transferrable, marketisable entities.

1.2 *Property and (modern) subjectivity*

This chapter, as explained above, is primarily concerned with the subjective processes by which reproductive bodily substances, capacities (Lafuente-Funes 2020) and infrastructures are propertised. The norm of the non-disposability and non-marketasation of the human body is highly relevant to this question. At the same time, it stands in clear tension with the objective development of ART economies, and is closely bound up with the notion of an autonomous, self-conscious, sovereign subject that is central to "Western" liberal modernity. Consequently, property and subjectivity are interwoven in myriad, often conflicting ways. The autonomous subject of "Western" modernity is based on the idea of self-ownership, with the exclusion of other people's rights of disposal over a person's body forming the foundation for individual freedom and self-determination. While the idea of "owning" one's body has its roots in the (pre)history of the Enlightenment, it also plays an important role in contemporary discourses and theories of bioethics (see Lettow's and Richardson's chapters in this volume) and has featured in both older and more recent feminist movements and struggles ("my body, my choice").

As has often been noted, the idea of self-ownership is highly paradoxical, as it introduces a division between "that which owns, and that which is owned" (Davies 1999, 333) into the subject. Inasmuch as self-ownership forms the normative basis for the liberal subject's freedom of contract, it also provides the foundation for systematic utilisation and exploitation of human productivity[9] in the context of "doubly free" wage labour under capitalism (cf. Marx 1887, 120). Accordingly, the modern subject depends on property in two respects. On the one hand, in order to earn a living, subjects are forced to put their labour power at other people's disposal, and hence to relate to themselves as objects. On the other, property mediates access to opportunities for participation, recognition and freedom—opportunities that are unequally distributed in modern capitalist societies. There is a close relationship between the quantity and quality of goods that individual subjects have at their disposal and their social status and agency (see e.g. Skeggs and Yuill 2019). Despite or even precisely because of this, the possession of certain objects can help subjects to build a secure personal identity (Miller 2010; Gehrlach 2020). Property can thus be understood as a central mode of securing and extending the self in modern capitalist societies (Belk 1988). Conversely, this means a subject's freedom to take decisions about themselves and their own body will increase in proportion not just to their *self*-ownership but also their ownership of *other* things—especially, in a capitalist society, objects with a high exchange value—whereas those who own little property, or whose property has no or only minimal exchange value, will possess limited autonomy, agency and self-determination.

9

1.3 *Some peculiarities of bodily donation*

Interestingly, the above-described relation between property, status and agency only applies to a limited degree in the context of ART/bodily donations. Many studies have shown that egg donors are typically individuals living in precarious circumstances, meaning that their agency is situationally limited (Rivas et al. 2018; Marre et al. 2018; Molas and Perler 2020; Nahman 2018). Although they are *de facto* owners of objects that possess high exchange value and are in high demand (namely: fertile eggs), donors often find themselves in a socioeconomically weaker position than the "propertyless" potential recipients from whom that demand stems (namely: people who want to become parents but lack fertile eggs). Put another way, there is a social divide between givers and takers in the ART economy such that ownership of property does not function the usual way.

This exception to the normal rule in the case of bodily donation (here, specifically, egg transfer) is probably due to the unusual character of the objects of exchange compared with everyday property and exchange relations. While other objects—from toothbrushes to stocks and shares—are typically first acquired and then (more or less lucratively) exchanged, the same is not true of bodily donations: donors of bodily substances only become property subjects in the context of the transfer itself. Although my body, in its material substance, of course "belongs" to me, in the normal course of everyday life that does not give rise to a consciousness of property nor a need for legal norms—except in specific circumstances such as medical procedures, high-risk activities or incidents of sexual or physical violence. Furthermore, in the case of bodily donations, a person's ownership of their bodily substances paradoxically only becomes visible in the moment when the subject relinquishes not only the related rights of disposal, but also the substances themselves. Ownership of one's body thus only becomes relevant *retroactively* and *ex negativo*. In conjunction with prevailing legal norms that define the right to dispose of one's own bodily substances as a matter of personality rights, and thus *not* as a matter of property, the subject who donates their bodily substances finds themselves in the contradictory position of simultaneously owning and not owning those substances. Additionally, by legally defining bodily donation as donation and therefore "non-work", the option of commodifying one's own labour power, which is linked to the self-objectification that regularly occurs in capitalist wage labour, is also constitutively restricted (Panitch 2016). Therefore, the transfer of a donor's bodily substances at most allows that donor to secure some symbolic (e.g. moral) status—which prompts the question of whether and to what extent moral "remuneration" can function as a surrogate for economic exchange.

1.4 Donation vs commodity exchange?

The difficulty of classifying the property relations constituted by bodily donations is due not just to the special character of bodily substances as objects, but also to the concept of donation. By contrast with other processes of exchange, donation is primarily associated with morally worthy action and virtues such as selflessness, benevolence, solidarity and empathy (Adloff and Sigmund 2005, 214 ff.). Thus, commodity exchange and donations are usually seen as radically opposed. At the same time, donation is not the same as gift exchange, described by Marcel Mauss (2005 [1923/24]) as a complex blend of binding norms of reciprocity and modes of group-specific identity formation (Degens 2016; Bensen and Carter 2008). Nonetheless, donations are usually assigned to the category of gift exchange; the terms "gift-giving" and "gift economy" are frequently used in the context of bodily donation (Titmuss 1971). Some even propose understanding donation as the ideal of a "pure gift", in which the giver expressly acts without expectation of any direct reciprocation (Strehle 2009, 146–147; Hillebrandt 2008, 4285).

The finer distinctions between these concepts are not central here; what matters is the general assumption that donations represent the antithesis of market exchange. It is precisely this assumption that underpins the protective function assigned to the construct of altruistic donation: namely, to shield bodily materials from commodification and propertisation. Commodities, by contrast, are primarily produced for the purpose of exchange itself (Strehle 2009, Appadurai 2014). Strictly speaking, these exchanges do not ground any social relations between the parties above and beyond that process of exchange, and hence have (economic) exchange value but no (social) use value. The opposite is true of donations; they are assigned great social (and hence also moral) value. At the same time, donations are considered uneconomic insofar as they do not serve traditional market-economy functions such as allocating goods or increasing efficiency.

There are various reasons to be sceptical about this supposed contrast, however. For example, Richard Titmuss (1971) argued that donations of bodily substances (specifically, blood) are more economically efficient than selling those substances at market rates precisely *because* they are donations (cf. Waldby and Mitchell 2006, 9 ff.). Similarly, it has been argued that altruistic donation or "pure gift-giving" may not be as far removed from commodity exchange as it appears at first glance. According to Paweł Łuków, for example, altruistic bodily donations have the following basic features: the donor and recipient are anonymous; the recipient is interchangeable; the donation is voluntary; and there is no obligation to reciprocate (Łuków 2020). Viewed in this way, donations do indeed exhibit certain parallels to market relations and commodity exchange (ibid., 101), which raises the question of whether altruistic bodily donations might perhaps serve not just a compensatory but *also* a directly economic function.

1.5 *The limits of moral dualism*

That (bodily) donations do not necessarily stand in binary opposition to capitalist economics and commodity exchange is a point that is often made in critical analyses of the expanding ART economy—particularly in arguments suggesting that the construct of altruistic donation may serve more as cover for, rather than an alternative to, dominant property and market logics (e.g. Reddy and Patel 2015, 229). According to these arguments, framing bodily transfers as altruistic donations makes it possible to minimise the cost of supplying the necessary bodily substances and capacities, hence allowing the (mostly private) clinics to reap higher profits (Lafuente-Funes 2020; Rivas and Jociles 2020; Hovav 2019).

While this relation is obvious for the "objective" side of economic appropriation or propertisation of bodily substances by ART clinics, matters are rather less clear for the "subjective" side, that is, when it comes to the views and motivations of the actors involved in the respective processes. Many studies (both quantitative and qualitative) have shown that egg donors' motivations do *not* conform to the officially mandated moral dualism—that is to say, their decision to donate their eggs is motivated *not just* by altruism, but *also* by financial considerations (Purewal and van den Akker 2009; Lucía and Núñez 2015; Lima and Álvarez Plaza 2019; Orobitg et al. 2013; Borgstrøm et al. 2018). Nonetheless, the way these studies are designed often emphasises the *centrality* of altruism as a motivation (see for instance Pennings et al. 2014; 2015). As a result, in the scholarly debate about egg donation the question of individual motivations for and against donating bodily materials is often confined to the alternatives "altruistic" vs "financial", while interest in subjective motivations is primarily focused on the donors. This perspective not only reduces the possible range of relevant motivations but also the field of relevant actors: if it is primarily donors and their motivations that are seen as crucial to the functioning of the reproductive economy's moral regulation, then the role and responsibility of other actors will recede into the background. Indirectly, this approach replicates the assumption, already implicit in the juridical-normative construct of altruistic donation, that the only way to control or limit processes of economisation is to encourage morally desirable motivations on the part of donors.

Here, in contrast, I want to look more closely at the relation between moral motivations in the field of egg transfer and the above-described growth in processes of economisation of human reproduction, *without* prioritising in advance one specific group of actors, categorically limiting the field of possible motivations or assuming that processes of economisation can be explained directly and exclusively by subjective judgements, experiences and desires. Nonetheless, the "subjective factor" does undoubtedly play a crucial role in the functioning of the ART economy, as I shall explore in more depth in the next section.

2. (Un)doing property in the field of egg transfer

Building on the general reflections set out in the first section, I shall now present an empirically informed analysis of the subjective dimension of propertisation in the context of egg donation. Given the central function ascribed to individual motivations in the normative regulation of this field, I begin by focusing on our interviewees' moral motivations. However, I take "moral" here in a very broad sense, rather than as referring to some extraordinary or especially remarkable practice (cf. Sichler 2020, 39). On this understanding, morality is at play wherever "people provide justifications for their actions, beliefs and emotional attitudes" (ibid., 36). This implies, firstly, that moral perspectives are not confined to a narrow set of issues and situations, but rather form part of social actors' everyday lives, and, secondly, that they are fundamentally diverse and cannot be restricted *a priori* to a certain register.

Accordingly, my analysis asks how, and by whom, moral articulations relating to property are expressed in the field of egg donation. I begin by briefly outlining the methodological approach (2.1), before presenting selected empirical findings (2.2). The section concludes with a discussion of the central insights gained from the empirical material in relation to this chapter's key research questions (2.3).

2.1 Methodological approach

In our study, we conducted a total of 43 problem-centred interviews with Spanish egg donors, German egg recipients and ART professionals from both Spain and Germany. We were especially interested in comparing field-specific moral perspectives on property across the different interviewee groups. In line with the methodology of grounded theory (Strauss 2004; Strauss and Corbin 1996), we then used a multistage coding process to identify key categories (Mey and Mruck 2011; Przyborski and Wohlrab-Sahr 2009, 195–205). This was supplemented by systematic case comparisons and theoretical memos. The presentation of our findings in the next section is structured around the following generative questions (Strübing 2019, 36), which were formulated based on the ongoing process of empirical and theoretical analysis:

Motivational dimension: What field-specific motivations are relevant to the interviewees' behaviour within the context of the egg donation economy? What questions, issues and problems are viewed through a moral lens and what form does this take? How is the construct of altruistic donation incorporated?

Process dimension: How is the transfer of bodily substances interpreted, experienced and legitimised? How are processes of propertisation and commodification of reproductive bodily substances perceived and evaluated?

Object dimension: Where and how do the interviewees acquire ownership of their own bodies/bodily substances or those of others? To what extent are reproductive bodily substances conceived as propertisable and/or marketisable objects?

Subject dimension: How is the right to dispose over (one's own or other people's) bodies/bodily substances experienced and interpreted? Where and how (if at all) does the idea of "self-ownership" feature in their interpretations? How does it relate to experiences of agency?

2.2 Empirical findings

As already mentioned, the topic of ownership does not appear to hold explicit relevance for most of our interviewees. For example, they did not tend to discuss who the eggs belong to, what rights and obligations existed between the various parties during the transfer process and what effect that had, or who can and cannot legitimately generate profits from their property titles. However, this does not mean that such questions were dismissed when they were posed, nor that more implicit or symbolic dimensions of ownership—relating to belonging, identity or kinship—play no role. The interviews also contain instances of moral reasoning not directly tied to ownership in the narrow sense. For instance, in all interviewee groups we encountered the narrative of a Spanish "culture of donation" (cf. Kroløkke 2014). So, although it did not come naturally to our interviewees to think about their experiences explicitly in terms of "property", once prompted they did articulate moral narratives on the topic. The concept of altruistic donation proved especially productive in their accounts, and interviewees' individual experiences and perceptions of gamete transfer also played a key role in sparking moral reflections.

Egg donors: flexible moral labourers

Almost all of the egg donors we interviewed were students or in a transitional phase between education and employment at the time of donation. Many reported financially precarious living conditions. They hoped the compensation would alleviate everyday hardships—such as paying rent or supporting family members—and/or help them to achieve independence. Some interviewees had donated years or even decades ago; others had done so more recently.

If their motivations could be summed up in a single word, it would be "varied". Not surprisingly, and in line with the discursive-juridical framing of egg transfers, the normative factor of altruism played an important role. However, this factor did not stand in isolation; rather, the donors worked it into (more or less affectively charged, depending on their personal circumstances) reflections on egg donation as a particular biographical experience, and retrospectively wove in a variety of moralising perspectives, articulating—sometimes in long narrative passages—their individual mix of moral motivations. One common theme was a desire to help other women become mothers. But the interviewees also mentioned other reasons for the decision to donate their eggs, such as needing a full gynaecological check-up or wanting to pass on their genes without becoming mothers themselves. Another motivation was to gain temporary respite from the pressure to be sexually active. Some were simply "curious" about the process. At several points, interviewees also expressed interpretations of egg donation as a means of increasing self-worth or self-empowerment. For instance, 29-year-old Olivia, who at the time of the interview was planning her fifth egg donation, said that, as well as helping other people, she wanted to feel valued. Carmen, who had donated eggs 17 years before the interview when she was aged 18, explained that she saw egg donation as "something [...] I could do for other people with my body. It almost felt like a feminist demand, to do what's in my power." Many of the interviewed donors clearly saw egg donation as a way to construct themselves, each in their own individual way, as a morally acting subject.

All interviewees in this group also consciously saw themselves as "owners" of their bodies, in the sense that they—and only they—get to make decisions about them. They rejected the idea that their bodies could be bought or sold. Even those interviewees who described the transfer as being a *de facto* sale did so with a notably critical or even bitter tone. Paloma, for instance, described how during the process of egg transfer she felt like an "egg-producing machine", a "uterus on legs". She summarised: "The way they treated us was so ... so cold. So yes, it was a sale." Sara, who had donated eggs three times, likewise drew a link between "coldness" and "selling": "You give me your eggs, I give you money. Done. Very cold treatment, you aren't seen as a human being." However, although experiences of "coldness" were often mentioned, that only rarely led to criticisms of economisation in the ART sector; where the clinics came up in the interviews, it tended to be with a focus on the professionals' intersubjective conduct during the process.

Interestingly, processes involving the propertisation of bodily substances—by contrast with the possibility of "selling" those substances—were seen as fairly unproblematic. In the egg donors' narratives, eggs are presented as transferrable objects, whose status varies according to the stage of the transfer process (cf. Appadurai 2014): prior to extraction, they were seen as a natural part of the body—abundant and therefore dispensable. Once extracted, they acquired a particular, "warm" value, enabling their transfer in the form of a donation. Lina explained it as follows:

For me, they're things I don't need and have no use for. [...] There's something appealing about the idea of my genetic material helping another person. The human factor ... you're helping someone very concretely. It's not like going to a supermarket and buying some beans. You know what I mean? It's not so cold.

Narratives of alienation and/or self-empowerment suggest that egg donors *want* to see egg transfer as both an altruistic practice *and* as an element of subjectivation and agency. However, this latter expectation is contradicted by their actual experience before and during the transfer process, since economic pressure and perceptions of an objectifying "coldness" strengthened their feelings of desubjectivation and reduced agency.

Overall, the egg donors in our interviews presented themselves not so much as "moral pioneers" (Rapp 1987) but rather as flexible "moral labourers" (cf. Siegl 2023)[10] who creatively rework the overarching norm of altruistic donation. Taking this norm as their starting point, the interviewees talked in detail about their experiences, feelings and motivations during the process of egg transfer, which they retrospectively wove into complex biographical narratives. The "warm–cold" dichotomy emerged as a kind of ordering system, into which the propertisation—commodification distinction was also inscribed. While the latter was universally rejected, the former was seen as largely unproblematic.

Egg recipients: vulnerable repropreneurs

The narratives shared by the egg recipients in our interviews centred on their desperate search for a way to become parents: from the painful realisation that they could not have children by the usual route, to (in some cases many) unsuccessful IVF attempts in Germany, to the process of selecting an ART clinic in Spain. At the time we spoke to them, our interviewees had gone through all or some of that process; almost all of them had successfully had a child or twins with the assistance of egg or embryo donation, either recently

10 In her anthropological study on surrogacy in Russia and Ukraine, Veronika Siegl deploys the notion of "ethical labor", which "rang[es] from rhetorical justification and persuasion, through protective care toward others and oneself, and affective labor on others, up to bodily and emotional work on the self" and is "employed to justify and uphold the morally contested practice of commercial surrogacy"; as such, Siegl contends that "ethical labor goes beyond the individual but rather constitutes an integral part of the moral economy of commercial surrogacy" (2023, 16). I essentially understand the concept the same way, but prefer the term "moral" to "ethical" because it is semantically closer to everyday usage.

or some time ago; the oldest of these children were primary-school age, the youngest a few months old.

Overall, compared with the egg donors, the recipients engaged in far less moral reflection on their motives. Rather, they framed the decision to use egg donation as one that was forced upon them by their tragic backstory. Accordingly, their field-specific motivations were primarily directed towards managing and alleviating their own suffering. The normative horizon of their actions was not altruism, but a belief that they were entitled to access reproductive medical services to fulfil their dream of having a child. Most of our interviewees in this group saw the egg donors as "technically" necessary for the goal of alleviating their suffering, but they held little relevance to them as actual people. When Annette, who had a son through egg donation and campaigns in Germany for people who are involuntarily childless, was asked what the egg donor meant to her, she explained:

> So I don't mean it the way it might sound, but she doesn't play a big role. I'm grateful to her. I'm grateful for the donation, but she doesn't play a role in my life.

At the same time, the recipients presented themselves in the interviews not just as vulnerable subjects, but also as self-assured "repropreneurs" (Kroløkke and Pant 2012) who adroitly navigate the international ART market and select the services suited to their individual needs. Many of them routinely adopted the clinics' marketing jargon, speaking of "guaranteed-pregnancy offers", weighing up the pros and cons of different "packages" or assessing the expected and/or actually experienced service quality at different clinics. Where clinics were mentioned, they were perceived on the one hand as service providers, on the other as legitimate economic actors with their own monetary interests. Ottmar, for instance, whose partner Frauke was pregnant at the time of the interview after her second transfer attempt in Spain, described a highly bureaucratic setting:

> It's all very medical, it's all very formalised forms, documents to sign, lots of people putting on gloves and masks, and there's a certain detachment.

One is reminded here of the repeated references to "coldness" in the interviews with egg donors. However, by contrast with the donors, Ottmar experienced this detachment expressly not as something objectifying or alienating, but rather as an inevitable corollary of professional medical treatment. Some interviewees in this group even described the clinics as places of warmth and humanity. Melanie, who became a mother in her mid-40s after an egg transfer in Spain, reported:

It was really sweet how they did it in the clinic. They show you the embryo again under a microscope on a screen and then a little [...] heart appears and a sign saying: good luck! And that was very emotional.

In these accounts, the "cold" character of the transfer is seen, on the one hand, as an unavoidable marker of efficiency and, on the other, as something that can be "warmed up" through the clinics' use of affective symbolism. The recipients do not see themselves as having paid for the eggs, but rather for the services and expenses of the clinic.

Despite that, it is interesting that for the egg recipients too, the idea that they *bought* the eggs is unsettling. Vera, for instance, who had had two donated embryos implanted and likewise found the clinic to be "very warm-hearted and friendly", explained,

No, I didn't buy them [the embryos]. Isn't that funny! [laughs] I've not thought about it that way. [...] But I don't feel like I bought them, no.

However, a little later Vera compared her decision to have embryos implanted to a spontaneous decision to buy a new top.

In the interviews with egg donors, logics of buying and selling were paradoxically regarded as both unacceptable and intuitively obvious—an ambivalence that extended to the eggs themselves, which were portrayed variously as an easily extractable resource, an invaluable gift or a risky investment requiring care and protection. At the same time, from the recipients' perspective, payment was not rendered for the eggs *per se*, but for the services and efforts of the clinic.

Altruism on the part of the donors was generally taken for granted by egg recipients, yet at the same time pragmatically reduced to the donors' voluntary consent to transferring their gametes. Altruism was regarded more as a "nice-to-have" extra and less as a precondition for the legitimacy of egg transfer. Its presence is, as it were, retroactively assumed. At the same time, egg recipients regarded the idea of property in the body, in the sense of complete self-ownership—and thus, self-determination—as intuitively obvious. However, by contrast with the egg donors, they applied this idea not so much to their right to dispose of their *own* bodies, but rather the *donors'* bodies. That was articulated especially clearly by Frauke, who saw egg donation as an expression of autonomy—perhaps even one with a rebellious, feminist character:

> Adult human beings [...] get told what they can do with or have done to their bodies. If I as a woman decide that I'd like to donate my eggs, then let me do it!

Here, the egg donor is viewed as an *a priori* empowered subject who possesses agency, is able to take informed risks and does not need special protection, and whose bodily substances can therefore be unproblematically appropriated by others. In this group too, commodification, even if it is also welcomed and justified, is regarded as more problematic than propertisation. The appropriation of other people's bodily substances is, in many respects, regarded as morally justified; logics of buying and selling, by contrast, are both affirmed and rejected. Overall, the recipients' central moral reference point appears not to be altruism but their own vulnerability. Both the agency ascribed to the donors and the recipients' self-perception as especially vulnerable feed into the hope universally articulated by this group that the social stigma attached to egg transfer will lessen in future.

Professionals: skilled facilitators

Unsurprisingly, the professionals that we interviewed (reproductive doctors, psychologists, fertility advisers, embryologists, marketing experts) are primarily motivated to treat donors and recipients in line with professional standards and legal requirements. They want to facilitate straightforward transfers with high success rates and minimal medical risks for donors and recipients alike. For Spanish professionals, the existence of a large private ART sector is taken for granted, as is the legal framing of egg transfer as a donation. German professionals, by contrast, more frequently voiced criticism of the restrictions resulting from legal prohibitions on egg donation. The question of altruism is also of central importance to the professionals. Most of the interviewees gave a clear answer when asked about egg donors' possible motives: they were said to be motivated by altruism plus monetary compensation. Some assumed that the donors' altruism was dependent on the level of compensation, as marketing expert Vela explained:

> If we raise it too high, then ultimately [donation] becomes something that people only do for money and not for altruistic reasons. [...] So it's also a question of mathematics, you have to calculate it effectively.

On the one hand, altruism is seen here as something that is simply and straightforwardly present and so can be "calculated effectively". On the other, the professionals also see altruism as something that they need to stimulate and encourage. In any case, the centrality of altruism for professionals must be understood against the background of clinics' and agencies' interest in attracting donors with higher social status, which means that donors with exclusively "economic" motivations are seen as less desirable.

The professionals we interviewed took a broad range of positions on questions of property, which could be seen as a sign that there is no strong imperative for them to reconcile their personal views with the requirements of their day-to-day professional life. At the same time, there was a notable tendency, especially among Spanish reproductive doctors, to reject the idea that the eggs are being sold. Spanish legislation, which unequivocally defines egg transfers as donations, clearly functioned here as a normative point of reference. Interestingly, a small subset of reproductive doctors from both countries would nevertheless regard selling eggs or bodily substances as unproblematic or even desirable. This position was formulated most clearly by Heinz from Germany:

> I mean, we always say, "Everyone can choose what to do with their own body." It's not like it's something bad. You're actually helping people. Why shouldn't I be allowed to get paid for it? […] Why shouldn't you sell your eggs, why shouldn't I sell my sperm, if the price is right? It's your decision, after all.

Most of the interviewees in this group understand egg transfer neither as a sale, nor as a gift, but as an unproblematic, non-commodified "barter exchange" (Chapman 1980): you give something and receive something in return. At the same time, interviewees do not see the clinics or themselves as participants in this exchange, but rather as intermediaries. The reproductive doctor Samantha, for instance, sees herself as

> an administrator of this … this biological product, to use that term. But I've never thought before about whether we doctors or the clinics are owners of this biological material. No. None of us have ever seen it that way.

One central idea in this context was a right of disposal over one's own body, which was understood as sufficient legitimation for the right to put substances from that body at the disposal of other people. Like the recipients, the professionals conceive of the donor as a self-determining, autonomous subject who has freely chosen to provide their bodily substances and been appropriately compensated for a negligible amount of work (even if it is not conceived as such) and a practically non-existent risk to their health. The reproductive doctor Aldara sharply rejected potential charges of exploitation and objectification:

> It's true that some people see it as exploitation of the body, but you have to wonder how well informed they are. [...] I have a very clear professional awareness of how we treat the young women—not as commodities or as lacking worth or anything else. Rather, we say that they're people who've made a free decision. And that's good.

What is interesting about this account is that in Aldara's view there are only two options: either you treat egg donors as "commodities" and hence as "lacking worth", or you treat them as fully free subjects whose agency is categorically *not* restricted. On the latter alternative, the commodity aspect disappears from view.

Although the professionals did generally take the eggs to have a special phenomenological character (due to their biological origin), they were fundamentally seen as an unproblematic, easily extractable resource whose property status is clear and free of doubt at every stage of the process. The process of egg transfer was, accordingly, likewise considered largely unproblematic, for two reasons. Firstly, it was repeatedly stressed, because the donors themselves have no interest in their eggs; secondly and above all, because their decision was assumed to be free and autonomous. However, several reproductive doctors reported having to persuade egg *recipients* that the eggs were really "their" eggs. For instance, Selma tells egg recipients to imagine the eggs as little "buttons" stored in "drawers", from which the ones most suitable for the recipient will be selected. This suggests that the *extraction* of eggs is seen as largely unproblematic, while the recipients' *accepting* the eggs as "theirs" is seen as a sensitive process that must be professionally facilitated; interestingly, this is done by emphasising the eggs' status as simple (property) *objects*.

The warm–cold narrative occurred in the interviews with the professionals too; it was especially relevant in the interview with marketing expert Vela, who develops campaigns to recruit egg donors. She explained that the goal of her work is to "give a soul" to the donors:

> We don't treat donors like [...] a number, but as a very important and valuable person. [...] [It's] really wonderful to make sure the whole thing isn't ... so cold, so medicalised and technical.

Here, the risk of "cold" objectification during the transfer process is explicitly addressed: through professional intervention, it is transformed into something "warm" and emotionally resonant. What appears intuitive in donor and recipient narratives—viewing the eggs as self-evidently "mine" or "not mine"—is here revealed to be the result of a process of professional guidance. In this sense, too, professionals position themselves as skilled facilitators of a complex transfer—conceived primarily in medical terms, but also involving emotional and symbolic dimensions. Property relations and processes of economisation, however, are rarely made explicit and even less frequently subjected to critique.

2.3 Summary

My review of the empirical findings has shown that moral perspectives were articulated across all levels and by all interviewee groups. However, the intensity and breadth of this moralisation varied. Different types of "moral resources" were combined (see Orobitg et al. 2013; Miner 2021): notions of possessive individualism were paired with ones of solidarity and gift-giving, as well as with cultural and gendered attitudes such as the assumption that, *as women*, egg donors are especially able to empathise with the plight of the involuntarily childless (see Almeling 2017; Lafuente-Funes and Pérez Orozco 2020, 367 ff.; Haylett 2012; Miner 2021). The interviewees also articulated emancipatory narratives of equality and self-empowerment, sometimes explicitly borrowing from the vocabulary of progressive social movements. Thematisation of vulnerability also played a key role: across all interviewee groups—but especially among recipients and professionals—the suffering of recipients emerged as a central moral reference point.

In other words, the focus was placed mainly on the "demand side". Most of our interviewees believe the involuntarily childless are legitimately entitled to fertility treatments, and that this entitlement justifies the required "property objects" being made available to them. Although the egg donors sometimes also described their own vulnerability—for instance, recounting experiences of alienation and objectification—they did not see that as grounding any explicit entitlements on their part. In the other two groups, the donors' (potential) suffering either goes completely unmentioned or is regarded as relatively easy to alleviate.

When comparing the three interviewee groups, the varying degree of moralisation is striking: while the egg donors reflected extensively on their motives and circumstances, and related them to their lived, often highly affectively charged experiences and to other actors in the field, the professionals primarily concentrated on norms codified in law or professional ethics standards. By contrast, the egg recipients' moral reflections were mostly confined to complaints about inadequate access to reproductive medicine resources and the perceived stigmatisation of egg transfer. The uneven distribution of *moral labour* appears inversely proportionate to socioeconomic status: the most socioeconomically vulnerable group, the egg donors, do extensive moral work, while the more privileged egg recipients do significantly less and the—likewise resource-rich—professionals tended to approach moral questions as routine aspects of managing medical and ethical procedures.

This moral stratification is also reflected in the cold–warm dualism that came up in all three interviewee groups. Pure economic-technical rationalities tended to be regarded as "cold", in sharp contrast to the "warm-glow-giving" of altruism (Andreoni 1990). The coldness manifests, firstly, in the process of transfer itself and, secondly and especially, where logics of "buying and selling" are at work. But while professionals address these perceptions of "coldness" by using marketing strategies to inject some "warmth" (cf. Bergmann 2014, 140) and some egg recipients were even expressly positive about the "cold" processes, the egg donors appeared to struggle more to accept the coldness or transform it into something more positive and warm. Thus, here too they had to bear a disproportionally high burden of moral labour.

The varying intensities of moralisation correspond to different views on the normative-juridical construct of altruistic donation. While this construct was an important horizon for the egg donors' reflections, it played no major role in the recipients'. Nor did the question of whether "selling" is actually a more accurate description than "donating". Although this question caused some unease at a few points in the interviews with recipients, it was clear that in most cases it had never crossed their minds before. The professionals, meanwhile, took it as given that the donors are motivated by a combination of altruism and financial motives, though they took a pragmatic view of this dualism and did not consider it problematic.

All in all, the moral motivations of egg donors—contrary to the simplified dichotomies often found in affirmative empirical research on donor attitudes—appear to be more complex and diverse than a simple dichotomy between "selflessness" and "economic self-interest" (Lafuente-Funes 2020, 210). Instead, donors take a relatively flexible approach to these principles, mixing and matching them according to the demands of different situations (Gilman 2022, 241). Thus, the field's socioeconomic, reproductive (Ginsburg and Rapp 1995) and transnational (Bergmann 2014, 149) stratifications are mirrored by a moral one, in which the donors' relative lack (whether acute or chronic) of economic *and* symbolic capital is counterbalanced by an intensification of flexible moral labour.

One widely shared assumption within the field I am analysing here is that people have a right to do as they wish with their own bodies—though this right is typically not framed in terms of property. For egg donors, it is mainly about *protecting* their own bodies from external control, while egg recipients deploy the notion to justify their *entitlement* to make use of other people's substances—retrospectively attributing autonomous decision-making to those people. Professionals, meanwhile, apply the principle of self-determination in both directions: bodily donation must be voluntary, which means any form of coercion or constraint (whether financial or psychological) must be ruled out. Provided this condition is met, the use of other people's bodily substances is considered unproblematic.

As already mentioned above, none of the interviewee groups made much mention of the ownership of clinics and infrastructure and the associated opportunities for profit. The clearest criticisms came from a handful of egg donors and (non-medical) professionals. Despite the sometimes exorbitant costs they incurred, egg recipients tended to emphasise the benefits of marketisation. Thus, the clinics' central role in the economisation of ARTs barely came up in the interviews, and they were virtually never discussed as *moral* agents. Taken together, all the interviewee groups regard eggs as an ambiguous yet ultimately unproblematic property object. In light of the above-discussed complaints about "coldness", it seems that propertisation and commodification—although closely interlinked in ART economies—are morally distinguished from one another: while commodification is seen as potentially problematic, propertisation is not—either because the transferred eggs' property character goes unrecognised or because it is taken to be self-evident and hence tolerated. Somewhat schematically, the interpretative schemas of the three interviewee groups can be broken down as follows:

	Egg donors	Egg recipients	Professionals
Focus on ...	Complex, individual life circumstances and personal motives	Individual story of suffering and the need for professional support	Experience with and management of professional standards and challenges
Central question	Should I do it?	(How) can I get it?	Does it work?
Degree of moralisation	High (extensive, complex, reflective)	Minimal (focus on describing processes)	Moderate (mainly relating to current legislation)
Function of altruism	"Horizon"	"Add-on"	"Simple fact"
Eggs are seen as ...	Surplus/gift	Gift/resource/investment	Biological material
and are ...	Generously given	Unquestioningly taken	Professionally transferred
Property in the body is understood as	Self-determination over one's own body, protection from external control	Self-determination, retroactively ascribed to the donor	Self-determination, guaranteed by absence of compulsion
Thematisation of economisation in the ART field	Mostly neutral	Mostly affirmative	Barely mentioned
Ideal type	**Flexible moral labourers**	**Vulnerable repropreneurs**	**Skilled facilitators**

Table 1: Interpretative schemas of the three interviewee groups

3. The moral economy of egg donation: provisional conclusions

To sum up our empirical findings: ownership of bodily substances is seen as largely straightforward and unproblematic, and was only rarely mentioned in relation to doctors', other professionals' and clinics' rights of disposal. Similarly, the (possibly economic and thus "self-interested") motives of actors other than the egg donors were rarely considered in the interviewees' subjective moral assessments (cf. Lafuente-Funes 2020, 222).

Based on the heuristic definition of property discussed at the beginning of this chapter (Carruthers and Ariovich 2004), we can say that the eggs and, relatedly, the donors' bodies come into view as property *objects*—but not the clinics, agencies or egg banks. Egg donors and recipients are thematised as property *subjects*—but not the doctors, clinic managers or owners of marketing agencies. In the interviewees' subjective accounts of egg donation, the *use* and *transfer* of property are interwoven—the eggs are transferred because they are needed for a certain use. At the same time, it is rarely mentioned that it is not just eggs or reproductive capacities that are used and transferred in ART contexts, but also productive and financialised capital (see Herb's chapter in this volume). The fact that *rules* around property and ownership—especially the construct of "altruistic donation"—strictly limit the earning opportunities for those who supply bodily substances but not for those who manage these substances and their transfer was generally seen as unproblematic.

Our findings thus show that divergences or convergences of moral and economic logics in the egg donation economy are not regarded as problematic or unproblematic *per se*, but rather are evaluated according to the relevant *sphere of action*: actors from the economic sphere, such as private clinic owners, are "permitted" to act in accordance with the economic logic of profit maximisation (and to appropriate bodily substances for that purpose), whereas the egg donors' "self-interest" must be curbed by regulations or deproblematised through the deployment of alternative moral resources, such as vulnerability, empathy or altruism. This gives rise to a moralism that is not just flexible yet stratified, but also *functionally differentiated*. As such, it can be readily adapted to the needs of specific actors, perhaps precisely because it reflects the reality of advanced capitalist society: the everyday experience of an economic logic that underpins every aspect of life is translated into situationally adapted forms of moral judgement and action.

This also means that the problem of the construct of "altruistic donation" is not just, as some critical analyses suggest, that it *conceals* value-creating labour or exploitation in the context of a capitalist exchange of biocommodities. Rather, it is that altruism *itself* is made profitable precisely *because* it is claimed to be strictly incompatible with capitalist economic principles. The (moral *and* economic) "value" of the altruistic "work" done in the context of egg donation lies, on this view, precisely in the fact that it is *not* work and is not experienced as such. If we follow the line of this argument, the relatively high degree of moralisation by egg donors can be understood as an attempt to deal with a situation involving various moral logics/spheres of action in a way that protects the donors' sense of self-worth: that is, as an attempt to deal, *firstly*, with the social consensus that people should *not* be forced to sell their bodies (or body parts) out of economic necessity; *secondly*, with their own actual socioeconomic situation at the time of the egg transfer; and *thirdly*, with cultural and gendered expectations of empathy, solidarity and selflessness. Accordingly, exchange value in the egg donation economy is generated not only by invoking or imposing altruism (Marre et al. 2018, 164) as a means to an end; rather, altruism *itself* is an object of appropriation, exploitation and circulation.

Based on the analysis presented above, I would like to conclude this chapter by formulating some overarching thoughts. They are structured around the concept of a "moral economy", which can provide a fruitful analytic perspective on the relationship between property, morality and the economy that goes beyond the register of methodological individualism. The notion of a "moral economy" is generally (and somewhat imprecisely, cf. Götz 2015, 158) attributed to the British social historian E. P. Thompson, who analysed the "food riots" that took place in England in the late eighteenth century as countermovements to the rise of capitalist market logics during the transition from the feudal system to industrial capitalism (Thompson 1971). According to Thompson, these struggles articulated a register of social norms and obligations whose moral force derived from rules and ideas of price formation, trade and fairness that had applied on local markets for centuries but were gradually hollowed out and "thoroughly demoralized" (Frevert 2019, 26) by the new ideology of "free markets". On Thompson's interpretation, the moral economy of the English farmers' riots attests to an (ultimately unsuccessful) *resistance* mounted by those with no or virtually no property to "all that is solid melting into air" (Marx and Engels 2002 [1848]).

An alternative approach understands the relation between morality and the economy as a constitutive *functional condition* of capitalist societies (Sachweh and Hilmar 2020, 169 ff.). On this view, capitalism fundamentally *depends* on processes of non-economic moral legitimation. Capitalism and (everyday) morality are thus not, as for Thompson, conflicting opposites, but work together in certain ways.

Two strands of this alternative approach can be distinguished. Firstly, one rooted in economic sociology that asks what role is played on specific markets by moral standards such as trust, honesty and friendship. One especially prominent example for the topic of reproduction is the work of Viviana Zelizer, who understands intimacy and the economy as systematically interwoven; intimate relationships, parent–child bonds and so forth involve monetary transactions of various kinds, without that necessarily being problematic or giving rise to conflict (Zelizer 2000).

Secondly, there is a strand of work that looks at the normative embedding of capitalism during the transitions to certain historical periods. Prominent examples are Max Weber's (2011 [1920]) famous study of Protestantism's role in the emergence of industrial capitalism and Luc Boltanski and Ève Chiapello's (2007) study on the importance of autonomy as a guiding normative principle in the transition to post-Fordism. Unlike the first strand, this line of inquiry assumes a fundamental difference between the economic and sociocultural spheres, yet it focuses on how the latter—particularly in the form of everyday morality—supports the functioning of the former. It does so by showing how capitalism incorporates the non-economic actions and moral judgements of its subjects. Moreover, the opposition of morality and capitalism is seen as playing a highly productive role in this process: "One of the essential aspects […] is the ability to give 'meaning' to one's actions: this meaning goes beyond the mere idea of generating profit" (Berland and Chiapello 2009, 32). What is especially significant here is that the *critiques* of capitalism, formulated for instance by social movements, are not seen as standing in opposition to capitalist innovation and transformation, but rather as an essential driver of it.

Applying the concept of a "moral economy", the interplay of everyday morality and the capitalist economy can thus be schematically understood in three possible ways: as *oppositional*, *functional* or *innovative*. Common to all three perspectives is that moral motivations are not held to be determined by economic or political structures, or vice versa. Rather, they assume that moral thought, judgement and action have their *own logic*, which systematically interacts with economic structures—whether by opposing, stabilising or animating them.

What does that mean for the moral economy of egg donation? The normative-juridical regulation of the field—centred on the notion of altruistic donation—can hardly be seen as a *countermovement* to the economisation of reproduction. Any dimension of resistance is, at best, difficult to discern—particularly given the lack of clarity as to what or whom such resistance would be directed against. Nonetheless, the opposition between economic and non-economic logics of action, which is central to both Thompson's concept of moral economy and to the work of Weber, Boltanski and Chiapello, has not disappeared. On the contrary, it fulfils a systematic *function* by facilitating the everyday understanding and legitimation of the ART industry's expansion within the existing juridical and normative framework. However, this bears little resemblance to the kind of innovative appropriation of social critique by social movements described by Boltanski and Chiapello (2007). Instead, it reflects a normative embedding of everyday action and moralisation into broader processes of valorisation and economisation.

The moral economy of egg transfer, as encapsulated in the juridical-normative construct of egg *donation*, thus proves to be *innovative* inasmuch as it not only contributes to ever more aspects of human and non-human nature being commodified and incorporated into the circuits of capital, but also serves to provide flexible moral legitimation, thanks to its relative openness of meaning. One is reminded here of Norbert Götz's observation:

"The 'moral' would thus no longer be something per se uneconomic or laudable, but an alternative way of 'utility maximisation' through the construction of altruistic meaning for economic transactions"

(Götz 2015, 158).

While he was speaking of the moral economy of capitalism in general, Götz's claim rings especially true for reproductive markets in particular. Seen this way, the special economic value of altruistic transactions involving bodily substances like eggs, sperm or uteruses may lie precisely in those transactions' supposed incompatibility with economic rules and principles. If that is the case, then egg donation is an ideal case study to illustrate how the *difference* between "capitalist" and explicitly "non-capitalist" moral orientations allows the latter to be an important element, or even driver, of the former.

Works Cited

Aderaldo, Janaina Ferreira, Beatriz Helena Dantas Rodrigues de Albuquerque, Maryana Thalyta Ferreira Câmara de Oliveira, Mychelle de Medeiros Garcia Torres and Daniel Carlos Ferreira Lanza (2023). Main Topics in Assisted Reproductive Market: A Scoping Review. *PLoS One*, 18(8).

Adloff, Frank, and Steffen Sigmund (2005). Die *gift economy* moderner Gesellschaften. In Frank Adloff and Steffen Mau (eds.). *Vom Geben und Nehmen: Zur Soziologie der Reziprozität*, 171–183. Frankfurt: Campus.

Almeling, Rene (2017). Paid to Donate: Egg Donors, Sperm Donors, and Gendered Experiences of Bodily Commodification. In Nina Bandelj, Frederick F. Wherry and Viviana A. Zelizer (eds.). *Money Talks: Explaining How Money Really Works*, 171–183. Princeton: Princeton University Press.

Andreoni, James (1990). Impure Altruism and Donations to Public Goods: A Theory of Warm-Glow-Giving. *Economic Journal*, 100, 464–477.

Appadurai, Arjun (2014). Introduction: Commodities and the Politics of Value. In Arjun Appadurai (ed.). *The Social Life of Things*, 3–63. Cambridge: Cambridge University Press.

Belk, Russell W. (1988). Possessions and the Extended Self. *Journal of Consumer Research,* 15(2), 139–168.

Benson, Michaela, and Denise Carter (2008). Introduction: Nothing in Return? Distinctions between Gift and Commodity in Contemporary Societies. *Anthropology in Action,* 15(3), 1–7.

Bergmann, Sven (2014). *Ausweichrouten der Reproduktion: Biomedizinische Mobilität und die Praxis der Eizellspende*. Wiesbaden: Springer.

Berland, Nicolas, and Ève Chiapello (2009). Criticisms of Capitalism, Budgeting and the Double Enrolment: Budgetary Control Rhetoric and Social Reform in France in the 1930s and 1950s. *Accounting, Organizations and Society,* 34, 28–57.

Boltanski, Luc, and Ève Chiapello (2007). *The New Spirit of Capitalism*. London: Verso.

Borgstrøm, Maria B., Siv S. Nygaard, Anne K. Danielsen and Ulrik S. Kesmodel (2019). Exploring Motivations, Attitudes and Experiences of Oocyte Donors: A Qualitative Study. *Acta Obstetricia et Gynecologica Scandinavica,* 98(8), 1055–1062.

Carruthers, Bruce G., and Laura Ariovich (2004). The Sociology of Property Rights. *Annual Review of Sociology,* 30(1), 23–46.

Castree, Noel (2003). Commodifying What Nature? *Progress in Human Geography,* 27(3), 273–297.

Chapman, Anne W. (1980). Barter as a Universal Mode of Exchange. *L'Homme,* 20(3), 33–83.

Cooper, Melinda, and Catherine Waldby (2014). *Clinical Labor: Tissue Donors and Research Subjects in the Global Bioeconomy*. Durham, NC: Duke University Press.

Davies, Margaret (1999). Queer Property, Queer Persons: Self-Ownership and Beyond. *Social & Legal Studies,* 8(3), 327–351.

Degens, Philipp (2016). *Geld als Gabe: Zur sozialen Bedeutung lokaler Geldformen*. Bielefeld: transcript.

Degli Esposti, Sara, and Vincenzo Pavone (2019). Oocyte Provision as a (Quasi) Social Market: Insights from Spain. *Social Science & Medicine,* 234, 112381.

EU (European Parliament and Council of the European Union) (2004). *Directive 2004/23/EC of the European Parliament and of the Council of 31 March 2004 on Setting Standards of Quality and Safety for the Donation, Procurement, Testing, Processing, Preservation, Storage and Distribution of Human Tissues and Cells*. https://eur-lex.europa.eu/legal-content/EN/TXT/HTML/?uri=CELEX:32004L0023.

Frevert, Ute (2019). Moral Economies, Present and Past: Social Practices and Intellectual Controversies. *Geschichte und Gesellschaft,* 26 (special issue), 13–43.

Gehring, Petra (2006). Kann es Eigentum am menschlichen Körper geben? Über einen Umbruch. In Petra Gehring (ed.). *Was ist Biomacht? Vom zweifelhaften Mehrwert des Lebens,* 35–54. Frankfurt: Campus.

Gehrlach, Andreas (2020). *Das verschachtelte Ich: Individualräume des Eigentums*. Berlin: Matthes & Seitz.

Gildemeister, Regine (2019). Doing Gender: Eine mikrotheoretische Annäherung an die Kategorie Geschlecht. In Beate Korkendiek, Birgit Riegraf and Katja Sabisch (eds.). *Handbuch Interdisziplinäre Geschlechterforschung*, 409–417. Wiesbaden: Springer VS.

Gilman, Leah (2022). The "Selfish Element": How Sperm and Egg Donors Construct Plausibly Moral Accounts of the Decision to Donate. *Sociology*, 56(2), 227–243.

Ginsburg, Faye D., and Rayna Rapp (1995). *Conceiving the New World Order: The Global Politics of Reproduction*. Berkeley: University of California Press.

Götz, Norbert (2015). "Moral Economy": Its Conceptual History and Analytical Prospects. *Journal of Global Ethics*, 11(2), 147–162.

Graefe, Stefanie (2019). *Resilienz im Krisenkapitalismus: Wider das Lob der Anpassungsfähigkeit*. Bielefeld: transcript.

Graefe, Stefanie (2023). The Discreet Charm of Catastrophe: Vulnerability, Resilience, and Critique in the Era of Multiple Crises. In Sebastian Eduardo Dávila, Rebecca Hanna John, Ulrike Jordan, Thorsten Schneider, Judith Sieber and Nele Wulff (eds.). *On Withdrawal—Scenes of Refusal, Disappearance, and Resilience in Art and Cultural Practices*, 279–296. Zurich: Diaphanes.

Haylett, Jennifer (2012). One Woman Helping Another: Egg Donation as a Case of Relational Work. *Politics & Society*, 40(2), 223–247.

Herb, Irina, and Zelda Wenner (2023). Who Owns and Controls the Means of Reproduction? Assisted Fertility and Pregnancy as a Multi-Billion Dollar Market. https://sfb294-eigentum.de/de/blog/who-owns-and-controls-the-means-of-reproduction-assisted-fertility-and-pregnancy-as-a-multi-billion-dollar-market/.

Hillebrandt, Frank (2008). Begriff und Praxis des Tauschens. In Karl-Siegbert Rehberg (ed.). *Die Natur der Gesellschaft: Verhandlungen des 33. Kongresses der Deutschen Gesellschaft für Soziologie in Kassel 2006*, 4279–4291. Frankfurt: Campus.

Hovav, April (2019). Producing Moral Palatability in the Mexican Surrogacy Market. *Gender & Society*, 33(2), 273–295.

Hudson, Nicky (2020). Egg Donation Imaginaries: Embodiment, Ethics and Future Family Formation. *Sociology*, 54(2), 346–362.

Hudson, Nicky, Lorraine Culley, Cathy Herbrand, Vincenzo Pavone, Guido Pennings, Veerle Provoost, Catherine Coveney and Sara Lafuente-Funes (2020). Reframing Egg Donation in Europe: New Regulatory Challenges for a Shifting Landscape. *Health Policy and Technology*, 9, 308–313.

Köhler, Bettina (2019). Kommodifizierung. In Jan Brunner, Anna Dobelmann, Sarah Kirst and Louisa Prause (eds.). *Wörterbuch Land- und Rohstoffkonflikte*, 189–196. Bielefeld: transcript.

König, Annika, and Heather Jacobson (2023). Reprowebs: A Conceptual Approach to Elasticity in the Global Assisted Reproduction Industry. *BioSocieties*, 18(1), 174–196.

Krawiec, Kimberly D. (2009). Price and Pretense in the Baby Market: Money, Morals, and the Neopolitics of Choice. In Michelle Bratcher Goodwin (ed.). *Baby Markets: Money and the New Politics of Creating Families*, 41–55. Cambridge: Cambridge University Press.

Kroløkke, Charlotte (2014). "West Is Best": Affective Assemblages and Spanish Oöcytes. *European Journal of Women's Studies*, 21(1), 57–71.

Kroløkke, Charlotte, and Saumya Pant (2012). "I Only Need Her Uterus": Neo-Liberal Discourses on Transnational Surrogacy. *NORA—Nordic Journal of Feminist and Gender Research*, 20(4), 233–248.

Kunow, Rüdiger (2015). Wertkörper. *PROKLA*, 178, 51–66.

Lafuente-Funes, Sara (2020). Shall We Stop Talking about Egg Donation? Transference of Reproductive Capacity in the Spanish Bioeconomy. *BioSocieties*, 15(2), 207–225.

Lafuente-Funes, Sara, and Amaia Pérez Orozco (2020). On (Global) Care Chains in Times of Crisis: Egg Donation and Domestic Work in Spain. *Tapuya: Latin American Science, Technology and Society*, 3(1), 354–376.

Lettow, Susanne (2015). Biokapitalismus und Inwertsetzung der Körper: Perspektiven der Kritik. *PROKLA*, 178, 33–49.

Lima, Natacha S., and Consuelo Álvarez Plaza (2019). Ovodonación: Bioeconomias emergentes en contextos de inequidad. https://www.aacademica.org/000-111/100.

Lucía, Cristina, and Rocío Núñez (2015). Revisión del perfil sociodemográfico de una muestra local de donantes de gametos, en España: motivación para la donación, procedencia de los donantes, ocupación. *Medicina Reproductiva y Embriología Clínica*, 2(1), 23–30.

Łuków, Paweł (2020). Pure Altruistic Gift and the Ethics of Transplant Medicine. *Bioethical Inquiry*, 17, 95–107.

Marre, Diana, Beatriz San Román and Diana Guerra (2018). On Reproductive Work in Spain: Transnational Adoption, Egg Donation, Surrogacy. *Medical Anthropology*, 37(2), 158–173.

Marx, Karl (1887): Capital. *A Critique of Political Economy. Volume I. Book One: The Process of Production of Capital*, 120. https://www.marxists.org/archive/marx/works/download/pdf/Capital-Volume-I.pdf.

Marx, Karl, and Friedrich Engels (2002 [1848]). *The Communist Manifesto*. London: Penguin.

Mauss, Marcel (2005 [1923/24]). Die Gabe. In Frank Adloff and Steffen Mau (eds.). *Vom Geben und Nehmen: Zur Soziologie der Reziprozität*, 61–72. Frankfurt: Campus.

Mey, Günter, and Katja Mruck (2011). Grounded-Theory-Methodologie: Entwicklung, Stand, Perspektiven. In Günter Mey and Katja Mruck (eds.). *Grounded Theory Reader*, 11–48. Wiesbaden: VS Verlag für Sozialwissenschaften.

Miller, Daniel (2010). *Der Trost der Dinge*. Berlin: Suhrkamp.

Miner, Skye A. (2021). "I Would Want to Pay Her": Challenging Altruistic Egg Exchanges in Canada through Moral Patchworks. *Social Science & Medicine*, 272. https://doi.org/10.1016/j.socscimed.2021.113733.

Molas, Anna, and Laura Perler (2020). Selecting Women, Taming Bodies? Body Ontologies in Egg Donation Practices in Spain. *Tapuya: Latin American Science, Technology and Society*, 3(1), 396–414.

Nahman, Michal (2018). Migrant Extractability: Centring the Voices of Egg Providers in Cross-Border Reproduction. *Reproductive BioMedicine & Society Online*, 7, 82–90.

Orobitg, Gemma, Joan Bestard and Carles Salazar (2013). El cuerpo (re) productivo: Interés económico y altruismo social en las experiencias de un grupo de mujeres donantes de óvulos. *Revista Andaluza de Antropología*, 5, 91–104.

Panitch, Vida (2016). Commodification and Exploitation in Reproductive Markets: Introduction to the Symposium on Reproductive Markets. *Journal of Applied Philosophy*, 33(2), 117–124.

Pennings, Guido (2015). Central Role of Altruism in the Recruitment of Gamete Donors. *Monash Bioethics Review,* 33(1), 78–88.

Pennings, Guido, J. de Mouzon, F. Shenfield, A. P. Ferraretti, T. Mardesic, A. Ruiz and V. Goossens (2014). Socio-Demographic and Fertility Related Characteristics and Motivations of Oocyte Donors in Eleven European Countries. *Human Reproduction,* 29(5), 1076–1089.

Przyborski, Aglaja, and Monika Wohlrab-Sahr (2009). *Qualitative Sozialforschung: Ein Arbeitsbuch*. Munich: Oldenbourg.

Purewal, Satvinder, and Olga van den Akker (2009). Systematic Review of Oocyte Donation: Investigating Attitudes, Motivations and Experiences. *Human Reproduction Update,* 15(5), 499–515.

Rapp, Rayna (1987). Moral Pioneers: Women, Men and Fetuses on a Frontier of Reproductive Technology. *Women Health,* 13(1–2), 101–116.

Reddy, Sunita, and Tulsi Patel (2015). "There Are Many Eggs in My Body": Medical Markets and Commodified Bodies in India. *Global Bioethics,* 26(3–4), 218–231.

Reitz, Tilman, Sebastian Sevignani and Marlen van den Ecker (2023). Eigentum im digitalen Kapitalismus: Ökonomie, Recht und Praxis. In Tanja Carstensen, Simon Schaupp and Sebastian Sevignani (eds.). *Theorien des digitalen Kapitalismus*, 264–284. Berlin: Suhrkamp.

Rivas, Ana María, and María Isabel Jociles (2020). ¿Ayuda o trabajo?: La perspectiva de las donantes de óvulos sobre su participación en la reproducción biológica. In Ana María Rivas and Consuelo Álvarez Plaza (eds.). *Etnografía de los Mercados Reproductivos: Actores, Instituciones y Legislaciones*, 95–156. Valencia: Tirant lo Blanch.

Rivas, Ana, Fernando Lores and Isabel Jociles (2018). El anonimato y el altruismo en la donación de gametos: La producción de biocapital en la industria reproductiva. *Política y Sociedad,* 56(3), 623–644.

Sachweh, Patrick, and Till Hilmar (2020). Moral Economy: Moral Forces in Economic Activity. In Milan Zafirovski (ed.). *A Modern Guide to Economic Sociology*, 166–185. Cheltenham: Edward Elgar.

Scheper-Hughes, Nancy (2001). Bodies for Sale—Whole or in Parts. *Body & Society,* 7(2–3), 1–8.

Sichler, Ralph (2020). Strukturanalyse normativ-praktischer Rationalität. *Journal für Psychologie,* 28(2), 34–55.

Siegl, Veronika (2023). *Intimate Strangers: Commercial Surrogacy in Russia and Ukraine and the Making of Truth*. Ithaca, NY: Cornell University Press.

Siegrist, Hannes (2006). Die Propertisierung von Gesellschaft und Kultur: Konstruktion und Institutionalisierung des Eigentums in der Moderne. *Comparativ,* 16(5–6), 9–52.

Skeggs, Beverly, and Simon Yuill (2019). Subjects of Value and Digital Personas: Reshaping the Bourgeois Subject, Unhinging Property from Personhood. *Subjectivity,* 12(1), 82–99.

Strauss, Anselm L. (2004). Methodologische Grundlagen der Grounded Theory. In Jörg Strübing and Bernt Schnettler (eds.). *Methodologie interpretativer Sozialforschung: Klassische Grundlagentexte*, 427–451. Konstanz: UVK.

Strauss, Anselm L., and Juliet Corbin (1996). *Grounded Theory*. Weinheim: Beltz Juventa.

Strehle, Samuel (2009). Jenseits des Tausches: Karl Marx und die Soziologie der Gabe. *Berliner Journal für Soziologie*, 19(1), 127–151.

Strübing, Jörg (2019). Grounded Theory and Theoretical Sampling. In Nina Baur and Jörg Blasius (eds.). *Handbuch Methoden empirischen Sozialforschung*, 525–544. Wiesbaden: Springer VS.

Thompson, Edward P. (1971). The Moral Economy of the English Crowd in the Eighteenth Century. *Past & Present*, 50, 76–136.

Titmuss, Richard (1971). *The Gift Relationship: From Human Blood to Social Policy*. New York: Pantheon Books.

Tober, Diane, and Vincenzo Pavone (2018). Bioeconomies of Egg Provision in the United States and Spain: Comparing Medical Markets and Implications for Donor Care. *Revista de Antropología Social*, 27(2), 261–286.

Tober, Diane, Vincenzo Pavone, Sara Lafuente-Funes and Nancy Konvalinka (2023). Eggonomics: Vitrification and Bioeconomies of Egg Donation in the United States and Spain. *Medical Anthropology Quarterly*, 37(3), 248–263.

Vertommen, Sigrid, Vincenzo Pavone and Michal Nahman (2022). Global Fertility Chains: An Integrative Political Economy Approach to Understanding the Reproductive Bioeconomy. *Science, Technology and Human Values*, 47(1), 112–145.

Waldby, Catherine, and Robert Mitchell (eds.) (2006). *Tissue Economies: Blood, Organs, and Cell Lines in Late Capitalism*. Durham, NC: Duke University Press.

Weber, Max (2011 [1920]). *The Protestant Ethic and the Spirit of Capitalism*. New York: Oxford University Press.

Wiel, Lucy van de (2020). The Speculative Turn in IVF: Egg Freezing and the Financialization of Fertility. *New Genetics and Society*, 39(3), 306–326.

Witzel, Andreas, and Herwig Reiter (2013). *The Problem-Centred Interview: Principles and Practice*. London: Sage.

Zeiler, Kristin (2014). Neither Property Right nor Heroic Gift, Neither Sacrifice nor Aporia: The Benefit of the Theoretical Lens of Sharing in Donation Ethics. *Medicine, Health Care, and Philosophy*, 17(2), 171–181.

Zelizer, Viviana A. (2000). The Purchase of Intimacy. *Law & Social Inquiry*, 25(3), 817–848.

IV
Reproductive Justice Perspectives on the ART Economy

Contested Property Relations: Feminist Debates on Labour, Biocapitalist "Land Grabbing" and Geneticised Kinship

Susanne Schultz

In recent years, there has been growing debate within gender studies about the right to make use of other people's reproductive bodies in the context of assisted reproductive technologies (ARTs). The debate engages with a range of complex and controversial issues, and has been sparked in part by the global expansion of the repro-industrial complex. Procedures that make use of "third-party" bodies,[1] in particular egg provision and surrogacy,[2] are gaining in popularity worldwide. But aside from this immediate contemporary relevance, the debate also touches on fundamental questions and critiques of power and domination.

We can distinguish, somewhat schematically, between three main categories of feminist positions. Firstly, there are liberal positions that emphasise the individual autonomy of both the "commissioning parents" and the individuals who choose to provide their eggs or carry a child on someone else's behalf; such positions also increasingly make reference to a right to biological or genetic parenthood for same-sex couples. Then there are opposing positions that regard these reproductive procedures as essentially patriarchal, capitalist and technological violence against those whose eggs are taken or whose children are "sold". They view the disempowerment of female "commodity providers" and mothers who already have a prenatal bond with their child as nothing short of scandalous. Finally, there is a growing strand of anti-capitalist positions that understand ART procedures in terms of global

1 In this case, the "first" party is the reproductive clinics that provide the service and the "second" is their customers (the commissioning parents).

2 I speak of egg provision and egg providers rather than egg donation and egg donors in order to avoid the euphemistic language of "donation", which ignores the dynamics of economisation that are at work here and invokes problematically normative notions of altruistic action.

labour relations and so hold that they should be regulated politically within the context of labour struggles.

However, there are also counterhegemonic, queer-feminist interventions that cut across these widely known positions. One example is *fem*ini*, the *feminist initiative against reproductive exploitation*, which I myself am involved in and which campaigns from a queer-feminist and anti-capitalist perspective for the ban on egg provision and surrogacy in Germany to be maintained.[3]

As this brief outline of the positions makes clear, the conceptual and analytical tools used to understand or frame these boundary technologies are strongly contested. In this essay, I will discuss three framings that play a key analytical role in the critical debate on the ART economy. These are firstly, framings that interpret reproductive medical procedures in terms of labour and exploitation; secondly, framings that emphasise biomedical or biocapitalist primary valorisation and commercialisation of bodies and bodily substances; and thirdly, framings that highlight (dis)continuities of genetic or biological kinship relations. Different positions in the debate vary in how much weight they give each of these framings and in whether or not they neglect problematic aspects that are highlighted in these framings. Of course, there is also political contestation *within* all three framings. Questions of property and ownership, which are the main topic of this anthology, run through all of these complex and conflicting framings. All three framings—emphasising, respectively, labour relations, biocapitalist "land grabs" and kinship relations—deal with (new or old) property relations in a broader or narrower sense. In particular, if we understand the establishment of such relations in terms of *processes*, we could say these framings deal with "propertisation" in different respects and that existing analyses reconstruct forms and relations of ownership or property in different ways. For instance, they differ with respect to whether they focus on property in the person, on the ownership of labour power, i.e. the ability to "sell" bodily services or commodified bodily substances, on ownership of genetic "information", on ownership of the embryo/foetus and the child after birth, or on, as I will discuss in part two of this article, on ownership of custody rights. Moreover, although this point is often neglected, the property owners in this context are not only the surrogates, egg providers and commissioning parents, but

3 The initiative's declaration is available in English at https://www.gen-ethisches-netzwerk.de/stellungnahmen/juni-2021/fuer-reproduktive-gerechtigkeit-reproductive-justice#english.

also the companies involved—such as reproductive clinics, agencies, and egg banks.

Despite the complex property issues that are at stake, feminist debates about reproductive medicine rarely deal explicitly with the topic of propertisation. Instead, these debates often highlight the commodification and commercialisation of the bodily substances and processes that are sold, and sometimes even raise concerns about "trade in children", while the question of property relations tends to be only addressed in passing, or brushed aside altogether. When it comes to property in the body or labour power, the debate is typically dominated by questions of individual autonomy and physical integrity. As a result, the dominant focus tends to be on the relationship between the individual who provides a bodily substance, service, or even a child, and the thing or service that is provided (see Schultz and Braun 2013). What is frequently overlooked are the complex, multilayered and structural dimensions of property relations, including—if we adopt a broader analytical lens—transformations in political-economic and social power relations. Moreover, there is often a tendency to focus narrowly on the explicit manifestations of commodification and commercialisation, thereby neglecting a more comprehensive consideration of property relations; for instance, the ownership of one's own labour power or the notion of one's "own" child. Embracing this broader perspective is essential, as it enables a critical examination of the genealogies of colonialism, racism, class hierarchy and the heteronormative family structure that underpin particular groups' domination over the reproductive labour of others—not merely as isolated individuals, but as constituted social collectives.

To make some first inroads into this complex terrain, I will explore the diverse forms and dimensions of property relations that are at least partly addressed in the three framings described above. My aim in this article is not to develop a completely new analytical framing, but rather to show that an approach focused on propertisation can provide helpful orientation in political debates about egg provision and surrogacy.[4]

4 Another complicating factor is that while egg provision and surrogacy procedures both involve reproductive instrumentalisation or exploitation of other people's bodies, they also differ in certain respects that are relevant to the present discussion. For instance, they involve different levels of physical burden and time commitment (from several weeks in the case of egg provision to many months in the case of surrogacy). Egg provision is concerned with a bodily substance (i.e. the egg) that is separated from the provider and with the genetic "information" it contains, whereas surrogacy is a service in which a person "rents out" their uterus and hands over the child after birth.

I will begin by examining the insights each of these framings offers and identifying the points of feminist contention within each of them. I then ask how the three framings relate to property, and which questions they ignore or leave open. In the final section, I examine how the interrelations between the three framings can contribute to a critical, intersectional feminist analysis attentive to power dynamics. The central aim is to demonstrate that limiting feminist analysis and political positions on egg provision and surrogacy to a single framing—as is often done in contemporary debates—results in significant gaps and blind spots in both critiques and interventions.

In recent years, interest in these topics has been fuelled by several major "turns" in gender theory and feminism, including "neo-materialist" and science and technology studies approaches, as well as a repoliticised debate about family abolitionism (Fannin et al. 2014; Lewis 2021; O'Brien 2023). With respect to property relations, however, I find the reproductive justice framing—which is gaining traction within counter-hegemonic, anti-racist, anti-ableist and anti-capitalist feminist movements—particularly illuminating. The concept of reproductive justice was introduced by Black United States feminists in the 1990s. Proponents of this approach call for a change in how issues around contraception, abortion, pregnancy, birth and parenthood are discussed. Instead of a pro-choice feminism that is strongly focused on abortion rights and often makes decontextualising, individualist demands for bodily autonomy, they draw attention to complex global power structures, institutional violence and social inequality in reproductive decisions and mothering/parenting (Ross 2017). Accordingly, they put great emphasis on an anti-natalist, anti-ableist politics of reproduction. However, the reproductive exploitation and instrumentalisation of other people's bodies is a dimension that extends beyond or cuts across the topic of multiple power relations that are a central topic of the reproductive justice approach, and which revolve around questions of whose children and whose parenthoods are socially desirable and whose are not, and which children should be born and which should not (Schultz 2023). Although the question of whose bodily substances/processes should be used to facilitate the birth of other people's children relates to a distinct problematic, it is closely connected to the questions raised in the reproductive justice framing and

Moreover, at present the standard global practice is that this child has no genetic "connection" to the surrogate; the embryos that are implanted come either from the "commissioning mother" or an "egg provider".

it cannot be discussed in isolation from them. This is because the practices of the ART economy are embedded within complex dimensions of stratified reproduction or "neoeugenics" (Ginsburg and Rapp 1995; Pande 2014, 104 ff.; see also Pande 2022).

1. Reproductive labour: the framing of reproductive exploitation

A first framing within the debate, which is particularly pertinent to the analysis of property relations, approaches the activities of egg providers and surrogates through a feminist, anti-capitalist lens—as forms of embodied labour. At its core, this perspective raises the question of how ownership over an individual's labour power, body, or even its personhood should be understood. This framing has gained increasing prominence in recent years (Cooper and Waldby 2015; Lewis 2021; Lafuente-Funes 2020), and one of its key strengths lies in its emphasis on the agency of the workers without whom the ART procedures described above would not be possible. Contra narratives of victimisation, this labour-based framing emphasises that egg providers and surrogates actively engage in these procedures, drawing attention to the myriad activities these procedures involve, the level of time commitment and exertion, and the burdens and stresses that egg providers and surrogates take on. By making their roles as workers visible, this framing opposes the notion of the body as "cheap nature" which is implicitly conveyed in ART procedures, i.e. the idea that the reproductive bodily substances or processes are freely available resources in the sense of a *terra nullius*. This idea presents women either as bodies to be "harvested" or property-owners of their bodies.

A crucial aspect of the reproductive labour framing is that it also highlights the temporal nature of the work involved in ART procedures. This work does not comprise one-off acts of handing over an egg or a newborn child, as bioethical contract models of informed consent at least suggest insofar as they focus on a single autonomous act of "delivery". This framing offers a clear view of the whole process, which takes several weeks in the case of egg retrieval (from the preliminary medical and psychological interviews to hormone treatment, the operation to extract the eggs and any necessary follow-up treatment) and many months in the case of surrogacy (from the preliminary interviews to hormone treatment, implantation of the embryo, pregnancy and birth, as well as treatment for any complications).

In addition, empirical analyses that apply this framing to explore labour conditions and forms of exploitation reveal social inequality structures that are crucial for understanding the global expansion of ART procedures. They show that the vast majority of body workers only engage in these activities in exchange for payment, that is, out of financial motivation or necessity. "Payment" can take various forms. Sometimes it involves covert forms of economisation, such as compensation or discounts for medical treatments (Braun and Schultz 2012). At other times, it is more overt—for example, service contracts with fixed prices in countries where commercialisation of the body is legally permitted. Narratives that present donation or altruism as the main motivation mostly disguise or downplay these economic aspects, and in places where "altruistic" regulations form the legal basis for ART procedures, workers are often pressured to endorse these narratives. For example, their financial motivations are rendered invisible or "discursively disappeared" during preliminary psychological interviews (Perler 2022, 170). Moreover, many empirical studies show that the supply of reproductive substances and services only comes close to meeting demand if workers are paid an attractive rate.[5] This means that ART markets can only establish themselves where there is sufficient social inequality, whether at a local or global level. Reproductive labour relations thus involve exploitation (in the Marxist sense) of surrogates or egg providers, as the business is fundamentally based on reproductive clinics extracting surplus value, i.e. paying or "compensating" the body workers considerably less than the clinics themselves earn from selling those workers' services. Furthermore, the fact that the wage relation is not formalised but is either disguised as altruism or operates via forms of precarious (pseudo-)self-employment results in the same overexploitation that typifies precarised work around the world more generally.

5 In Spain, the country with by far the most "egg donations" in Europe, the "donors" receive 800 to 1,300 euros per cycle (Lafuente-Funes et al. 2023). In the United Kingdom, compensation was increased from 250 to 750 pound in 2012 to make up for a "shortage" of eggs. And in countries like Austria that only permit reimbursement of documented expenses, the number of registered "egg donations" remains low several years after legalisation (46 documented cases in 2022, Kern et al. 2023).

1.1 Bodily aspects of reproductive labour

The analytic focus on wage labourers' agency prompts an understanding of egg providers and surrogates as what Marx calls "labourers who are free in a double sense": on the one hand, they "freely" decide to enter into a specific wage relation, but on the other they are forced to do so to earn a living. However, this framing is marked by certain blind spots, leading to the distinctive characteristics of these labour relations being neglected. In some debates framed through the lens of work, inadequate and sometimes misleading comparisons are made with other forms of "embodied labour" (most commonly sex work). These comparisons are often combined with critiques of "prohibitionist" laws. The argument is that the best way to deal politically with the exploitative conditions is through workers' self-organisation and labour struggles, rather than through state-imposed restrictions or bans (see Waldby and Cooper 2008; Lewis 2021).[6]

In my view, one key distinguishing feature in the case of egg provision and surrogacy centres on how we are to understand the bodily processes that accompany these procedures and, indeed, constitute their very purpose, i.e. the maturation of eggs or development of a baby. In contrast to other bodily activities, these processes cannot be actively controlled, meaning the worker does not have agency over them. Egg provision, for instance, is based on hormonal stimulation that causes multiple oocytes to mature and which sets in motion hormonal processes that are either irreversible or can only be halted by biomedical means at the cost of failing to achieve the work's intended goal. Similarly, once a surrogate pregnancy has begun, it cannot be stopped for nine months, short of having an abortion and so undermining the very purpose of the work. The fact that these biomedically initiated bodily processes constitute the essential purpose of this "work" is a specific feature that cannot simply be reduced to the general notion that all human labour is, of course, embodied and may entail physical costs beyond the activity itself.

Waldby and Cooper offer an analysis inspired by Marxist value theory that subsumes these bodily processes under the concept of labour. They argue that these bodily processes themselves can be understood as productive and

6 Arguments for "prohibitionist" regulations can be made within the "labour framing" too: in particular, arguments for health and safety regulations. ART procedures do involve physical risks, stresses and potential harms, which could support the conclusion that this work should be banned on health and safety grounds.

as creating extractible surplus value (2008). Elsewhere (Schultz and Braun 2013), Kathrin Braun and I argue that this interpretation entails a problematic, vitalist, and essentialising view of value-creating labour. It is based on ontological and ahistorical readings of Marx's concept of labour and overlooks formulations in which Marx identifies wage labour as a historically specific, objectified social relation. In any case, the value relation does not stem inherently from the productive capacity of bodily processes that transcend specific modes of production, but must be grasped as the objectified expression of social power relations that demand critical and historical reconstruction.

1.2 Propertisation through unfree labour

How are these elusive, blurred boundaries between activity on the one hand and irreversible bodily processes on the other relevant to the question of propertisation? The "labour framing" construes property relations in terms of relations to a worker's labour power, or to their body as a whole. If we apply the Marxist idea of "doubly free" wage labour, then egg provision and surrogacy workers are able to freely dispose of their embodied labour power, while simultaneously being forced to sell that labour power to earn a living. At the moment of signing a contract, they can in principle decide whether they want to enter into that specific labour relation rather than another. But if we take the irreversible bodily processes to be central to these (labour) relations, we need to ask whether and at what point in time exactly workers are free in a double sense. Melinda Cooper (2015) raises some important points in her analysis of how surrogacy contracts negotiate the boundaries between family and employment law. She notes that, unlike in other employment relationships, the surrogate cannot terminate the contract by offering a financial compensation, such as returning fees or already-paid wages, as is otherwise customary in contract law. Around the world, surrogacy contracts typically stipulate a requirement of "specific performance of service" (ibid., 18)—namely, the obligation to hand over the child after birth—even before the embryo has been implanted in the surrogate's uterus. Cooper explores how family and custody law is positioned vis-à-vis contract law in the context of surrogacy, although the ways in which the boundary between them is drawn can vary. This peculiarity of surrogacy contracts reveals the unfree nature of the work involved. With regard to the war in Ukraine, for example, journalist Alison Motluk described the "her body—my baby conundrum" (Motluk 2022) from the perspective of the intended parents, emphasising the fact that the surrogates commit to a nine-month process that they cannot get out of. However, from the perspective of reproductive clinics and commissioning parents, "my body—my baby" would be a more accurate description, as the surrogate is no longer regarded as a fully autonomous person, but rather as a body enclosing an embryo or foetus.

Viewed through the lens of ownership, what is at stake is not merely the alienation of the surrogate's labour power; rather, the surrogate—temporarily and after first "freely" consenting to the contract—places herself in a position akin to that of a "serf". Or, to phrase matters more cautiously and avoid falsely invoking historical feudal contexts, surrogacy is situated within the "semantic field of serfdom" (Schrupp 2016). Thus, if debates on decolonial and racial capitalism are taken into account, it becomes evident that the labour of surrogates and egg providers fits into complex analyses of the global genealogies of unfree labour (see Barrientos et al. 2013; Davis 1998). Waldby and Cooper (2008) anticipated this point in their analysis of the history of wet nurses and domestic slaves, and Eva von Redecker's concept of "phantom possession" could likewise be used to describe the phenomenon. "Phantom possession" in the theory that the fact that although the members of certain social groups are formally free legal subjects, our social relations and conceptions of rights to make use of their bodies, labour and lives continue to be shaped by their historical classification as unfree labourers, slaves, serfs, servants, or housewives (see von Redecker 2020, 32 ff.). However, even setting aside the question of whether von Redecker's focus on imaginary property rights places undue emphasis on the economic dimensions of complex processes of subjectivation and power relations, I argue that the specific qualities of unfree labour I have described go beyond what she terms "phantom possession". It is not merely that the use of the bodies of individuals from certain social groups appears to be considered legitimate in reproductive medicine worldwide; rather, for a certain period, there is an explicit form of actual ownership over the surrogate's individual body. Depending on the wording of the contract, the commissioning parents may hold legal entitlements to demand that the surrogate behave in specific ways, reside in designated places, and comply with other conditions—obligations from which the surrogate cannot withdraw during the term of the contract. For example, when the war in Ukraine started in February 2022, Ukrainian surrogates were pressured to either move to another country where surrogacy is legal or to return to Kyiv to give birth (Motluk 2022; Siegl 2022). While some contracts may be more stringent and restrictive than others—in terms of how the surrogate is required to behave, where she is permitted to live, and similar conditions during pregnancy—the surrogate is, in all cases, obligated to carry the pregnancy to term and relinquish the child afterwards. This unfree labour relationship also applies, to some extent, to egg providers—albeit for a much shorter period. Once hormonal stimulation has begun, the egg provider can likewise no longer freely dispose of her labour power: she cannot unilaterally terminate the contract, and for the duration of the process may be at risk of potentially harmful complications, such as ovarian hyperstimulation syndrome (OHSS). By intervening inside the body and initiating irreversible physiological processes, ARTs produce a distinctive constellation of unfree labour—or, more pointedly, a form of temporary "serfdom".

These points make it clear that the labour framing (in the sense of double freedom) is inadequate for fully understanding and politically addressing the relations of domination, power, and property involved in egg provision and surrogacy, even though the labour dimension is one that must not be overlooked. I will therefore now turn to the other two analytical framings: biocapitalist "land grabs" and geneticised kinship.

2. Biomedical procedures beneficial only to others: the framing of biocapitalist "land grabs"

A second key analytical framing in the political debate on the ART economy is that of biocapitalist "land grabs", which places greater emphasis on the irreversible bodily processes initiated by ART procedures and the extracted bodily substances or "products" themselves. Understanding these procedures not only in terms of labour but also in terms of the biomedical and biocapitalist instrumentalisation of bodily processes, substances or "products" is, moreover, the most intuitively straightforward way to comprehend the property relations at play. What is at stake is whether and how property relations can be conceived in relation to either bodily substances (specifically, eggs) or the embryo/foetus and ultimately the child that is to be handed over.

The concept of "biocapitalist land grabs" draws on analyses showing how the body's interior is increasingly becoming a site of primary valorisation (Lettow 2015; Sunder Rajan 2006), on recent feminist theories of ongoing primitive accumulation and on the thesis that capitalist growth is always dependent on gaining access to domains considered "natural" or "non-economic" (see Federici 2004).

These biocapitalist land grabs cannot be understood without reference to transformations of statehood. In the case of egg provision and surrogacy, they are made possible by specific forms of biomedical regulation and bioethical legitimation of ART procedures. This requires two main regulatory limitations to be overcome: it is necessary to legalise and provide bioethical legitimation for, firstly, the other-benefiting nature of these biomedical interventions and, secondly, the primary valorisation of the resulting "products" (i.e. the eggs), the rented uterus and the handover of the child produced through surrogacy.

Let us start with the first point. Egg provision and surrogacy are medically invasive, potentially harmful interventions in the bodies of individuals who cannot expect any health benefits from the treatment themselves, yet are exposed to risk, pain and physical stress. As such, these procedures violate the Hippocratic oath, "*primum non nocere*" (first, do no harm): a basic norm of medical ethics which requires that the benefit to the person being treated must outweigh the harm. There are, of course, other biomedical procedures in which the person undergoing the treatment receives no medical benefit from it, such as living organ transplants and clinical research (both of which also have their own problems of economisation and so on; see for instance Sunder Rajan 2006). These procedures are legitimised by weighing up the medical costs and benefits in a way that looks beyond the individual case: for instance, by arguing that the health benefit for another person (in the case of living organ donation, where the benefit is often the survival of the recipient) or the general public (in the case of medical research) legitimises the "harm" to the organ donor or clinical trial subject. In consequence, for "reproductive treatment" to be legitimised as a medical benefit for others (the commissioning parents), fulfilling the wish to have children must also be considered a "medical benefit". The ground for this was laid by the World Health Organization (n.d.) categorising infertility as a disease, so that some (though by no means all) "non-reproductive" bodies came to be classed as sick and in need of treatment, and life without biological children as a pathological condition rather than a matter of social circumstances.

The second strategy for overcoming regulatory and bioethical boundaries concerns the economic valorisation of bodily substances and processes. It is supported by the discursive interpretation of altruism. In Europe, commercialisation of the human body and human body parts explicitly contravenes Article 3 of the European Union Charter of Fundamental Rights and Article 21 of the European Convention on Bioethics. The narratives of altruism and donation described earlier in this article undermine this regulatory restriction on biocapitalist "land grabs". "Altruistic" regulatory interpretations systematically weaken and undermine the ban on commercialisation, and thus enable the elaborate and expanding political economy of the repro-medical complex. In European countries where egg provision and/or surrogacy are legalised on the grounds of "altruism", reproductive clinics are able to offer these procedures on private, explicitly commodified markets despite the ban. These profit-oriented dynamics have profound implications for the expansion of such procedures (Herb and Wenner 2023).

Which feminist lines of conflict are connected to the political framing of egg provision and surrogacy as biocapitalist land grabs? In liberal feminist positions advocating for the legalisation of these procedures, the justification typically rests on the individual motivations and autonomy of egg providers and surrogates. This approach often rhetorically sidesteps the issue of biomedical procedures that offer no medical benefits to their recipients. At the same time, there is strong discursive investment in downplaying the medical burdens and risks of these procedures or framing them as "manageable" (see e.g. Wiesemann 2023). The idea of a person who "owns" their body and has the right to have it burdened or harmed by biomedical procedures for the benefit of others is thus set against bioethical boundaries such as the Hippocratic oath and bans on commercialisation. Furthermore, in the political debate around the ban on commercialising the body, advocates of ART often reinforce narratives of altruism and refer to quantitative studies demonstrating individuals' altruistic motives (e.g. Bracewell-Milnes et al. 2016).

The *double* economisation involved in ART procedures is rarely recognised in these perspectives. Double economisation refers, firstly to the individual egg donors and surrogates providing their labour in exchange for payment; and, seecondly, it pertains to the sale of reproductive medical services and products by companies within the reproductive medical complex. The political debate focuses almost exclusively on the former aspect, and various strategies involving "altruistic" regulation have been proposed to avert criticisms of commercialisation, which is interpreted as being preventable. Meanwhile, the second dimension—that is, the political economy of the reproductive industry—is largely neglected in the feminist debate. As a result, it is mistakenly suggested that the only economic actors in egg donation and surrogacy are the individuals involved—egg providers or surrogates versus the commissioning parents. However, the significant profits made by companies within the largely private global reproductive industry are often overlooked.

Like liberal positions that invoke the ideas of self-ownership or autonomy to deflect criticisms of procedures that provide benefits only for other people, anti-capitalist positions that focus on labour relations also tend to neglect the infringements of biomedical boundaries needed for biocapitalist land grabs, i.e. treatments that provide no medical benefits for their recipients and the commercialisation of bodily substances/processes. They often argue, rather fatalistically, that the dynamics of capitalist land grabs can in any case not be curbed by government-imposed restrictions and, moreover, that domestic regulation cannot halt the transnational dynamics of global outsourcing. This touches on major questions about the state or statehood as a field of conflict, about appropriate abolitionist perspectives and about the crucial need for transnational feminist political strategies, which it is not possible to discuss here in detail. I will, however, note that a simplistic anti-prohibitionism does not adequately address these questions, but runs the risk of simply feeding into liberal projects of biocapitalist deregulation.

Indeed, feminists that support prohibitionist politics including—and problematically in my view—in relation to sex work are often strongly opposed to the commercialisation of bodies and biomedical procedures that provide no medical benefits to their recipients. These feminist positions and their respective theoretical traditions are certainly complex, but they often converge in strongly emphasising the victimisation of egg providers and surrogates as vulnerable, generally powerless commodity suppliers. There is, to be sure, an important anti-capitalist protest against biocapitalist land grabs and instrumentalisation of bodies at their core. However, one problematic aspect of these positions is that surrogacy is often reductively (mis-)interpreted as "child trafficking". Moreover, these feminist positions often reinforce conservative notions of "natural" female embodiment and motherhood that must be defended against technological and capitalist encroachments, which are understood as external threats. Declarations like those of *Stop Surrogacy Now* (n.d.) or, in the German context, *Terre des Femmes*

(2020) make reference to a "natural" or "biological" prenatal bond between mother and child that must be protected. It seems problematic that this bond is implicitly imagined in terms of a positive sociality that transcends social power relations. These positions are potentially capable of feeding into conservative norms of biological motherhood and a general delegitimisation of alternative forms of family and social parenthood.

2.1 Propertisation of bodily substances and custody rights

The concept of self-ownership or ownership of one's reproductive labour power is central to positions that advocate for the legalisation of egg provision and surrogacy procedures. Property-based notions of autonomy either explicitly challenge the bioethical limitations of procedures beneficial to others or, more often, simply dethematise them. In this context, the dynamics of biocapitalist land grabbing, the valorisation and commodification of bodies and the political economy of reproductive medicine are either completely ignored, de-thematised or presented as unstoppable, "natural" developments under capitalism.

In light of this, it is important to understand the property relations that structure egg provision and surrogacy practices without ignoring the systematic differences between them. In the former case, the biomedical process of extracting eggs makes them a materially isolable and separable object. It is only through this disentanglement from the body that eggs can be commodified, that is, in Marxist terms, that they can become an alienable commodity. An implicit or explicit exchange value can then be assigned to this commodity by the reproductive medicine industry. As already mentioned, it is important to distinguish more precisely between the various actors involved in these commodity exchange relations and complex value chains, which extend from the process of recruiting the egg provider, to possible cryopreservation and storage in egg banks, to the legal advisors and agencies that take their cut of the profits, to the reproductive clinic's sale of the eggs to a customer. A crucial aspect of egg provision, which makes property relations particularly complex in this- case, is that it is not just the physical substance of the egg that is relevant in these transactions but also the genetic "information" associated with it (see Perler 2022; Bergmann 2015). The various owners (the egg provider, the clinics, the banks, etc.) accordingly also position themselves in relation to the supposed genetic "qualities" of the egg provider that are being sold along with the egg—and to the implications of that sale.

Donna Dickenson (2006; 2007) was among a handful of feminist authors to recognise at an early stage the complex dimensions of property and ownership in relation to egg provision. Like Cooper and Waldby (2008),[7] she referred to John Locke's concept of property, noting that it allows property to be conceived as a product of labour. Indeed, she can be regarded as an early proponent of the "labour framing" that enables a focus on workers' rights and opposes the idea of their bodies as a readily available *terra nullius*. An interesting aspect of Dickenson's interventions is that she adopts Locke's notion of a "bundle of rights" to bodily substances (2006, 9–10). She asks what specific political rights egg providers as property owners who transfer these rights might have concerning the various ways their eggs could be used in biomedical transactions. However, if we take the condition of the doubly free wage labourer to intersect with the aspect of unfree subjection to the bodily processes that are the very purpose of these procedures, we should also question the bundle theory of property,[8] and ask which other critiques of domination and propertisationmight be more productive in this context—for instance, one that considers the simultaneous processes of exploitation and expropriation and develops a more nuanced perspective. Such an approach would allow us to address the extractivist nature of inner land grabs without denying or overlooking the agency of the body workers in the moment of entering into a contract. Furthermore, a perspective on the embodied self is needed that critically addresses the separation between the active body owner/worker and their body/labour power without lapsing into crude models of a bodily integrity that must be siloed off or defended.

The property relations are different in the case of surrogacy. Instead of a bodily substance becoming commodified property, the ultimate purpose of the economic transaction is the resulting child. Besides the agency of the surrogate worker that I have already discussed above, the commodification also extends to the surrogate providing her uterus and related bodily processes for an embryo that is already constructed as someone else's future child at

7 Cooper and Waldby show that Locke's concept of property can be used in this context to undermine the liberal regime of property that he himself supported by revealing the egg providers' and surrogates' contributions to have the form of labour rather than a freely available *res nullius*: "If the contribution of labour is explicitly recognised, then this level of expropriation becomes illegitimate under the liberal terms of property" (2008, 67).

8 See also the chapter by Susanne Lettow in this volume.

the time of implantation. Certain parallels to the logic of state bans on abortion can be seen here: whereas in the case of abortion it is the right to life of an embryo construed as independent of the pregnant woman that is set against her agency, in the case of surrogacy that function is served by the reproductive clinics' and commissioning parents' claim to an embryo or foetus that has already been constructed as independent "property".[9]

But the question of how the child that is to be handed over to the commissioning parents after birth, should be understood in terms of ownership is a complex issue. In fact, it makes little sense to describe the child itself as a commodity because even before conception the child is conceptualised as the commissioning parents' "own child" and their right to custody of it after birth is guaranteed. I suggest that we speak here of a commodification of the right to custody, a topic that has not yet received much attention or discussion within legal scholarship. With the agreement to hand over the child to the commissioning parents after birth, which is usually made in the surrogacy contract prior to the pregnancy, custody becomes a commodity that can be purchased before a child is even conceived. This undoubtedly falls within a tradition of stratified reproduction and reproductive injustice, as already addressed in many critical studies of anti-natalist politics and global power imbalances. These studies draw attention to social ascriptions of who has the right to care for and raise children (Ginsburg and Rapp 1995). However, future custody becoming a commodity even before a child is born adds a new dimension. This is not about the right under family law to raise existing children, as in the case of parental custody, foster care or adoption (which are also very much embedded in commercialised global markets), but the right to purchase custody rights in advance. This also has implications for the question of disentanglement. Although the child does not become a commodity, this advance sale of custody does mean that even during pregnancy the embryo/foetus is already conceived as separable from, and as not belonging to, the surrogate's body.

Geneticisation also plays a key role in the political economy of surrogacy practices, albeit with important differences from the role it plays in egg provision practices. Generally speaking, the purchased custody right is underpinned by the idea of a genetic relationship between the commissioning parents and the future child, so that even in legal situations where the surrogate

9 According to Schrupp (2022, 79 ff), this separation fails to account for how pregnancy is a state involving neither "one" nor "two" entities, but rather "two in one".

not to know, the right to information and the right of contact. Debates usually centre, on the one hand, on the right of the future child to know about its genetic origin and, on the other, on the commissioning parents' desire to be encumbered with as few claims as possible from the side of the genetic "mother".[11] In contrast, there is little discussion about the egg provider's right to (not) know about and (not) have contact with the children resulting from the egg provision. Debates about legal regulations are instead more concerned with questions of human genetics and biopolitics: for example, laws intended to prevent "too many" genetic "half-siblings" descended from a single egg provider.

By contrast with egg provision, the rights of the surrogate in her (non-)relationship with the child figure more prominently in political discussions. As mentioned above, more conservative positions, such as that of *Stop Surrogacy Now*, support their calls for a ban on surrogacy with general assumptions on prenatal bonds, and a child's right to its biological mother. These positions likewise assert a priority of biological over social motherhood, albeit to different ends, which runs counter to queer-feminist critiques of such assertions and positions that support alternative social models of creating families. Proponents of different positions can draw on a variety of empirical studies on how surrogates see their relationship to the child to support their case, as there is considerable variation in the needs articulated by surrogates from around the world. For instance, Amrita Pande (2014) found that Indian surrogates wanted an ongoing relationship with the child and the commissioning family, while the Russian surrogates interviewed by Veronika Siegl (2015) often expressed a view of themselves as workers and took a more pragmatic attitude, seeing their job as done once the child was handed over. There are also case studies of conflicts in both directions, which have sometimes been subjects of extensive media coverage: there are surrogates who did not want to give up their child (see Cooper 2015, 19 ff.), while others were forced to either take care of the child themselves or give it up for adoption in cases where the commissioning parents decided not to take the child after all (see Siegl 2015, 99; Siegl 2023).

Above, I have discussed relations of property or ownership based on genetics in terms of the commercialisation of future custody rights and genetic "information". In what follows, I will consider to what extent the idea of a

11 Anonymity remains a marketing advantage, as illustrated by the high number of egg providers in Spain (see Perler 2022, 78).

child that is genetically or biologically "one's own" can be understood as a relation of "ownership" broadly construed. With regard to property relations in surrogacy, a distinction should be drawn between the commissioning parents' rights to make use of the surrogate's body during pregnancy (as discussed earlier) and custody relations after birth based on the idea of a child that is genetically "one's own". As I have shown, the need for legal certainty with regard to one's "own child" even before an embryo is created enables a state of unfree labour relations. But even if surrogates can officially only decide after the birth whether they want to give up the child, the situation remains precarious. Although regulations of this kind create a legal uncertainty and tend to undermine the foundations of the reproductive medicine business, the situation is nevertheless not comparable to adoption.[12] Even without a prior guarantee of the commissioning parents' custody rights, the geneticised relations and the fact that the contract was concluded with a specific intention before gestation and on the basis of an unequal relationship, weigh too heavily. By contrast with adoption, surrogacy does not involve a child who already exists and needs care, and who only at this point enters into the economising logic of adoption markets. It seems as if, even without legal certainty, the claim to ownership that is constructed through the surrogacy relation prior to pregnancy and based on genetics outweighs any possible kinship claims of the surrogate.

The idea of being able, thanks to reproductive medicine, to design a child that is genetically and/or biologically "one's own", as well as the desire for this "child of one's own", is embedded in the world of a nuclear family order in which parents have power and control over "their" children. This world assigns clear social roles and has established inheritance relations with diverse connotations, ranging from qualities conceived as "genetically" inherited to the inheritance of wealth and social status. The idea of a "child of one's own", and hence of ownership of children, is not specific to reproductive medicine, but is reproduced by its procedures, animated by a politics of desire and supported by legal moves to establish a fundamental right to one's own child (see Wagenmann 2014). In my view, this effect is far stronger than Sophie Lewis claims in *Full Surrogacy Now* (2021). Lewis suggests that giving up a child after birth anticipates postcapitalist conditions of a universal social and communitarian parenthood, and thus a society where there are no claims of owner-

12 Siegl (2015) describes how the surrogacy business has become established in Russia even though legally speaking the woman who gives birth is initially recognised as the mother.

ship over a child and where the question of who gave birth to a child is not central to its well-being and the constitution of social relationships of care. In the here and now, however, the geneticising and biologising basis of ART procedures and the unequal labour, commercialisation and custody relations have so much more weight that invoking this framing of postcapitalist "surrogacy" strikes me as almost cynical.

From a reproductive justice perspective, however, the key question concerns the context within which the right to choose to have children and raise them in good conditions is hierarchically organised. In contrast to anti-natalist or eugenicist programmes, in which this right is denied by preventing reproduction among certain social groups and for certain children, egg provision and surrogacy are about making certain reproductive bodies productive for other people's reproduction—while denying the surrogates and egg providers rights to ownership and use of their own bodies and reproductive relations at various points throughout the process. The property relations involved are complex, but culminate in the birth of a "child of one's own" to whom the workers, the temporary "serfs" or the suppliers of genetic traits, no longer have any relationship. These property relations are mediated by a political economy of reproductive medicine that rarely comes under scrutiny in current political debates.

4. Conclusion

In this article, I have reconstructed property relations in the ART economy in terms of three framings deployed in an often fiercely contested feminist debate about egg provision and surrogacy. This reconstruction has revealed the complex the dynamics of propertisation, which touch on an array of different forms of ownership—from "one's own child", to ownership of one's labour power, to access to unfree labour, to the purchase of custody rights, and the commodification of eggs. The current feminist debates described here tend to marginalise or ignore many of these property relations, although all three framings, and hence all three dimensions—relationships of exploitation, extractive inner "land grabs" and geneticised kinship—explore crucial aspects of processes of propertisation. These framings are intertwined and need to be understood and addressed *together* through a reproductive justice lens.

A labour-based framing draws attention to the doubly free labourer who, on the one hand, owns their capacity for reproductive labour and sells it voluntarily (at least in theory) under economic conditions of social inequality, while, on the other, conditions of unfree labour are established, since the purpose of the medical procedures is to initiate bodily processes that workers have no control over. These workers thus become temporarily unfree "serfs", or "owned bodies", of the reproductive industry. The framing of biocapitalist land grabs makes it clear that this is not just a matter of exploitation but also, in this specific conjunction, of extractivism. These land grabs are enabled by the shifting boundaries of biomedical statehood. They establish property relations to bodily substances (in the case of egg provision) or future custody rights (in the case of surrogacy) that are put up for sale. Moreover, egg provision involves not just a material object but also the idea of transferring genetic information, while surrogacy involves not just working for nine months of pregnancy and then giving birth, or other people having rights over embryos/foetuses while they are inside the surrogates' bodies, but also custody rights to the commissioning parents' "own child". Both facts point to a long-term temporality that endures beyond the transient aspect of labour and bodily extraction.

Having geneticised and biologised kinship as both the ground and the goal of ART procedures adds further dimensions to the already complex property relations at stake: the ownership of genetic information and the evaluation of the genetic "qualities" of an egg (and hence of the person who provided it) are governed by hierarchised social norms that shape the egg's commodity form. In surrogacy, meanwhile, the future custody right itself becomes a commodity whose ownership is transferred. Here, too, the question of ownership involves complex negotiations of boundaries; in this case, not only between exploitation and extractivism or between agency and bodily processes, but also between the market context on the one hand and the custody and kinship relations to "one's own child", governed by family law, on the other.

Previous studies have analysed the exploitation of body workers from a de- or postcolonial perspective as an expression of continuing colonial, racist, class-hierarchical and gendered genealogies of unfree reproductive labour, involving the use of wet nurses, domestic workers and house slaves, as well as closely related genealogies of children being taken away from their parents (see Waldby and Cooper 2008; Briggs 2021). Egg provision and surrogacy could likewise be understood as a continuation of these genealogies or as a claim to "phantom possession", within which the reproductive capacities and children of certain social groups have always been organised as available to others.

At the same time, the configurations of ownership associated with biocapitalist land grabs targeting reproductive bodies are also specific and new. The specific nature of temporary *de facto* serfdom goes beyond claims to "phantom possession". And the fact that these land grabs play out at the regulatory level in the field of biomedical institutions and practices, with negotiations of boundaries between biocapitalist dynamics and state regulation of biomedicine playing a role, is crucial to understanding this battlefield and the negotiations over property relations.

Any political engagement with these complex phenomena from a reproductive justice perspective must therefore include all three dimensions and their interrelationships, so that a radical critique of property relations old and new can be advanced. However, the way in which the political debate is currently structured is inadequate for this goal. On the one hand, there is an anti-capitalist position focused on labour rights, whose anti-prohibitionist tendency ultimately leads it down the same path as neoliberal demands for deregulation couched in the language of an individualist, pro-choice feminism. On the other hand, there are traditionalist conservative positions that defend "natural" family set-ups and biological motherhood and, in a spirit of anti-technological essentialism, deploy the framings of land grabs and geneticised kinship in problematic ways.

This binary structure of the debate means that many issues are either ignored or are only articulated by one political camp. It gets overlooked that what is at issue here is a set of complex politico-economic processes that need to be analysed from a broad, intersectional, feminist-materialist perspective rather than the individualised perspective focused on decontextualised relationships between commissioning parents and body workers that dominates public discourse. However, a queer-feminist position that weighs up bioethical questions and still sees in egg provision and surrogacy the promise of transforming heteronormative kinship relations, despite the recognition that "such achievements are not made without extracted biomaterials, labours, and other resources" (Mamo 2018, 27), likewise prevents a more radical interrogation of these processes of propertisation. Loretta Ross, a key proponent of the Black feminist concept of reproductive justice, expresses matters clearly when she asks, "What the hell makes your DNA so special?" and calls for a strengthening of social parenthoods (Ross 2023). She gestures towards another open question in the debate, which I have only touched on in passing, namely that of how to engage with global biocapitalist statehood in a way that is both radical and nuanced (see Schultz 2023, 129–130). Transnationally organised statehoods are the battlefield on which these struggles, whether we intend it or not, are being fought, and must be understood in terms of all three framings and their specific contradictions. This requires us to develop a reflective abolitionism that opposes state repression and familialist power relations, while also being aware that what we need to fight for are "anti-reformist reforms"—not neoliberal deregulation that supports reproductive exploitation, biocapitalist land grabs and geneticised kinship relations.

Works Cited

Barrientos, Stephanie, Uma Kothari and Nicola Phillips (2013). Dynamics of Unfree Labour in the Contemporary Global Economy. *Journal of Development Studies*, 49(8), 1037–1041.

Bergmann, Sven (2015). Assisted Authenticity: Naturalisation, Regulation and Enactment of "Race" through Donor Matching. In Venetia Kantsa, Lina Papadopoulou and Giulia Zanini (eds.). *(In)fertile Citizens: Anthropological and Legal Challenges of Assisted Reproduction Technologies*, 231–246. Mytilini: University of the Aegean.

Bracewell-Milnes, Timothy, Srdjan Saso, Shabana Bora, Alaa M. Ismail, Maya Al-Memar, Ali Hasan Hamed, Hossam Abdalla and Meen-Yau Thum (2016). Investigating Psychosocial Attitudes, Motivations and Experiences of Oocyte Donors, Recipients and Egg Sharers: A Systematic Review. *Human Reproduction Update*, 22(4), 450–465.

Braun, Kathrin, and Susanne Schultz (2012). Oöcytes for Research: Inspecting the Commercialisation Continuum. *New Genetics and Society*, 31(2), 135–157.

Briggs, Laura (2021). *Taking Children: A History of American Terror*. Oakland, CA: University of California Press.

Cooper, Melinda (2015). Reproduktion neu denken: Leihmutterschaft zwischen Vertrag und Familie. In Kitchen Politics (ed.). *Sie nennen es Leben, wir nennen es Arbeit*, 49–77. Münster: Edition Assemblage.

Cooper, Melinda (2015). Rethinking Reproduction—Between Contract and Family Law. https://www.academia.edu/27637549/Rethinking_Reproduction_Between_Contract_and_Family_Law.

Davis, Angela Y. (1998). Surrogates and Outcast Mothers: Racism and Reproductive Politics in the Nineties. In Joy James (ed.). *The Angela Y. Davis Reader*, 210–222. Oxford: Blackwell.

Dickenson, Donna (2006). The Lady Vanishes: What's Missing from the Stem Cell Debate. *Journal of Bioethical Inquiry*, 3(1–2), 43–54.

Dickenson, Donna (2007). *Property in the Body: Feminist Perspectives*. Cambridge: Cambridge University Press.

Fannin, Maria, Julie MacLeavy, Wendy Larner and Wenfei Winnie Wang (2014). Work, Life, Bodies: New Materialisms and Feminisms. *Feminist Theory*, 15(3), 261–268.

Federici, Silvia (2004). *Caliban and the Witch*. Williamsburg: Autonomedia.

Ginsburg, Fayne D., and Rayna Rapp (1995). Introduction. In Fayne Ginsburg and Rayna Rapp (eds.). *Conceiving the New World Order: The Global Politics of Reproduction*, 1–18. Berkeley: University of California Press.

Herb, Irina, and Zelda Wenner (2023). Who Owns and Controls the Means of Reproduction? Assisted Fertility and Pregnancy as a Multi-Billion Dollar Market. https://sfb294-eigentum.de/de/blog/who-owns-and-controls-the-means-of-reproduction-assisted-fertility-and-pregnancy-as-a-multi-billion-dollar-market/.

Kern, Reinhard, and Dominika Mikšová (2023). *IVF-Register Jahresbericht 2022*. Vienna: Gesundheit Österreich.

Lafuente-Funes, Sara (2020). Shall We Stop Talking about Egg Donation? Transference of Reproductive Capacity in the Spanish Bioeconomy. *BioSocieties*, 15(2), 207–225.

Lafuente-Funes, Sara, Christina Weis, Nicky Hudson and Veerle Provoost (2023). Egg Donation in the Age of Vitrification: A Study of Egg Providers' Perceptions and Experiences in the UK, Belgium and Spain. *Sociology of Health & Illness*, 45(2), 259–278.

Lettow, Susanne (2015). Biokapitalismus und Inwertsetzung der Körper: Perspektiven der Kritik. *PROKLA*, 45(1), 33–49.

Lewis, Sophie (2021). *Full Surrogacy Now*. London: Verso.

Lindemann, Johanna, and Gen-ethisches Netzwerk e.V. (GeN) (eds.) (2023). *Reproduktive Gerechtigkeit: Kinderwunsch und Elternschaft in Ungleichen Verhältnissen. Gen-ethischer Informationsdienst*, 266.

Mamo, Laura (2018). Queering Reproduction in Transnational Bio-Economies. *Reproductive BioMedicine & Society Online*, 7, 24–32.

Mamo, Laura, and Eli Alston-Stepnitz (2015). Queer Intimacies and Structural Inequalities: New Directions in Stratified Reproduction. *Journal of Family Issues*, 36(4), 519–540.

Motluk, Alison (2022). Ukraine's Surrogacy Industry Has Put Women in Impossible Positions. *The Atlantic*, 1 March. https://www.theatlantic.com/health/archive/2022/03/russia-invasion-ukraine-surrogate-family/623327/.

O'Brien, M. E. (2023). *Family Abolition, Capitalism and the Communizing of Care*. London: Pluto.

Pande, Amrita (2014). *Wombs in Labour: Transnational Commercial Surrogacy in India*. New York: Columbia University Press.

Pande, Amrita (ed.) (2022). *Birth Controlled: Selective Reproduction and Neoliberal Eugenics in South Africa and India*. Manchester: Manchester University Press.

Perler, Laura (2022). *Selektioniertes Leben: Eine feministische Perspektive auf die Eizellenspende*. Münster: Edition Assemblage.

Redecker, Eva von (2020). *Revolution für das Leben: Philosophie der neuen Protestformen*. Frankfurt: Fischer.

Ross, Loretta J. (2017). Reproductive Justice as Intersectional Feminist Activism. *Souls: A Critical Journal of Black Politics, Culture, and Society*, 19(3), 286–314.

Ross, Loretta J. (2023). Was macht Deine DNA so besonders? *Gen-ethischer Informationsdienst*, 266, 8.

Schnieder, Laura (2020). *Transjektorien der Sorge: Zur Konstitution von Versuchspersonen am Beispiel der Psoriasis-Forschung*. Weilerswist: Velbrück.

Schrupp, Antje (2016). Ist Leihmutterschaft Arbeit? *Der Standard*, 15 April. https://www.derstandard.at/story/2000034835237/ist-leihmutterschaft-arbeit.

Schrupp, Antje (2022). *Reproduktive Freiheit: Eine feministische Ethik der Fortpflanzung*. Münster: unrast.

Schultz, Susanne (2022). *Die Politik des Kinderkriegens*. Bielefeld: transcript.

Schultz, Susanne (2023). *Reproductive Racism: Migration, Birth Control and the "Specter of Population"*. London: Anthem Press.

Schultz, Susanne, and Kathrin Braun (2013). Procuring Tissue: Regenerative Medicine, Oocyte Mobilisation and Feminist Politics. In Andrew Webster (ed.). *The Global Dynamics of Regenerative Medicine: A Social Science Critique*, 118–149. Basingstoke: Palgrave Macmillan.

Siegl, Veronika (2015). Märkte der guten Hoffnung: Leihmutterschaft, Arbeit und körperliche Kommodifizierung in Russland. *PROKLA*, 45(178), 99–115.

Siegl, Veronika (2022). Die "Leihmütter" der Ukraine: Wer bestimmt über den schwangeren Körper? *Gen-ethischer Informationsdienst*, 261, 32–35.

Siegl, Veronika (2023). *Intimate Strangers: Commercial Surrogacy in Russia and Ukraine and the Making of Truth*. Ithaca, NY: Cornell University Press.

Stop Surrogacy Now (n.d.). Statement: Stop Surrogacy Now Campaign. https://cbc-network.org/wp-content/uploads/2015/05/Stop-Surrogacy-Now-Statement-with-Signatories-LOCKED-English.pdf.

Stüwe, Taleo (2021). Rassismus im Kontext von "Eizellspende". *Gen-ethischer Informationsdienst*, 258, 17–18.

Sunder Rajan, Kaushik (2006). *Biocapital: The Constitution of Postgenomic Life*. Durham, NC: Duke University Press.

Terre des Femmes (2020). TDF Positionspapier zu Leih- bzw. Mietmutterschaft. https://frauenrechte.de/fileadmin/Redaktion/Unsere_Arbeit/Sexuelle_und_Reproduktive_Rechte/Reprod-Materialien/2020_0708_TDF_Positionspapier_zu_Leih-_bzw._Mietmutterschaft.pdf.

Wagenmann, Uta (2014). Reproduktionsmedizinische Feldbestellung. *Gen-ethischer Informationsdienst*, 224, 29–31.

Waldby, Catherine, and Melinda Cooper (2008). The Biopolitics of Reproduction. *Australian Feminist Studies*, 23(55), 57–73.

World Health Organisation (n.d.). Infertility Factsheet. https://www.who.int/news-room/fact-sheets/detail/infertility.

Wiesemann, Claudia (2023). Pro Eizellspende: Das Verbot der Eizellspende in Deutschland sollte aufgehoben werden. *Ethik in der Medizin*, 35, 437–444.

Abortion, Surrogacy and Propertisation: Unthinkability as Analogy's Negation

Penelope Deutscher

Judge Cites 1849 Slavery Law in Ruling Embryos Can Be Considered Property .

One bioethics professor called the use of an antiquated law by a Circuit Court judge in Fairfax, Va., "reprehensible and offensive."

New York Times, 16 March 2023[1]

"We've seen this a long time ago with issues around trying to stop enslaved people from being free in the states where they escaped to and states trying to enforce their laws across the borders," said David Cohen, a professor at Drexel University's Kline School of Law. "I think we're going to see the same thing here with anti-abortion states trying to make sure that people in their state can't go out of state to get abortions."

Washington Examiner, 4 May 2022[2]

Law proceeds by analogy.

Janice G. Raymond, Women as Wombs[3]

Policies enabling access to abortion in the United States have sometimes been linked to the history and afterlife of chattel slavery, thus invoking an association that—construed a certain way—implies unthinkability. This

---

1 Hauser 2023: "A Virginia judge relied in part on a 19th century law that defined enslaved people as property in a recent decision to allow a divorced woman to pursue using embryos that she shared with her former husband—a ruling that has drawn criticism [...]. While previous cases asking for the division of frozen embryos have been considered within the legal context of splitting up marital property, the judge wrote in February, Ms. Heidemann was already divorced from her former husband, Jason Heidemann. So Judge Gardiner took a different approach, delving into earlier versions of Virginia's current property law on 'goods or chattels' to see whether embryos could be divided as property between people who are no longer spouses. One version, an 1849 code, categorized 'slaves' as property that could be divided and sold. The judge cited it to draw a parallel to the human embryo case, saying the code used 'language almost identical' to current law."

2 Morrison 2022.

3 Raymond 1993, 67.

analogy was drawn, for instance, by Justice Samuel Alito in the Supreme Court *Dobbs v. Jackson* decision that revoked the constitutional protection of abortion in 2022. As Melinda Cooper put it, "Alito [went] out of his way to represent the foetus as a natural person who has been subject to a long and egregious history of persecution comparable to that of African Americans" (Cooper 2024, 373). Alito recalled the unthinkable legal interpretations once used by United States courts to deny personhood, equality and citizenship to African Americans, a body of law so repudiated that it forms the core of the nation's jurisprudential "anti-canon" (Greene 2011). By implication, as Cooper notes, "Alito is suggesting that anyone who recognizes the civil rights of African Americans should be prepared to extend those rights to fetuses too" (Cooper 2024, 373).

This analogy has been a longstanding trope in pro-life activism.[4] The history of chattel slavery is frequently instrumentalised in pro-life rhetoric to deny the pregnant person's bodily autonomy, by suggesting the latter is trumped by a separable foetal right to life. But when the womb is effectively likened to the plantation (Sexton 2015, 171), the subtext does more. Invoking slavery as the threshold of unthinkability and forging a (pretended) alliance with the cause of racial justice serves to legitimise condemnations of abortion (ibid., 170; Sernett 1980, 461). Further, this invocation serves as a way to avoid engaging with the actual substance of racial justice arguments, making the tactical role of the analogy even clearer. The resulting arguments are more likely to present the granular detail of abortion (with the aim to provoke shock and outrage) than that of the Black lives, past or present, to which they refer to support their pro-life position.

This was vividly illustrated in Justice Alito's invocation of a discredited pro-life argument that legal abortion has disproportionately led to the termination of Black foetal life (in this connection, he also made reference to a past opinion from Justice Clarence Thomas (*Box v. Planned Parenthood*)).[5] Again,

4 For discussions of the use of this analogy in pro-life politics, see for example Sexton 2015, 171; Cooper 2024, 322. Other similar analogies have been deployed elsewhere. When the French health minister Simone Veil, whose parents and brother were killed in Nazi concentration camps, successfully presented her proposal in 1974 to the French Assembly for a conditional decriminalisation of abortion, the political opposition's arguments included a likening of abortion to the Nazi gas chambers (Veil with Cojean 2004, 76–77). See also Cooper 2024, 555, n. 68, for a discussion of an analogy between abortion and Nazi genocide in a Black Panther context.

5 *Dobbs v. Jackson Women's Health Organization*, 597 U.S. at 30 (and see the concurring opinion of Clarence Thomas in *Box v. Planned Parenthood of Ind. & Ky., Inc.*, 587 U.S. (2019).

the effect is to legitimise the pro-life position by laying claim to racial justice credentials, while treating Black lives as mere argumentative devices, mere placeholders for foetal lives. In recent years, Thomas and Alito have taken advantage of every opportunity to erode previous Supreme Court decisions intended to promote racial justice in the United States. When claims about a double unthinkability are made (linking the lives of enslaved people who were deprived of their rights to the assertion that there are aborted reproductive lives that are likewise so deprived), it serves an obscuring function that is particularly telling in one further respect. The arguments presented by both judges disdained to mention, let alone answer, the case made in supporting literature and amicus briefs and by dissenting justices concerning the harmful and racially disproportionate impact of revoking abortion's legality on pregnant people's health and lives.[6] At the exact point of intersection of race and reproduction to which their arguments would seem to point, one finds instead a disregard for the historical and continuing relationship of Black women to reproductive injustice that has been widely analysed within Black feminist theory (for example, by Dorothy Roberts (1997; 2002; 2022) and Michele Goodwin (2020)[7]).

But the malleability of the work of analogy, particularly at the point on which this double unthinkability hinges, necessitates attention to a further usage. Sometimes the conduct, policies or techniques of anti-abortion politics, that have most heavily impacted Black pregnancies, are themselves described by critics of those pro-life policies as evoking the period of legal slavery in the United States. That conduct includes the criminalisation and monetisation of the womb, the forcing of pregnancy or child removal. As will be seen in the examples considered in this chapter, this is not the same use of analogy. But it does raise the question of how these two usages are related.

This chapter seeks to replace a generalised critique of the use of such analogies with an interrogation of its more specifically combinatory role. I show that the analogies at work in the field of reproductive politics are not, in fact, comparisons between distinct and different forms of violence or their

6 The dissenting justices countered that it was, in fact, illegal abortion that has disproportionately impacted the health and mortality of Black women (Justices Breyer, Sotomayor and Kagan, dissenting, *Dobbs*, 597 U.S. at 39). Their dissent also makes reference to a bibliography of supporting evidence that was disregarded in the majority decision.

7 Both Roberts and Goodwin speak of the systemic under-resourcing, surveillance, targeting and criminalisation of Black women's pregnancies. As their work makes clear, one can recognise the afterlife of slavery without rendering the latter a source of analogy.

historical contexts. Jared Sexton—invoking a further sense of unthinkability that is distinct from those discussed in this chapter—says that racial slavery is a "way of suffering that has no analogy" (Sexton 2015, 167). This is another reason for shifting from a critique of analogies that invoke human propertisation to an analysis of the role that they play. Put another way, in this chapter "unthinkability" is understood as a device that is used to render certain forms of critique unintelligible. This can be seen, for example, in its deployment in the jurisprudence of Thomas and Alito. Here, and in respect to its use in a number of legal decisions leading up to the *Dobbs v. Jackson* decision, a helpful question to ask is: "Within what kind of power structure is this analogy embedded?" When it is deployed in the ways discussed in this chapter, I suggest it be analysed as a "hinge" of power. In other words, since the analogy hinges together a number of different tactics, our analysis should focus on their mutual coordination. The first of these moves, as we will see, consists in insinuating proximity to something deemed unthinkable by those acting in that way while obscuring the fact of doing so. The second displaces responsibility for the perception of that unthinkability onto critical antagonists (a group that includes the targets of everyday institutional or legal violence). This displacement seeks to establish that it is the critique of power itself which is epistemically irresponsible. In short, as elaborated below, the hinge between the construction of milieus of negated "unthinkability" and the displaced blameworthiness that coordinates with it has emerged as a characteristic technique in debates about the regulation of reproduction. In the United States, such hinged analogies have been a means of exploring, while at the same time repudiating, reproduction as propertisation, as can also be seen in a series of laws concerned with the regulation of reproduction dating back—for the purposes of this discussion—to the 1980s.

When Mary Beth Whitehead, a white defendant, fled the state of New Jersey in 1986 to avoid surrendering "Baby M" to the couple with whom she had entered into a surrogacy contract,[8] a number of commentators perceived echoes of the historical forms of fugitive resistance to chattel slavery's forc-

8 *In Re Baby M*. The case concerned a surrogacy contract that Whitehead entered into with Elizabeth and Robert Stern, with Whitehead also acting as egg donor. Whitehead sought to break the contract and claimed consideration of her parental rights. Her right to do so was eventually upheld by the court; however, custody was awarded to the Sterns. One memorable aspect of the case was the negative commentary on Whitehead's conduct as a "mother", which the judge said weakened her claim.

ing women into alienable reproduction for profit.[9] The question was taken up in Black feminist commentary, for instance in wary analyses of early surrogacy contracts by Dorothy Roberts (1997) and Anita Allen (1991). Commenting retrospectively on views expressed during that period, Alys Weinbaum (2019) remarks that it seemed to contemporary commentators—particularly when a state supreme court considered the case of a Black woman, Anna Johnson, who sought, unsuccessfully, to terminate a surrogacy contract[10]—as though "a world was being recalled". Weinbaum refers back to the position of Lorraine Stone (1988):

> For Stone and others, in transferring a child from the woman who gave birth to it to a second party the court's actions undercut its ruling, as its actions recalled a world, supposedly long gone, in which slave women reproduced living commodities for others. As the journalist Katha Pollitt mused [...] "Judge Sorkow is surely the only person on earth who thinks [that] William Stem paid Mary Beth Whitehead $ 10,000 merely to conceive and carry a baby and not also to transfer that baby to him."
>
> *Weinbaum 2019, 46*[11]

But how was this idea of "recall" understood? Were critics *likening* surrogacy to enslavement?[12] Or were they making a different point, namely that the governance and milieu of surrogacy had simultaneously embedded a sinister insinuation that the person who carried a surrogate pregnancy was a disposable means to producing alienable life for the benefit of others and, to add insult to injury, further degraded the surrogate by using historical associations on which that insinuation could slyly draw?

---

9 While repudiating this argument, Anita Allen has suggested (as has Dorothy Roberts) that the analogy is more apt in the reverse direction: "American slavery was analogous to a de facto system of surrogacy. Slave owners were recognised not only as the owners of the slaves but they were also owners of the natural children to which the slaves gave birth. These ownership rights allowed the children to be bought or sold to third parties, regardless of the wishes of the natural mother" (Allen 1991, 17). On this point, Allen refers to Walker 1989; see also Roberts 1997.

10 In this case, the egg donor and Johnson, as the gestational carrier, were deemed to have equal claims to maternity under California law. It was decided that "she who intended to procreate the child—that is, she who intended to bring about the birth of a child that she intended to raise as her own—is the natural mother under California law". (It is notable that motherhood is associated here with a kind of creative intent.)

11 Weinbaum is referring here to Stone 1988 and Pollitt 1987. For relevant commentary on surrogacy from the period, see Allen 1988, 1990 and 1991; these pieces also provide further references to contemporaneous public commentary, including the *New York Times* article headlined "Mothers Urge Ban on Surrogacy as Form of 'Slavery'" (*New York Times*, 1 September 1987, A13, col. 1, cited in Allen 1990, 47, n. 8).

12 See Allen 1990 for her clarification that this was not, of course, how the analogy was intended.

Or, adding to these alternatives, we could ask a different question: what is the specific technique of power that operates through a milieu that both implies and repudiates such proximity? How is the hinge between these two elements (proximity and repudiation) then mobilised to create effects of epistemic irresponsibility through negation (of the insinuation) and displacement (of its perception)? The analogies discussed in this chapter have haunted post-*Roe* legal cases, and either indicate or draw on, an afterlife of propertisation within reproductive politics. That term refers, in this context, to the (systemically repudiated) possibility that there are regimes and regulations of reproduction which situate pregnancy not *as* (productive of humans-as-)property but *"as if"* reproduction propertised human life and pregnant people, in addition to dehumanising and undermining the latter's rights.[13]

To trace the sequence of analogisation extending from the 1980s to the 2022 *Dobbs v. Jackson* decision and its fallout,[14] I shall draw a connection between the use of analogies in two early cases, respectively concerning surrogacy and a revision of abortion's legality in the United States. With a view to how concerns about reproductive propertisation are represented in this context, I then ask the same question of pro-life initiatives in the post-*Dobbs* environment, including the effort to restrict interstate travel undertaken for the purposes of obtaining a legal abortion in another state when it is illegal in a person's state of residence.

13 See Goodwin 2020 for her extensive analysis of pregnancy being used as a pretext for a range of rights being removed in the United States, in many cases inflected by race, class and age.

14 With the 2022 *Dobbs v. Jackson* decision, the United States Supreme Court revoked the right to abortion which had been established as constitutionally protected by *Roe v. Wade* in 1973. This allowed roughly half the federal states to render abortion entirely illegal, or illegal with varying but limited exceptions. Other states either kept abortion legal, or in some cases improved protections and support. The result is a national patchwork of different legal regimes that vary from state to state. This patchwork situation has fuelled a massive increase in abortion-related travel and/or procurement of medication across borders as a means of accessing medical services that are illegal in people's own states. As discussed below, the efforts by some anti-abortion states to discourage or impede this cross-border travel/procurement, and the resulting legal conflicts, have sometimes been compared to an earlier period in United States jurisprudence when slaveholders sought to force the extradition of enslaved people who had fled to abolitionist states; then as now, conflicting legal regimes meant that rights could only be accessed by crossing state borders.

1. What is "historical continuity"?—techniques of historical callback and the role of negation

Claims about historical continuity do not necessarily draw analogies between the phenomena they seek to link together. In the field of Black feminist theory, this distinction can be seen when, for example, Roberts and Goodwin describe the violence and death arising from what Roberts calls a "systematic, institutionalized denial of reproductive freedom" that "uniquely marked Black women's history in America" (Roberts 1997, 4) dating back to reproduction under slavery. How is this continuity understood? Goodwin's *Policing the Womb* describes a passage from chattel's slavery's extractive propertisation (which includes the propertisation of reproduction[15]) to the impacts of post-slavery on Black women's pregnancies. Those impacts have included heightened mortality in pregnancy, forced or impeded pregnancies and a tendency to criminalise the conduct of pregnant people. According to Goodwin's characterisation, the many aspects of post-slavery include a passage from "private" ownership of enslaved women (often advertised or monetised under the regime of slavery in terms of their protected reproductive potential) to "public" techniques of reproductive domination, erosion and control of Black women's pregnant bodies still at work more than 150 years after Emancipation:

> For Black women in Texas, Louisiana, Alabama, Georgia, West Virginia, and elsewhere, not only is their reproductive freedom illusory, but staying alive during pregnancy is not a guaranteed, foregone conclusion. Private reproductive bondage in these former slave states is now public. That is, where planters once controlled Black women's reproduction on their plantations and elsewhere, now the state controls what Black women (and others) may do with their bodies during pregnancy.
>
> *Goodwin 2020, 8*

If we briefly interrupt the discussion with a framing question—how is Goodwin construing power in this context?—we might conclude she is describing the continuation of domination via a transfer of control to alternative techniques for exercising it. Her aim is not to flatten the differences between reproduction under chattel slavery and the contemporary regimes of reproduction that she critiques. Rather, she wants to focus scrutiny on the pat-

15 Jennifer Morgan has argued that this has been chronically downplayed in histories of chattel slavery. See Morgan 2004 and 2021.

terns of contemporary policing and punishment of the pregnancies of low-income women, particularly women of colour, which for decades did not receive broad public attention.[16] Goodwin and Roberts have suggested these patterns are linked to a longer history that also includes reproductive extractivism under slavery; torturous medical treatment of and experimentation on Black women and their pregnancies; negligent or coercive reproductive healthcare; and forced sterilisation. These patterns have also included hypercritical surveillance of Black and poor people's pregnancies, medical care that has doubled as a mode of policing and racially disproportionate prosecution of those criminalised as a result. Roberts has shown how these patterns can also be observed in sceptical assessments of Black women's ability to care for children and pregnancies, which in turn manifest in racially discriminatory approaches to child custody removal (Roberts 2022).

These analyses of how inequalities of treatment as continuities of racial domination are linked to the regimes of chattel slavery and Jim Crow do not blur the distinctions between them. That is evident in Goodwin's discussion of forms of medical care that present themselves as concern for ensuring healthy pregnancies, but devolve into an imposition of medical inspection, hospitals reporting to police and arrests. The examples discussed by Goodwin include those of Regina McKnight and Paula Hale, who turned to hospitals in the southern United States for prenatal care, but were instead targeted by medical professionals and subsequently arrested on "foetal endangerment" charges. Women whose pregnancies are already constructed as "irresponsible" in advance by differentially vigilant medical scrutiny continue to be treated by a medical protocol[17] whose techniques combine *de facto* profiling, invocations of care and concern,[18] surveillance, legally inept medical practitioners acting as a policing auxiliary, bodily searches that also amount to a deprivation of rights, condescension or humiliation, forms of treatment that are unwanted or invasive, carceral punishment and continuing medical neglect. This nexus already comprises a cluster of heterogeneous forms and

16 Foetal endangerment laws have resulted in additional grounds for arrest on suspicion of drug use. But the wide range of instances discussed by Goodwin also includes cases of people being arrested for suicide attempts, falling down stairs, continuing to work while pregnant, declining caesareans and other medical interventions, prescribing medical treatments such as chemotherapy and even, as Boone and McMichael (2021) note, failure to wear a seatbelt.

17 Goodwin (2020) offers a detailed study of a practice that relies on annexing medical professionals as de facto judicial and policing auxiliaries.

18 On the role of care, see *Ferguson et al. v. City of Charleston et al.* (2001).

techniques of power and authority. But Goodwin observes a further technique at work here: corporeal methods of arrest and detention that create a further effect of historical callback, an insinuating echo of the past. Again, her point is not to deny the differences within these regimes, for it is because of these differences that the use of analogies, within a certain context, plays an important role in asserting the connection between different forms of power. But the question is: what kind of role? Goodwin gives the example of the use of leg irons, shackles and chains binding the abdomen to detain the pregnant Black prisoners in the case she discusses (Goodwin 2020, 110):

> Regina [McKnight]'s case is illustrative of a broader pattern in South Carolina, where dozens of poor pregnant women suffered similar fates. Paula Hale, also a rape victim from South Carolina,[19] likely did not expect that, by carrying her pregnancy to term rather than aborting, she would be "dragged out of the hospital in chains and shackles." Lynn Paltrow, Executive Director of National Advocates for Pregnant Women (NAPW), compared the disturbing images of law enforcement entering hospitals, separating Black babies from their mothers, and carting the women off in shackles and chains, to the cruelty embedded in antebellum slavery.
>
> *ibid., 16; see also 145; and Roberts 1997*[20]

Linette Collins and Mali Park have also discussed this use of restraint or shackles: "a problem", as they observe, "for any birthing person". What intensifies the abuse in these cases is that "the shackling of Black birthing people has a specific cultural history related to forced gynecological experimentation and the lasting material vestiges of chattel slavery" (Park and Collins 2021). As with Goodwin's analysis, it is helpful to distinguish critique that seeks to establish analogies, from critique that exposes the effect of a putatively care-oriented medical—carceral nexus that insinuates those analogies. Goodwin, Collins and Park describe techniques of institutional milieus in which a relationship with longstanding racial histories is implied, all while maintaining plausible deniability. An echo of debasement is secured from claims to equivalency. That it cannot be said that these milieus are "like" (in the sense of "equivalent to") slavery is their very point. Any such suggestion is immediately repudiated by those broadly responsible for these forms of detention. If the point here is not degrees of likeness, it is

19 Along with 28 other Black women, she was "dragged out of the hospital in chains and shackles". See Goodwin 2010/2011.

20 As Goodwin observes, "enforced isolation and solitary confinement" is said to be "for the sake of 'protecting' the pregnancy" (2020, 175).

because a hinge between the repudiation of likeness with enslavement and the contextual insinuation of proximity serves a further function.

In other words, when these techniques of echoing further combine with a disavowal of the analogy that is being situationally implied, this also offers a means of discrediting in advance the critics and targets of these techniques of detention, who can easily see the intensified effect of debasement through milieus of implied analogy. In this example, the "plausible deniability" concerning the milieu created by detaining Black women using chains and shackles (as is evident in replies to the effect that these techniques are in general use and their application is race-neutral) makes it easy to repudiate as tasteless or extreme the criticism that these practices insinuate an analogical association with the era of enslavement.[21] The further effect, then, is a displacement of perceptual responsibility from milieu to individual,[22] producing the latter's epistemic irresponsibilisation. As Park and Collins put it, another "womb"—of wandering "hysteria"—is also displaced onto detainees and critics, who are blamed for exaggeration when they claim to see this echo effect in the contemporary practices that present themselves as medical care or child/foetal protection.[23] In short, as a hinge of power coordinating two apparently opposed operations, epistemic irresponsibilisation draws on these operations' heterogeneity to at once stimulate and discredit the perception of the effect, thereby implying that critique itself signals a mismanagement of a person's own critical faculties.

Through displacement and redirection, a vestige of a historically anterior state is implied, stimulated, irresponsibilised. Moreover, a sense of menace is generated by the echoes of past violence in these milieus in a further sense. Again, the point is the vagueness of the implications of affinity in the relevant practices. While it is implied that some remnants of past violence might be revivable, it is left unclear to what extent that might be the case. A

---

21 For their discussion of the implied meaning of these carceral techniques, see Park and Collins (2021).

22 Saidiya Hartman (1997) describes how many of the apparent freedoms delivered to freedmen and freedwomen after the Emancipation Proclamation constructed a burdened individuality through techniques that continued racial domination. In those contexts too, responsibility was rerouted from a milieu of racial domination to one of individual blameworthiness.

23 For a suggested alternative, see also Weinbaum's discussion of commercialised surrogacy as belonging to a post-slavery constellation (Weinbaum 2019). She suggests this term as a means of situating commercialised surrogacy within a post-slavery context without drawing analogies or equivalencies.

general revocability—of equality, rights, dignity—hovers all the more effectively through the use of "*not*". To repudiate the unthinkable leaves yawningly open exactly what is being implied in its stead. The further insinuation (also repudiated in advance) is that some part of freedom, citizenship, subjectivity and epistemic credibility is revocable—but to an undetermined degree. In short, the revocability at work here is at once epistemic (an imputation of non-credibility), moral (an overriding accusation of irresponsibility), ontological (threatening to insecuritise status and being) and anticipatory: revoked futures are threatened, despite (and because of) their negated non-definition and consequent open-endedness.

How could we further, but laterally, connect the complexity of this reproductive governance with the disdain expressed by the Supreme Court majority for those warning of the impending destructive impact[24] of revoking a right to abortion that, by 2002, had been in place for 49 years? The decision particularly disregarded arguments concerning the historically differential impact depending on race. Moreover, negation played a further role by envisioning a further loss of rights that might ensue, in combination with the assessment and declaration that this would *not* happen. For example, Justice Brett Kavanaugh gave his opinion, in the guise of reassurance, that the *Dobbs* decision would "*not*" threaten cross-border travel for abortion access: "May a State bar a resident of that State from traveling to another State to obtain an abortion? In my view, the answer is no based on the constitutional right to interstate travel."[25]

Alito opened a broader gate of possibility with this same gesture of raising a possibility while at the same time nullifying it,[26] in this case the possibility that other unenumerated rights judged, in a series of previous legal decisions, to be protected by the Fourteenth Amendment (including same-sex marriage, contraception and other reproductive decision-making[27]) might

24 Described by the dissenting justices, in the oral hearing and in amicus briefs, and extensively supported by literature and detailed empirical evidence.

25 Justice Kavanaugh, concurring, *Dobbs*, 597 U.S. at 10.

26 To this should be added the further comments of Justice Thomas, who in his assenting opinion indicated his openness to revisiting these established interpretations of the due process clause of the Fourteenth Amendment (Justice Thomas, assenting, *Dobbs*, 597 U.S. at 2–3).

27 Interracial marriage, established as a constitutional right in 1967, is omitted from the list of Fourteenth Amendment rights that Thomas, in his separate and assenting opinion, suggests (at first by way of the negation: "are not at issue"), could, eventually, be revisited. His ominous comment is: "In future cases, we should reconsider all of this Court's substantive due process precedents, including Griswold, Lawrence, and Obergefell" (Justice Thomas, assenting, *Dobbs*, 597 U.S. at 2–3)

in the future be similarly revoked. Specifically, Alito declared: "Nothing in this opinion should be understood to cast doubt on precedents that do not concern abortion."[28] The destabilising ambiguity of the work done by negation was underscored by a separate assenting opinion from Justice Thomas, who denied the broader implications of the decision while also indicating that he was open to reviewing them.[29]

2. The negative licence of analogy

Against this backdrop, and in light of the looming horizons of revocability, we can reassess the consequential United States legal decisions that began to address the legal basis of surrogacy contracts in the 1980s and early 1990s—the same period in which the basis for the constitutional right to abortion was also being reconsidered.

Firstly, *Johnson v. Calvert*. This case from early jurisprudence concerning surrogacy is also an example of how a repudiated unthinkability was deployed in determinations of the enforceability of surrogacy contracts.[30] Anna Johnson sought unsuccessfully to break a surrogacy contract into which she had entered to carry to term the foetus for which both sperm and egg were provided by Mark and Crispina Calvert. Deciding against Johnson, Judge Parslow mobilised analogies to legitimate, to negate and to legitimate via negation. He repudiated the possible affinity of enforced surrogacy contracts with enslavement that was raised by Johnson's lawyer[31] (and that was a topic of public debate in this period: see Allen 1991). In question was the enforceability of a type of contractual commitment that in many other contexts is prohibited. Judge Parslow proposed that gestational surrogacy could more properly be likened to foster care (cf. Raymond 1993, 66): "It has

referring to the decisions that established the right to use contraception; to engage in private, consensual sex acts; and the right to same-sex marriage.

28 *Dobbs*, 597 U.S. at 66.

29 There was no indication that the decision on abortion would lead to implications for in vitro fertilisation (IVF), a possibility broached by a state court some two years later.

30 See *Johnson v. Calvert*. The contract allowed for payment of 10,000 dollars and a life insurance policy. Johnson was judged to have no parental or visitation rights, and the surrogacy contract she had entered into was upheld.

31 See the account offered by Roberts 1997, 282, and, on this point, see Roberts' reference to Behrens 1990, 1, 15.

been suggested that gestational surrogacy may run afoul of prohibitions on involuntary servitude. [...] We see no potential for that evil in the contract at issue here, and extrinsic evidence of coercion or duress is utterly lacking."[32]

When Parslow repudiated the connection between an enforced surrogacy contract and an unthinkable form of enforced servitude, he did so with a whiff of reproof. The evidence for that link was not only said to be absent but "utterly" lacking. Enslavement is reversed into a distancing point of reference, serving to license the surrogacy contract through its negation.

Of course, other factors were said to safeguard these arrangements from devolving into involuntary servitude. One of these was Johnson's right to choose to terminate the pregnancy[33]—for this was the early 1990s and Johnson was assumed to have access to legal abortion. And yet, arguably, a counter-future lurked in the background, for it was also true that abortion rights had just been revised and weakened by the Supreme Court.[34] Some 30 years later, the Supreme Court's *Dobbs v. Jackson* decision would revoke the

32 The passage in full reads as follows: "It has been suggested that gestational surrogacy may run afoul of prohibitions on involuntary servitude. (See U.S. Const., Amend. XIII; Cal. Const., art. I, § 6; Pen. Code, § 181.) Involuntary servitude has been recognized in cases of criminal punishment for refusal to work. (*Pollock v. Williams* (1944) 322 U.S. 4, 18 [88 L. Ed. 1095, 1104, 64 S. Ct. 792, 799]; see, generally, 7 Witkin, Summary of Cal. Law (9th ed. 1988) Constitutional Law, §§ 411–414, pp. 591–596). We see no potential for that evil in the contract at issue here, and extrinsic evidence of coercion or duress is utterly lacking. We note that although at one point the contract purports to give Mark and Crispina the sole right to determine whether to abort the pregnancy, at another point it acknowledges: 'All parties understand that a pregnant woman has the [5 Cal. 4th 97] absolute right to abort or not abort any fetus she is carrying. Any promise to the contrary is unenforceable.' We therefore need not determine the validity of a surrogacy contract purporting to deprive the gestator of her freedom to terminate the pregnancy", *Johnson v. Calvert* 5 Cal. 4th 84 at 784.

We can note the association that is drawn here between a pregnancy, which is not considered involuntary servitude, and the "absolute right" the plaintiff retains to abort it. On the question of whether the foetus under these circumstances should be understood as alienable property, analogous to intellectual property, see Justice Joyce Kennard's dissenting opinion concerning this construal of surrogacy: "Just as children are not the intellectual property of their parents, neither are they the personal property of anyone, and their delivery cannot be ordered as a contract remedy on the same terms that a court would, for example, order a breaching party to deliver a truckload of nuts and bolts. [...] A pregnant woman intending to bring a child into the world is more than a mere container or breeding animal; she is a conscious agent of creation no less than the genetic mother, and her humanity is implicated on a deep level. Her role should not be devalued [...]. I cannot agree with the majority's devaluation of the role of the gestational mother" (Justice Kennard, dissenting, *Johnson v. Calvert*, 5 Cal. 4th 84 at 115–116).

33 See note 33.

34 See the discussion of *Planned Parenthood v. Casey* below.

right that Parslow had cross-referenced as securing pregnancy from forced continuation—as his means of using the negation of forced servitude as a technique of legitimation. In the interim, instrumentalised references to historical enslavement would continue to be invoked in debate[35] about the legal regulation of reproductive interventions. These malleable references have frequently been used to serve a legitimation function.

Thus, in a number of the decisions on surrogacy during this period, its acceptability turned on the repudiated analogy with human life as property under slavery. Did surrogacy contracts surrender newborns in return for payment? In response, legal decisions determined that surrogacy amounted instead to payment for services. A supposition that gestated life was alienable, combined with the prospect of having to continue an arrangement under forced conditions (out of economic coercion, or even where a surrogate had changed their mind[36]), seemed to create the disturbing "recall of a world".[37]

How should we understand the spectre of propertisation here? While it does not concern a literal (e.g. legal) conversion of human life into property, it is more than an analogical substitute for legal property. It is more tellingly understood as a negatively hinged relationship that simultaneously binds together and holds apart: *"this" is not "that"*. This hinge is used to

35 See for example Smith 2019 and Crockett 2016. To quote from the latter: "Rep. Louie Gohmert (R-TX) invoked the Supreme Court's Dred Scott decision to suggest—as many Republicans and conservatives often do—that abortion is like slavery because women treat fetuses like 'property.'" The same report also describes a House Judiciary Committee hearing on abortion. One of the witnesses at the meeting was Kierra Johnson, "executive director of URGE (Unite for Reproductive and Gender Equity), a black woman and the panel's only pro-choice witness, [who] made clear how offensive many women of color might find [...] remarks [comparing abortion to slavery] to be [...] Johnson's response to that idea [...] was: 'It's interesting that we're bringing up slavery in this space. When you own somebody's decision-making, you own them.'" In other words, the abortion–slavery analogy (as used by figures such as Gohmert) implies that in pregnancy Black women attain an ability to control life akin to that of slave*owners*. But to use the analogy in this way specifically occludes the point that under slavery, Black women were forced into pregnancy and childbirth and had their children stolen.

36 In the view of multiple critics, including some feminist critics, the conditions of surrogacy's acceptability should include provision for a surrogate to withdraw from the agreement during pregnancy. Some surrogacy contracts in India appear to allow a limited provision for change of mind if costs are reimbursed to the contracting couple; see Pande 2014 and also Allen's early essay on the topic, Allen 1988.

37 We have seen how negation can function as an anchoring point in this regard: in other words, a possible similarity is invoked only to be repudiated, and by this means is understood to give licence to what is therefore *not* "that".

project the maximal understanding—which bears the status of greatest unthinkability—of the conversion of humans into property, so as to secure, by means of the conjoined negating repudiation, the alternative that is thereby differentiated and licensed.

To further illuminate this point, we can turn to two recent arguments, respectively from Eva von Redecker and Alys Weinbaum, about contemporary propertisation. Both carefully interrogate the role of analogy that is so often at work when the present is situated relative to historical forms of domination. Addressing the analogies invoked at the time of *Johnson v. Calvert,* Weinbaum definitively repudiates models of likeness in her own analysis: "The black feminist argument that I take up and to which I add is *not* that biocapitalism and chattel slavery are the same and or that they ought to be treated as analogical" (Weinbaum 2019, 8, her emphasis).

Instead, and reversing the direction of the question, Weinbaum suggests that the history of enslavement, forced reproduction, and extreme white supremacist violence, introduced a new type of conceivability, posited as a "prior" condition of possibility. That condition of possibility continues to be detectable in contemporary regimes of reproduction, which include commercial surrogacy arrangements. According to Weinbaum, they share with chattel slavery the sheer *thinkability* which allows reproduction, its gestational labour and (today) its biomaterials to be considered alienable in a wide range of profit-making contexts (from literal trade to other forms of monetisation and speculation). She argues that what connects contemporary surrogacy and slavery is not likeness, nor a direct historical continuity, but rather a prior condition of possibility: the alienability of reproductive life for the purposes of commercial profit.

Considering this argument, one can further scrutinise the role that *un*thinkability continues to play. Assuming that an epistemic condition of possibility must coalesce, making it minimally conceivable that women, and others who are capable of pregnancy, could reproduce alienable human life for the purposes of commercial profit, then the point is not exactly that this thinkability continues as an underlying condition of the surrogacy arrangements of the twentieth and twenty-first centuries. If it persists, it does so as part of a complex hinge connected to the operations of negated "unthinkability", as described in this chapter.

This point can also be seen in von Redecker's treatment of propertisation. She has developed the concept of phantom possession to mobilise the distinction between dominion and domination, while also pointing to the role of analogy as linking them. If it can be said that the forms of dominion over people and their bodily capacities pertaining to the periods of chattel slavery and patriarchal coverture were replaced by modern sex- and race-based domination, the propertisation of modern times retains a phantom relationship to dominion. Von Redecker uses the metaphor of a "phantom limb" to characterise those who might expect to inherit race and gender privilege but instead perceive themselves as if that privilege had been amputated. The aim of race and sex domination is, she argues, compensatory in relation to the phantasmatic belief in lost dominion.

First, we should stipulate that this loss is, again, retroactively constituted. The perception of privilege's loss is projected onto a phantasmatic "lost" past, in which (it is tacitly believed) legal or state-authorised racial or sexual dominion delivered a secure right to capture, control, and dispose over enslaved persons, their labour, and reproductive capacities. The phantasmatic belief in loss that can be seen in white or male privilege obscures the friction, paradox and resistance inherent to all phenomena and projects of dominion.[38] When group-based oppressive relations allow some people to be treated, by virtue of sex, race or reproductivity, as if they were "analogous to property" (von Redecker 2020, 33, 49), domination would appear to analogically substitute for dominion. But, since the loss is phantasmatic, phantom possession aims at an impossible "restoration" of control of humans and their capacities that has never belonged to those who perceive it as lost. What operates the analogy is not a comparable quantity (as if domination were somewhat like, but less than, dominion and might deliver some of its projected satisfactions). Rather, the analogical dimension is grounded by the impossibility of the substitution, moreover, it could be said that its construction of anteriority implicitly recognises that it produces the "loss" it resents.

Furthermore, von Redecker's analysis points to domination's capacity to treat multiple groups in parallel or cross-referenced terms, as if they were analogous to each other. The conduct of domination can assert the interrelation of group-based oppressions, as when sex, race and immigration status become pretexts for people being treated disposably in service of privilege's perceived interests (ibid., 56). To be sure, there are many differences between race-based violence perpetrated by white supremacists, the detention of immigrants and "border regimes, detention centers, prisons, and abor-

38 Von Redecker 2020 references Hartman, who has given particular emphasis to this point.

tion bans" (ibid., 56–57 and see 35). But these practices can make reference to each other's techniques, or means of producing vulnerability, as if to insinuate that, in their substitutability, such affinities are a mutually augmenting humiliation.[39] But if the seeming effort to insinuate proximity or likeness, in this further sense, also results in echoes of conduct, by drawing analogies to milieus of domination, this asserted substitutability concurrently reminds us that while domination may be interminable its outcome never fully arrives; instead, it threatens further substitutions to come.

Originally, and with self-renewing effect, propertisation creates a fundamental effect of plausibility: obscuring, by familiarising, something that should remain critically accessible, namely the preconditions under which someone—or something—could conceivably become "property" at all. And so, in dialogue with those (from W. E. B. Du Bois to Cheryl Harris) who have shown how the entitlements of whiteness function as if it were akin to valuable property (Du Bois 1935, 700; Harris 1993), von Redecker interrogates the meaning of privilege in phantom property. The latter presupposes the self-evidence of what can be *done* with property and, by extension, with all that is asserted to be "like property". Propertisation thus creates effects of a right of conduct, as if the fact that something could plausibly be property thereby also grants others unlimited rights of use. It further obscures, by familiarising "ownership's" (and, phantom possession's) having come to mean a licence to treat something, or someone, disposably instead of (to mention just one of many possible alternatives) implying a role of custodianship (von Redecker 2020, 41).[40] Thus, to the extent that domination accomplishes a treatment of others *as if* they were property, the work of analogy continues to naturalise, again retroactively and reversibly, the very plausibility of so treating them.

Phantom property can be at work in socially tolerated violence, and in differences of treatment that are tacitly accepted as appropriate or adequate, without converting humans into property. And in this regard, von

39 The same could be said of the intense victimisation of trans men and women by right-wing politicians that has emerged in recent political campaigns; these campaigns have either resulted from, substituted for or augmented (or all three) concurrent attacks on immigration and abortion rights in the United States and elsewhere.

40 On a more complex understanding, propertisation is also seen as retroactively changing the meaning of what is propertised, in addition to changing the meaning of property itself (insofar as it could ever have included humans as property) and retroactively creating the "-isation" effect: the very conceivability of humans and reproduction as propertisable. On this retroactive time, and its intersection with gender and genealogy, see also Spillers 1987.

Redecker's account also touches on the negation at work in the techniques that produce those differences. For one thing, phantom property is effected "not by individual fictitious owners, but by the order erected around [propertied groups]" (ibid., 56). This order is, she suggests, more than a symbolic repetition of an archaic form of power. As the order erected around groups particularly reveals itself in differences of conduct associated with permissibility, self-authorisation and a claimed authority over others, it also becomes clear (particularly from the examples cited in this discussion[41]) that it further mobilises the heterogeneous techniques and materially productive formations of power that, albeit couched in a Foucauldian vocabulary, would include securitisation, biopolitics, discipline and subjectivation, while doing so in terms that repeatedly instrumentalise negation. Examples include the contradictory sexual objectification and responsibilisation (and hence culpabilisation) of female undocumented immigrants (ibid., 56–57) and von Redecker's astute observation that the multiple ways of people being treated *as if* they were property include treating them as if they did not have sufficient authority to "protect" others (ibid., 34). This also gives rise to moralising alternations, articulated in the register of care, between those deemed more, or less, capable. Such differentiations may present themselves in the guise of an interest in maximising care, while also attaching to another kind of power: namely, the power to deprive people of the right to care for others. We could further recall here Goodwin's and Roberts's meticulous studies of post-Emancipation forms of domination, which included repeated invalidation of the adequacy of lower-class and Black women's "care" for pregnancies and children, an invalidation that might otherwise seem baffling in light of the disinterest exhibited by those levelling such charges in ensuring better levels of the care that is claimed to be deficient.

Of course, these are modern forms of domination that gain legitimacy by being distinguishable from dominion. To put it another way, dominion and domination are not two different morphologies of power in a substitutive relationship. If we were to ask of phantom propertisation, "What kind of power is this?" we would encounter the legitimating hinge that asserts: this "*may not*" be. To whatever extent that domination—in its construction of order, policing of care, disparagement of interest or culpabilisation of

41 See in particular Jacqueline Rose's discussion (2019) of the punitive and subjectivising techniques used to detain undocumented immigrants, which again mobilise the structure of negation (discussed in von Redecker 2020, 56–57).

management—ever appears to stand in for a phantasmatically lost dominion, its effects and techniques are licensed by the self-evidence on which they hinge concerning what is *not* the case. To the extent that social, bureaucratic, institutional, policing, vigilante, carceral or even caretaking practices treat others disposably, or "like property", according to their sex, race or immigration status, these practices claim to be distinguishable from historically repudiated forms of dominion. While this hinge is a licensing mechanism, rather than a historical substitution of regimes or techniques, it may nonetheless operate *as if* there had been a replacement. For an illustration, we can turn to another instance of the combined regulation and management of reproduction.

3. Negations of propertisation I: the power that "*may not*" be

What role did such hinges of thinkability and unthinkability play in the series of legal reassessments of abortion rights in the decades following the *Roe v. Wade* ruling?[42] That question can be applied to *Planned Parenthood v. Casey* (1992),[43] which resulted in one of the most important reformulations of abor-

42 In the landmark *Roe v. Wade* decision of 1973, the United States Supreme Court held that the "unenumerated" rights protected federally by the United States constitution included the right to abortion. This built on a number of interpretations established cumulatively in the years leading up to the *Roe* decision, including the *Griswold v. Connecticut* decision (1965) that a married couple's right to use contraception was protected by the right to privacy, followed by *Eisenstadt v. Baird* (1972), which extended the same right to unmarried couples. In their deliberations on the latter decision, the judges had anticipated the imminent claim that abortion was similarly protected by the constitution. Nonetheless, the basis on which abortion's constitutionality was established has sometimes been seen as fragile by advocates of reproductive justice. The same applies to the conditional terms in which the right's protection was formulated. The *Roe* ruling led to decades of pro-life and conservative activism, including numerous court challenges and coordinated bureaucratic and political erosion of abortion access, culminating in the nullification of *Roe* by the Supreme Court in 2022.

43 After *Roe* was passed in 1973 by the Supreme Court, a number of United States state courts began to challenge the decision, often with mutually coordinated strategies. *Roe* had established that abortion was protected as a constitutional right to privacy. State courts sought to erode this right, for example by allowing limiting conditions on health workers who could provide abortion; by imposing onerous conditions on abortion provision such as waiting periods, foetal viability tests or requiring that parents or partners be notified or that the person seeking abortion be provided with information about alternatives, shown images of the foetus or made to listen to its heartbeat; or by prohibiting certain methods in favour of procedures that were more costly or onerous for the

tion rights during this period. The decision also included an ambiguous representation of a seeming passage from private to public forms of power, and from dominion to domination.[44] By then, it was thinkable that the Supreme Court justices who heard *Casey* might revoke *Roe*, given the strength of opposition among their ranks in the early 1990s to the 1973 decision. Instead, a compromise was found through which the court could reaffirm, and yet restrict, abortion's constitutional protection.[45] As it did so, a hinge of unthinkability was put to work that would later resurface in *Dobbs*.

Planned Parenthood v. Casey may have unexpectedly reaffirmed the right to abortion,[46] but revisiting *Roe v. Wade* the court determined that it was, nonetheless, not unconstitutional to impose bureaucratic and procedural

pregnant person. The question arose: did such conditions infringe a pregnant person's federally guaranteed, constitutional right to abortion? These repeated challenges gave an increasingly hostile Supreme Court the opportunity to revisit the terms of abortion's constitutional protection in a group of cases prior to *Dobbs*. In *Webster v. Reproductive Health Services* (1989), the Supreme Court ruled that a right to abortion did not amount to a right to government-funded abortion provision. Previously, in *Harris v. McRae* (1980) it had upheld the Hyde amendment, which excluded the use of federal funding for abortion, rendering the procedure near inaccessible for some of those who were pregnant and in economically challenged and precarious circumstances. See also Roberts 1997 for the reminder that there are multiple facets of reproductive injustice: abortion, sterilisation and contraceptive implants, have also been (coercively) imposed in the United States by assorted medical and state agencies. Those impacted were disproportionately Black and Latinx women of low socioeconomic status.

44 See also *Planned Parenthood v. Danforth*, which among other things deliberated on whether it was constitutional for abortion to require a husband's written consent.

45 Like *Webster*, the *Casey* case asked whether the constitutional protection of the right to abortion was compatible with states setting numerous restrictions and limits on the accessibility and availability of abortion. Did *Roe* render it unconstitutional to institute a range of bureaucratic requirements designed to obstruct abortion access? In response, the *Casey* decision introduced the expression "undue burden". The judges argued that conditions, restrictions and limitations could be imposed by states provided that pregnant people still retained a reasonable degree of access to the procedure. Under the "undue burden" standard, it should, therefore, have been illegal to introduce limits, conditions and restrictions whose "purpose or effect" was to "place a substantial obstacle in the path of a woman seeking an abortion of a nonviable fetus". Instead, the decision gave rise to decades of efforts by anti-abortion activists to weaken the sense of "undue burden" and thereby erode abortion rights, creating abortion deserts in many states well before the *Dobbs* decision formally revoked *Roe*. Other contributing factors were successful efforts by right-wing politicians to prohibit the use of federal or state government funding (including Medicaid) for abortion, despite its legality.

46 Despite the Supreme Court majority's lack of enthusiasm in 1992 for the 1973 decision, the principle of *stare decisis* was invoked, which enjoins future courts to respect major decisions on which the public has come to rely and to respect the logic of the court's prior decision-making, though not unconditionally.

conditions on abortion that were not required for medical interventions involving an equivalent degree of risk for the patient (these conditions included mandatory waiting or "cooling-off" periods, counselling, notification and reporting duties and clinics having to present alternative options to abortion and notify patients of supposed "health risks", while a separate decision permitted withholding federal or state funding for abortion provision). Instead, the judges in *Casey* claimed that the decisive question was whether such conditions imposed an "undue" burden on the pregnant person's ability to obtain an abortion.[47] But a strange reflection on forms of power was also at work in the argumentation.

In some extended passages, the *Casey* decision reflected on the form of power associated with women's historical property-like subordination to their husbands, and with the subordination of children to the authority of their parents. What, then, was the nature of these parental and spousal interests in relation to the pregnant person, as construed by *Casey*? When considering whether it would infringe the constitutional rights of underaged pregnant people seeking abortions to oblige them to first notify their parents, the argument was not that parents might have an overriding interest in the foetal life in question. Rather, parents were assumed to have a degree of authority over the decisions taken by their children. Since other (though not all) medical procedures on underage patients required parental consent, this was not necessarily a case of pregnancy being used as a pretext for setting aside the rights a pregnant person would otherwise have.

However, the *Casey* judges' determination that parents did have a right of prior notification concerning these decisions performed a dual role, and also demarcated a type of power that the judges both named and explicitly claimed must be denied to husbands: "A State *may not* give to a man the kind of dominion over his wife that parents exercise over their children".[48]

---

47 *Casey* also repudiated the "three-trimester" framework introduced under *Roe*, according to which abortion was legal in the first trimester; in the second trimester it could be more strictly regulated but only on the grounds that it was in the interests of the pregnant person's health; and in the third trimester states had an "interest" in "potential life" and were allowed to restrict abortion, so long as exceptions to those restrictions were in place (for instance, to protect a pregnant person's life if they were endangered by the pregnancy).

48 *Planned Parenthood v. Casey*, 505 U.S. at 898 (*emphasis mine*). This had previously been decided in *Planned Parenthood v. Danforth*. Post-*Roe*, the state of Missouri introduced, in addition to other conditions, a requirement that pregnant individuals obtain the consent of their husbands before proceeding with an abortion. The Supreme Court ruled that this requirement was unconstitutional, arguing that the state could not "delegate to a spouse a veto power which the state itself is

The decision also addressed the unthinkable consequences that would ensue if a husband's interest in a foetus could outweigh those of his wife.[49] But the care taken to declare that women did not lose their constitutionally protected freedoms by marrying was not matched by an equivalent degree of caution about the *state's* possible interest in the foetuses they might bear.[50] To the contrary, *Casey* allowed that the state could act (although with limitations) throughout the pregnancy to protect its "interest" in a foetus,[51] whereas *Roe v. Wade* had limited any such imposition to the third trimester.[52]

How, if at all, did this relate to *Casey*'s expressed concern about intolerable exercises of patriarchal power in modern marital relationships? And how did that concern relate to the state's interest? There are several ways of understanding this. The *Casey* decision did not mean to suggest that patriarchal rights (here associated with domination, private control, histories of domestic and sexual violence, making decisions *about* women and a husband's traditional authority over his wife) had been replaced with an alternative, public kind of right (even if circumscribed) to control, under certain circumstances, pregnant bodies. The decision does not refer, in that sense, to a transfer of authority over pregnancy from "private interest" to "public interest". It is more helpful to recognise these as different construals of interest. Moreover, it was explicitly declared that a state could not now delegate to husbands a

absolutely and totally prohibited from exercising during the first trimester of pregnancy" (*Planned Parenthood v. Danforth*, 428 U.S. 52 at 72).

49 *Planned Parenthood v. Casey*, 505 U.S. at 898.

50 The term "state interest" played a role in *Roe v. Wade*, but to a different end. Given that it was already held that regulations could limit an individual's fundamental rights only where there was a "compelling state interest", *Roe* asked whether the state had an overriding interest in "areas of health and medical standards" or "in protecting the woman from an inherently hazardous procedure"—here judging that legal abortion did not present such dangers. But *Roe* did recognise a state's interest in foetal life but limited the legitimacy of that competing interest to the third-trimester. Later decisions, including Casey, deemed that third-trimester limit incoherent.

51 According to the *Casey* decision, while the state's interest did increase in the course of pregnancy, it could also be exercised from the outset, so long as the methods used to do so were not unduly obstructive.

52 Ian Shapiro and Alicia Steinmetz (2023, xxi) describe Justice Blackmun's reference in *Roe* to the state's interest in "the potentiality of human life" as a "throwaway" remark that would not only "come back to haunt him" but constitute the stake "drive[n] into Roe's heart", first by Chief Justice Renquist in *Webster v. Reproductive Health Services* (1989), who saw no basis for limiting the state's interest to the final trimester only. However, when *Casey* referred, without trimester restrictions, to the state's interest in life, it nonetheless recognised a different limiting principle: the state could not place an "undue burden" on women seeking abortions. This was then dismantled in 2022 when *Roe* was entirely revoked.

type of power over women the state did not possess. Although the state was described as having an interest that could, eventually, override a pregnant person's choice, it was not claimed that this imposition expressed a transfer of the dominion that husbands had historically sometimes been granted by structures of patriarchal power? Even if both types of interest might align in some cases, such as when an attempt to legally obstruct a particular abortion satisfies the expressed interest of a male spouse or father in that outcomes, they were nevertheless not being described as equivalent. Instead, when "interest" replaces a more legitimate exercise of authority, it neither exercises the same kind of power, nor even targets the same object. And yet neither does it entirely abandon dominion over women (or, to speak in terms that go beyond the patriarchal imaginary of power's own conceptual apparatus, over pregnant people). This is demonstrated when Ian Shapiro and Alicia Steinmetz note the incoherence in the *Casey* ruling's "seem[ing] to run together the quite different considerations of trying to ensure that the woman makes a well-thought-out decision (in the sense of not being one that *she* would subsequently come to regret) and the state's right to further *its* interest in potential life by regulating the woman's abortion choice" (Shapiro and Steinmetz 2023, xxvi).

The different language with which the state's interest is articulated is also telling. The state's right of obstruction is represented as protective responsibility for health and well-being, including an interest in protecting and optimising the quality of environment for both the foetus and the pregnant person. "Interest" is, in other words, presented in terms that theorists of biopolitics would readily identify as a project to optimise life.

"Interest" might refer to the state's predictive and trend-based management of populations or to interest in the life of a foetus that is projectively individuated as a potential person, or its bureaucratic responsibility for the conduct and services of medical facilities and for individual and public safety, or to the appeal by politicians, judges, and legislatures to moral questions or religious understandings of life. These are just some examples showing how variously the term "interest" is understood, and how it is not necessarily always applied to the same object. All of these understandings, and more, can be observed in state laws passed to regulate and restrict abortion access. A Foucauldian framework is not inappropriate for deciphering within such decisions a reconfiguration of "interest" into "biopower". That can include an interest in regulating overall behavioural trends; in a disciplining evaluation of the responsible conduct expected of pregnant persons in abortion decision-making; in either expanding or limiting medical power and its reach and facilities; and in creating environments that influence the likelihood of certain actions being taken within them. Each of these might be understood as different governmental commitments to well-being, and they might very well seem to replace the historical exercise of dominion by patriarchal authority that *Casey* repudiated. Yet to see this as a replacement would be to conceive of power in terms that merit closer scrutiny.

State interest hinges together a claimed responsibility for life and a claimed authority over life. That becomes clearer if we return to the question: what might be the *relationship* between the repudiation of husbands' superannuated dominion over women and the affirmation of a legitimate interest attributed to the state? What if we think of this, not as a replacement, but as a scene of replacement? In other words, what if we mark the difference between, on the one hand, a transfer of power, and, on the other, the social, legal, or political effect of *representing* a transformation of power (whether asserted or negating—for example, as anachronistic, superannuated, revoked, replaced, etc).

Certainly, there is a type of power that one part of the *Casey* decision sought to repudiate. Portraying the traditions of patriarchal marriage as still exposing women to domestic violence, rape and other forms of abuse-as-control, *Casey* affirmed that women did not "lose their constitutionally protected liberty when they marry".[53] Therefore, any obligation to notify their husbands before they sought abortions would unacceptably limit their autonomy, and moreover amount to a recognition of the dominion of husbands over their wives, even though this argument was instead intended to declare that dominion had been officially revoked. In 1976 it had been necessary for the Supreme Court to invalidate a Missouri state law that required women to notify their husbands about an intended abortion.[54] In 1992 this proved necessary again in relation to a similar law passed in Pennsylvania in 1982.[55]

53 *Planned Parenthood v. Casey*, 505 U.S. at 898.

54 Missouri's imposition of this condition was ruled unconstitutional in *Roe v. Danforth*.

55 At issue in *Casey* were the requirements of the Pennsylvania Abortion Control Act (passed in 1982): to wit, that a pregnant person must provide informed consent prior to abortion and be provided with "certain information at least 24 hours before the abortion is performed"; that parental consent must be obtained for minors; that married women seeking abortions must sign a statement indicating they had notified their husband; and that facilities providing abortion must comply with certain reporting requirements.

Moreover, as Justices O'Connor, Kennedy and Souter argued in notable detail, with six pages and many citations on the topic,[56] marriage was a milieu that exposed women to chronic domestic violence. They elaborated that obliging women to notify their husbands only increased that exposure. Thus, violence, and fear of violence, could obstruct women's exercise of their constitutionally protected right. However, if we give renewed attention to the judges' statement that "the husband's interest in the life of the child his wife is carrying does not permit the State to empower him with this troubling degree of authority over his wife",[57] we can see more than the announcement of a defunct form of power. It is true that the Supreme Court declared that states had no authority to attribute property-like rights over women to their husbands. Some parts of *Casey's* argumentation suggest that the exercise of such power had become unthinkable in modern times, despite the efforts of some state legislators to accord patriarchal rights to husbands and their indifference to the domestic violence mentioned in this decision.

But what did this mean for the nature of the propertisation (or, von Redecker might say, the phantom possession) that remained at issue? To argue (returning to Casey's wording) that *husbands* "may not" be granted spousal or private dominion over women is not to say that women and pregnant people or foetal life can no longer be propertised in the senses suggested by Weinbaum and von Redecker. In fact, the latter might describe domestic violence in just those terms. That being the case, the real question is how contemporary forms of power hinge together with the declaration that some are now impossible, and that "*this*" is not "*that*".

To ask what is the *relationship* between the repudiation—as superannuated—of husbands' dominion over women and the affirmation of a legitimate interest attributed to the state is to ask what is facilitated by the declaration that there are forms of power (in this case, patriarchal dominion) that "*may not*" be accorded to husbands. It is the repudiation of the "troubling" authority over women that legitimates, as if by securing an alternative to that authority, the state's claim of responsibility for care and concern for life.

A more extreme version of this was seen in 2022. It is notable that the Supreme Court *Dobbs* ruling included the majority's reference to the political equality and agency of modern women. This effectively amounts to an assertion that revoking the constitutional right to abortion *cannot* be the form

56 *Planned Parenthood v. Casey*, 505 U.S. at 888–894.

57 *Planned Parenthood v. Casey*, 505 U.S. at 898.

of power we call "dominion", nor "domination".[58] The decision made reference to pregnancy-based discrimination, the perception of illegitimate pregnancy as shameful and the role of pregnancy in impairing women's economic equality and rights as if these were all historical matters.[59]

The decision represents a further example of legitimation by dissociation. This dissociation is possible because the alternative forms of power with which state interest was expressed (the decision included examples of biopolitics, disciplining, securitisation and the creation of milieus of discouragement)[60] form a hinge with its demarcation of the supposedly obsolete sovereign forms of power over female and pregnant bodies.

"Care" for lives, concern for life, standards, well-being, order and security, the assumption of responsibility for overall trends in reproductive conduct or for the differential population impact or morality of abortion are neither a continuation nor a replacement of the sovereign forms of power conceived of as dominion. They produce different objects, different bodies and different problems. But they do hinge together with a force that is instrumentalised as negative, and that provides licence by always finding ways to declare that *this is not that*. If there is a sly implication of likeness (from the use of chains and shackles discussed by Goodwin, to the historical comparisons drawn concerning the women and pregnant people left with no choice by Dobbs but to resort to trans-border legal evasion), it is always accompanied by a claim to unlikeness, a claim that is put to work as legitimating: whether that be expressed in the policing of bodies under the pretext of "concern for foetal life", or whether it be declared a legal matter of state interest.

58 Thus, Alito's mention of the recourse now available to women (to turn to the ballot box in their states to get new laws passed) was not just a replacement of federal overreach with renewed respect for state decision-making.

59 We could also see this move as being undermined by Alito's concurrent willingness to cite as a point of reference jurisprudence from the period in which women and enslaved people were not legally recognised as citizens with equal rights.

60 I have elsewhere (Deutscher 2024) discussed how the *Dobbs* decision makes extensive reference to these heterogeneous forms and techniques of power.

4. Negations of propertisation II: the "*may not* be" of obstructing cross-state travel for abortion

In 2020, this mechanism of the "*may not* be" was also deployed in new legal efforts to impede pregnant people from crossing state borders to obtain abortion. Mary Elizabeth Coleman, at that time a Missouri state representative, was responsible for one of the earliest of several attempts by pro-life Republican politicians to prevent their states' citizens from evading state-level abortion bans.[61]

One journalist characterised Coleman's attempt to stop pregnant Missourians from going to another, abortion-providing state, as "drawing a subtle difference [. . .] from actually stopping people" (Kitchener in Powers and Kitchener 2022). The convolution of Coleman's own explanation included a common pro-life ambiguity, as if the aim were instead care—for adults and foetuses who were both referred to as Missourians: "I'm working on trying to deal with what happens in Missouri so Missouri residents who are harmed outside of the state have legal recourse for [sic] those who are trying to aid

61 As a more indirect initiative, Coleman sought to impede Missouri residents from crossing state borders to obtain an abortion by targeting those who assisted them, and by targeting abortion providers operating beyond Missouri's borders. But there was also a use of "unthinkability", since the effort further drew on Coleman's ability to point out this was *not* a matter of detaining those seeking to cross borders. A further strategic measure in this and other states has been to foreground the issue of teenage abortions. Instead of attempting to physically detain underage teenagers, this alternative targets everyone who sought to assist them, including their parents and abortion providers. Deterrent milieus have been put in place in multiple states through legislation techniques modelled on SB8, introduced in Texas in 2021. Coleman sought to repeat the latter's distinctive structure, which, rather than criminalising those who seek abortion, legalises civil action lawsuits against anybody assisting a pregnant person to obtain an abortion. Because of the ambiguous scope of the term "assistance" and the unpredictability of open-ended exposure to civil lawsuits, these laws have been highly successful in pre-emptively deterring assistance and medical treatment, even where the corresponding prosecution might never have succeeded. A number of states have since introduced copycat laws and similar strategies to impede their citizens and residents from accessing abortion medication and procedures outside, as well as within, their borders.

and abet people who are not following the laws of Missouri" (quoted in Morrison 2022).[62]

Numerous journalists, legal scholars and politicians have—albeit hesitantly—noted echoes of laws passed in the 1850s to deter slave fugitivity at a time when enslaved people could be recognised as free in the Northern states to which they escaped, despite continuing to be deemed legal property in the states from which they had fled. According to Michael Hiltzik:

> The Fugitive Slave Act[63] was a federal law. Yet several red states are prepared to replicate it on their own books. The quarries this time aren't Black slaves, but those who assist pregnant women to seek abortions out of state, including employers who pay for the travel and others who help them.
>
> *Hiltzik 2022*

Historian Kate Masur has referred to the "talk of a new 'Underground Railroad' that conjures clandestine networks helping people to flee their home states in search of the freedom to end a pregnancy" (Masur 2022; see also Rascoe 2024).

So, we can recognise a technique with a specific morphology in Coleman's distancing of her project from equivalences with the mid-nineteenth century efforts to prevent enslaved people from escaping across borders. As Coleman herself remarked:

> you know, it's really technically difficult to do because I certainly don't want to limit people's freedom of movement. That's not just illegal, I think that's pretty immoral. That's not something you want to be doing.
>
> *Quoted in Powers and Kitchener 2022*

Using the device of negation, Coleman sought to legitimise her proposed laws by pointing out that they were in fact *not* like the historical laws impeding slave fugitivity. In other words, *a* was not like *b* (moreover, she further

62 The identity of these protected state "residents" is clear in her comments that it was "disheartening to think of how many people are going to lose their lives in that clinic across the river" and further references to foetuses as "citizens" and harmed "children" who merited the state's "care": "If our children are being harmed in this state or in another state, Missouri still has the ability to take care of that" (quoted in Powers and Kitchener 2022).

63 The Fugitive Slave Act was a federal law passed by Congress in 1850 in response to the legal ambiguity of slavery remaining legal in some states although illegal in others. It determined that previously enslaved men and women who escaped to free states could be claimed legally by and forcibly returned to their former slaveowners from southern states.

implied, to suggest otherwise would be obfuscation). Nor would *a* lead to *b* (to suggest otherwise, it was often said at the time, would amount to paranoia). As projects powerfully organised by their "*not*", there is a linkage between the work of negation in creating effects of revocability, and the work of negation in allowing some analogies to both imply and discredit an association. Coleman's statement could also be taken as saying: if *you* interpret these forms of governance as analogous to antebellum attempts to restrict freedom of movement, that is a matter of your own irresponsible epistemic misconduct.

What licence was generated by this double motion of negation? Coleman's question about cross-state abortion procurement: "How do we stop this?" combined the aim of "impeding" people with the expression of care and concern for them. "What can we do to try to *protect* Missourians from this?" (quoted in Powers and Kitchener 2022, *my emphasis*).

More speculatively, let us attribute to Coleman the further implication: *you* have erred by confounding a technique that operates to deter the likelihood of behaviour by acting on milieu with sovereign forms of power that literally restrict freedom of movement. *This* is not *that*. When Coleman claims her bill does not aim to do something everyone would agree is "immoral", the point is not the degree of comparability to, or echoes of, the archive of nineteenth-century fugitivity laws. For if there are any echoes, they operate as a revoked form. Where attention should be directed is to the action of that negation, the legitimation of the *may not be*. The claim to moral legitimation represented by Coleman's saying "I certainly don't want to limit people's freedom of movement" underscores the obstructive and deterrent milieu whose techniques of power are not the same as those of a ban. In fact, such techniques had already resulted in a state of affairs in which Coleman could claim that Missourians were no longer seeking abortions.

In short, while the forms of order created around pregnant people are certainly distinguishable from literally impeding their physical freedom, what "*may not be*" is annexed as a point of demarcation, with an emphasis on "interest", "concern", and "care", and thereby licensed as "*not*" domination. Given this unthinkability, the question "How do we stop this?" is not quarantined by its repudiation, but instead authorises, by negation, the strategies of cross-state impediment.

By contrast, in the *Dobbs* decision, Kavanaugh's and Alito's affirmation that the decision would *not* or could *not* lead to a further loss of rights[64] doubled as a negative indication of the further fields of *possible* revocability opened up by the decision. But techniques for removing rights can assume a variety of other forms. In fact, in the wake of the decision, the right to contraception has come under challenge, but *not* because the Supreme Court is likely, at least in the short term, to revoke the constitutional right to the use of contraception. Rather, it is being eroded by other means.[65] All this serves to illustrate that a key dimension of these negative declarations can be more precisely pinpointed by asking "What kind of power is this?" This allows us to attend more closely to what the declarations facilitate. And to consider one more variation: it is sometimes the case that when the licence of the *will not be* connects itself to the realm of projected possibility, its negation is all the more threatening because its future scope is unknown.[66]

5. Could *not* follow

In February 2024, one of the many open legal consequences that it had seemed in 2022 could *not* follow from the Dobbs decision, namely the granting of legal personhood to embryos, briefly became less unthinkable. The Alabama Supreme Court declared all frozen embryos "extrauterine children" who had the rights of persons irrespective of their developmental stage, a decision allowing for prosecution and private lawsuits on the grounds of disposal or mistreatment of embryos. The judges claimed that test tubes are the equivalent of nurseries and that destroying their contents is "like"

64 Justice Alito said that the decision would *not* call into question other rights protected by the Fourteenth Amendment, including rights to contraception and to sex/marriage irrespective of gender or race.

65 The right to use contraception was established for married couples by *Griswold v. Connecticut* (1965) and for unmarried couples by *Eisenstadt v. Baird* (1972). It has most recently been undermined through coordinated initiatives seeking to revive a law that would prohibit delivery of contraceptive products by post and similar methods, to reduce funding for contraception, to make it more difficult to access contraception, to reclass some forms of contraception as abortifacients and so on.

66 Post-*Dobbs*, there have also been efforts at state court level to revoke the Federal Drug Agency's approval of the abortifacient mifepristone in terms that would have limited its access nationwide.

homicide.[67] How did this up the ante concerning the role of "unthinkability" as a hinge of power?

Deeming a blastocyst to be the equivalent of a child gave rise to newly (in)conceivable embodiments, as well as new possibilities for labelling people as irresponsible parents. Comedians explored the (sometimes absurd) implications of this revision of the boundary between thinkable and unthinkable. There was more than a grain of truth in Desi Lydic's joke that under these circumstances just starting a family would amount to a murderous act (Lydic and Chieng 2024). She reminded her audience that she was not allowed, when last she checked, to store her children in the freezer. Ronny Chieng, meanwhile, expressed high hopes for the paternity benefits he might derive as the father of a test tube. How could seeing a blastocyst as a child further exacerbate the burden of expectations associated with reproduction and raise to a nonsensical register the ways in which those expectations produce (ir)responsibilised subjects?

This incident served as a reminder that there are other means of understanding the unthinkability that hovers around the laws, politics and activist strategies at work in the regulation of reproduction. Revocability works in other ways, sometimes making it possible to reveal its own reversibility. This returns us to one of the chapter's starting points. Jared Sexton responded to the pro-life analogy between a womb and a plantation by showing how it opened up an unthinkability that could be amplified to the point of conceptual self-destruction. As he asked, what did it really mean for the pro-life lobby to claim that the "most dangerous place to be Black was in a womb?"[68] Does the analogy between a womb and a slave plantation make the birth canal the Underground Railroad? What, then, is "abolitionism", if we follow this analogy to its conclusion? Would it not mean the abolition of pregnancy? In

67 Alabama Supreme Court ruling in the consolidated cases LePage v. Center for Reproductive Medicine and Burdick-Aysenne v. Center for Reproductive Medicine.

68 See the concluding chapter in Cooper 2024.

My warmest acknowledgments go to Stefanie Graefe, Irina Herb, Sophie Jossi-Silverstein and particularly Susanne Lettow for their generous input and to Übersetzungsbüro Denzig, Cologne, for the highly professional copy-editing. Thank you also to Astrid Deuber-Mankowsky and Eva von Redecker for their vigorous conversations about this material, to Christoph Menke for the opportunity to hold a workshop on the broader project and to the participants of the Praktische Philosophie seminar at Goethe University Frankfurt. At IAS, thanks to Nadia Marzouki, Clara Latham and Darryl Li for their valuable feedback on earlier versions and to the members of the memorable IAS (23–24) working group: Wendy Brown, Zahid Chaudhary, Joan Scott, Antonio Vázquez-Arroyo and Gary Wilder.

other words, this deployment of unthinkability also contains the potential of its own rupture.

Works Cited

Allen, Anita L. (1988). Privacy, Surrogacy, and the Baby M Case. *Georgetown Law Journal*, 76(5), 1759–1792.

Allen, Anita (1990). Surrogacy, Slavery, and the Ownership of Life. *Harvard Journal of Law and Public Policy*, 13(1), 139–149.

Allen, Anita (1991). The Black Surrogate Mother. *Harvard Blackletter Journal*, 8, 17–31.

Behrens, David (1990). It's a Boy! But Whose? Surrogate and Genetic Parents in Tug-of-War. *New York Newsday*, 21 September.

Boone, Meghan, and Benjamin J. McMichael (2021). State-Created Fetal Harm. *Georgetown Law Journal*, 109(3), 479–522.

Cooper, Melinda (2024). *Counterrevolution: Extravagance and Austerity in Public Finance*. New York: Zone Books.

Crockett, Emily (2016). Congress Members Casually Compare Abortion to Slavery, Black Genocide, and Killing Puppies. *Vox*, 23 September. https://www.vox.com/identities/2016/9/23/13029778/congress-abortion-puppies-genocide-slavery-steve-king.

Deutscher, Penelope (2024). Revocability, Exception, Disqualification: Grammars of Power after Dobbs. *Critical Times*, 7(1), 66–93.

Du Bois, W. E. B. (1935). *Black Reconstruction in America: An Essay toward a History of the Part Which Black Folk Played in the Attempt to Reconstruct Democracy in America, 1860–1880*. New York: Harcourt.

Goodwin, Michele Bratcher (2010/2011). Reproductive Carrots and Sticks. *S&F: The Scholar & Feminist Online*, 9(1–2). https://sfonline.barnard.edu/reproductive-carrots-and-sticks/3/.

Goodwin, Michele (2020). *Policing the Womb: Invisible Women and the Criminalization of Motherhood*. Cambridge: Cambridge University Press.

Greene, Jamal (2011). The Anticanon. *Harvard Law Review*, 125(2), 379–475.

Harris, Cheryl I. (1993). Whiteness as Property. *Harvard Law Review*, 106(8), 1707–1791.

Hartman, Saidiya (1997). *Scenes of Subjection: Terror, Slavery, and Self-Making in Nineteenth-Century America*. Oxford: Oxford University Press.

Hauser, Christine (2023). Judge Cites 1849 Slavery Law in Ruling Embryos Can Be Considered Property. *New York Times*, 16 March. https://www.nytimes.com/2023/03/16/us/virginia-slave-laws-embryos.htm.

Hiltzik, Michael (2022). Threats to Criminalize Out-of-State Abortions Are a Scary Reminder of 1850s America. *Los Angeles Times*, 12 July. https://www.latimes.com/business/story/2022-07-12/threats-to-criminalize-out-of-state-abortion.

Lydic, Desi, and Ronny Chieng (2024). Alabama's New Reproductive Law Considers Embryos Children. *The Daily Show*, 21 February. https://www.youtube.com/watch?v=ICtioqgEmFI.

Masur, Kate (2022). What Pre-Civil War History Tells Us about the Coming Abortion Battle. *Washington Post*, 14 July. https://www.washingtonpost.com/made-by-history/2022/07/14/what-pre-civil-war-history-tells-us-about-coming-abortion-battle/.

Morgan, Jennifer (2004). *Laboring Women: Reproduction and Gender in New World Slavery*. Philadelphia: University of Pennsylvania Press.

Morgan, Jennifer (2021). *Reckoning with Slavery: Gender, Kinship, and Capitalism in the Early Black Atlantic*. Durham, NC: Duke University Press.

Morrison, Cassidy (2022). Post-Roe Interstate Legal Warfare Echoes Fugitive Slave Litigation. *Washington Examiner*, 4 May. https://www.washingtonexaminer.com/news/1177134/post-roe-interstate-legal-warfare-echoes-fugitive-slave-litigation/.

Pande, Amrita (2014). *Wombs in Labor: Transnational Commercial Surrogacy in India*. New York: Columbia University Press.

Park, Linette, and Mali Collins (2021). Black Women Giving Birth in Prison Face Surveillance Disguised as Medical Care. *Truthout*, 27 July. https://truthout.org/articles/black-women-giving-birth-in-prison-face-surveillance-disguised-as-medical-care/.

Pollitt, Katha (1987). The Strange Case of Baby M. *The Nation*, 23 May, 667–688.

Powers, Martine, and Caroline Kitchener (2022). The Next Abortion Fight Is over State Lines. *Post Reports*, 8 July. https://www.washingtonpost.com/podcasts/post-reports/preparing-for-a-postroe-america/.

Rascoe, Ayesha (2024). What the Alabama IVF Ruling Means for Parents Going through IVF. *NPR*, 25 February. https://www.npr.org/transcripts/1233771248.

Raymond, Janice (1993). *Women as Wombs: Reproductive Technologies and the Battle over Women's Freedom*. New York: HarperCollins.

Redecker, Eva von (2020). Ownership's Shadow: Neoauthoritarianism as Defense of Phantom Possession. *Critical Times*, 3(1), 33–67.

Roberts, Dorothy (1997). *Killing the Black Body: Race, Reproduction, and the Meaning of Liberty*. New York: Random House/Pantheon.

Roberts, Dorothy (2002). *Shattered Bonds*. New York: Hachette.

Roberts, Dorothy (2022). *Torn Apart: How the Child Welfare System Destroys Black Families—and How Abolition Can Build a Safer World*. New York: Basic Books.

Rose, Jacqueline (2019). Agents of Their Own Abuse: The Treatment of Migrant Women. *London Review of Books*, 41(19), 37–40.

Sernett, Milton (1980). The Rights of Personhood: The Dred Scott Case and the Question of Abortion. *Religion in Life*, 49(4), 461–476.

Sexton, Jared (2015). Unbearable Blackness. *Cultural Critique*, 90 (Spring), 159–178.

Shapiro, Ian, and Alicia Steinmetz (eds.) (2023). Introduction. In Ian Shapiro and Alicia Steinmetz (eds.). *Abortion: The Supreme Court Decisions 1965–2022*, 4th ed., 2–23, New York: Hackett.

Smith, Kate (2019). Alabama Politicians Compare Abortions to the Holocaust in Proposed Legislation. *CBS News*, 23 April. https://www.cbsnews.com/news/alabama-abortion-bill-alabama-politicians-compare-abortions-to-the-holocaust-in-proposed-abortion-law-2019-04-23/.

Spillers, Hortense J. (1987). Mama's Baby, Papa's Maybe: An American Grammar Book. *Diacritics*, 17(2), 64–81.

Stone, Lorraine (1988). Neoslavery— "Surrogate" Motherhood Contracts v. the Thirteenth Amendment. *Law and Inequality: A Journal of Theory and Practice*, 6(2–3), 63–73.

Veil, Simone with Annick Cojean (2004). *Les Hommes aussi s'en souviennent: Une Loi pour l'histoire.* Paris: Editions Stock.

Walker, Alice (1989). What Can the White Man ... Say to the Black Woman? *The Nation*, 22 May. Republished at https://www.thenation.com/article/archive/what-can-white-man-say-black-woman/.

Weinbaum, Alys (2019). *The Afterlife of Reproductive Slavery*. Durham, NC: Duke University Press.

Cases

Box v. Planned Parenthood of Ind. & Ky., Inc., 141 S. Ct. 187, 207 L. Ed. 2d 1112 (2020).

Center for Reproductive Medicine v. Burdick-Aysenne, No. 24–127 (U.S. 2024).

Dobbs v. Jackson Women's Health Organization, 142 S. Ct. 2228, 213 L. Ed. 2d 545 (2022).

Eisenstadt v. Baird, 405 U.S. 438 (1972).

Ferguson et al. v. City of Charleston et al., 532 U.S. 67, 121 S. Ct. 1281 (2001).

Griswold v. Connecticut, 381 U.S. 479, 85 S. Ct. 1678 (1965).

Harris v. McRae, 448 U.S. 297, 100 S. Ct. 2671 (1980).

In Re Baby M, 217 N.J. Super. 313, 525 A.2d 1128 (Ch. Div. 1987).

Johnson v. Calvert, 5 Cal.4th 84, 19 Cal. Rptr. 2d 494, 851 P. 2d 776 (Cal. 1993).

LePage v. The Center for Reproductive Medicine, No. SC-2022-0515 (Ala. 2024).

Planned Parenthood of Missouri v. Danforth, 428 U.S. 52, 96 S. Ct. 2831 (1976).

Planned Parenthood of Southeastern Pa. v. Casey, 505 U.S. 833, 112 S. Ct. 2791 (1992).

Roe v. Wade, 410 U.S. 113, 93 S. Ct. 705 (1973).

Webster v. Reproductive Health Services, 492 U.S. 490 (1989).

Life, Liberty or Property: Reparative Reproductive Justice without Self-Ownership

Elizabeth Lanphier

Reproductive justice is a theoretical framework and activist movement concerned with reproductive choice and freedom. It expands beyond a narrow conception of reproductive "rights" that is often aligned with choices against pregnancy (e.g. choosing to take contraception or have an abortion) but that fails to pay attention to the conditions necessary to enact those choices. First theorised by Black feminist scholars and activists, reproductive justice is also a critique of second-wave feminist approaches to reproductive rights that historically focused on—and only met—the reproductive needs of a subset of well-off, often white, women, while continuing to marginalise the reproductive needs of others.

Reproductive justice adds two additional domains of reproductive freedom: the ability to become a parent, and access to safe communities in which to raise children. These three pillars of reproductive justice (being able to choose not to become a parent, being able to choose to become a parent and being able to raise children safely), when understood as a framework for justice, point to the ways in which reproductive freedom is not only a negative liberty to be *free from* interference in reproductive choices and goals, but also a positive liberty to be *free to* make reproductive choices aligning with one's goals. A justice-based framework entails not only that individuals have rights but that other individuals and institutions are accountable to those rights. Reproductive justice is therefore about creating conditions necessary for people to achieve reproductive freedom as a matter of justice, including through social, political and healthcare policy.

I have previously critiqued the notion of "self-ownership", which represents a popular theoretical and colloquial understanding of bodily rights and reproductive autonomy. On my view, the idea that we "own" our bodies and therefore control them does not capture the positive liberties necessary for reproductive freedom (Lanphier 2021a). It also builds on a philosophical history that reinforces the very injustices reproductive justice works to undo. My previous critique focused on how self-ownership fails to address access to the goods and services necessary for people to make reproductive choices against pregnancy or parenthood. However, I left open whether the same framing addresses other pillars of reproductive justice, including the ability to choose pregnancy or parenthood. In this chapter, I revisit my previous argument against bodily self-ownership as a conceptual framework for reproductive justice. I then pick up where that argument left off and consider how it interacts with reproductive technologies that often operate on logics of bodily ownership and control: specifically, ownership of gametes or embryos and contracted surrogacy.

Based on an exploration of reparative approaches to justice that were posited by Olúfẹ́mi Táíwò (2022) and connected to reproductive justice by Desiree Valentine (2023), I suggest a view of "reparative worldbuilding" as one way of rethinking a reliance on property that may be fruitful for reproductive justice. This notion focuses, in part, on the impact of historical and ongoing trauma—individual and collective—and oppression as grounds for enacting reparative worldbuilding. Táíwò asks, "What if building the just world *was* reparations?" (Táíwò 2022, 3), introducing the idea that reparative justice and worldbuilding are approaches that address historical harm not only by paying past debts of injustice, but by pursuing and enacting better structures and systems in the present and future.

This reparative worldbuilding formulation introduces new questions that allow us to think about reproductive justice not only intersectionally but also internationally, and to reflect on access to and regulation of reproductive technology. In conclusion, I sketch a view of trauma-informed reparative reproductive justice. I briefly describe the concept of trauma-informed care, which is not only a model of direct care delivery, but also a framework for creating healing environments. In other words, it is a kind of reparative worldbuilding. Trauma-informed care responds to the prevalence and heterogeneity of trauma as a subjectively experienced disruptive phenomenon, which can be individual or collective, physical or psychological, acute or ongoing. It can also provide guidance for developing ethical policies and practices regarding the use of and access to reproductive technologies on a local and global scale.

Importantly, a trauma-informed framework resists a prescriptive account of the necessary or sufficient conditions for justice, which may not be attuned to context-dependent histories, opportunities or constraints. This is not an argument for moral relativism, but rather for moral humility, recognising that the content of reproductive justice needs to adapt to context. As such, a relational, trauma-informed approach demands attuning to social, historical and political context.

1. The problem of self-ownership

There is a lineage within Anglo-American political philosophy that is built on a rhetoric of bodily self-ownership, running from the social contract theory of John Locke (1988 [1689]) to the libertarianism of Robert Nozick (1974) and continued by their commentators. This rhetoric has been used to defend private property and the concept of ownership, including ownership of goods and territory by individuals and nation states, but also bodily autonomy. This includes autonomy as conceptualised within biomedical and reproductive ethics. Being a "self-owner" is a means of self-determination, at least on a proceduralist view of autonomy. It implies that we have exclusive control over our bodies, just as we have exclusive control over the property we own. This discussion arises out of social contract theory and the view that the creation of institutions is necessary to either establish (Hobbes) or protect (Locke) private property.

According to Locke, because individuals have a right to self-preservation, they also have a right to acquire the means necessary for self-preservation, including appropriating things for themselves (i.e. acquiring property). In Locke's time, that included goods such as the food a person eats and the land necessary to produce it. According to Locke, because a person owns their body, they can take ownership over anything which they mix with their body through labour. He claims that a person can amass or acquire exclusive control over whatever they can directly produce and consume. The reliance on an individual's body to establish an entitlement to property, through either consumption or embodied labour, rests on a prior commitment to bodily "self-ownership" that continues to be both developed and refuted within philosophical literature, including as a formulation for bodily autonomy.

The language of self-ownership is used not only in social and political philosophy, but also within reproductive rights activism. The slogan "my body, my choice" was popularised by the United States second-wave feminist movement in the late 1960s and early 1970s, a period when feminists and the United States Supreme Court reshaped rights to contraception and abortion. It continues to be used to this day in the United States and globally (Lanphier 2021b). The concept of self-ownership also permeates recent reproductive rights advocacy, such as the "Bans off Our Bodies" campaign by United States reproductive and sexual health provider Planned Parenthood, which included slogans like "when we own our bodies, we are powerful." I have previously critiqued the idea of grounding concepts of reproductive autonomy in the notions of private property and self-ownership by focusing on three of its shortcomings: it gives an insufficient account of the initial acquisition of property; it involves inequitable access to ownership, including self-ownership; and the notion of ownership does not adequately entail correlative duties (Lanphier 2021a).

The first critique underscores how the philosophy of private property relies on flawed views of the just initial acquisition of property—that is, of how anything (including the body) becomes property that can be owned. While there are adequate theories of how property can be justly transferred once acquired, the same is not true when it comes to theories of how things come to be property in the first place (Thomson 1990). That is to say, once property is owned, there are legitimate philosophical and legal ways to understand the right to transfer said property (purchase, inheritance, gifting, etc.). But theories of how property initially came to be owned require either a leap of reasoning (e.g. accepting, as Locke does, an unfounded presumption of divinely commanded self-ownership) or an acceptance that the origins of ownership are unjust. The latter can be seen in histories of forceful or deceitful initial acquisition: for example, territorial acquisition in colonial periods by colonising powers that asserted forceful control over inhabited territories and claimed ownership.

Secondly, the historical connection between bodily and property ownership systematically excludes some individuals from recognition as self-owners or property owners and is fraught with racism and sexism. Locke, who argued that because we own our bodies we come to own the land that we toil with them, nonetheless permitted some people to own others' bodies and to claim ownership over the land worked by their serfs or slaves. Similarly, in the English context within which Locke formulated his theory, women were property that was transferred at marriage, and were barred from owning property themselves. Viewed through the lens of these historical injustices of ownership, there is understandable interest in reclaiming property and bodily self-ownership as a form of resistance. For women and people of colour who were structurally and conceptually prohibited from ownership, or whose bodies were themselves owned, to assert self-ownership as a form of control is powerful. However, it does not solve the problem of the unjust origins of property, or the conceptual incoherence of the origins of self-ownership.

Even if self-ownership and bodily property were decoupled from their conceptual problems and redirected solely towards an activist agenda of reproductive freedom, the notion of self-ownership would still fall short. The third critique of using this notion to advance the cause of reproductive justice is that it only makes a claim on negative liberties, or the right to be free from interference and obstacles. Isaiah Berlin (1969) distinguished between "two concepts of liberty" that run through political philosophy. According to the first, negative liberty, freedom is the absence of obstacles or constraints, while according to the other, positive liberty, freedom is the internal or external capacity to realise one's choices. While other theorists draw various conceptual distinctions regarding the scope and content of positive liberties, for the purposes of this chapter I am going to simply take positive liberties to be enabling conditions.

These two concepts of liberty entail different expectations and obligations. If I own something, I get to control it. There is a negative freedom from control over my property, and a positive freedom to (mostly) do what I like with my property. But my ownership does not entail that anyone else is obligated to assist me in managing or exercising control over my property, only that they must not interfere. As much as non-domination remains an urgent demand for reproductive rights, it does not go far enough to ensure reproductive justice. We are reliant on others—on systems, structures and policies—to create the conditions in which we can realise reproductive choices. In other words, reproductive justice requires positive liberties to enable and achieve reproductive freedom.

In response to this third point, one might say that ownership also requires positive liberties. We rely on the availability of resources and systems to take care of our property. While this is true, ownership does not confer a positive right to that assistance. For example, if I own my house, I have a right to control it, but must also maintain it. But no one else is obligated to provide the goods, services, or conditions needed for me to do so (even if I can be held liable for failing in my duty of maintenance). If a pipe breaks, I do not have a right to a plumber, though I hope one will be available at an affordable price. Governments or civic authorities provide some goods and services, such as emergency medical care, ambulance and fire services or maintenance of utilities. However, these are valuable services for the entire community or society that people receive by virtue of being members of it, not by virtue of owning property within it.

A more plausible objection to the third critique might be that the activist assertion of "my body, my choice" is not only decoupled from a property rights history; it is, furthermore, not making a claim about *owning* but rather about having a particular *relationship to* one's body. According to this objection, slogans about *my* body point to a relational claim entailing certain rights, privileges and obligations. Similarly, I might talk about *my* children not because I own them but because I stand in a relation to them such that I have duties to care for them and special rights to make decisions on their behalf.

The ways in which we relate to our bodies are part of what is at stake in reproductive activism and reproductive justice. However, even on this relational view, "my body, my choice" focuses exclusively on the right to non-interference. In the example of the relationship to children, this is precisely why the third pillar of reproductive justice asserts a right to raise children in safe and supported communities. Merely standing in relation to something or someone does not, by itself, entail obligations on the part of other people or society to support systems that enable one to take care of that person or thing. I have obligations to my children, but that relationship does not obligate others (systems, societies, communities) to provide adequate support to help me meet those obligations. The third pillar of reproductive justice specifically asserts that it should not fall entirely on parents—indeed, *cannot* fall entirely on parents—to create the conditions necessary to support children. Parents have positive rights that entail corollary duties on society to meet the demands of reproductive justice.

2. Freedom to become a parent

Thus far, I have discussed how two of the three pillars of reproductive justice, the freedom not to become a parent and the freedom to raise children in safe and supported communities, require us to reject views of reproductive autonomy based on notions of self-ownership and property rights. But what about the freedom to become a parent? For some individuals, the freedom to become a parent primarily requires non-interference in their reproductive capacity, e.g. freedom from forced contraception or sterilisation or from controls on their sexual activity. Access to affordable medical care and a healthy environment further supports the freedom to become a parent but may not be essential to it in all cases.

For other individuals, and for certain groups, the freedom to become a parent requires access to either medical interventions or social processes such as adoption. For those with access to effective reproductive technologies (meaning that the technologies already exist and are financially and logistically accessible), a reproductive rights approach may *seem* sufficient because all they want or need is non-interference in their use of the available technologies. However, reproductive justice recognises that for some individuals without the practical and financial access to assisted reproductive technology (ART), non-interference is insufficient. Being able to make positive rights claims to use and benefit from ART (or become an adoptive parent) is a matter of justice. Thus, just as with choosing against parenthood, the logical framework of a property-based account or a system based on self-ownership and reproductive *rights* protects negative liberties and not positive ones in ways that fall short of justice.

But does a view based on bodily property or self-ownership prove useful in other ways, when considering the kinds of reproductive technologies on which one might be reliant to realise reproductive choices to become a parent? Is a self-ownership framework potentially necessary for practical and ethical reasons in relation to ART, especially when it comes to allocating or constraining rights? In this section, I consider a potential asymmetry between the justification for abandoning a property rights view of self-ownership as it applies to not becoming a parent versus becoming a parent, before considering ways out of such an asymmetry.

I take ART for the purposes of this chapter to refer to a broad set of technologies that currently exist. These include processes for the storage, sale, purchase or donation of reproductive material, such as eggs, sperm and embryos, as well as processes for engaging or becoming a gestational surrogate. In practice, using many of these technologies requires various forms of access: awareness of the technologies, logistical and geographic access to them and the ability to afford to use them or to be compensated for contributing to them. They also entail disparate burdens: the burdens on one's own body or resources in order to use ART, and the burdens on another's body if they become a gamete donor or gestate a surrogate pregnancy.

To varying degrees, all these forms of ART engage contractual systems or have concepts of ownership—ownership over the self or parts of the self, but also the exchange of goods and ownership—embedded into the relevant processes. Even in cases in which a mixed-sex couple contribute their own reproductive material (egg and sperm) for a process of in vitro fertilisation (IVF) after which the fertilised embryo will be transferred to the female partner, this process involves agreements with their IVF providers regarding the storage and handling of their gametes and embryos. As I write, there is an active debate in the United States about whether embryos are understood, for the purposes of the law, as property or persons (see e.g. Daar 2020; Merelli 2024).

As Judith Daar observes, embryos have until now primarily been treated as property under the law, particularly in legal cases brought against ART providers due to negligent loss or destruction of embryos, though people also often have an emotional attachment to their embryos and may extend moral status to them (Daar 2020). This is not unlike the ways in which a house that someone owns may be property but also a source of emotional connection. Daar notes that "not infrequently, patients fail to pay storage fees and become unreachable by ART clinics and warehousing facilities, shifting the cost of perpetual maintenance to those in possession of the know-how and materials" (ibid., 61). Clinics may be unwilling to discard unclaimed embryos despite guidance from the American Society for Reproductive Medicine Ethics Committee that it is permissible to do so after a certain period. This reluctance is due to a "perception by some" that embryos are persons, which "collides with their treatment by others as property" (ibid., 61).

According to Daar, the "strict classification" of embryos "as either person or property has its obvious drawbacks, but so does the intermediate approach where embryos are unclassified (that is, neither person nor property) but given special respect because of their potential for human life." In cases of negligent embryo destruction, Daar proposes a "balancing approach" that can address the loss of property (granting monetary compensation to cover costs related to lost embryo storage or the need to obtain new embryos) and award damages for "emotional distress" (which are otherwise "rarely awarded in breach of contract and damage to property cases") such that embryos could be, for the purposes of legal regulation, both property and something more than property (ibid., 61–62). The point is that embryos remain conceptualised as property that is owned and controlled (or abandoned), even if they are also construed as more than mere property.

A property-based account may be a practical approach to regulating gamete and embryo management, including their storage, sale or donation.

Similarly, if embryos are goods possessed by individuals, then those individuals have obligations to safely store or dispose of their property. Understanding them as property confers obligations on those engaged in agreements to manage or store this property and can entail protections for owners if duties are not adequately discharged. There are tangible, material benefits to a property-based account of reproductive material.

Surrogacy introduces another related set of questions and concerns for the body-as-property view. Reproductive labour intersects with property rights in the form of contract surrogacy, where someone is engaged (directly or via an agency) to carry a pregnancy. Not only is the surrogate compensated, but the purchaser of this service pays for any related care—just as an owner pays for the maintenance of their material property. The work the surrogate does, including fertility treatments, attending medical appointments, maintaining their health while pregnant and carrying and delivering a baby, is inextricably linked to the surrogate's body. This work can be variously construed as a form of labour or commodification or exploitation, just like many other forms of labour involving a person's body that place the worker at physical and psychological risk. The idea of "my body, my choice" here implies that the surrogate's body is something they own and have the right to use as they like. A property rights argument may support negative rights to non-interference to justify the idea of minimal or no regulation of a person's ability to enter into a surrogacy agreement. I shall return to this free-market logic of surrogacy later on, when I discuss how it may fail to capture the unique dynamics of this work in terms of the risks and vulnerabilities associated with pregnancy.

But even if there are productive uses of a property rights view of the body, or parts of the body, in relation to ART, these technologies raise substantial questions about the extent and limits of such a view for justice-based accounts of ART. This applies especially to disparities in access to ART. For relatively wealthy individuals who want non-interference in their ability to use ART, rights to non-interference may be sufficient. However, a property-based account is insufficient to contend with the significant inequities in terms of who has access to ART, and on whom ART places the greatest burden. It cannot capture the positive liberties required for reproductive justice, which includes the freedom to become a parent.

I shall now turn to a reparative approach to reproductive justice that seeks to address the redistribution of goods while building a more just world for reproduction.

3. Reparative reproductive justice

In this section, I describe the concepts of reparative worldbuilding and reparative reproductive justice. In the next section, I shall then apply these concepts to the relationship between ART and property. A reparative account of reproductive justice might at first appear to support a property-centric view of reproductive rights if we consider reparations to be the redistribution of property. But Valentine (2023), building on Táíwò's (2022) account of reparative worldbuilding, argues for a kind of worldbuilding that creates the conditions for reproductive justice to flourish rather than merely redistributing existing resources. Táíwò takes reparations to be neither reconciliatory nor restitution for past harms but part of a forward-looking project of *worldbuilding* that he describes as "constructivist". This view is particularly attentive to the disparate vulnerabilities that present people experience, or that future people will experience, due to inherited advantage or disadvantage (not just inherited property). These vulnerabilities necessitate structural responses to address unjust distributions of benefits and harms. Táíwò takes climate justice as a model for, and necessary case of, constructivist reparations, because those made most vulnerable by climate change are also those least responsible for contributing to it. Moreover, they are often marginalised and minoritised populations.

Building on this view, Valentine argues that both reparative justice and reproductive justice are frameworks attentive to the impact of historical, intergenerational and present harms, and "are about building just conditions, not simply responding to injustice in the moment" (Valentine 2023, 111). She says that both frameworks "prioritize the reshaping of infrastructure and norms of access and inclusion over abstract, individual, and isolated 'choice'" yet they also "emphasize self-determination as a key target of justice" (ibid.). Part of Valentine's target is the structural conditions necessary to create the reproductive freedom to become a parent. She catalogues numerous contributors to disparities in the United States that inhibit procreative freedom. These include the impact of stress on communities experiencing economic instability or racism, which cause "difficulty conceiving and gestating"; exposure to environmental toxins; and structural barriers to accessing ART if state-funded insurance programmes, which disproportionately provide healthcare to lower-income communities, fail to cover ART. Valentine takes these to be examples of how the "state *deprives* procreation [...] when it fails to protect individuals from being rendered infertile and when it refuses to help such individuals regain fertility" (ibid.).

Attention to the role of the state is important for understanding the extent—and limits—of the constructivist worldbuilding view. This is especially the case when considering how to understand reparative worldbuilding globally in relation to ART. Táíwò's reparative worldbuilding, while attentive to disparate vulnerability, is focused on distributive targets, both national and international, as remedies. Some of these involve action by the state (payments within and between nation states, taxation structures) while others involve action at the level of smaller groups or even individuals (divestment from harmful entities, shifting power and control of resources to communities).

While still distributive in nature, worldbuilding here primarily represents a shift in control of and participation in material goods to adjust for the benefits and burdens entailed by historical advantages and disadvantages. This kind of redistribution of resources does not take the form of a compensatory direct payment, but rather the restructuring of a system, including material distribution and control of resources. An important takeaway from this view, for the purposes of reconsidering the role of bodily property in reproductive justice, is that the worldbuilding account of reparations is not focused on which groups or people have some of the resources allocated to them redistributed to others, but rather on producing the conditions that permit more just access to resources in the first place to mitigate disparate vulnerability.

Reparative worldbuilding for reproductive justice, according to Valentine, is part of a programme for creating the conditions necessary for reproductive freedom, attuned to historical reproductive harms and disadvantages that leave some individuals and groups more vulnerable to reproductive *injustice*. Valentine is interested in "a redistribution of reproductive self-determination as well as the 'tools' of reproduction, which include basic necessities like food, water, housing, healthcare, and education" (ibid., 105). These are tools for basic flourishing, above and beyond reproductive flourishing, which underscores Ruha Benjamin's view that we should think "well beyond the body—so often the site of trauma and exploitation—to encompass the full range of life-affirming practices" (Benjamin 2018, cited in Valentine 2023, 105).

A more just world would also be a more reproductively just world. Valentine describes a need for the worldbuilding of a basic structure of society that addresses disparate vulnerabilities, environmental stressors and shortcomings in basic life necessities. She also specifically invokes the disparate trauma and exploitation historically imposed on Black women's bodies in the United States that:

> [I]ncluded not only the horrific rape, impregnation, and forced gestation of enslaved women and the separation of families, but the *medical bondage*, as Deirdre Cooper Owens (2017) puts it, of reproductive medicine itself being born through experimentation on enslaved women's bodies. The medical knowledge produced here was in turn essential to the maintenance of slavery and an enslaved population. This forced *reproductive labor*—labor that propels and regenerates the present work force—often goes unacknowledged and certainly uncompensated.
>
> *Valentine 2023, 107*

In my conclusion, I will return to this important point by Valentine about the contribution of historical, intergenerational and cyclical trauma to reproductive injustice. This is a different kind of inheritance—not of property, but of vulnerability. But first I should note that Valentine only in passing discusses the implications of reparative worldbuilding for reproductively just policies and practices in relation to ART. She asks: "In what ways might we retool policies related to [...] ARTs in terms of both access to ARTs and accountability to ART collaborators?" (ibid., 114). This question, however, falls outside the scope of her immediate project. In the next section, I begin to flesh out a plausible answer, since this question returns us to the notion of body-as-property for ART purposes, including the utilisation of gametes, embryos and surrogates to meet reproductive goals and potentially enable the freedom to become a parent. While Valentine's arguments suggest the capacity to access ART is a matter of justice, this entails obligations on others to fulfil such rights. What corollary duties can this liberty reasonably entail and for whom? And how does this relate to the structures necessary to more justly distribute reproductive property and vulnerability?

4. Vulnerability, privilege and exploitation

Access to ART could encompass a range of goods and services: from available and affordable IVF providers to donor gametes to gestational surrogates. Selling reproductive materials or labour can be construed as a matter of reproductive liberty to use one's body and reproductive potential in self-determined ways. But it can also be construed as a form of coercion and exploitation, undermining the very idea that such choices are self-determined. There is no single policy or practical solution that will allow us to navigate this landscape and find a reproductively just approach to the disparate benefits and burdens of ART, especially across societies with vastly different social norms, economic contexts and political views. Here, I consider three kinds of cases, which respectively involve people who want to use their own reproductive material and carry a pregnancy aided by ART; people who are unable to carry a pregnancy; and people who could potentially carry a surrogate pregnancy. In the concluding section, I suggest taking a trauma-informed approach to adapt the goals of reproductive justice to actionable policy that is sensitive to the local and global contexts of ART.

In the United States context in which I am writing, there is growing understanding of disparities in access to abortion across race and income divides, particularly in the aftermath of the *Dobbs v. Jackson Women's Health* Supreme Court decision that removed federal protections for abortion. This decision has allowed states to impose sometimes severe abortion restrictions, meaning that entire regions of the country now have no access to abortion (except in some limited cases). This has brought heightened attention to how abortion prohibitions impact anyone who can become pregnant, but at the population level most significantly affect people of colour and those on lower incomes who may not be able to access the abortion care they need locally nor to travel for it. Similarly, as noted in the previous section, significant disparities also exist regarding procreative capacity, often along similar racial and economic lines. People of colour face structural injustices that impact on their infertility *and* structural injustices that impact on their ability to access potential remedies. One retrospective study of birth records from 2011 to 2019 in the United States showed that "Black and Hispanic women had about 70 % lower likelihood of receiving any infertility treatment" (Dongarwar et al. 2022).

Globally, disparities in access to ART also exist within and between countries. One review of international reports on ART showed that in many lower and middle-income countries (LMICs), ART was available only within "private clinics" that were "providing ART access to the more economically affluent population" (Chiware et al. 2021, 223). The kinds of ART discussed in that paper include intrauterine insemination, artificial insemination and similar or related procedures, but not access to surrogacy. The authors note multiple factors contributing to ART access in LMICs, including cultural and religious norms, stigma around infertility and local policy, but suggest that the World Health Organisation is poised to propose guidelines for providing accessible ART in LMICs and for promoting the development of lower-cost yet effective ART options.

One approach to reparative worldbuilding for reproductive justice would be for governments to promote policies that enhance the accessibility of ART, in ways that will improve access for those systemically excluded from them due to historical oppression and vulnerability. This could take the form of policies to support research into lower-cost ART, policies that incentivise opening ART clinics in new areas to increase geographical access and policies that require government and private insurance to finance at least some access to ART. These are in many ways more traditionally distributive targets. However, as noted by Táíwò, the focus on structural distribution is not about debiting some to credit others but rather about building structures (e.g. affordable cost schemes) and redistributing benefits and burdens such that those who have been historically most vulnerable would benefit the most from policy change.

This policy change could run concurrently with actions aimed at reducing disparate burdens of infertility within populations, for instance the impact of infertility-causing pollutants on communities. Importantly, these are population-level targets. Promoting reproductive freedom to procreate is not a guarantee that it would be a realisable goal for every individual, and supporting procreative potential is not to say that any one individual is owed unlimited ART resources as a matter of justice. Moreover, ART access polices can only ever be one piece of a larger programme for reproductive justice that concurrently fosters other ways of becoming a parent, including the imagining, and realisation, of more expansive social visions of parenting and kinship relationships.

So far, I have considered justice-oriented frameworks for accessing reproductive technologies to enable people to make choices to become biological parents and gestate pregnancies. What about individuals who want to become biological parents but lack the capacity to gestate a pregnancy? The set of relevant ARTs in those cases is more expansive, including access to donor eggs and gestational carriers. Camisha Russell (2018) analyses whether reproductive justice can and should apply to gay men and their reproductive interests in becoming parents. Some gay men looking for gestational surrogates become, or see themselves as, “reproductive refugees”, due to financial or regulatory barriers to using a surrogate in their home context, which brings "the question of justice in[to] stark relief" (ibid., 133).

Gay (or bisexual/queer) men's access to surrogacy, particularly as reproductive travellers in global contexts, illustrates the negative and positive liberty dichotomy between reproductive rights and reproductive justice. Members of this population may have a right to enter into a surrogacy contract somewhere in the world—provided there remain, as there currently are, nations that permit surrogacy agreements. That does not mean, however, that they have a right to a surrogate's reproductive labour and body-as-property, but only that, in permissive states, surrogates have a right to contract out their bodies and services. As Russell puts it: "Free-market rights are essentially negative rights—they offer freedom from interference in the marketplace. People are not prevented from buying those things that are offered on the open market, so long as they can afford those things and are willing to pay the amount asked" (ibid., 134). Similarly, Russell points out, on this logic those interested in selling goods—including their eggs or their services as surrogates—should not be impeded.

This treats surrogacy similarly to other kinds of property rights. If a good is understood as something that can be owned, it can be justly transferred, and so if potential gestational carriers own their bodies, then they can, presumably, transfer the use of those bodies through a market-based process to the person seeking their services as a surrogate. A property rights account suggests a general freedom from interference with a person's right to buy or sell property, provided they follow relevant laws and norms governing the just transfer of that property. But the right to purchase (or rent) property does not entail that there is property available to purchase (or rent), as the great number of cities with housing shortages makes evident, nor does it entail a right to afford the prices the market can sustain in terms of the cost of the purchase or rental (again, as many cities with housing shortages and extremely high housing costs illustrate), nor does it mitigate the exploitation or coercion a person might experience in deciding to sell their property under market conditions.

Negative liberty does not create an "obligation to make the desired good affordable or to assist any particular person or group in buying the desired good;" it only ensures that "the ability to buy, where it already exists, is not impaired" (ibid.). The property-based market logic of *rights* to ART only supports reasonably privileged populations who can navigate and afford the market-based system. Well-off gay men may see themselves as reproductive refugees due to their inability to obtain the reproductive care they seek in their home setting. But they may in fact be reproductive luxury tourists, able to mobilise financial and other forms of privilege when seeking surrogacy services. Many people cannot afford those things, even when a free market is available on which they can be purchased. Does this mean that, *as a matter of justice*, people have a positive right to access the resources of donor eggs or embryos, or the services of a surrogate?

In this case, the property rights account again fails to accommodate a justice-oriented view, if reproductive justice includes the freedom to become a (biological) parent, because on this market-logic approach there is no positive liberty to be able to access the market goods necessary to do so. At the same time, the free-market logic leaves potential donors and surrogates exceedingly vulnerable. Thus, this approach is doubly harmful. One way to avoid the problem is to follow Russell and deny that the inability of gay men to have "biological children without assistance" is a source of injustice; this inability, according to Russell, "is not a punishment that society has issued against them [...] it is a lived reality that may be experienced as a hardship, but not as a result of injustice" (ibid., 136). In other words, the structure of society does not render gay men unable to have biological children, though norms and features of society may structure biological kinship as preferred or ideal. Russell notes this same logic applies to straight individuals who are "naturally infertile", as opposed to those infertile due to structural injustice, such as heightened exposure to environmental toxicity as a result of structural racism; they are not owed, as a matter of justice, a remedy for infertility via ART (ibid.).

Russell leans into a naturalistic argument in ways that are at odds with some accounts of justice, and which are difficult to apply in practice. Practically, determining who is "naturally infertile" versus who has been made infertile by structural injustice may be challenging if not impossible. And as a matter of justice, we might be reticent to view justice as bound to biological destiny. Disability justice affords a loose corollary for how the demands of, and obligations entailed by, justice shift depending on which model of disability we operate with, whether medical, social or a hybrid of both (Wasserman and Aas 2023). Regardless of the model of disability we favour, justice demands that society build a liberatory world in which disabilities are not deficits. If someone is infertile, whether due to their physiology or their social identity and relations, this does not negate their interests in reproductive freedom and liberation.

Russell recognises that infertile individuals have, at a minimum, interests in procreative liberty that are in solidarity with reproductive justice. Comparing this to disability rights and liberation might suggest that whether infertility is due to medical, social or hybrid reasons will affect the nature of the demands and potential obligations entailed by one's interests in reproduction, but not one's interests in liberation. For Russell, procreative liberty involves understanding reproduction expansively, in ways that go beyond the biological, and broadening our concepts of kinship and family. This is a form of worldbuilding, though Russell does not describe it in those terms. This example illustrates the utility of a reparative worldbuilding approach to reproductive justice that focuses less on what is owed due to deficits and more on how to create systems and structures that support liberation and respond to various kinds of vulnerability.

This worldbuilding project still bumps up against questions of what can reasonably be demanded of others as matters of liberty or justice. In building a world in which people can exercise a freedom to become parents, including those historically excluded from parenthood or those requiring assistance to exercise the choice to become a parent, what positive liberties can be expected or owed? One might have a right to purchase goods on the free market but not have a right to those goods being available to purchase or to anyone making their goods available for purchase. The reproductive freedom to become a parent cannot compel anyone else to take on burdens associated with their parenthood, such as donating their eggs or gestating a pregnancy. Compensation for such activities when they are undertaken raises concerns about what constitutes an adequate and fair level of compensation, and whether accepting compensation in exchange for taking on such significant risks and burdens can ever be fair, or freely chosen in the context of oppressive background conditions.

Thus, the market logic of property rights and market constraints remains relevant to understanding ART access. The limits on the demands of justice could look different in a world where other technologies, such as artificial wombs, were a real option. In the meantime, creative and justice-oriented solutions to market-based problems, such as embryos that are abandoned when owners fail to pay for storage or make a disposition plan, could be pursued according to a reparative scheme. For example, governments could create repositories for discarded embryos so that existing resources are made more equitably accessible without imposing new burdens, and in so doing prioritise the pooling of resources rather than replicating market-based structures and create allocation schemes designed to redistribute benefits and burdens in connection with reproductive (in)justice.

Available resources for ART lead us to the third concern, which is linked not only to the vulnerability and privilege of those seeking to *use* ART, but to the vulnerability of those *contributing* their reproductive materials and labour to it. Critiquing oversimplified views of the global market for ART resources and labour, Alison Bailey notes that Western rhetoric tends to commodify the bodies of non-Western women who sell their reproductive resources. She says that the "rhetorical focus here is on opportunity, choice, and fair exchange", which suggests that women have the right to be market agents and should be free to do so (Bailey 2011, 719). However, according to Bailey this overlooks the ways in which broader contexts of injustice shape why someone might be compelled to become a surrogate: the "characterization of surrogacy work as a legitimate choice for some women is accurate", but a focus on free choice also "obscures the injustice behind these choices: the reality that, for many women, contract pregnancy is one of the few routes to attaining basic social goods such as housing, food, clean water, education, and medical care" (ibid., 722). This list is similar to the basic resources Valentine says ought to be part of a comprehensive account of reproductive justice.

What is reproductively just for the vulnerable individual at risk of exploitation when contracting out their reproductive labour on a free-market model? Does enabling the sale of genetic material or gestational capacity afford individuals participating in this market a source of power and control to extricate themselves from unjust background conditions? Or is it a form of exploitation because it offers only an unjust option in response to structural oppression? Would regulating or prohibiting this practice be a new source of injustice, because it would inhibit a means of financial liberation without providing alternatives?

When thinking through the obligations of states, or international bodies like the World Health Organisation, to provide guidelines for and regulation of global ART markets, a narrowly market-based approach again bumps up against practical and logical constraints. It invites competing accounts of rights without factoring in background contexts of (in)justice. Bailey's analysis of global ART markets through a reproductive justice lens aims to straddle the divide between paternalistic moralising and moral absenteeism and develop ethical guidelines that recognise the limits of any one-size-fits-all approach to the very nuanced realities of individuals and populations across time, space and social contexts.

Bailey describes reproductive justice as a "conversation starter, not a moral theory" (ibid., 734), yet it does provide guidance for applying moral theory. Examples include Valentine's argument for reparative reproductive justice and Russell's solidaristic approach to procreative liberty and reproductive justice, which does not pit rights holders against each other in terms of who has rights to reproductive resources, but seeks to produce "a fuller re-imagining of procreation and family" that would ideally "imagine (and ultimately enact) broad guidelines for ensuring that all people in our society have not simply the right, but actual concrete access to [...] a much wider variety of protected and supported family formations" (Russell 2018, 139). In the next section, I consider how we can build on these accounts by incorporating principles of trauma-informed care.

5. Trauma-informed reparative worldbuilding

Despite my arguments that property offers a flawed logic for reproductive justice, I am not convinced that we will get out from under it in the context of ART. There remain unresolved questions about rights to buy, sell, store or use gametes and embryos. Processes for, and expectations regarding, the buying or selling of surrogacy services are likely to endure. Analogously to Bailey's observation about a focus on practical decision-makers diverting attention from their unjust choices, a property rights and market-based approach to matters such as global surrogacy places the focus on whether one is an autonomous self-owner able to enter freely into a contract, which obfuscates a broader set of justice-based considerations that are relevant to how to understand that question. Asserting that women are self-owners for the purposes of autonomously selling their surrogacy services, even though at the same time they do not autonomously own any of the other resources that they need to sustain themselves, shows the very unstable logic of a selective assertion of ownership. To disentangle the ways in which ownership frameworks perpetuate systems of injustice requires at a minimum taking complementary approaches that can mitigate injustice.

Valentine presents reparative reproductive justice as a conceptual framework that needs to be fleshed out. Conceptualising reparative worldbuilding through ART policy and regulation is one way to start to do so in practice. My further claim is that this worldbuilding should be trauma-informed. This is a normative point about the conditions for justice. But it also includes a descriptive point about how the world is structurally unjust in ways that reflect and perpetuate individual and collective trauma. Reparative worldbuilding is concerned with building worlds in response to disparate distributions of advantages and disadvantages, attending to how these "build up over time" and addressing "past and present harms" (Valentine 2023, 110). Similarly, trauma-informed care responds to past and present impacts of trauma, seeking to minimise retraumatisation and interrupt future trauma through principles that build a trauma-informed world.

Valentine describes experiences of individual and collective trauma as sources of reproductive injustice that demand reparative reproductive justice. While I cannot give a full account of, or a full argument for, trauma-informed care (TIC) as a framework for justice here, by drawing on my previous work on structural care as a matter of justice (Lanphier 2021c) and trauma-informed ethics (Lanphier 2023), I will suggest that TIC affords principles for managing the scope, terms and targets of a worldbuilding approach that is both reparative of past harm *and* seeks to mitigate current and prevent future harm.

The Substance Abuse and Mental Health Services Administration (SAMHSA) defines "trauma" as the subjective experience of an event, series of events or environment that an individual or group experiences as having lasting adverse effects on them, including by disrupting or inhibiting their coping mechanisms. Trauma-informed principles include the promotion of physical and emotional safety, peer support, inclusion and collaboration, voice and choice, trust and attention to culture, bias and oppression (SAMHSA 2014). TIC is intended as a universal precaution applied to all individuals and groups, which recognises the pervasiveness and frequency of trauma at the population level. This is not to say it is a universalising framework, in the sense of a framework that flattens difference (Young 1990). Instead, it is one that flexibly attunes to particularity (Walker 1991). For some, this particularity involves histories of trauma. But TIC is also about preventing trauma. My point in arguing for a TIC approach to ART policy and practice is not to say that such policy only applies to those who have experienced trauma, or to suggest that using or contributing to ART as a prospective parent or as a contributor of reproductive material or labour is necessarily due to trauma, is done by those with trauma histories or is traumatising. Instead, my intention is to suggest principles that respond to the interconnections that can exist between trauma, reproduction and choice, but at the same time constitute a set of justice-oriented principles that are focused on safety, trust, support, inclusion and empowerment, while also being sensitive to the many historical and contemporary barriers and injustices that prevent their realisation.

Layering trauma-informed principles onto a reparative worldbuilding approach shifts the conversation from the competition between certain rights (like the right to sell or buy surrogacy services or the right to use, store, destroy or access gametes) that a property rights account promotes, and focuses instead on how to make practices attentive to past and present vulnerability (including in relation to trauma, but also to injustice more generally) and build worlds that promote trauma-informed principles. Such principles may require the distribution or redistribution of material resources in the more traditional sense of reparations in order to meet goals like flattening out hierarchies or creating and supporting safety. I am not suggesting that we can disentangle the complex relationships between property and capital, bodies and trauma, inheritance of goods and (dis)advantage, as separate from material conditions. Rather, I am arguing against property as the exclusive or best model for what is at the core a set of relationships: to and between past and present, to our bodies and their interactions with social structures and policies, to our reproductive choices and desires, and to others locally and globally.

For example, policies to regulate surrogacy agreements cross nationally might not only attune to the "rights" of surrogates to monetise their services or the rights of those willing and able to purchase them, but also consider the necessary conditions for safety, inclusion, collaboration and trust in the *relationships* formed through surrogacy. The mere fact of having a surrogacy contract does not ensure safety, inclusion, collaboration, or trust. These are features that need to be carefully and thoughtfully address within such a contract, and the broader policies and norms guiding the practice. TIC might fundamentally shift the practices for developing surrogacy contracts, for example by shifting who is understood as a stakeholder in the contract, by embedding peer support resources for surrogates and potential parents in volved in contract processes, by adopting different culturally sensitive techniques or processes for negotiation, or by thinking through how to level hierarchies that may inhibit voice, choice, and empowerment in contract negotiations. Trauma-informed ART policies might start by systematically including the voices and experiences of all ART participants in the development of ART, with awareness of how some voices and experiences have until now been marginalised in such discussions, particularly across lines of nationality, economic status and family composition.

Identifying specific trauma-informed policies is, in part, an empirical question. Recognising the importance of such policies, however, invites further participatory research into the kinds of practices that support TIC principles such as safety, trust or empowerment in a given context, both for surrogates and for potential parents, in full recognition of particular cultures and histories that may disproportionately make one group more vulnerable than another, or certain members within those groups more vulnerable than others. A trauma-informed reparative reproductive justice holds together the distributive and relational levels and provides a flexible yet systematic set of principles for building a world, and a basic structure of society, that provides forms of care *as a matter of justice*—reproductive, reparative and relational.

Works Cited

Bailey, Alison (2011). Reconceiving Surrogacy: Toward a Reproductive Justice Account of Indian Surrogacy. *Hypatia*, 26, 715–741.

Berlin, Isaiah (1969). Two Concepts of Liberty. In Isaiah Berlin. *Four Essays on Liberty*, 118–172. London: Oxford University Press.

Bridges, Khiara (2021). Beyond Torts. *Columbia Law Review Association*, 121(3), 1017–1074.

Chiware, Tendai M., Nathalie Vermeulen, Karel Blondeel, Roy Farquharson, James Kiarie, Kersti Lundin, Thabo Christopher Matsaseng, Willem Ombelet and Igor Toskin (2021). IVF and Other ART in Low- and Middle-Income Countries: A Systematic Landscape Analysis. *Human Reproduction Update*, 27(2), 213–228.

Cooper Owens, Deirdre (2017). *Medical Bondage: Race, Gender, and the Origins of American Gynecology*. Athens: University of Georgia Press.

Daar, Judith (2020). Legal Liability Landscape and the Person/Property Divide. *F&S Reports*, 1(2), 61–62.

Dongarwar, Deepa, Vicki Mercado-Evans, Sylvia Adu-Gyamfi, Mei-Li Laracuente and Hamisu M. Salihu (2022). Racial/Ethnic Disparities in Infertility Treatment Utilization in the US, 2011–2019. *Systems Biology in Reproductive Medicine*, 68(3), 180–189.

Lanphier, Elizabeth (2021a). A Problem of Self-Ownership for Reproductive Justice. *Cambridge Quarterly of Healthcare Ethics*, 30(2), 312–327.

Lanphier, Elizabeth (2021b). With Abortion Heading Back to the Supreme Court, Is It Time to Retire the "My Body, My Choice" Slogan? *The Conversation*, 4 August.

Lanphier, Elizabeth (2021c). An Institutional Ethic of Care. In Elizabeth Victor and Laura K. Guidry-Grimes (eds.). *Applying Nonideal Theory to Bioethics: Living and Dying in a Non-ideal World*, 169–193. Cham: Springer International Publishing.

Lanphier, Elizabeth (2023). Trauma-Informed Ethics. In Mortimer Sellers and Stephan Kirste (eds.). *Encyclopedia of the Philosophy of Law and Social Philosophy*, 3489–3494. Dordrecht: Springer.

Locke, John (1988 [1689]). *Two Treatises on Government.* Cambridge: Cambridge University Press.

Merelli, Annalisa (2024). Embryo Loss Is Integral to IVF: Alabama's Ruling Equating Embryos with Children Jeopardizes Its Practice. *STAT News*, 22 February. https://www.statnews.com/2024/02/22/alabama-frozen-embryo-ruling-threatens-ivf-clinics/.

Nozick, Robert (1974). *Anarchy, State, and Utopia*. New York: Basic Books.

Russell, Camisha (2018). Rights-Holders or Refugees? Do Gay Men Need Reproductive Justice? *Reproductive BioMedicine & Society Online*, 7, 131–140.

Substance Abuse and Mental Health Services Administration (SAMHSA) (2014). SAMHSA's Concept of Trauma and Guidance for a Trauma-Informed Approach. HHS Publication No. (SMA) 14–4884.

Táíwò, Olúfẹ́mi (2022). *Reconsidering Reparations*. London: Oxford University Press.

Thomson, Judith Jarvis (1990). *The Realm of Rights*. Cambridge, MA: Harvard University Press.

Valentine, Desiree (2023). Reproductive Justice as Reparative Justice. *Social Philosophy Today*, 39, 101–118.

Walker, Margaret Urban (1991). Partial Consideration. *Ethics*, 101(4), 758–774.

Wasserman, David, and Sean Aas (2023). Disability: Definitions and Models. In Edward N. Zalta and Uri Nodelman (eds.). *The Stanford Encyclopedia of Philosophy*, autumn 2023 edition. https://plato.stanford.edu/archives/fall2023/entries/disability/.

Young, Iris Marion (1990). *Justice and the Politics of Difference*. Princeton: Princeton University Press.

Authors

Kathrin Braun is a political scientist affiliated with the University of Stuttgart's Department of Social Sciences and the University of Hannover's Department of Political Science. Her research interests lie in the fields of critical biopolitics studies, the politics of biomedicine, biopolitics and historic justice and, more recently, the political techno-economy of computational architecture, planning and construction. Kathrin is also forum editor of *Critical Policy Studies*.

Katherine Carroll is Associate Professor in the School of Sociology at the Australian National University. Her research interests include the sociology of perinatal medicine and the lactation sciences. Her most recent research, funded by the Australian Research Council, has engaged health professionals and bereaved parents from across Australia in examining bereaved lactation care experiences and practices after stillbirth and infant loss. Katherine has worked with health professionals, hospitals and leading national breastfeeding and grief advocacy organisations to help reshape policy and practices to enhance lactation care for bereaved parents after infant loss.

Daisy Deomampo is Associate Professor of Anthropology at Fordham University. She is a cultural and medical anthropologist whose research investigates constructions of race and gender in relation to reproductive politics and technologies. She is the author of *Transnational Reproduction: Race, Kinship, and Commercial Surrogacy in India* (NYU Press, 2016).

Penelope Deutscher is Joan and Sarepta Harrison Professor in the Department of Philosophy at Northwestern University. Her research areas include biopolitics, reproductive politics and the intersections of 20th century French philosophy and gender and sexuality studies. Her publications include *Foucault's Futures: A Critique of Reproductive Reason* (Columbia University Press, 2017).

Stefanie Graefe is a sociologist at the University of Jena. Her main research interests are social theory and sociology of the present; governmentality of work and subjectivity; and biotechnologies, digitalisation and qualitative research. Since 2021, she and Susanne Lettow have led the research project "Property in the human body in the context of transnational economies of reproduction", a subproject of the Collaborative Research Centre TRR 294 "Structural Change of Property".

Irina Herb is a doctoral researcher in the project "Property in the human body in the context of transnational economies of reproduction", a subproject of the Collaborative Research Centre TRR 294 "Structural Change of Property", based at the University of Jena. Her dissertation explores Marxist feminist approaches to social reproduction, with a focus on the commodification of fertility and pregnancy. She is a member of the Politics of Reproduction Network (PRiNa) and has written in academic and non-academic publications on reproductive justice, social reproduction theory and the financialisation of fertility treatments.

Charlotte Kroløkke is a professor at the University of Southern Denmark's Department of Culture and Language. She is principal investigator of several interdisciplinary research projects on reproduction and reproductive technologies, including the Ice Age project (which focuses on interdisciplinary perspectives on the cryopreservation of reproductive cells and tissue). She was editor of the *Nordic Journal of Feminist and Gender Research* from 2020 to 2022 and has authored or co-authored more than 50 peer-reviewed journal articles, as well as several books and book chapters.

Sara Lafuente-Funes is a feminist sociologist, currently working in the Sociology: Methods and Theory department at Universidad Complutense in Madrid. Her doctoral thesis (2012–2017) was on assisted reproduction in Spain. She continued working on that topic in the EDNA project (2017–2020), which compared egg donation in the UK, Belgium and Spain. Her more recent work, as part of the Cryosocieties project (2019–2024) based at the University of Frankfurt, has focused on cryopreservation technologies.

Elizabeth Lanphier is a faculty member in the Ethics Centre at Cincinnati Children's Hospital Medical Centre and in the Department of Paediatrics at the University of Cincinnati College of Medicine, with affiliations to the University of Cincinnati's Department of Philosophy, Women, Gender, and Sexuality Studies and Centre for Public Engagement with Science. Her research interests include shared and collective responsibility for healthcare, feminist ethics, trauma-informed care and narrative medicine.

Susanne Lettow is a philosopher at Freie Universität Berlin. Her fields of research include feminist philosophy and gender studies, political philosophy, philosophy of technology and history of science and philosophy. Since 2021, she and Stefanie Graefe have led the research project "Property in the human body in the context of transnational economies of reproduction", a subproject of the Collaborative Research Centre TRR 294 "Structural Change of Property".

Rebecca Rahe is trained as a sociologist with a master's degree from the University of Jena. She has researched labour struggles and union campaigns in social services. Her interests lie in Marxist feminism, labour studies and the commodification of the human body in the reproductive economy. She is based in Berlin and currently works as a trade union secretary at *Gewerkschaft Nahrung-Genuss-Gaststätten Ost: Region Berlin-Brandenburg,*.

Janice Richardson is Associate Professor at the Faculty of Law, Monash University. Her research interests lie at the overlap between feminist philosophy and law: for example, feminist applications of Spinoza and feminist critiques of the social contract tradition. She has published four single-authored books, the latest of which was Routledge in 2023: *Law, Selfhood and Feminist Philosophy: Monstrous Aberrations* (Routledge, 2023).

Susanne Schultz is a sociologist at the Goethe University Frankfurt. She has held visiting professorships in Frankfurt, Vienna, Graz and Erfurt. Her research interests are stratified relations of reproduction and reproductive injustices, migration regimes, bio- and necropolitics of population, intersectional feminist theories and movements, family policies, reproductive technologies and human genetics. She is active in feminist anti-racist movements in Berlin and the queer-feminist editorial collective Kitchen Politics, and is a board member of the Gen-Ethical Network (GeN), the Rosa Luxemburg Foundation and fem*ini (feminist initiative against reproductive exploitation).